NEW YORK SHORT STORIES

Mario Schneider

NEW YORK SHORT STORIES

Mario Schneider

KEHRER

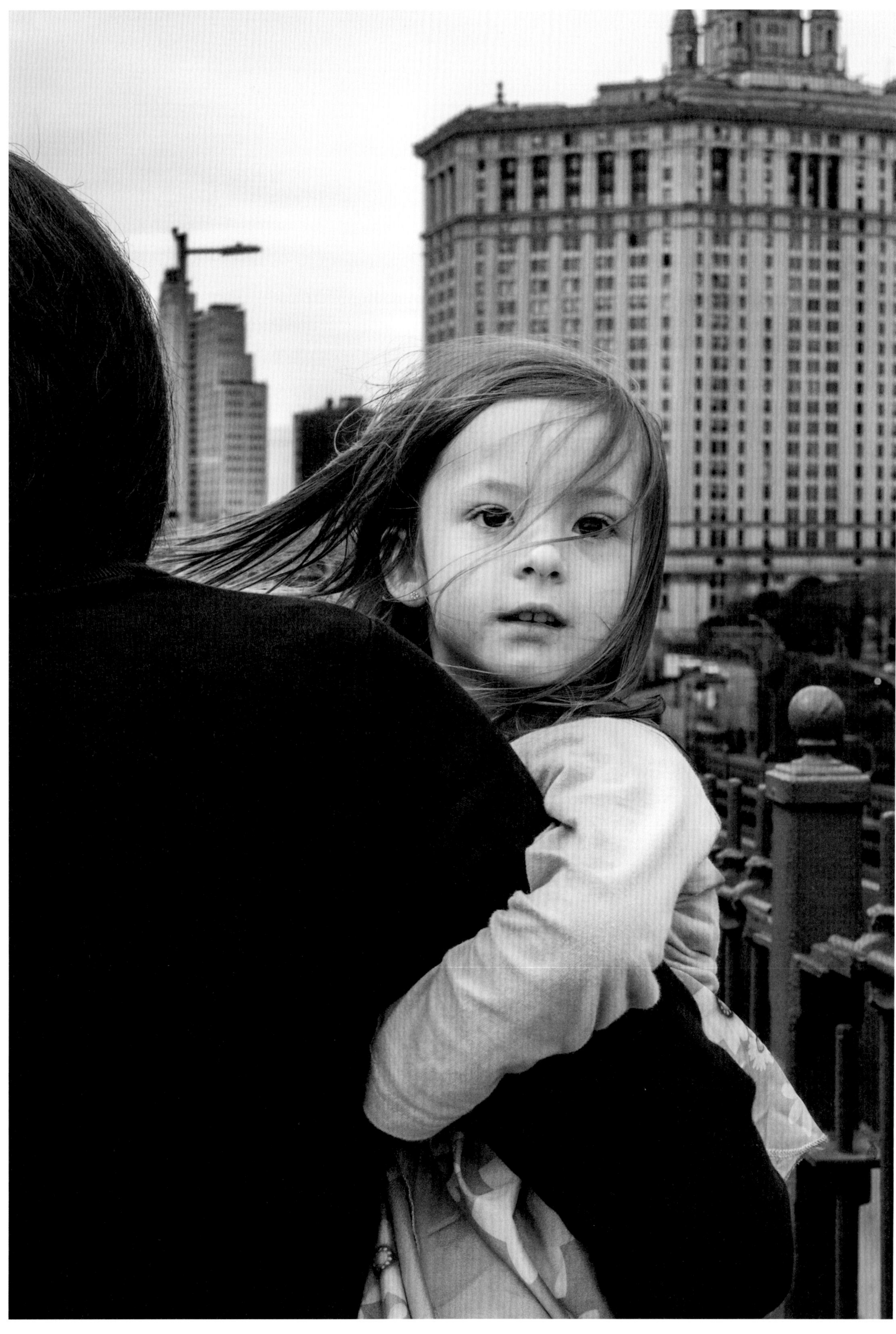

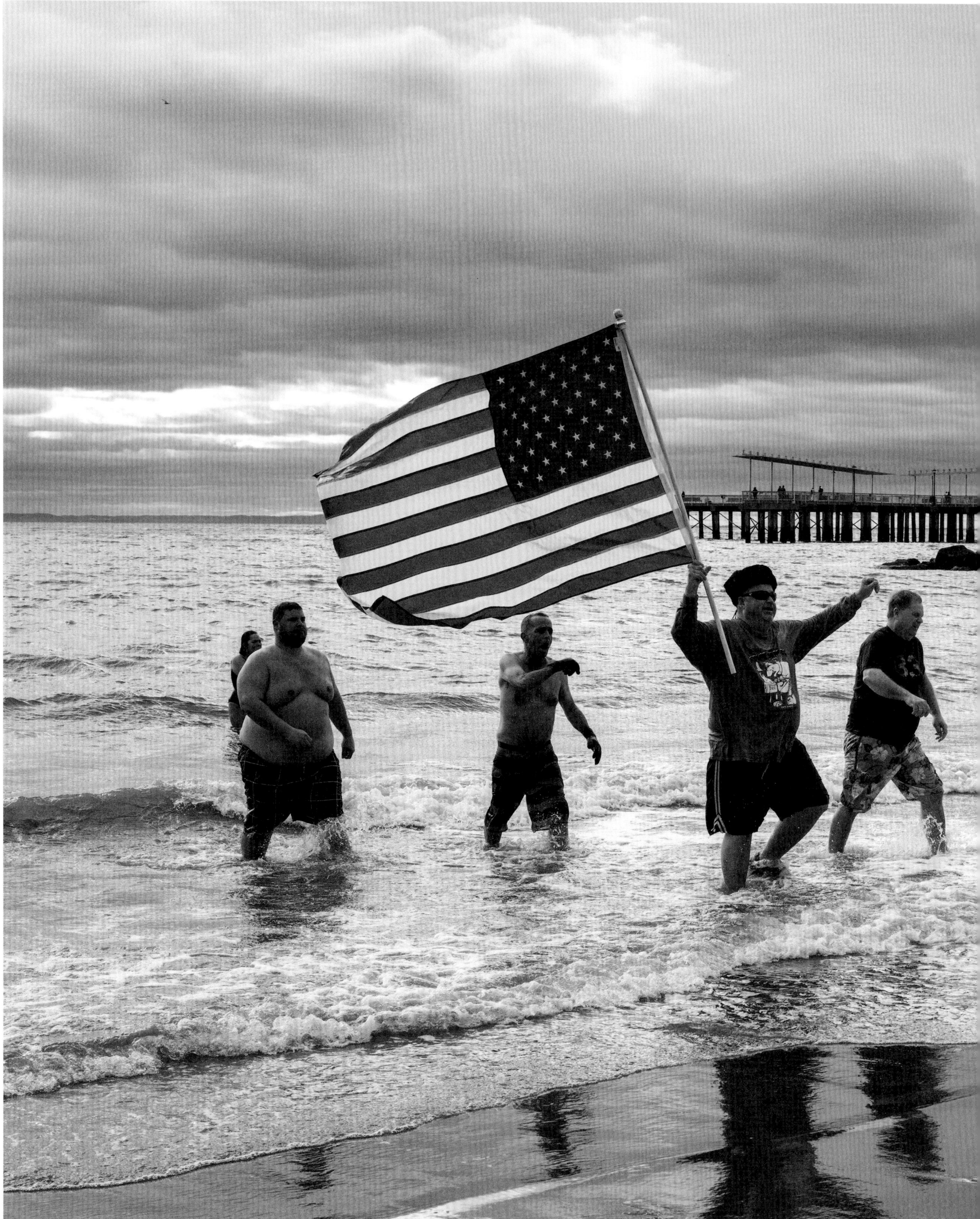

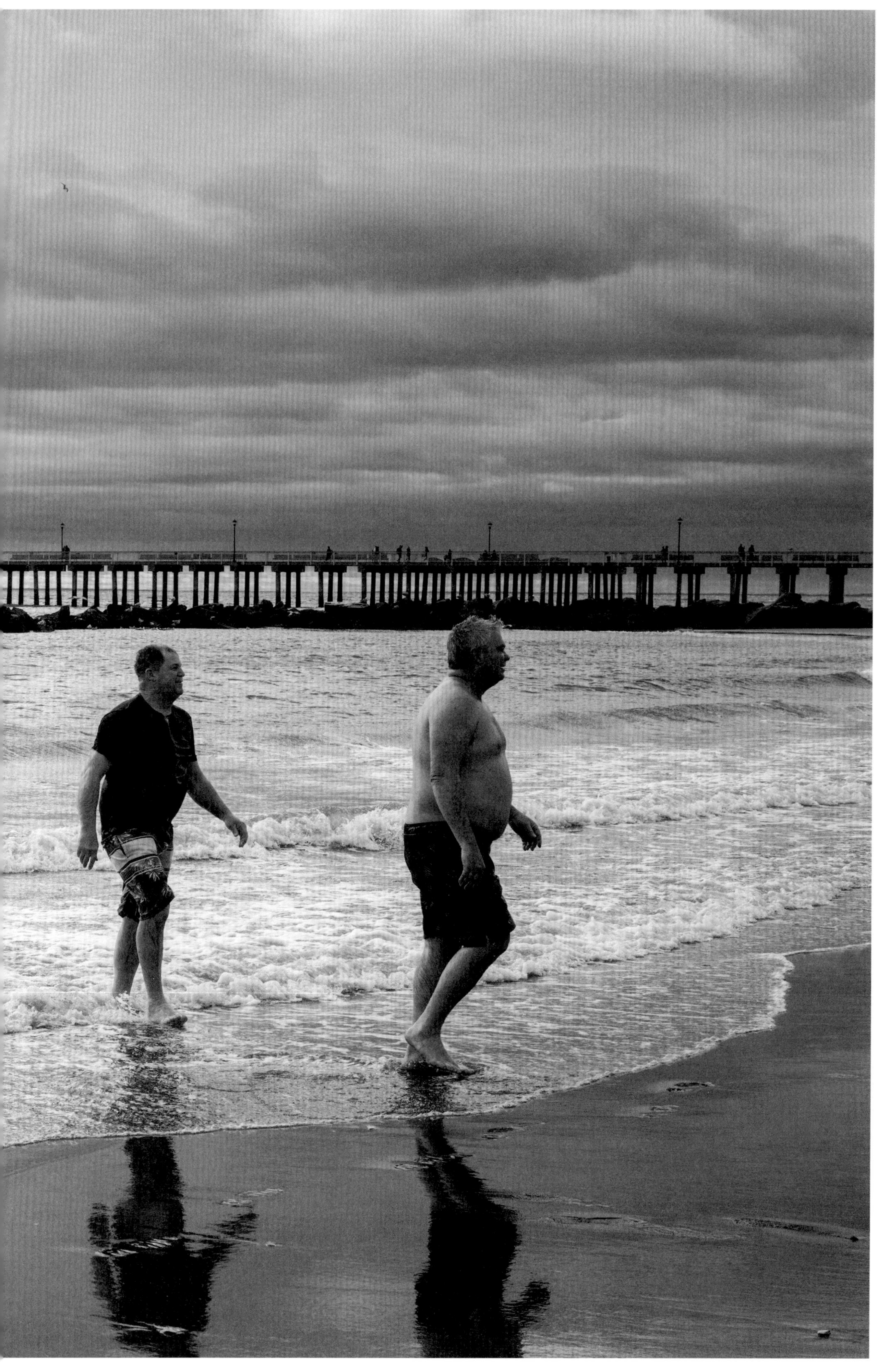

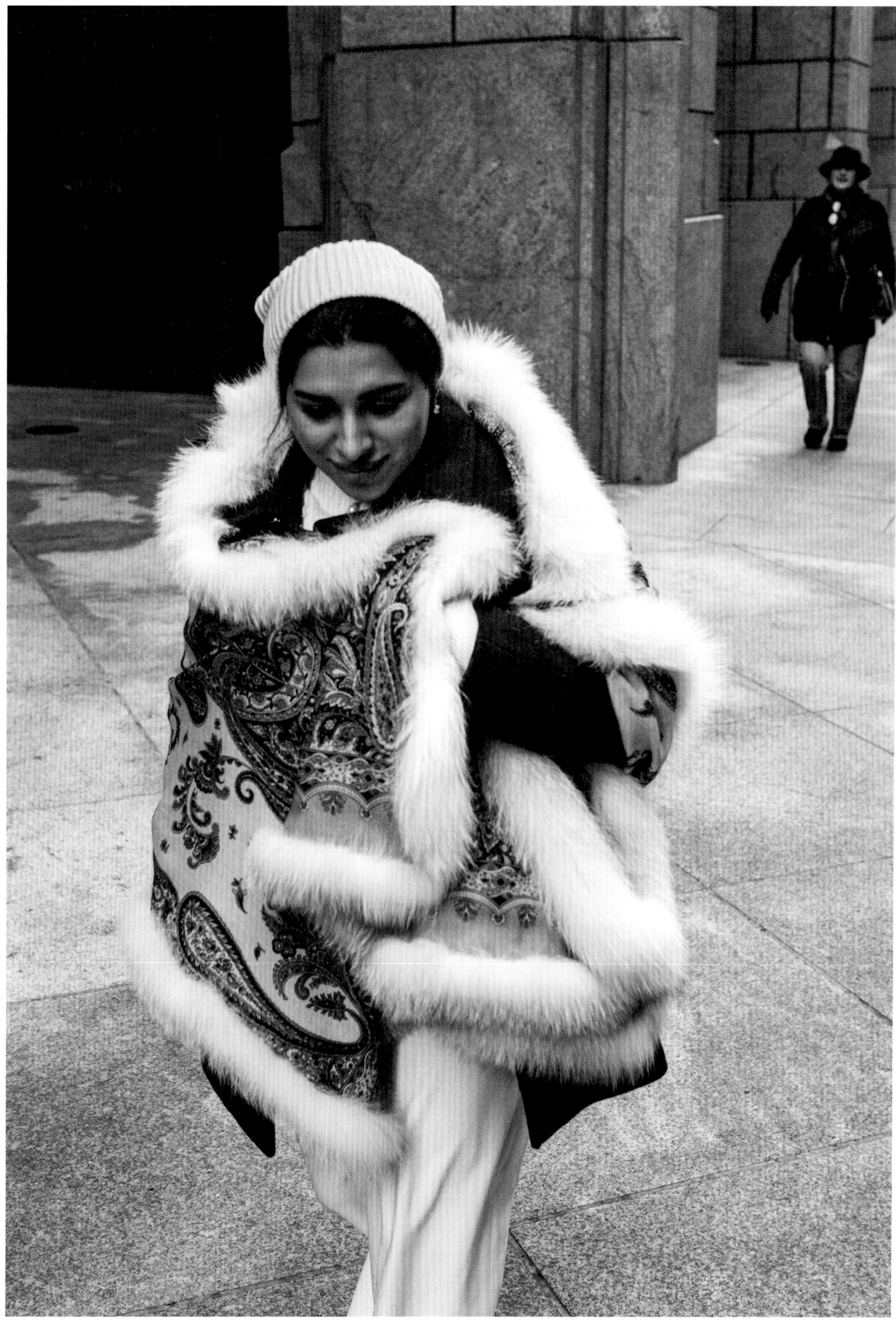

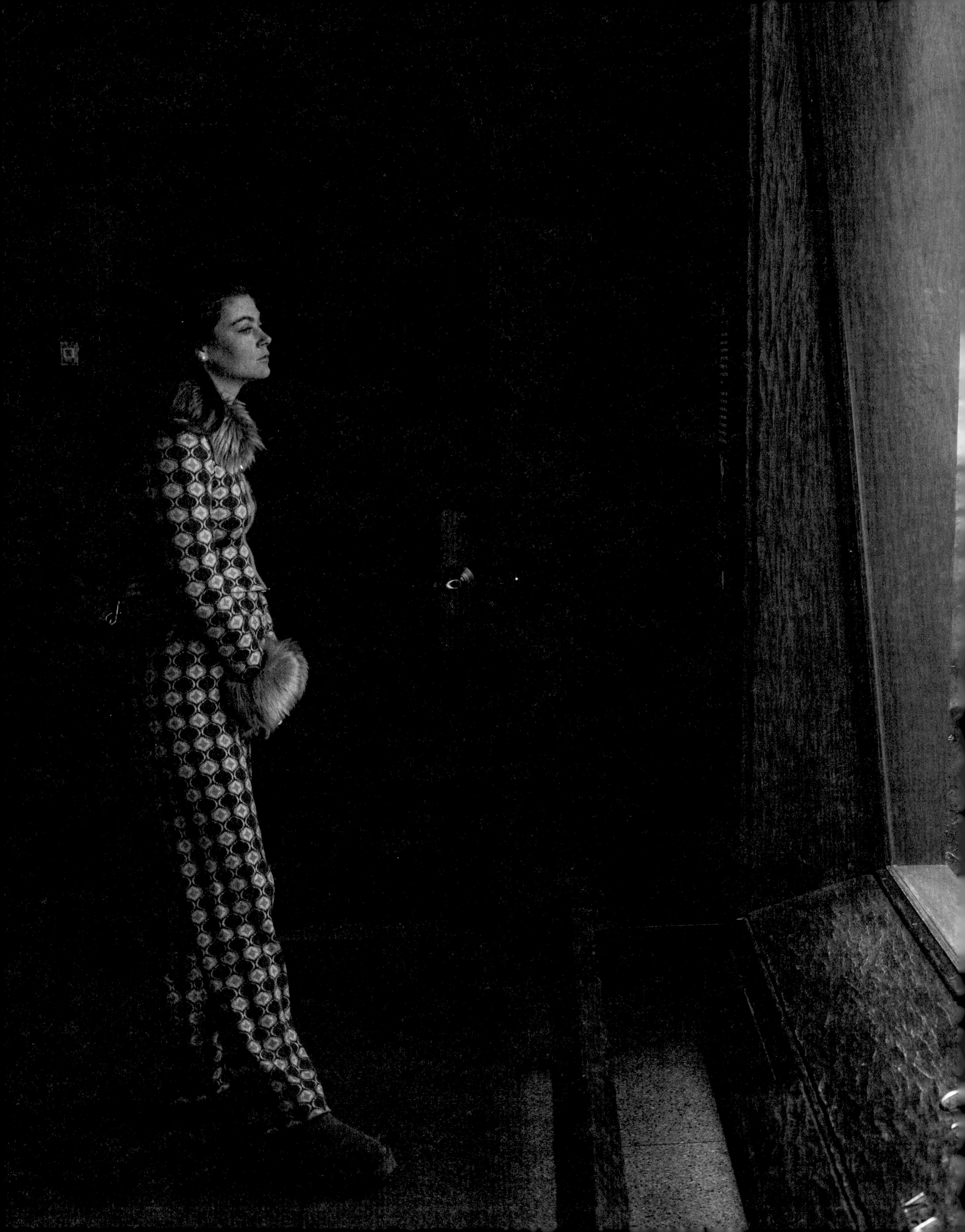

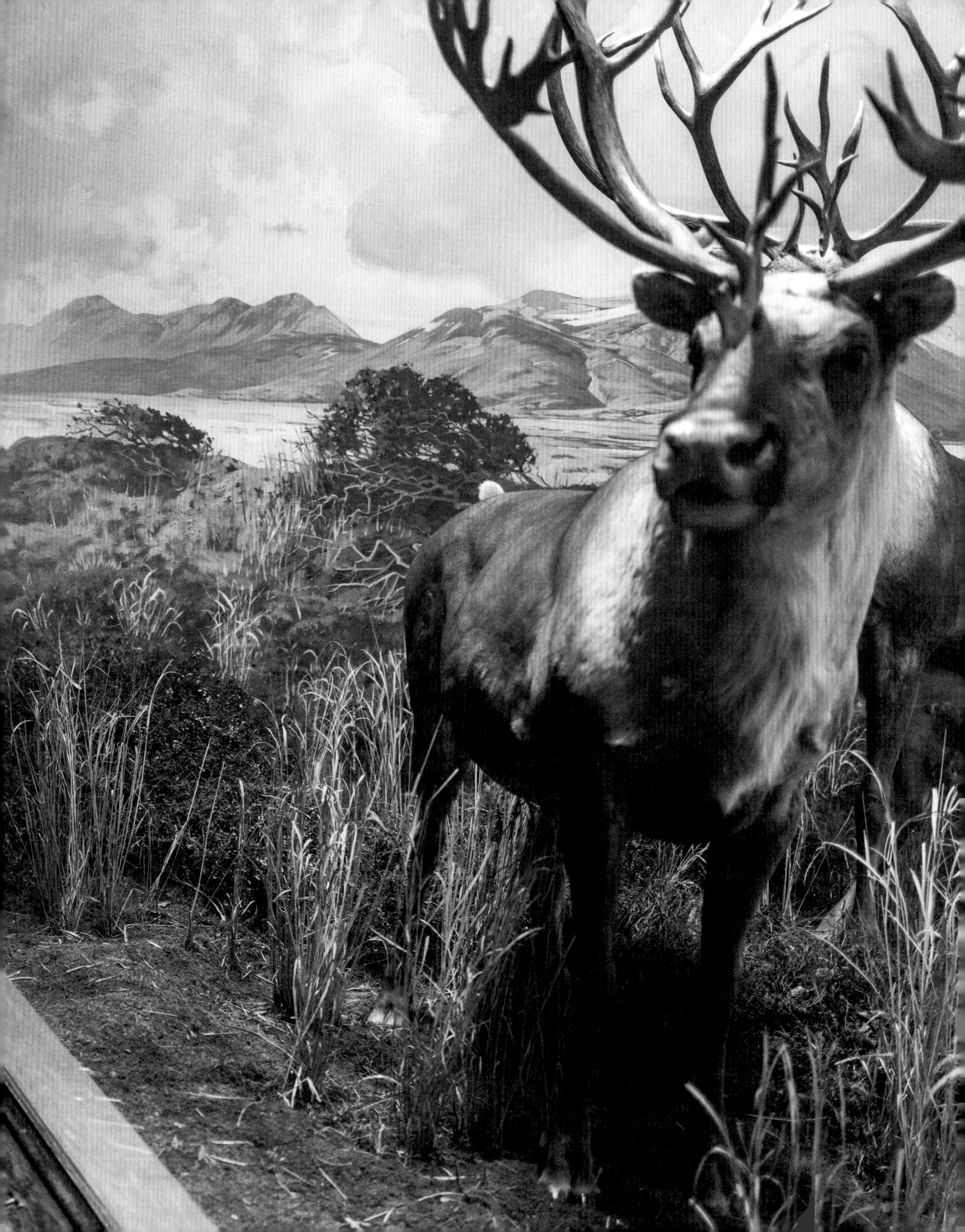

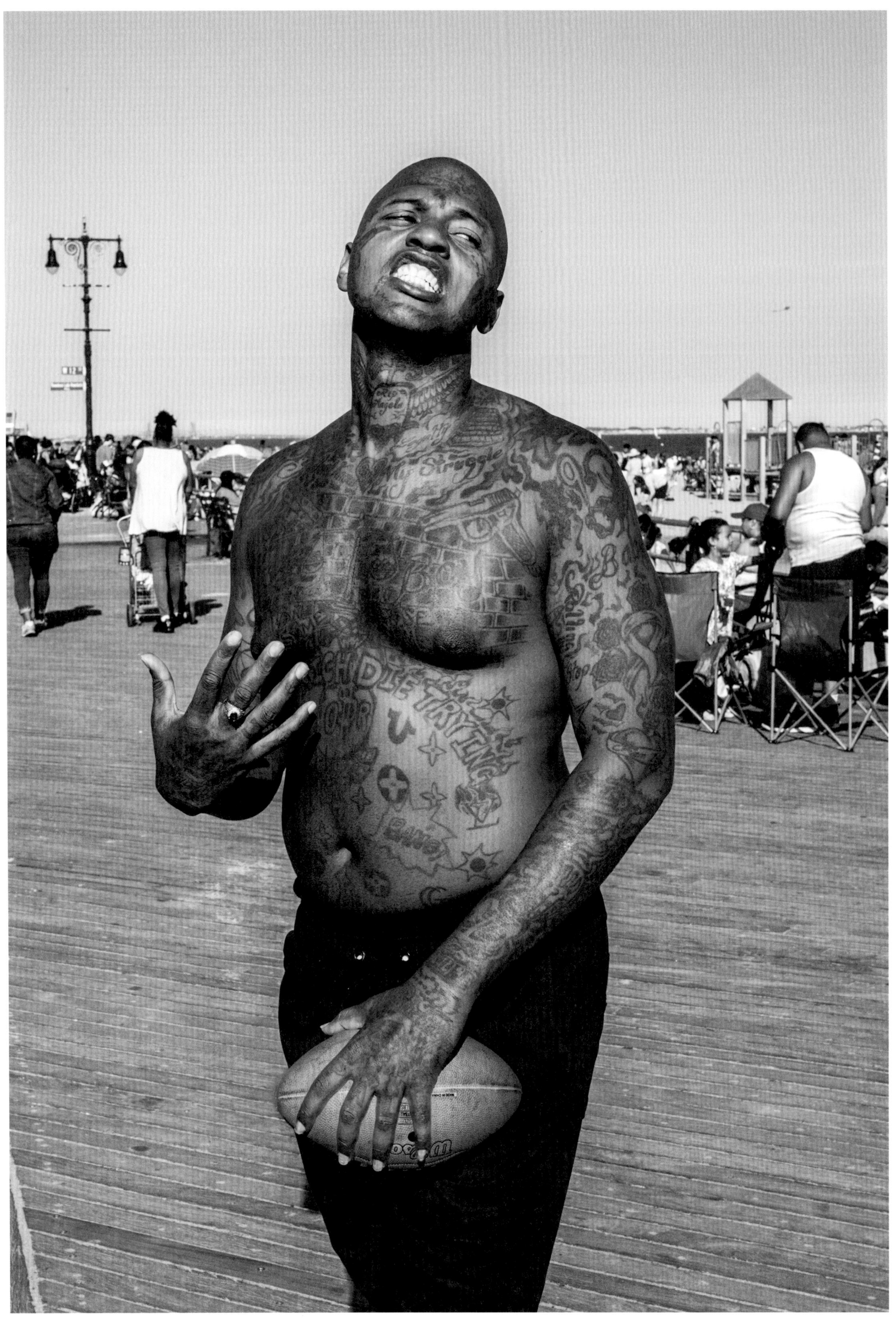
My Struggle
DIE TRYING

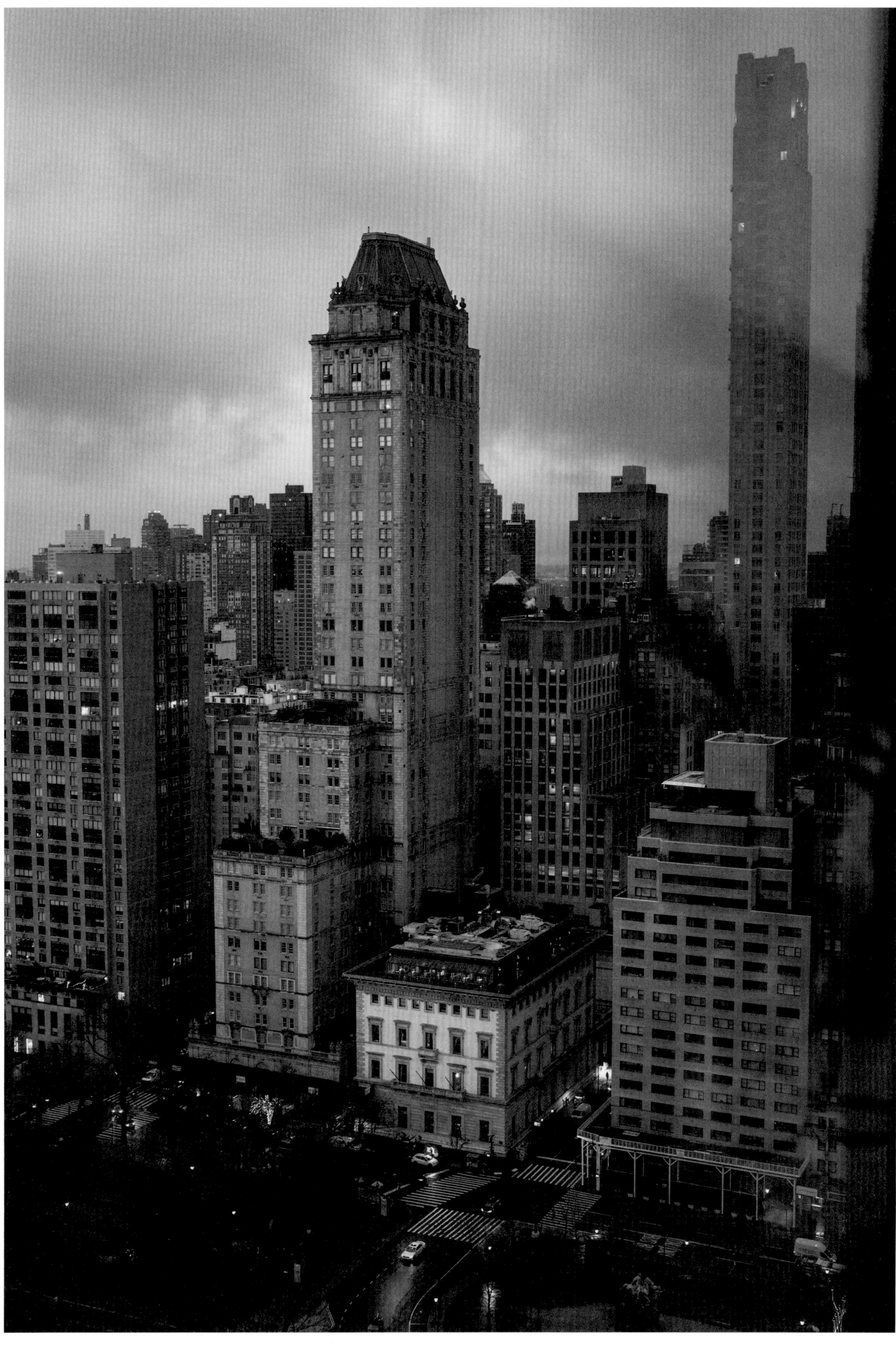

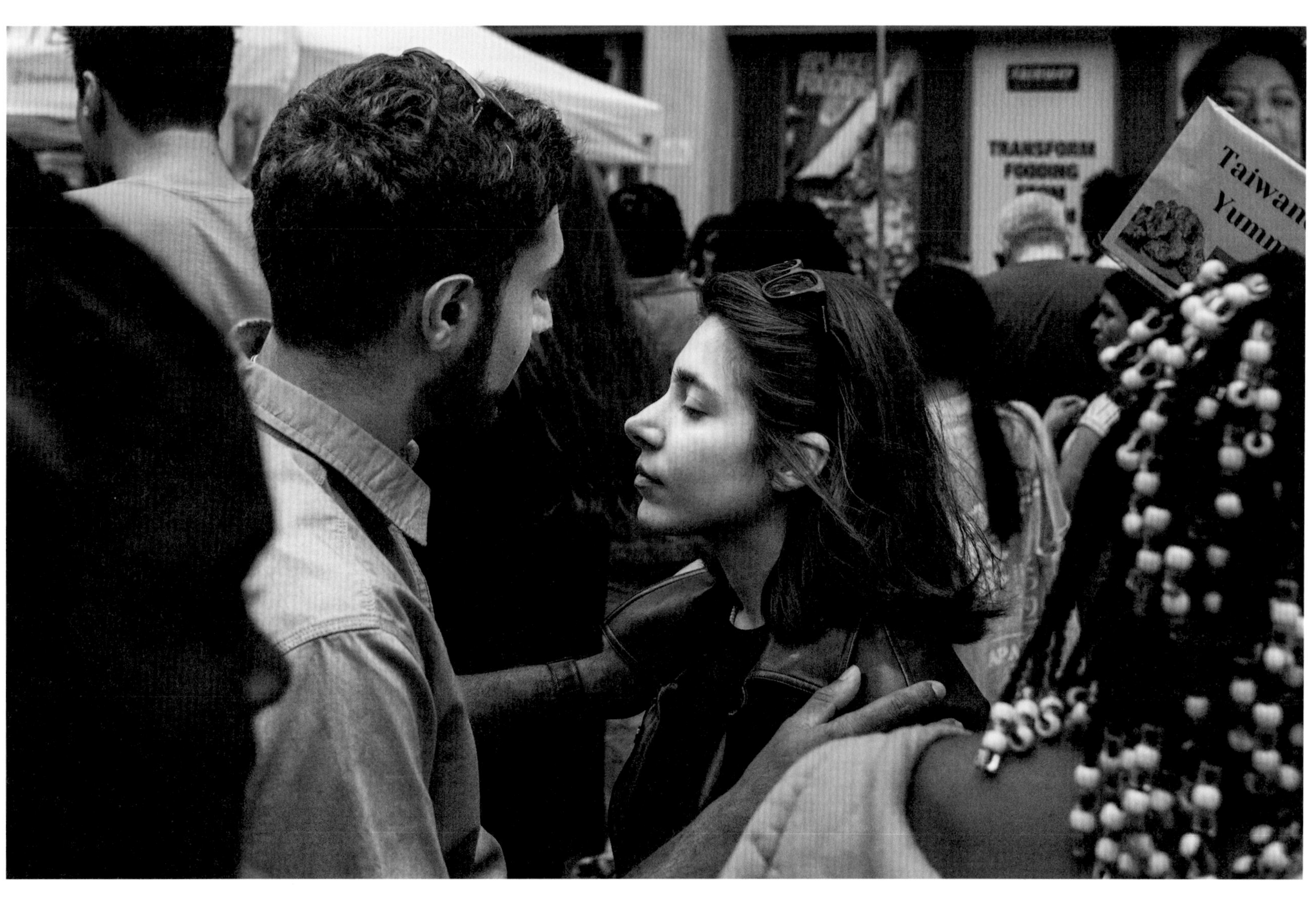
TRANSFORM
FOODING

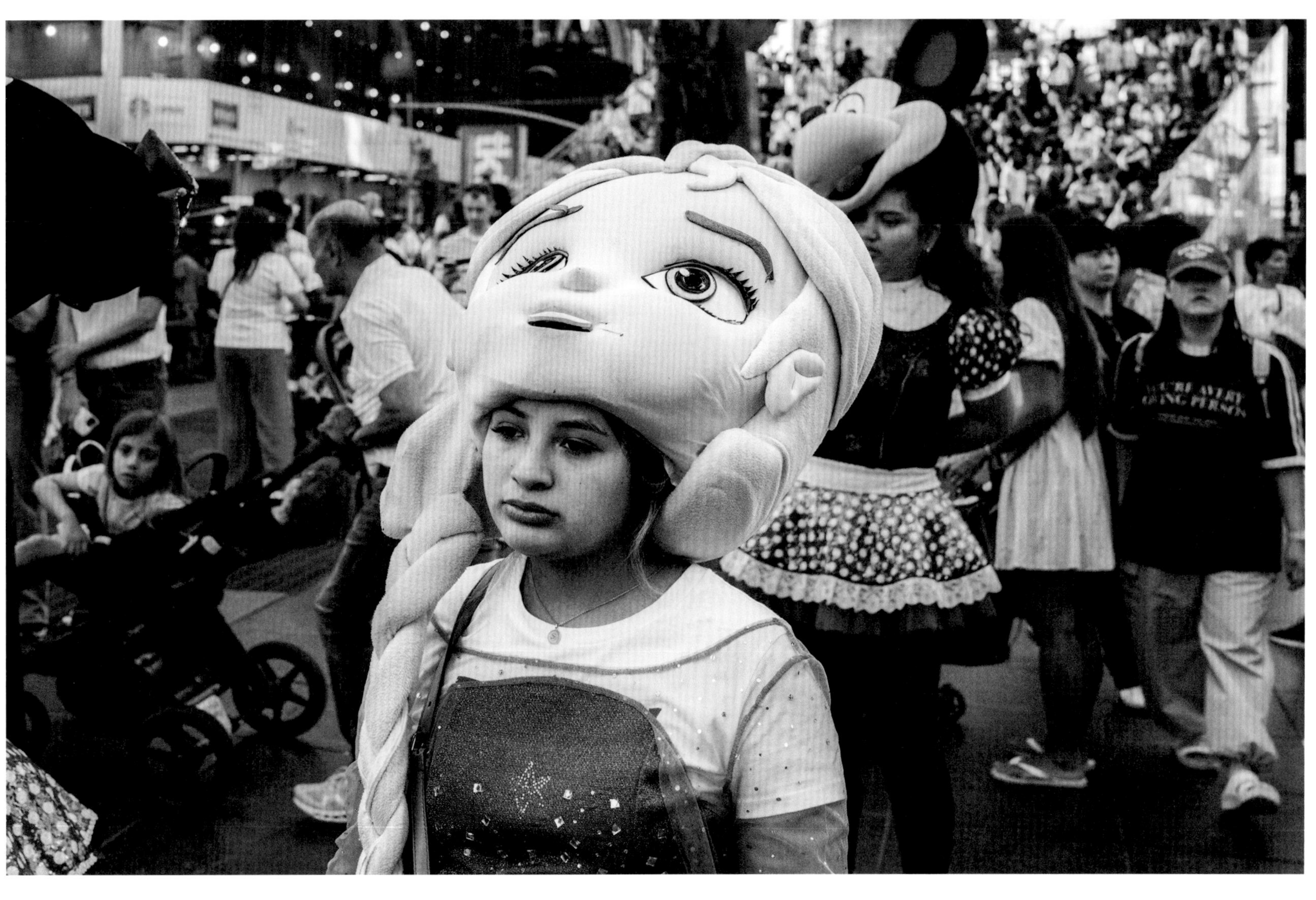

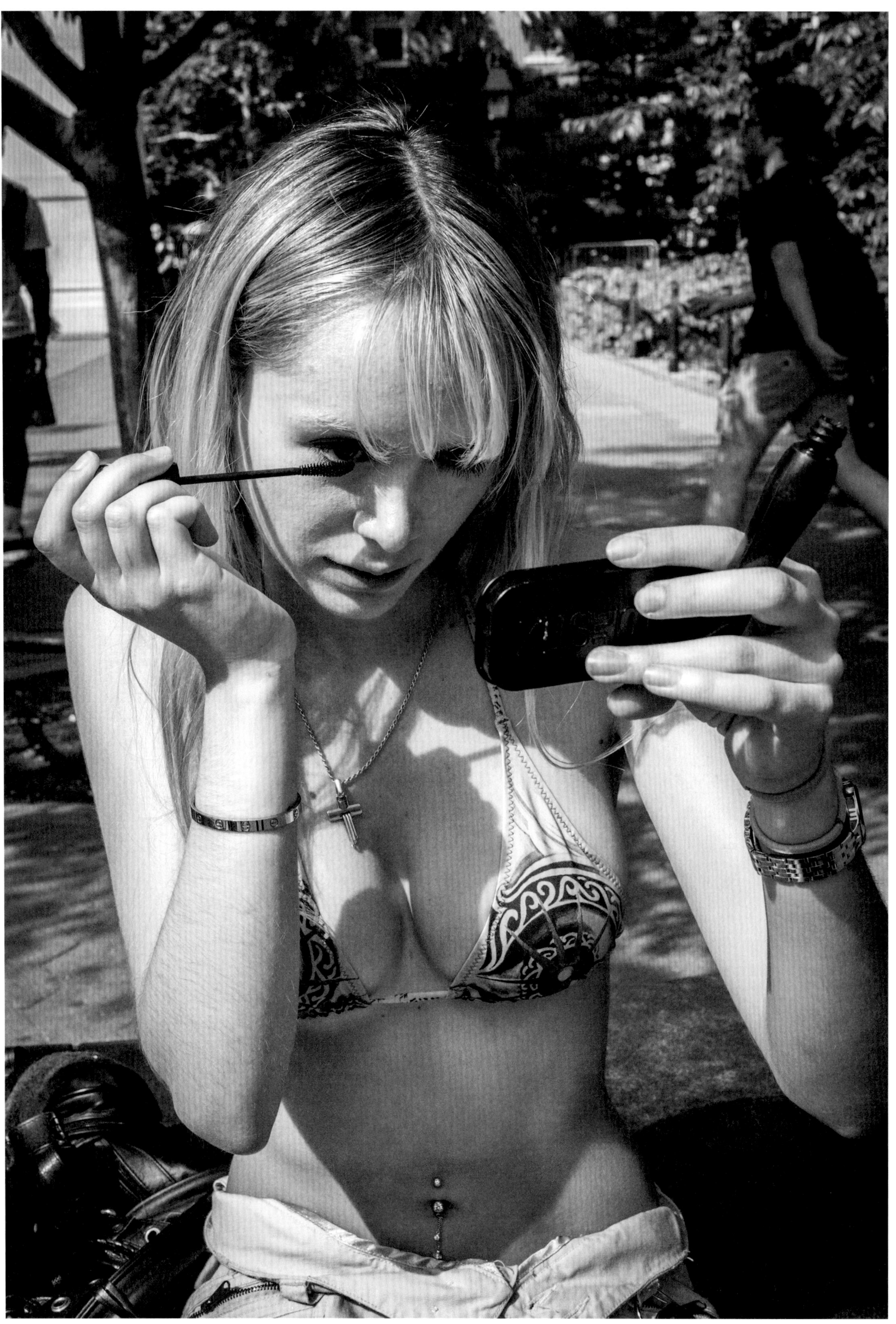

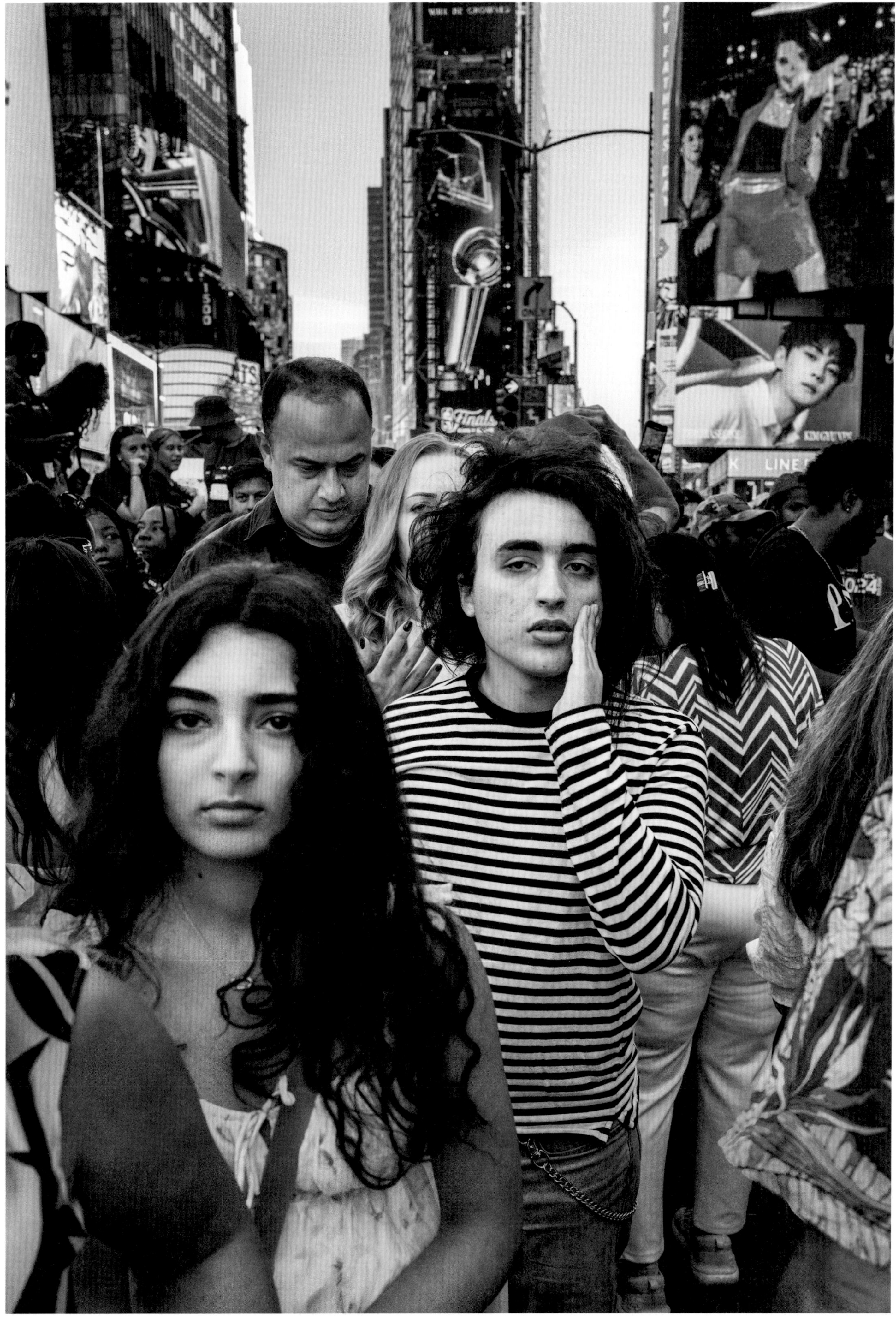
1500
ONLY
Finals

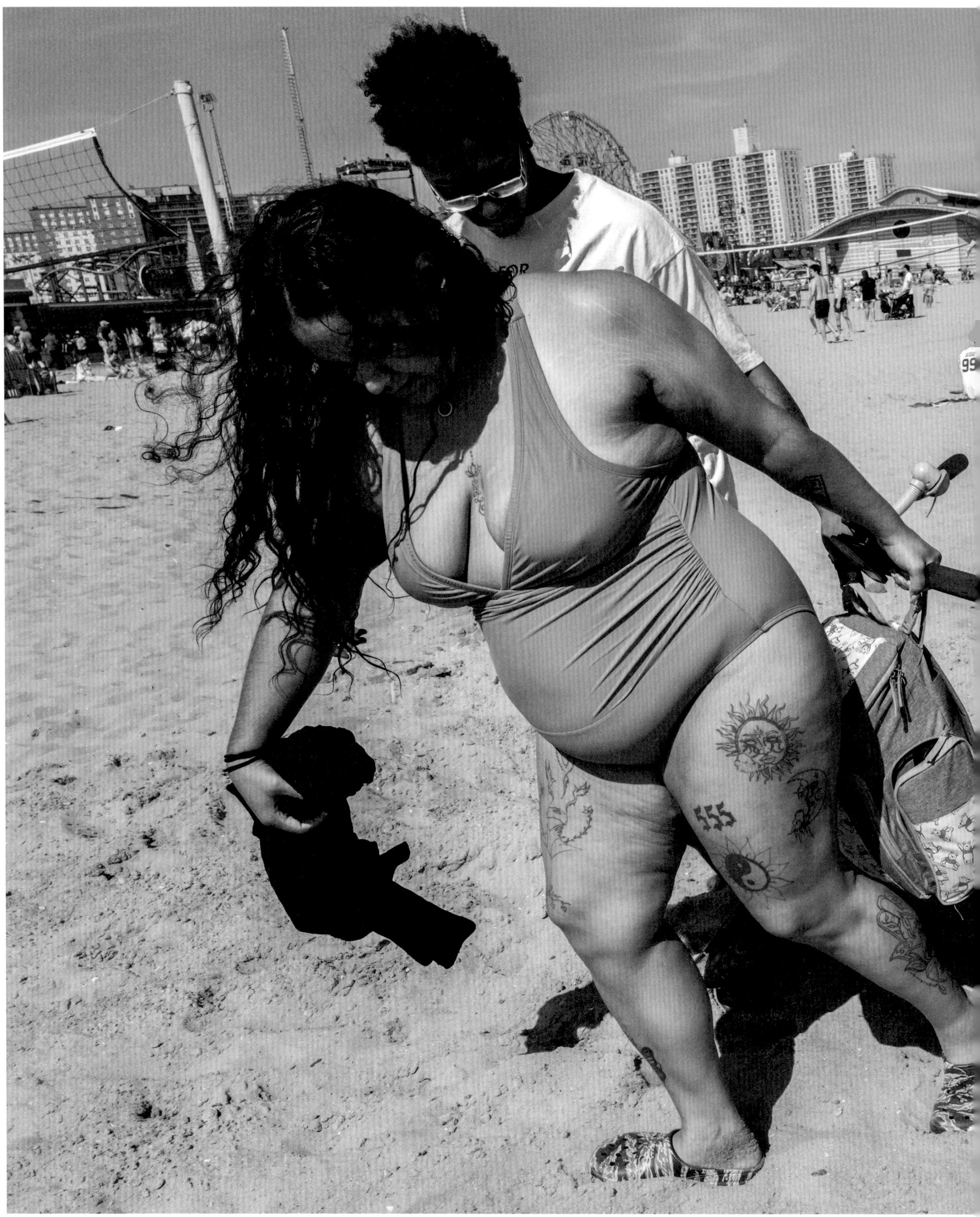
FOR
555
99

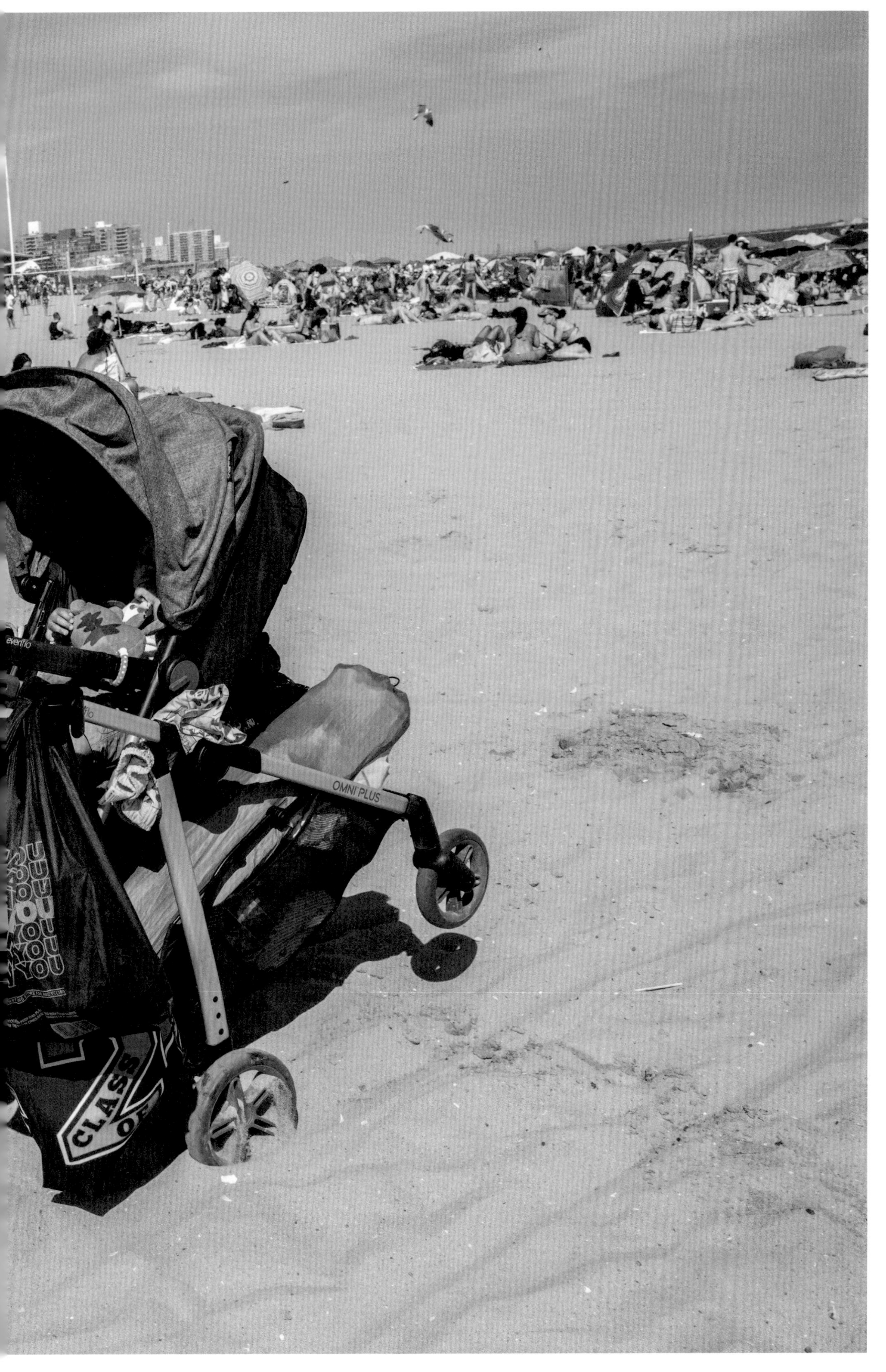
eventflo
OMNI PLUS
CLASS
OF

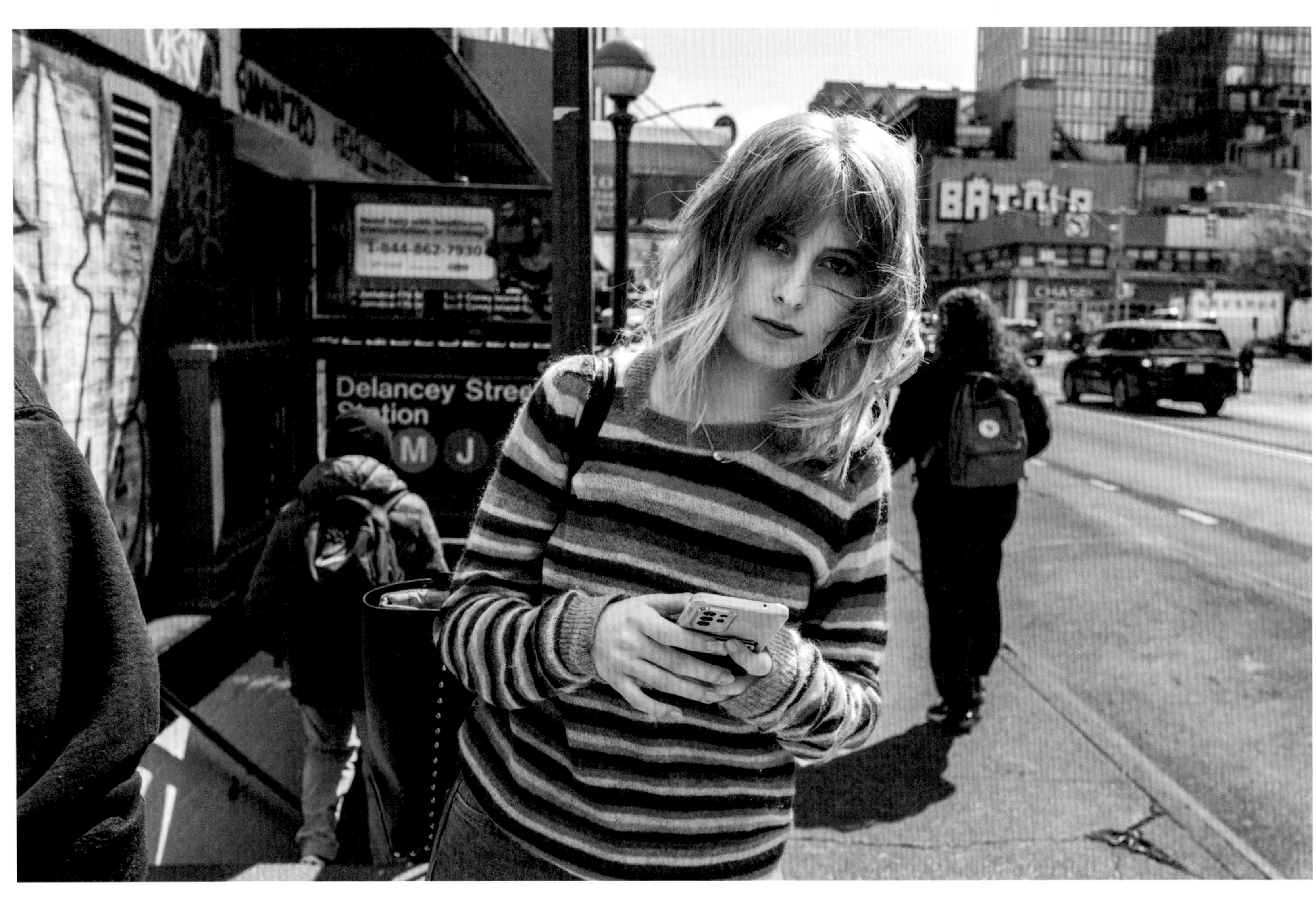
1-844-862-7930
Delancey Stree
M
J

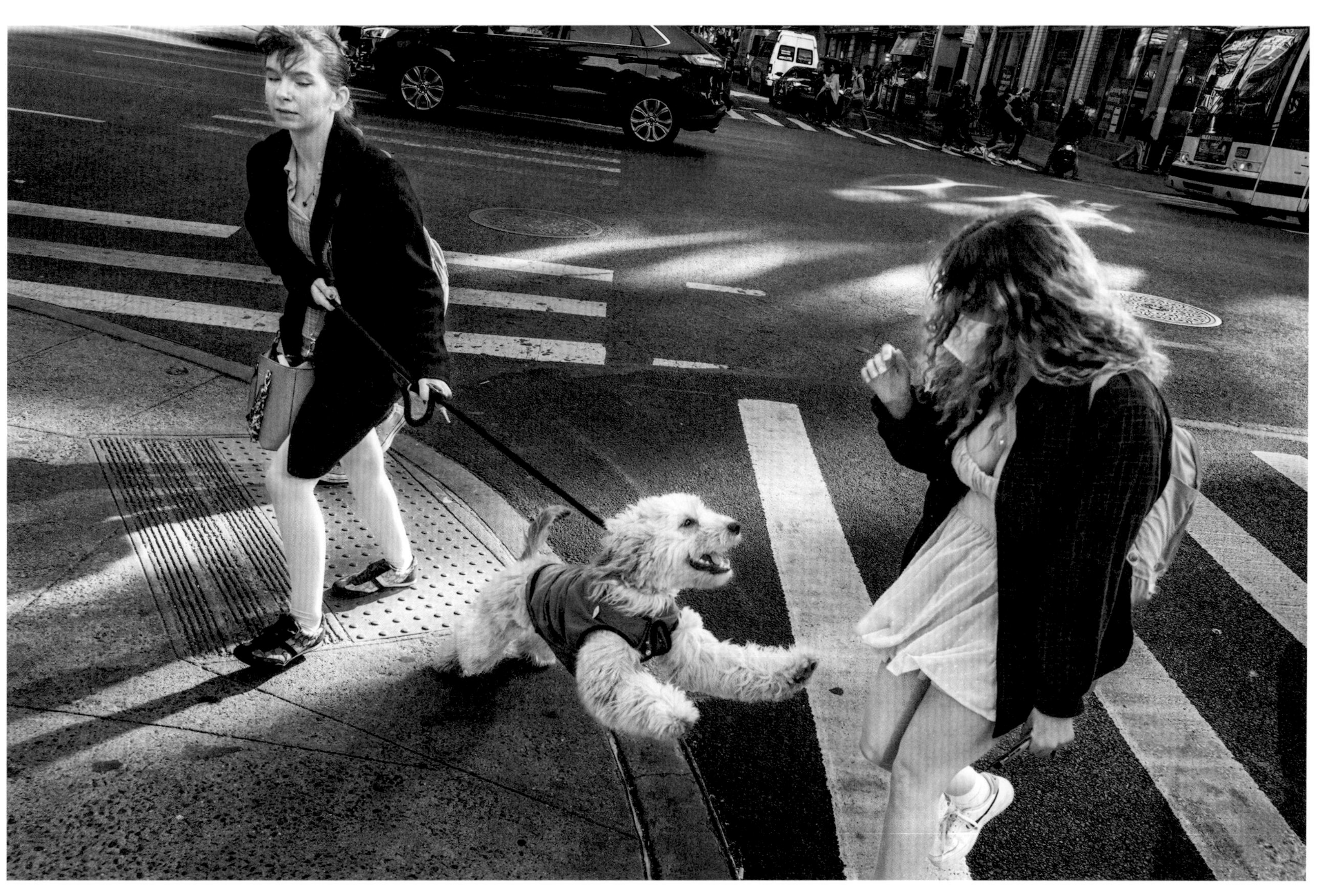

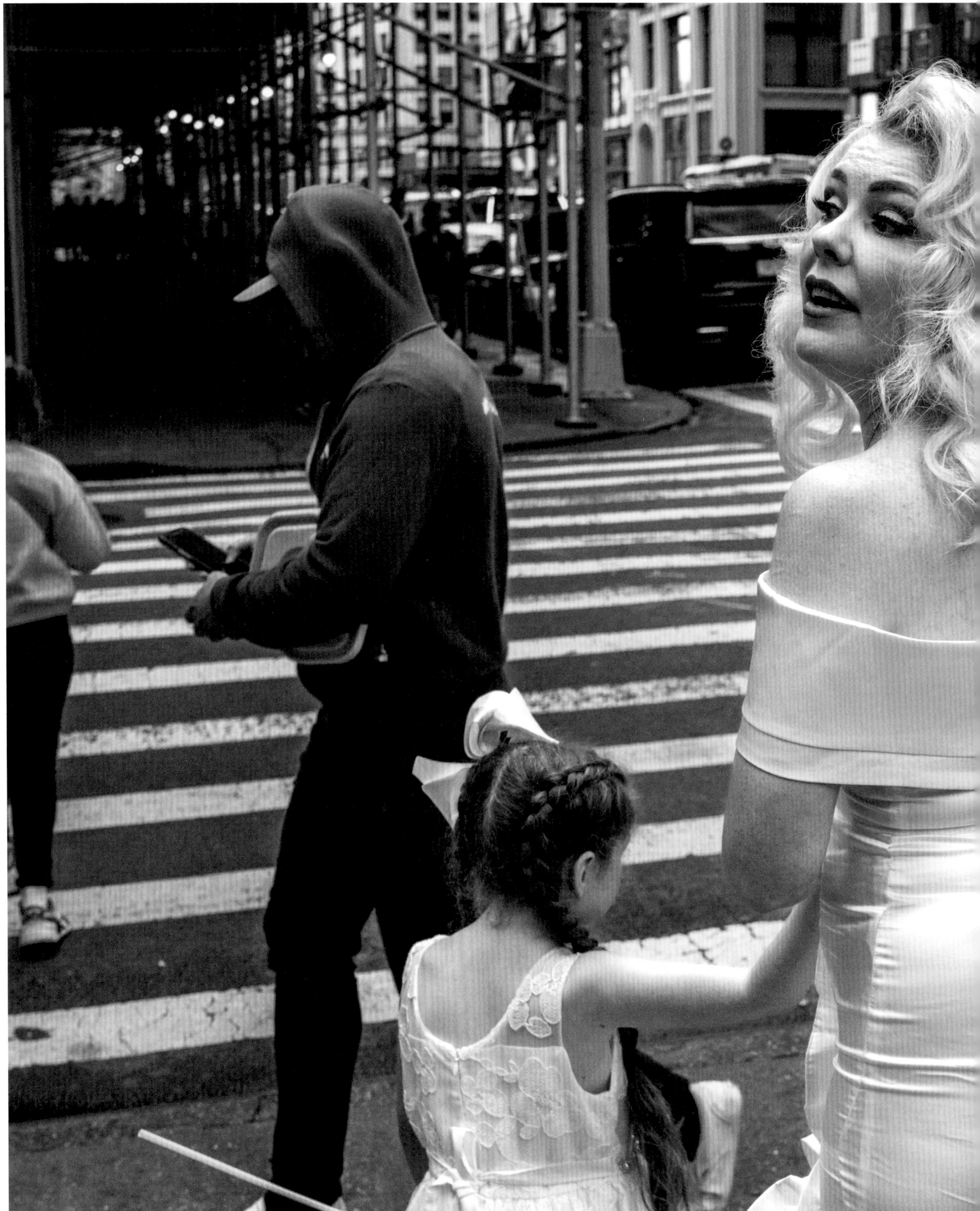

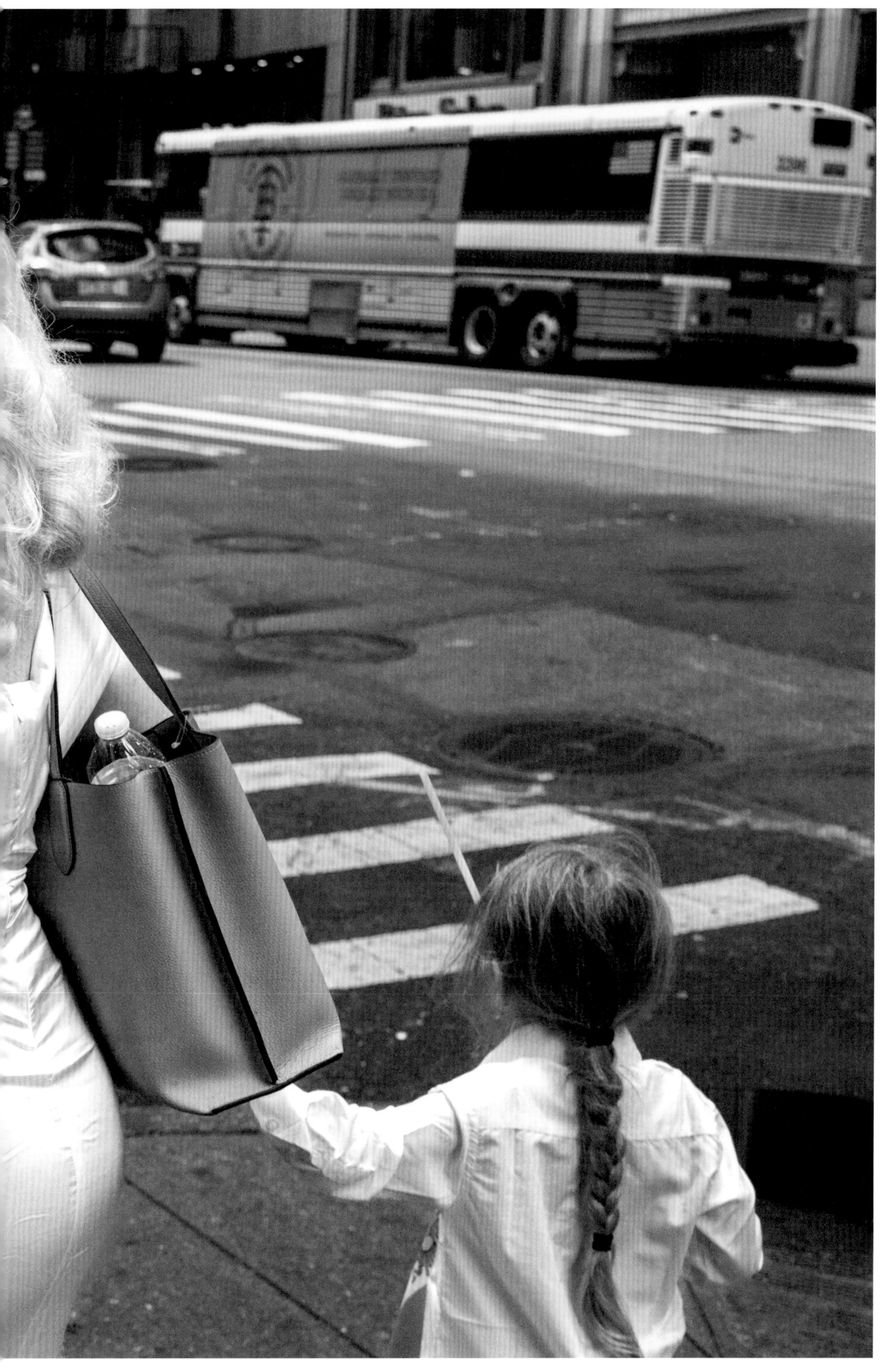

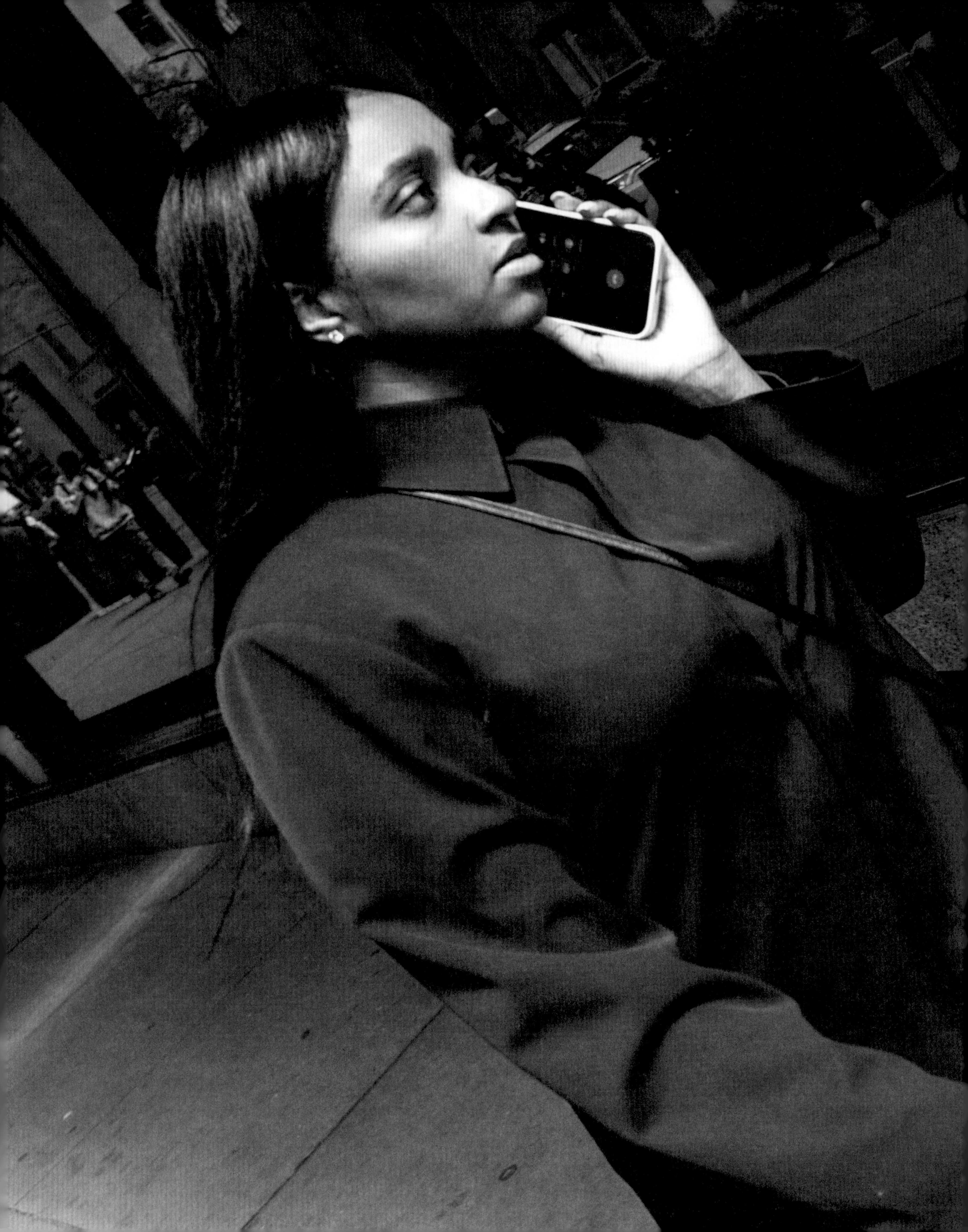

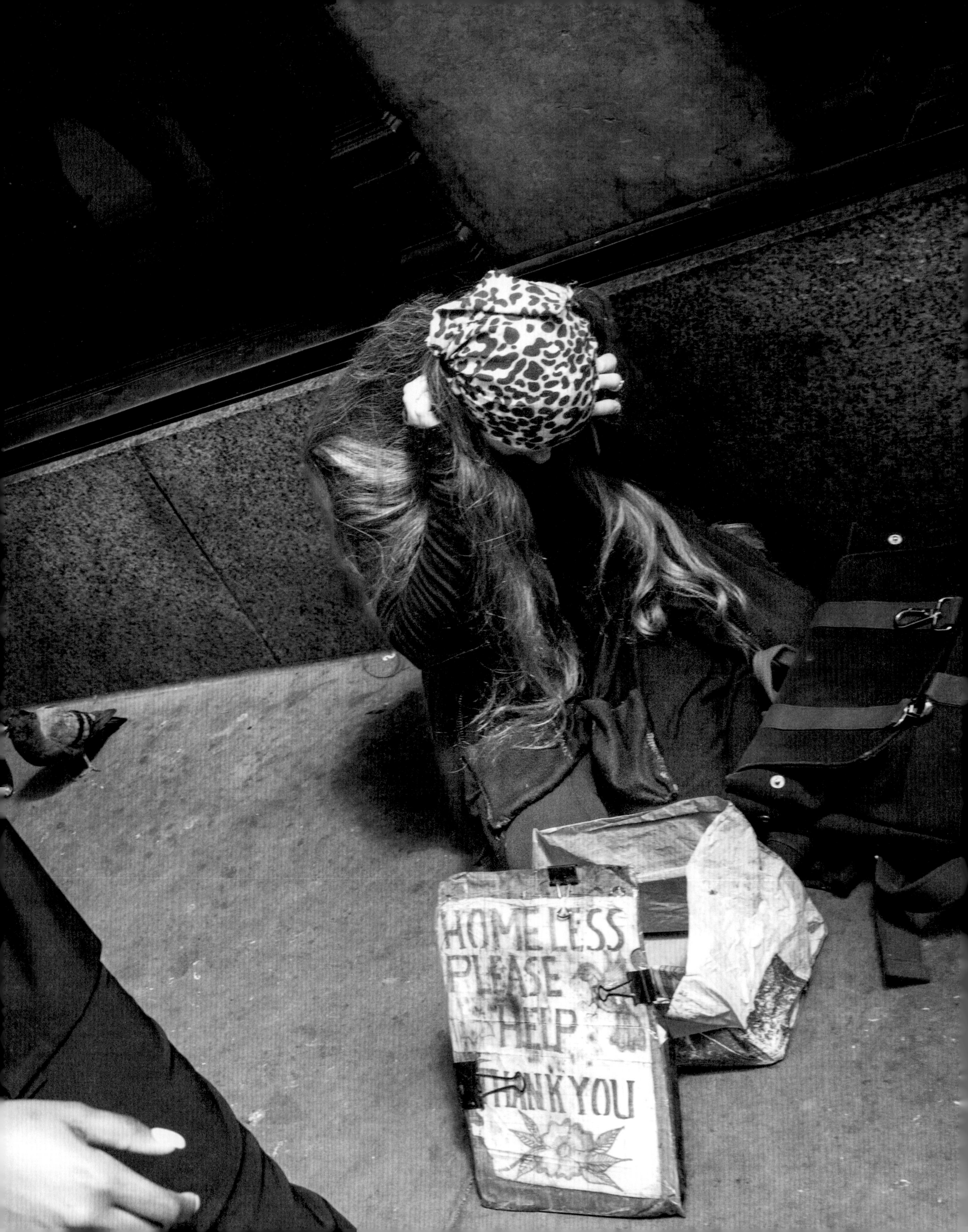
HOMELESS
PLEASE
HELP
THANK YOU

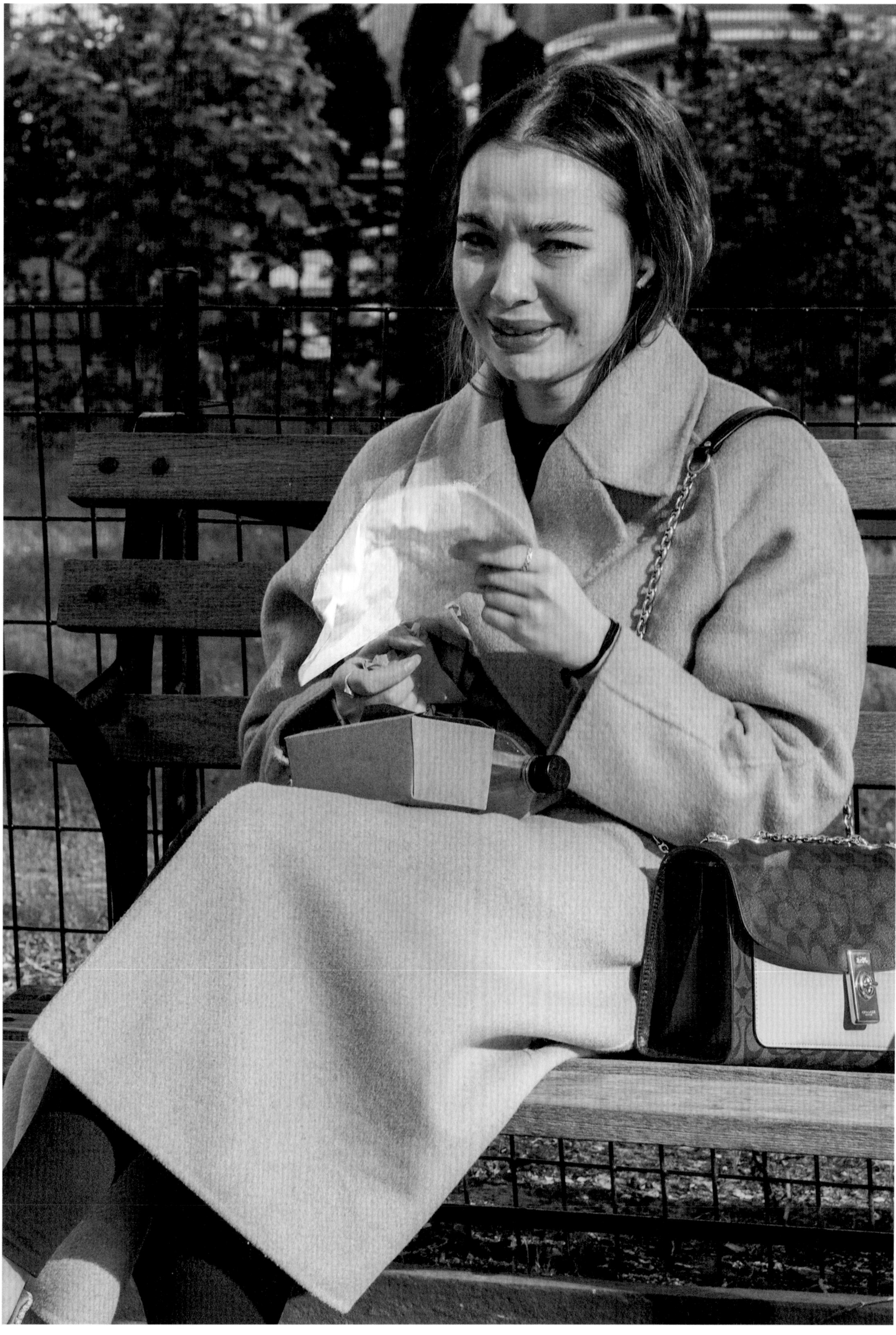

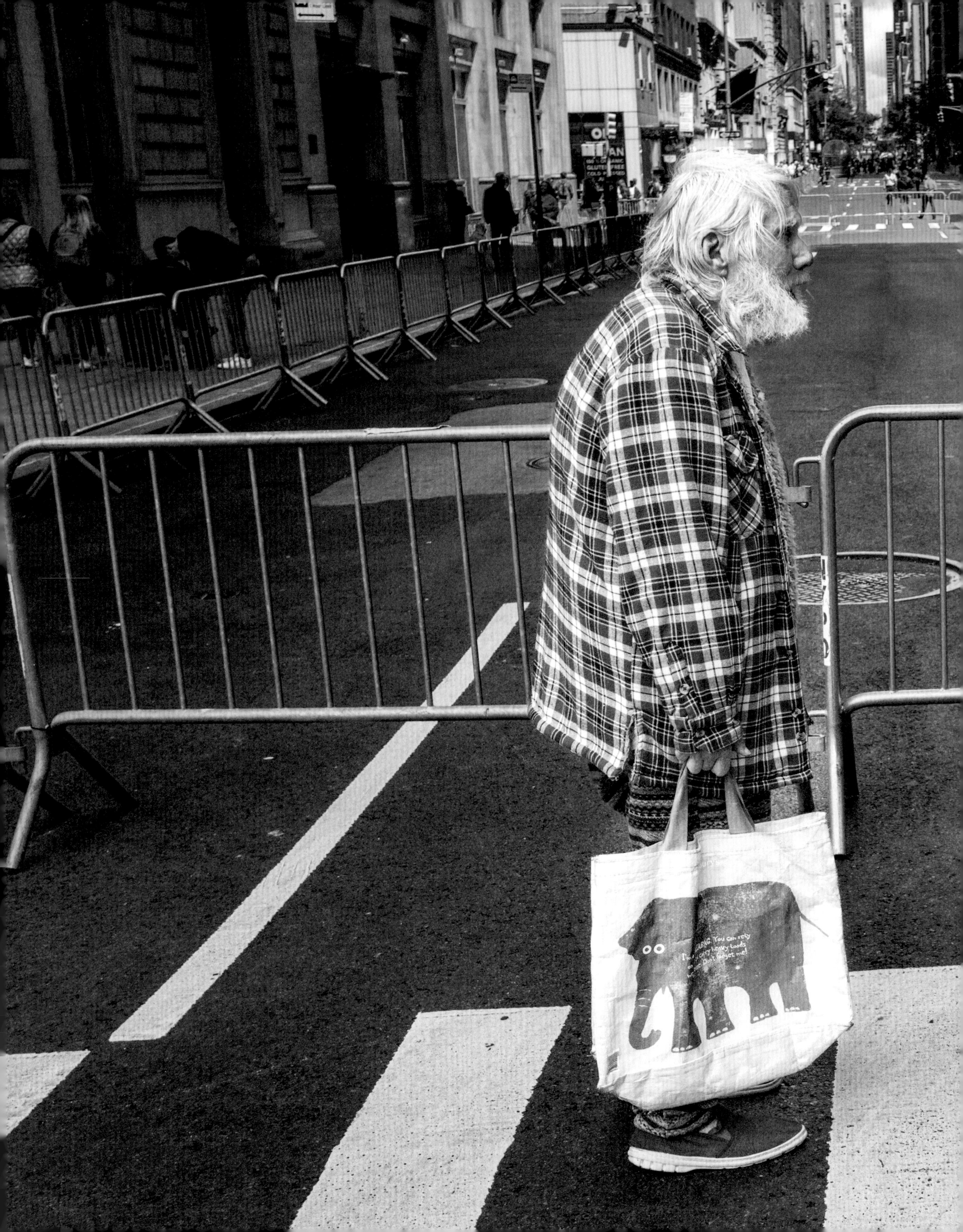
You can rely
carry heavy loads
Don't forget me!

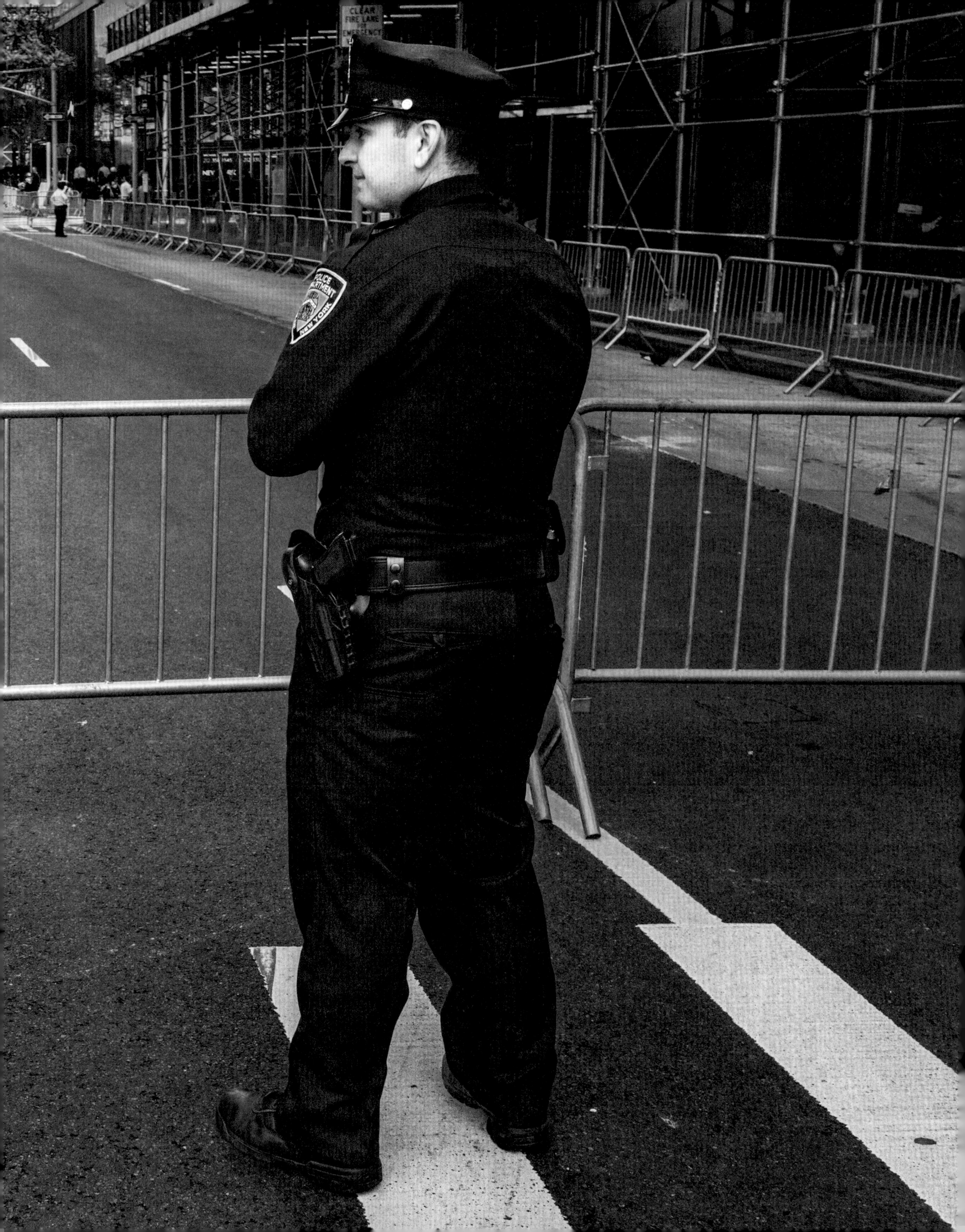
CLEAR
FIRE LANE
POLICE
NEW YORK

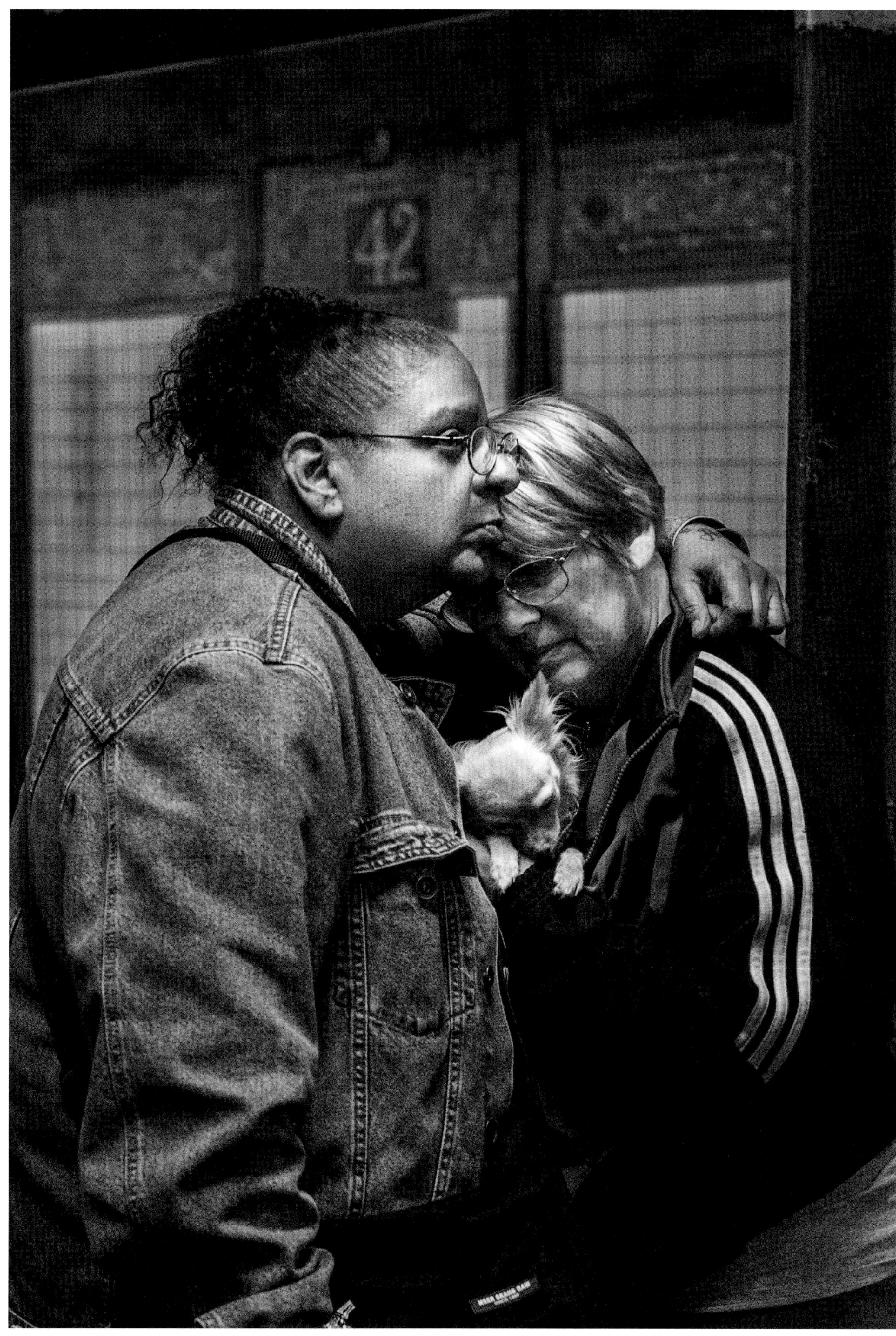
42

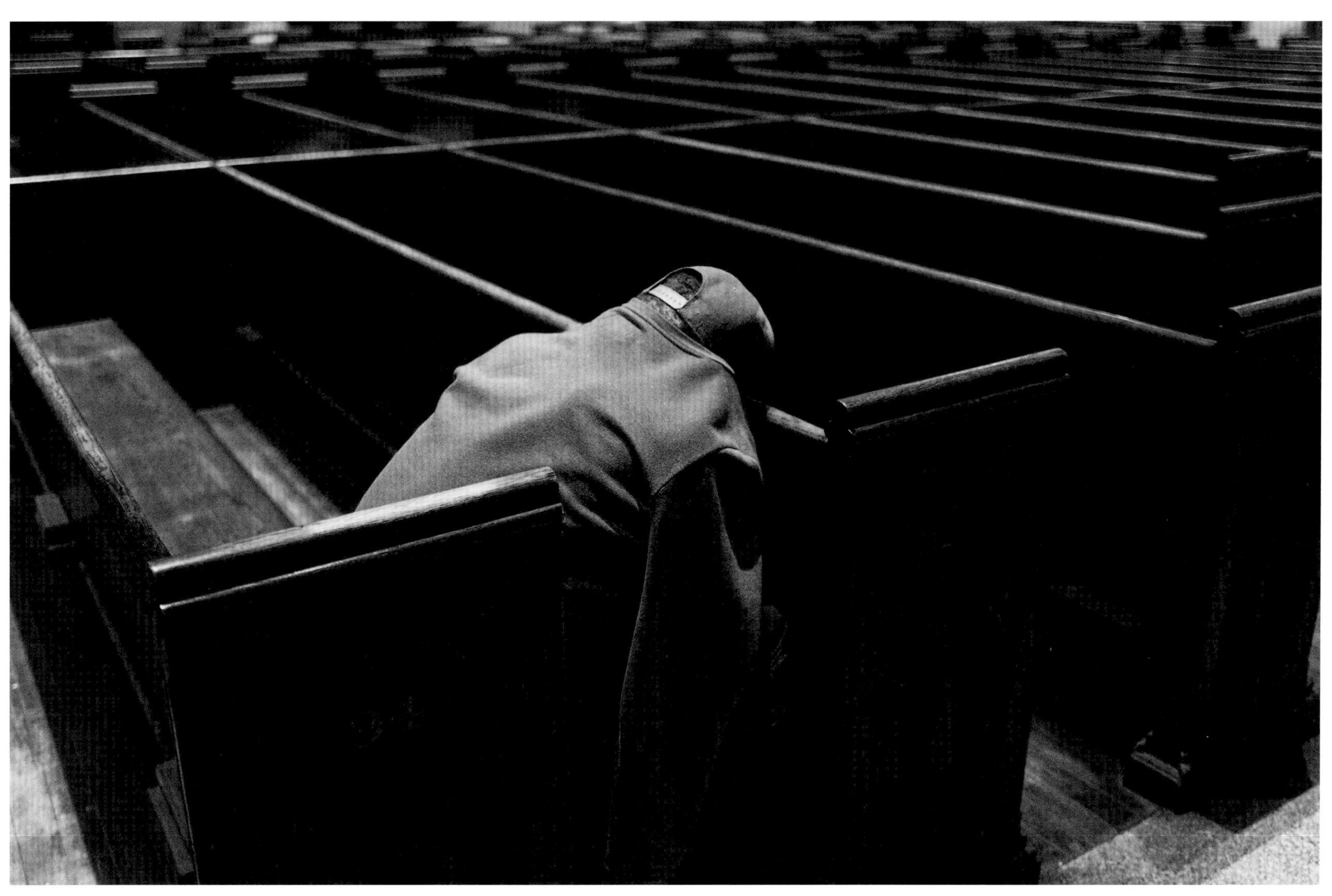

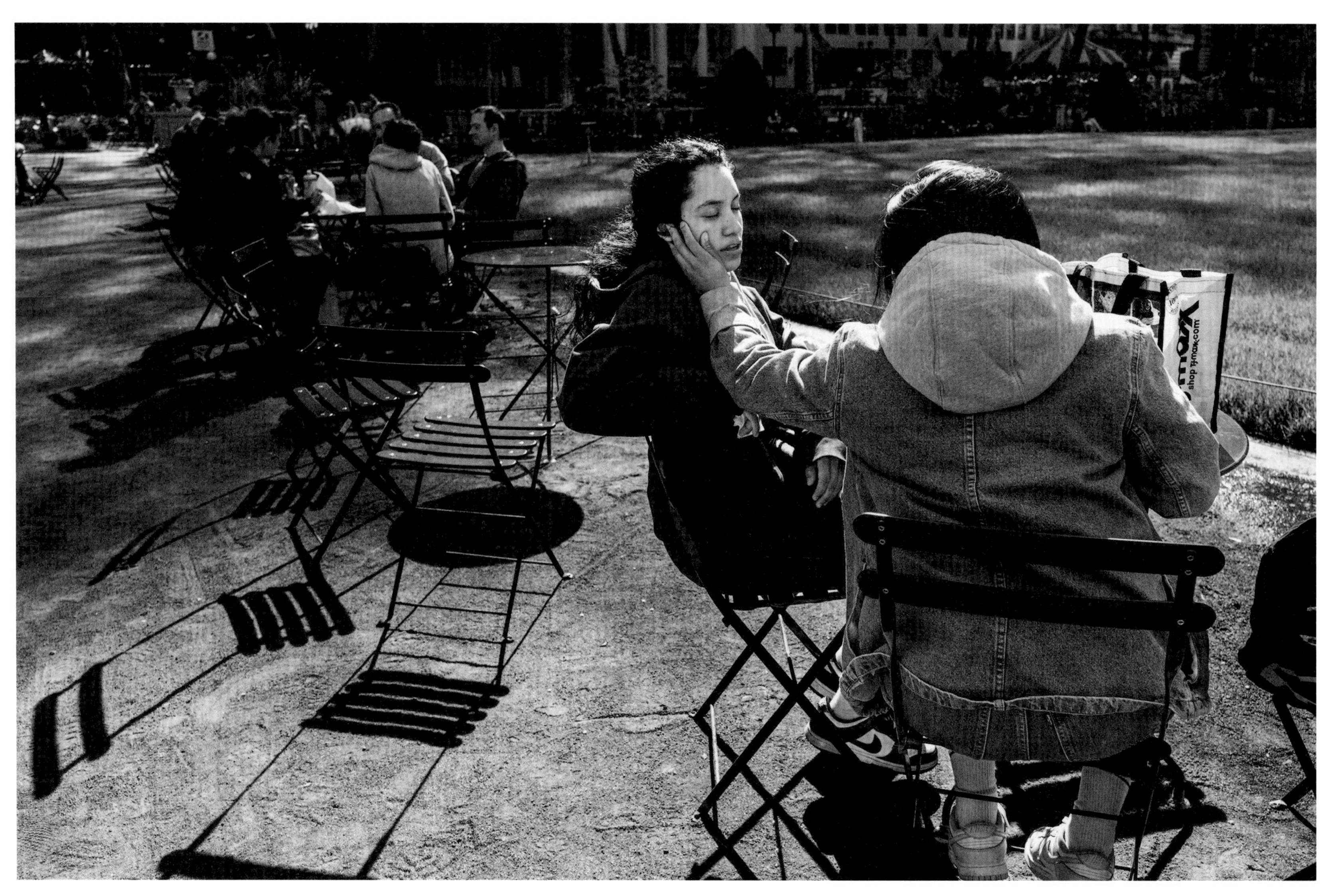
shop tjmaxx.com

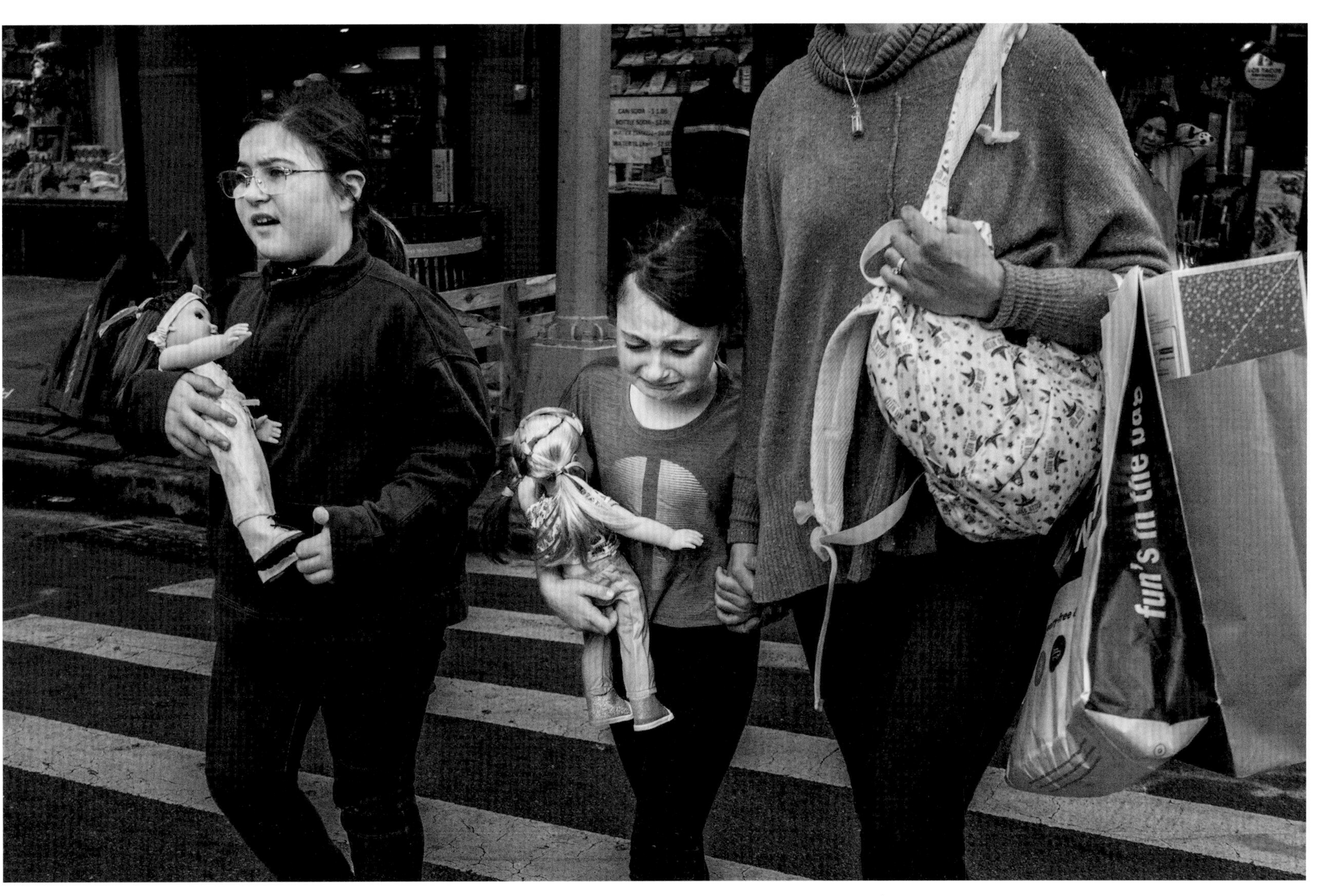
fun's in the

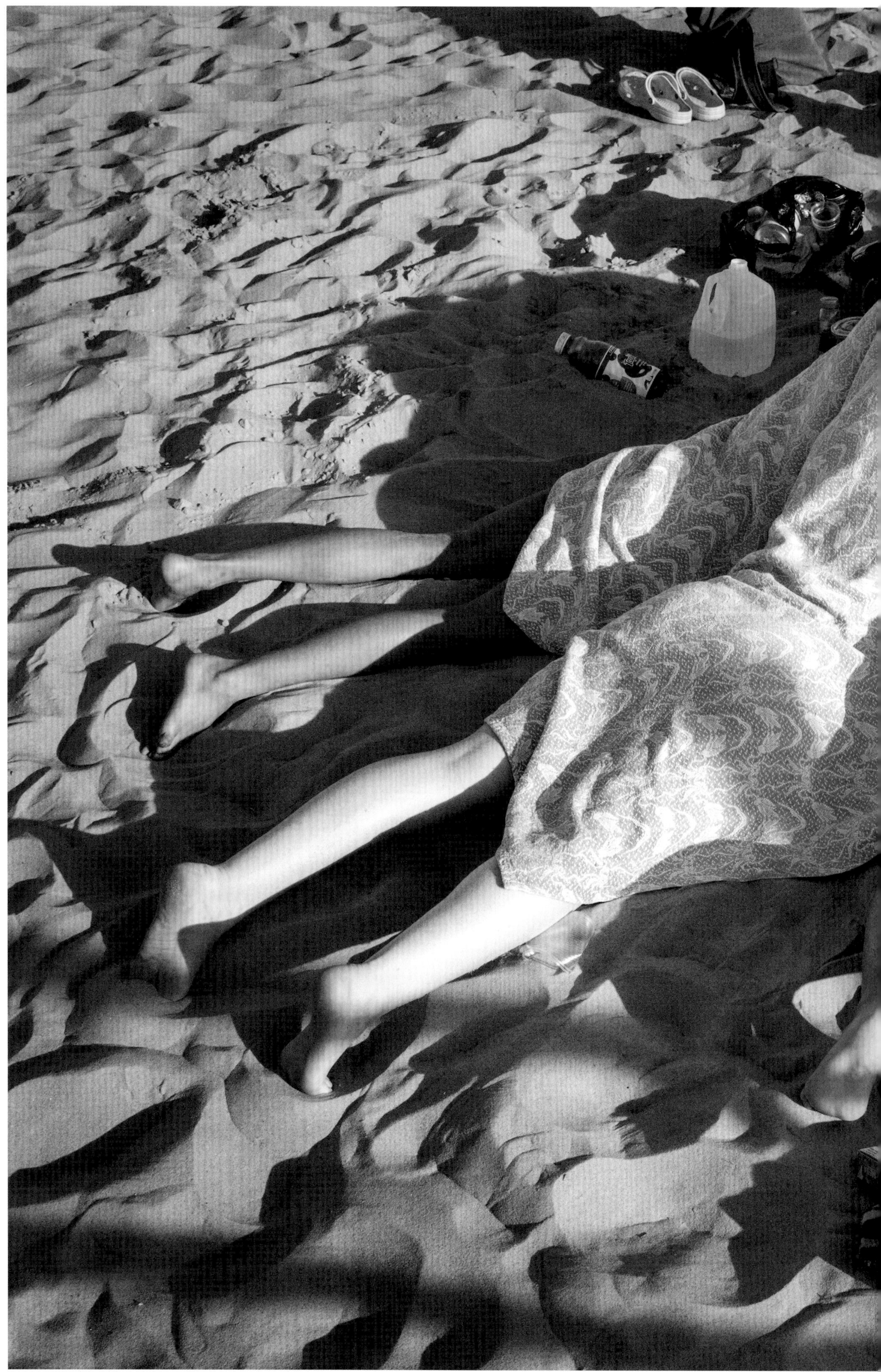

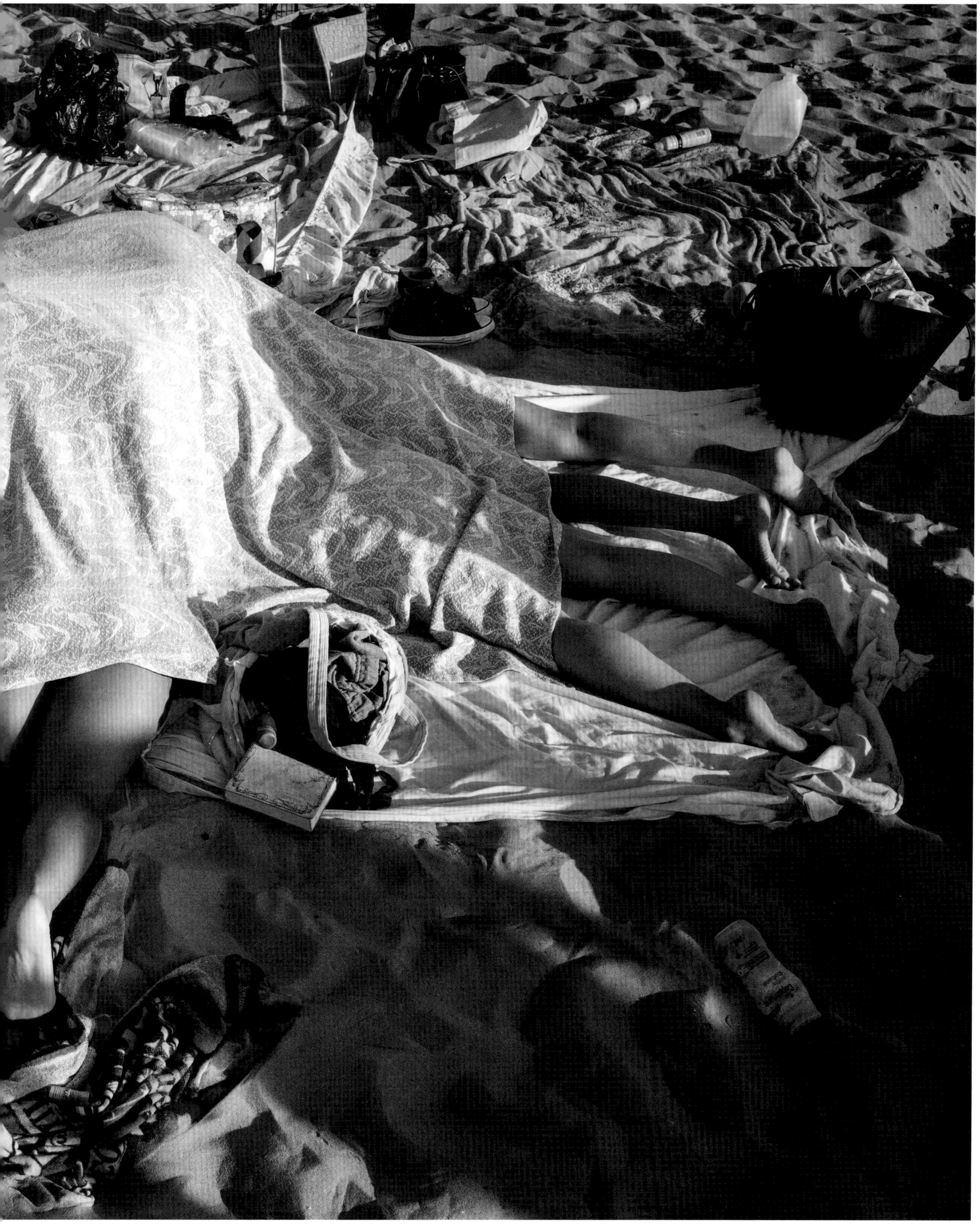

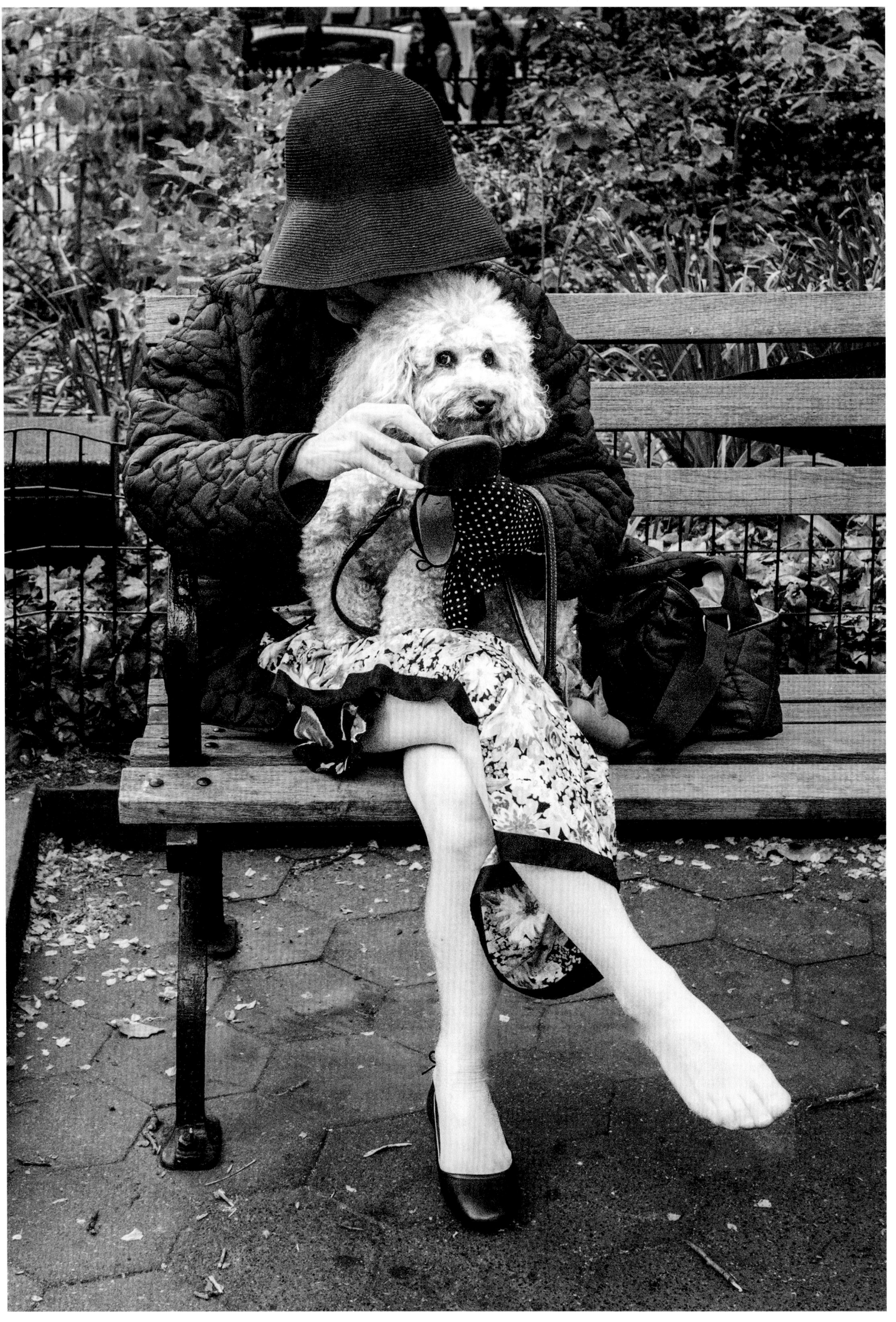

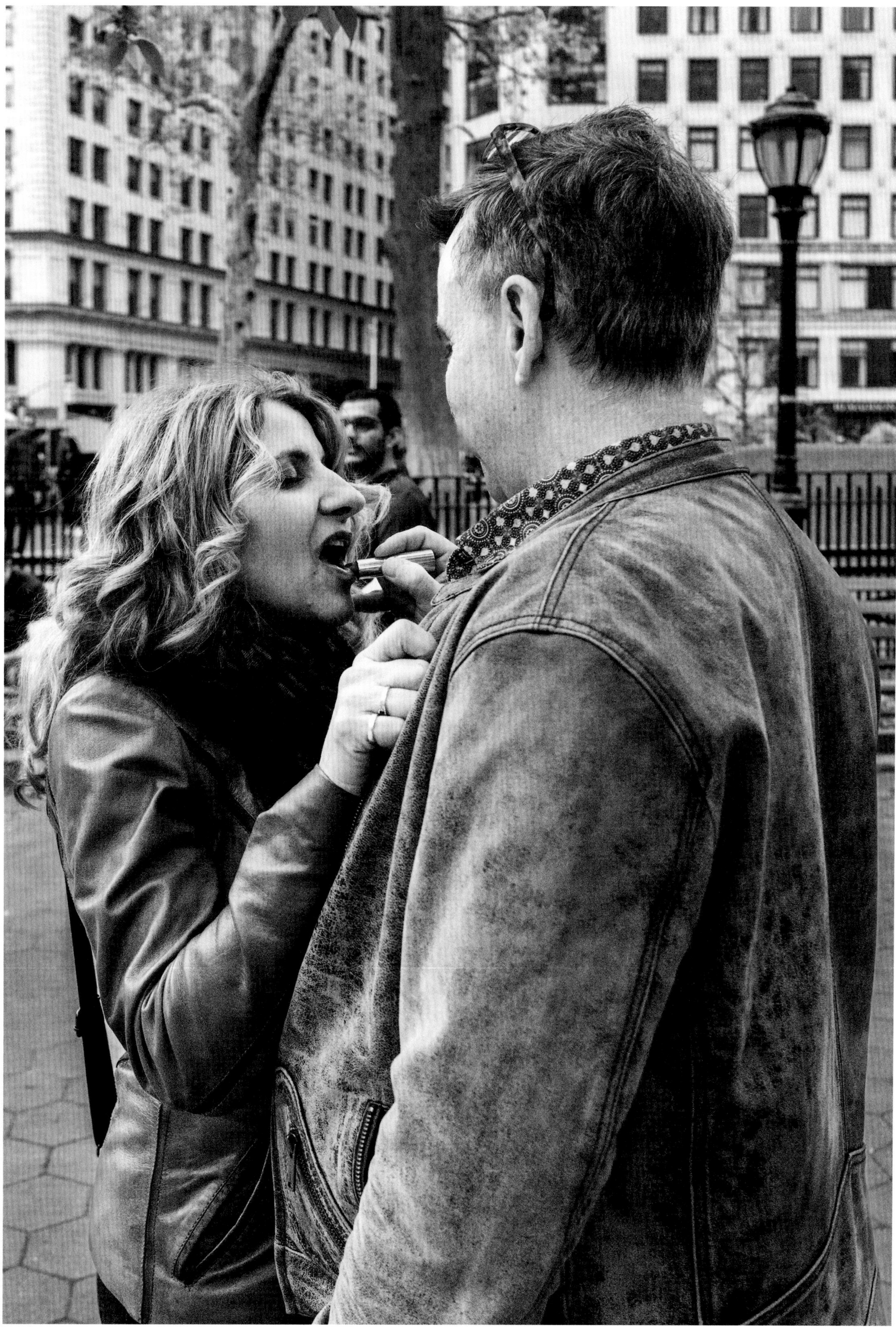

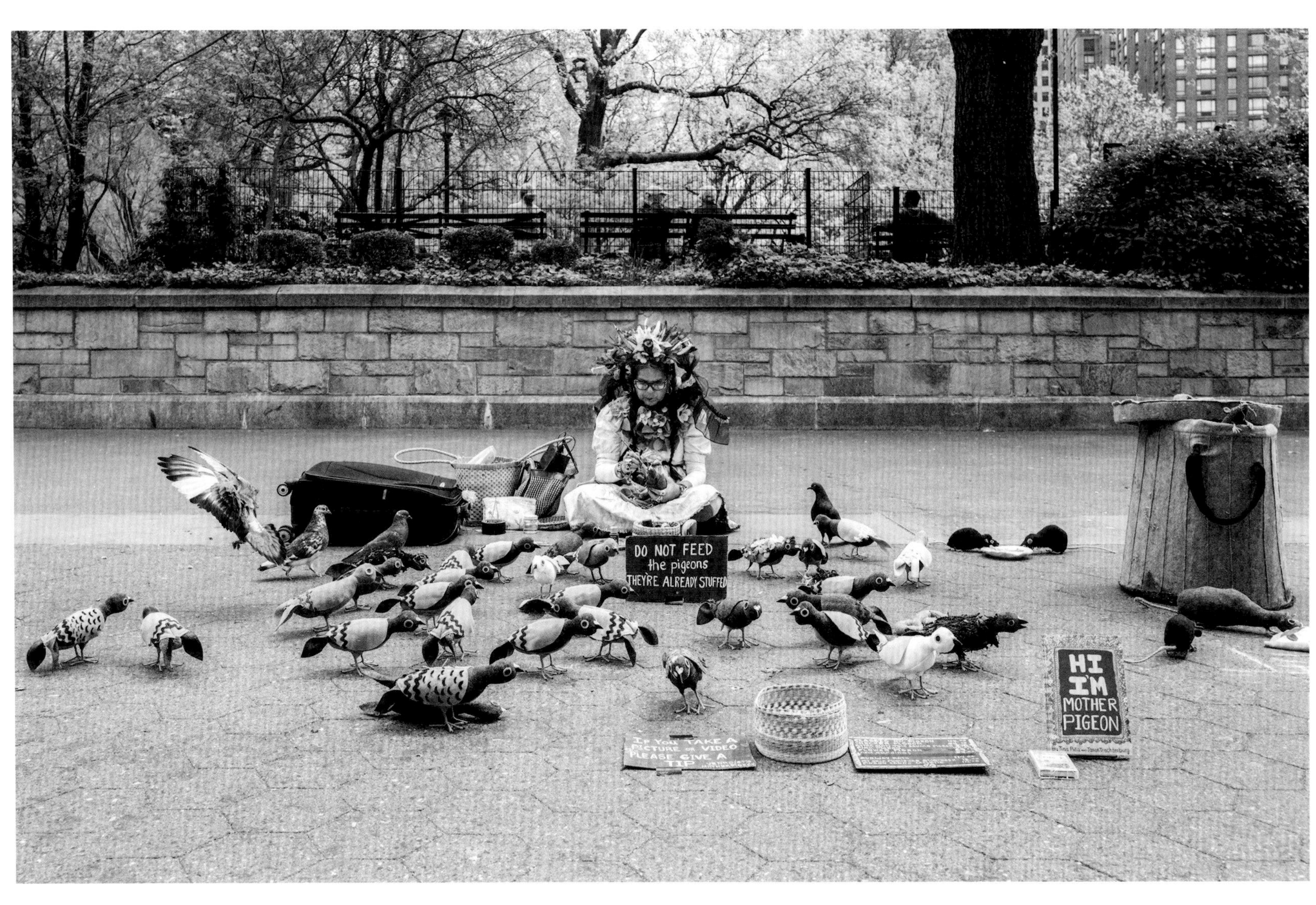
DO NOT FEED
the pigeons
THEY'RE ALREADY STUFFED
IF YOU TAKE A
PICTURE or VIDEO
PLEASE GIVE A
TIP
HI
I'M
MOTHER
PIGEON

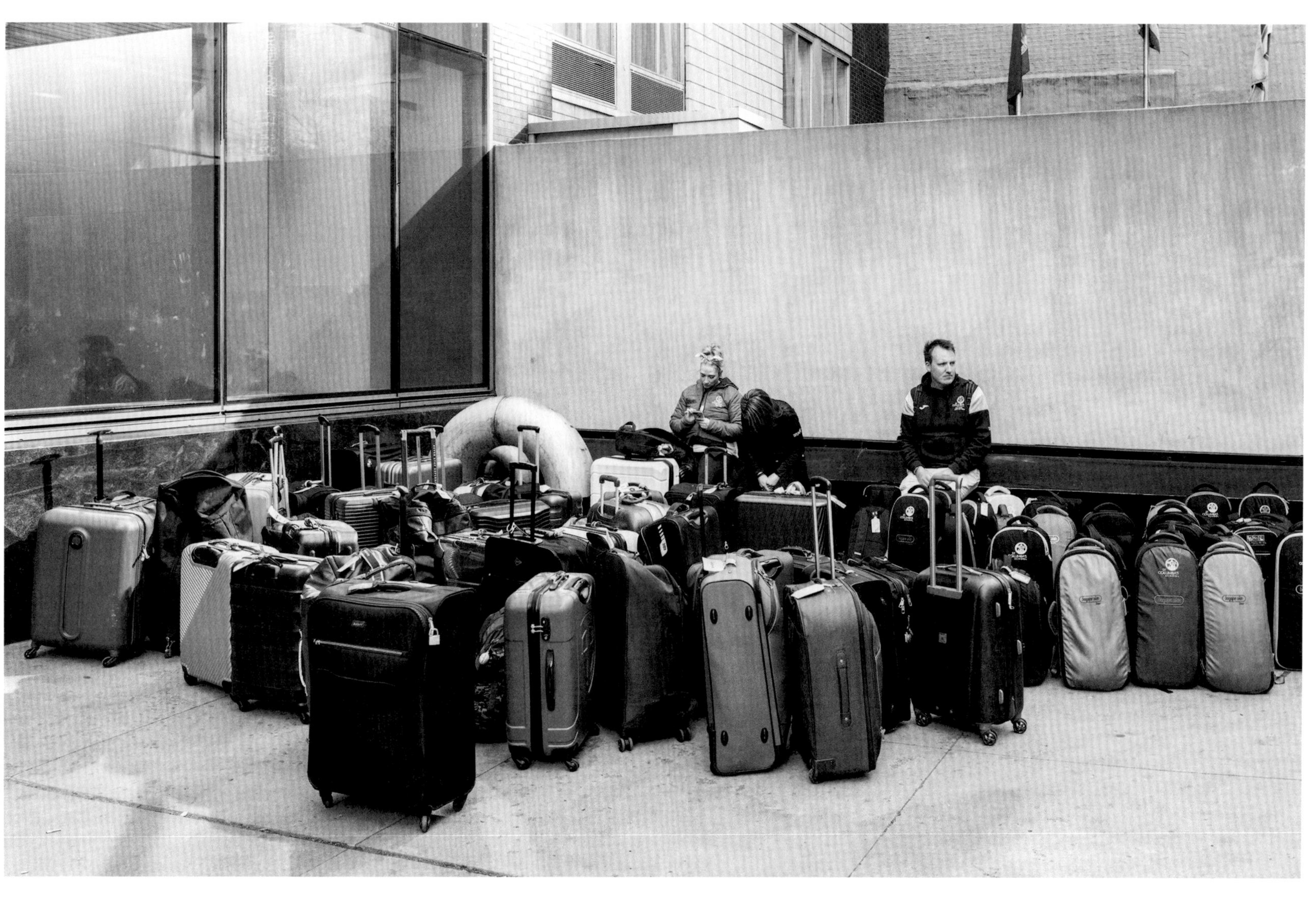

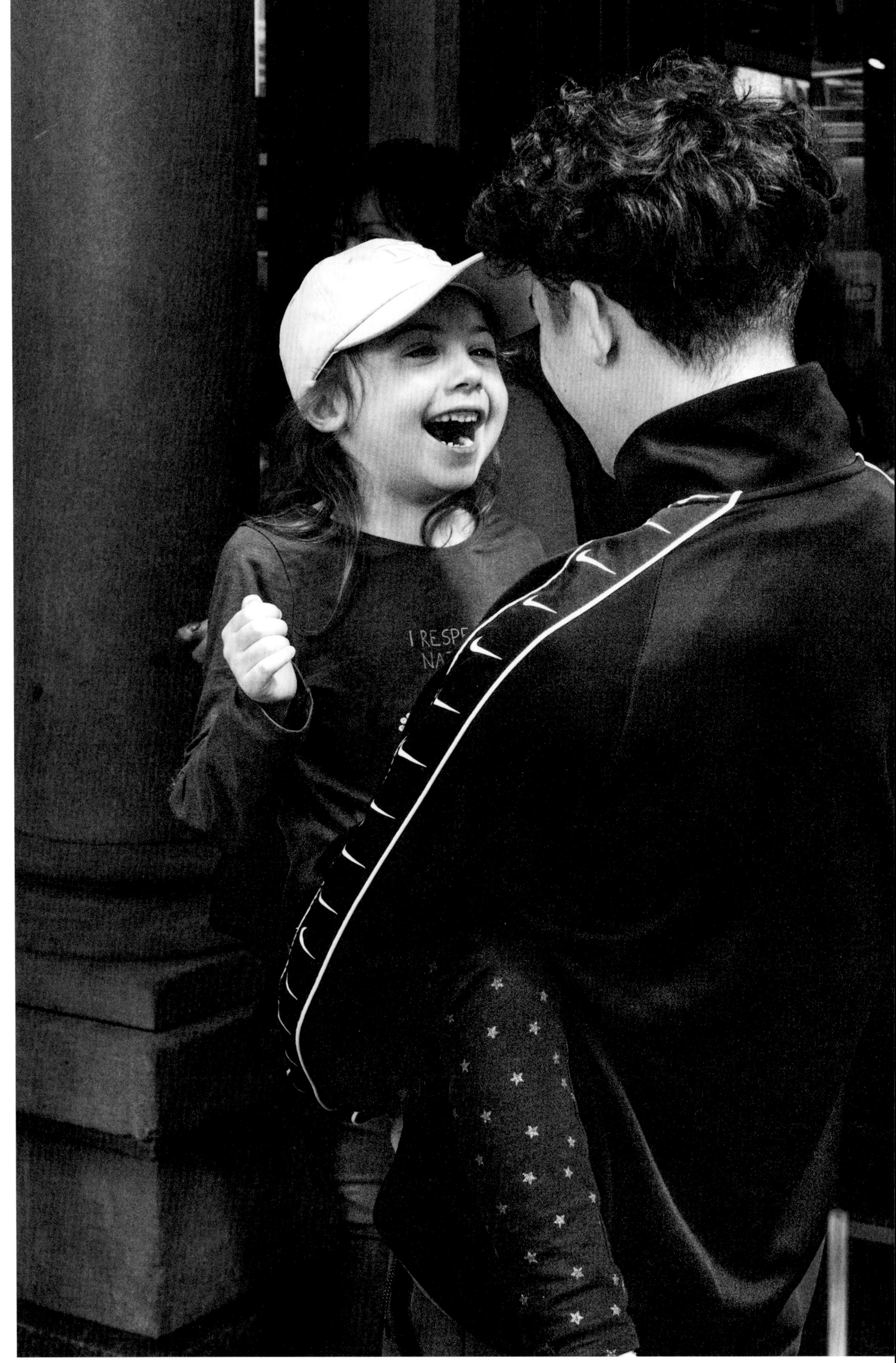

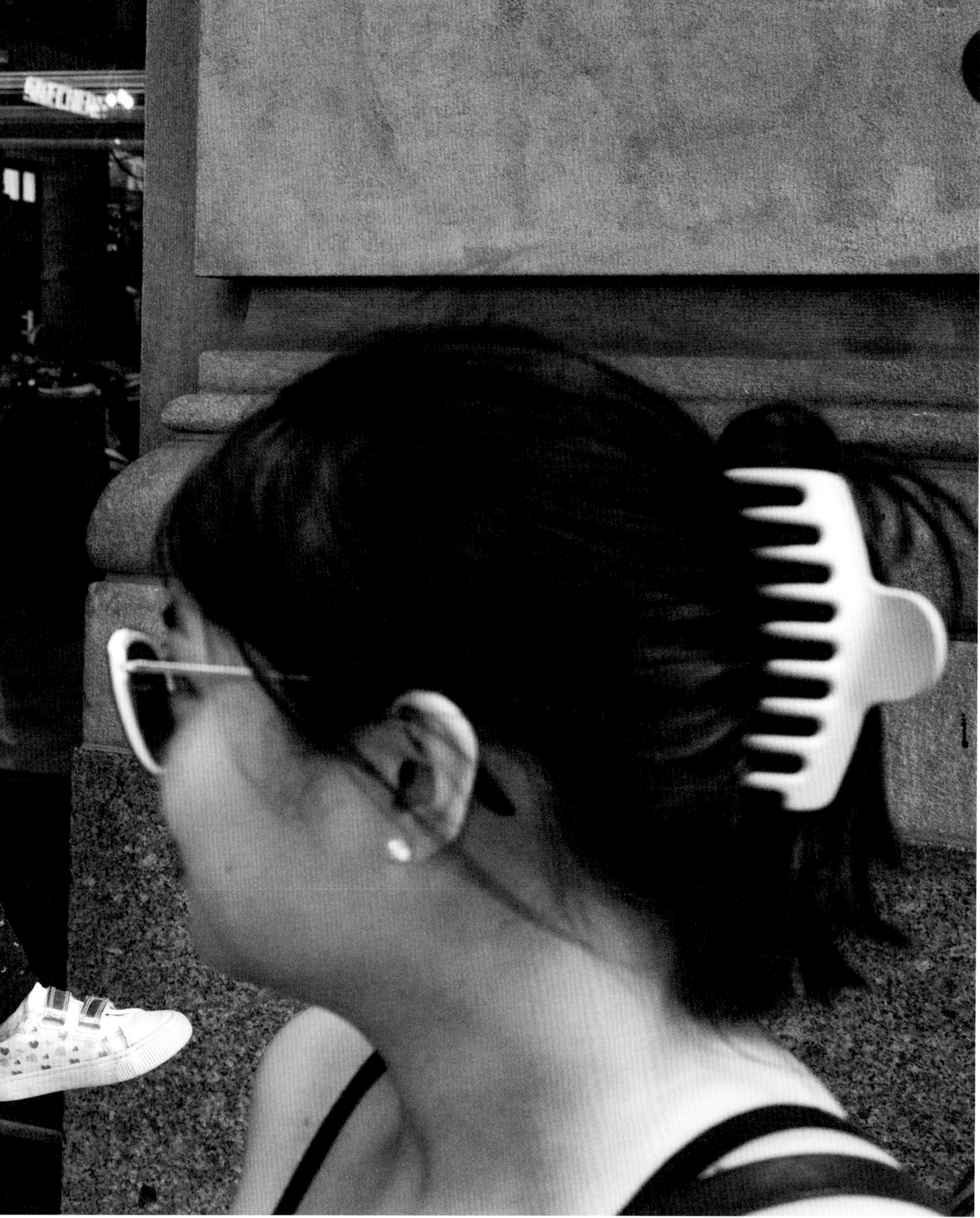

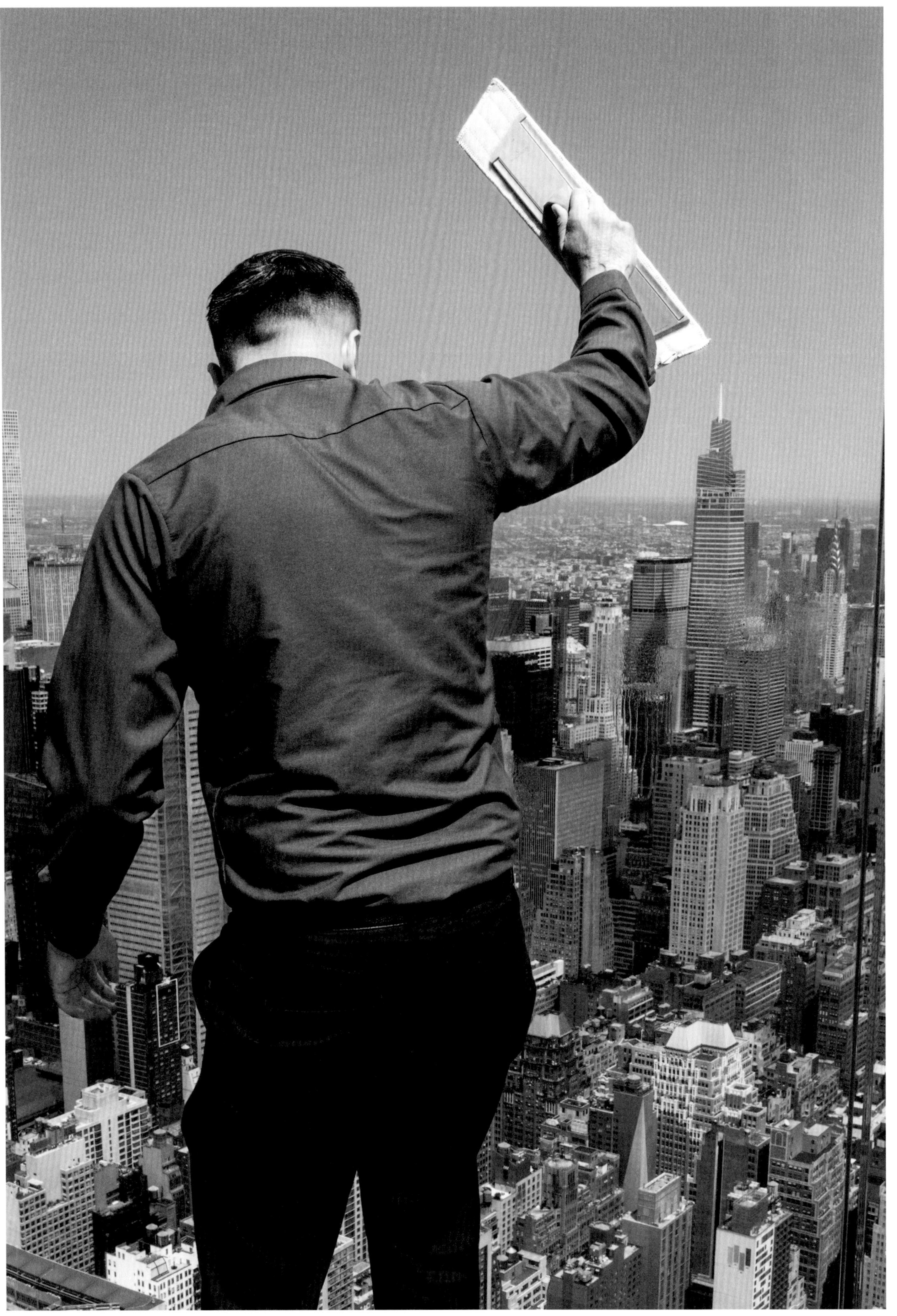

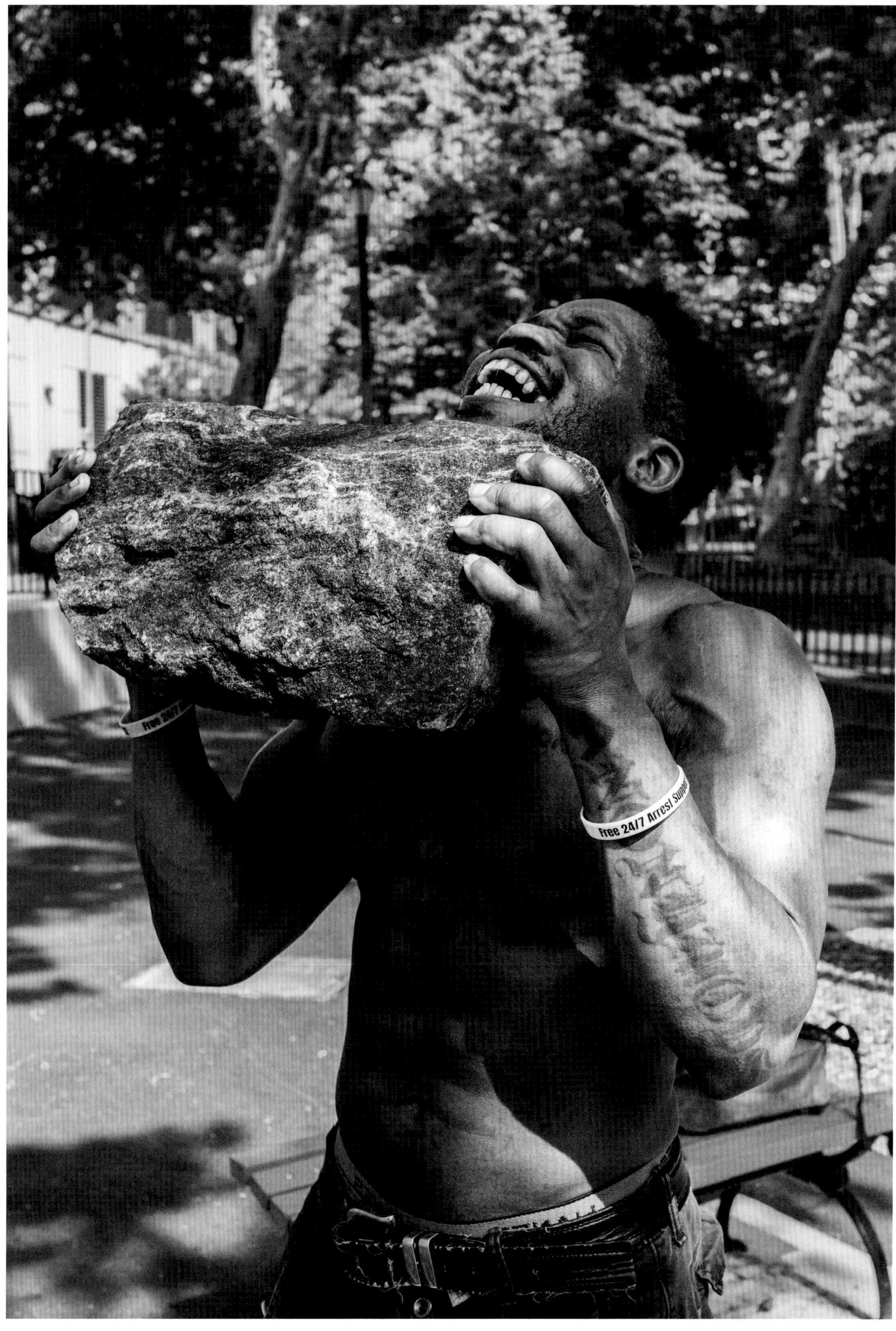
Free 24/7 Arrest

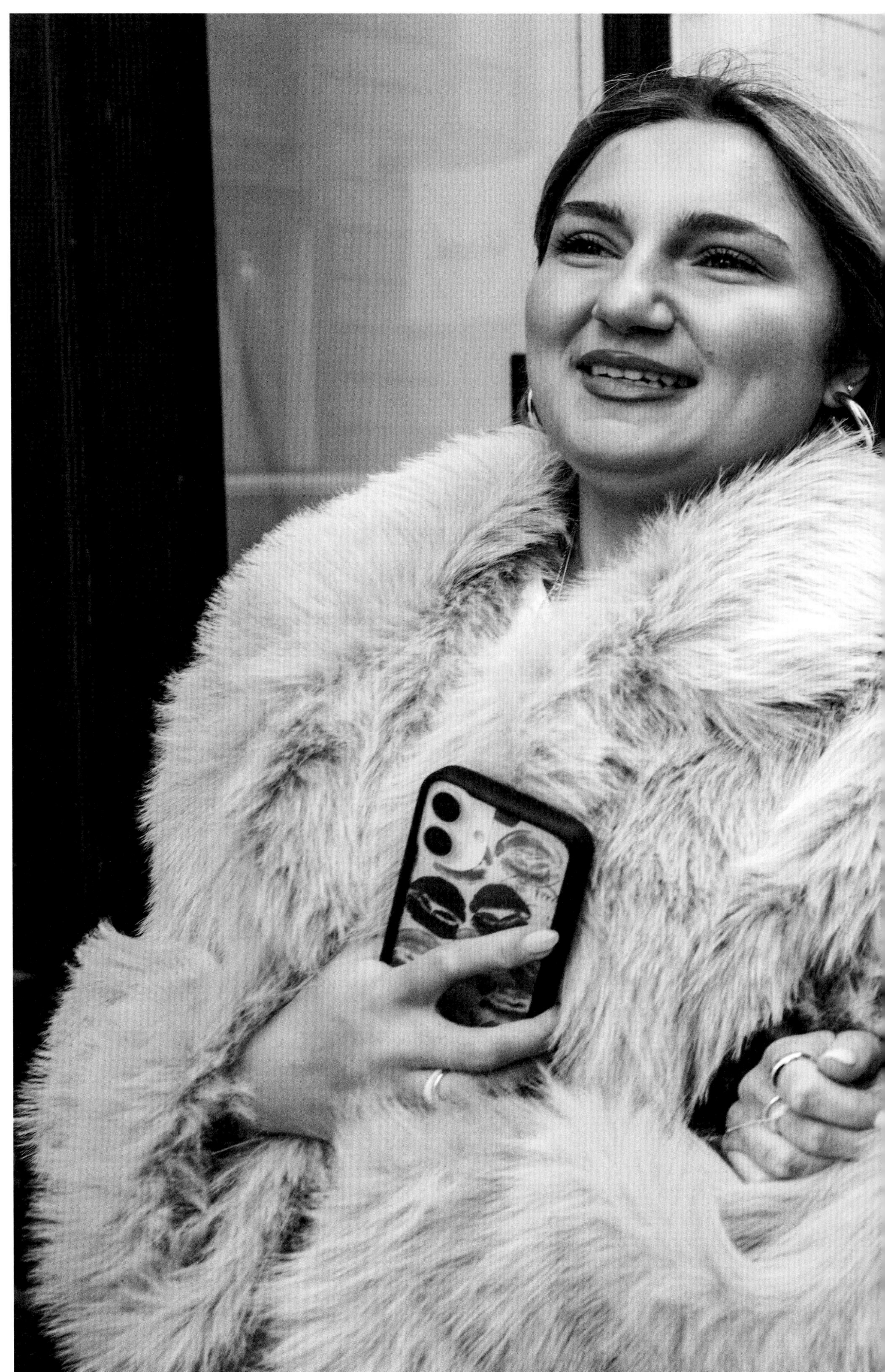

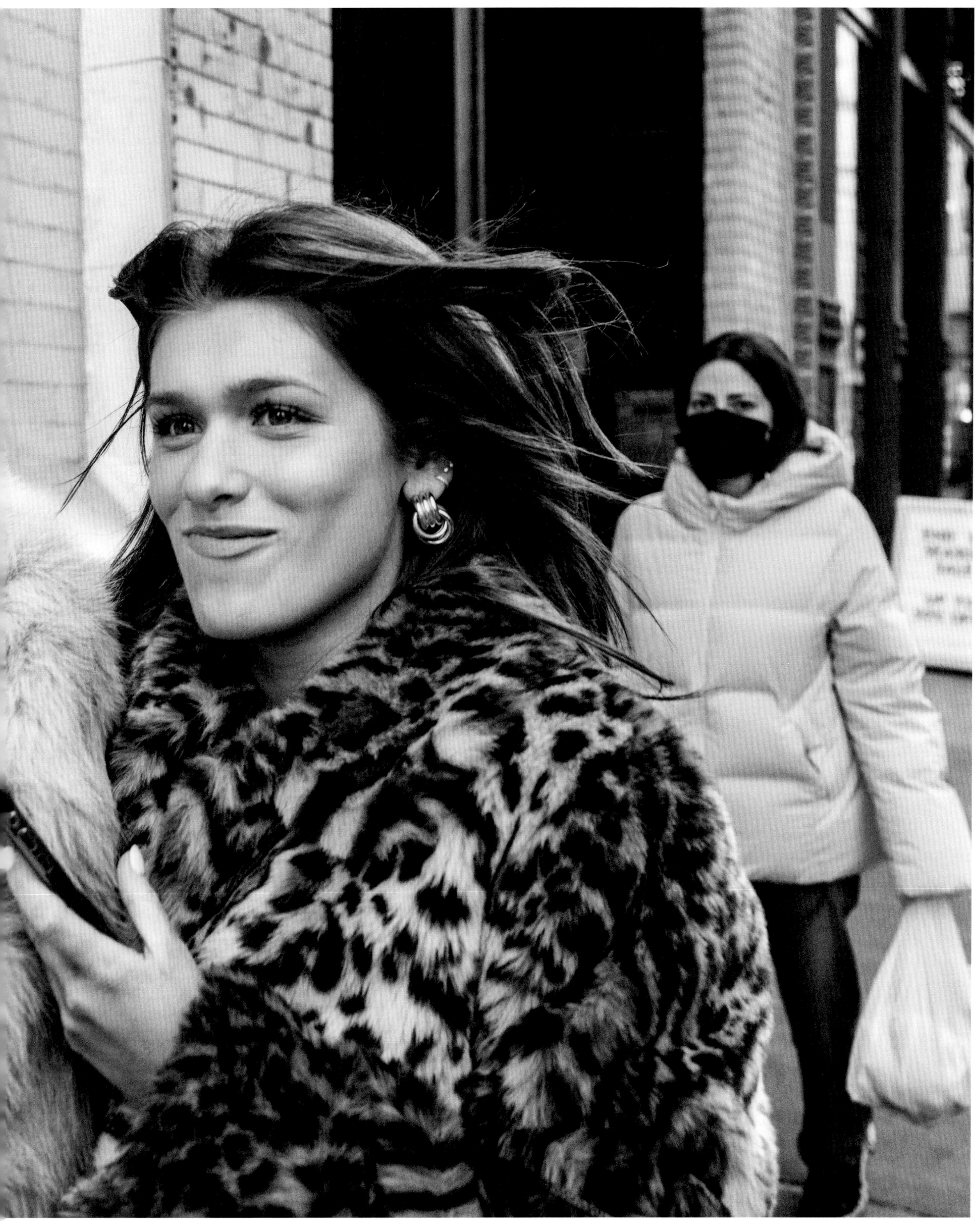

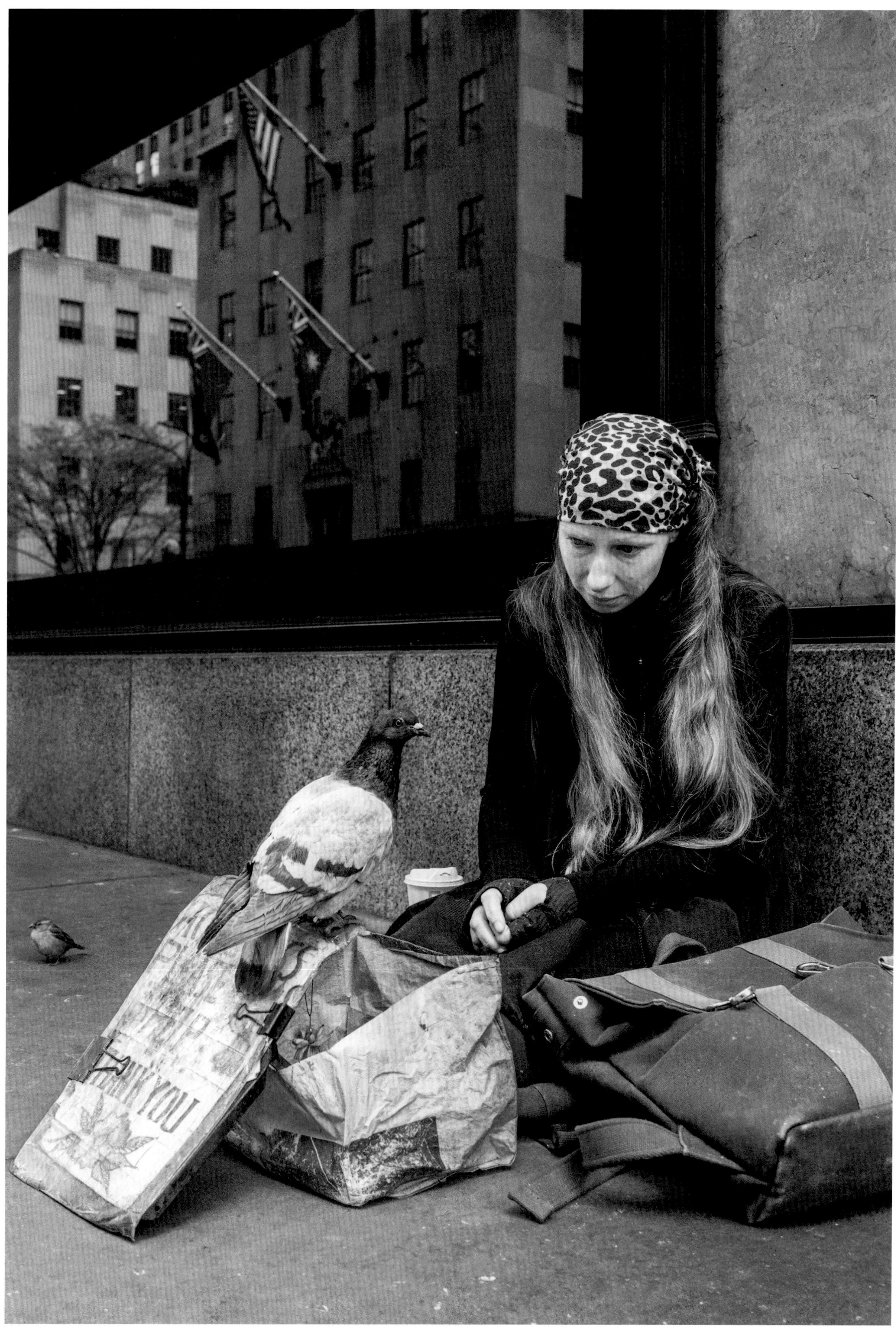

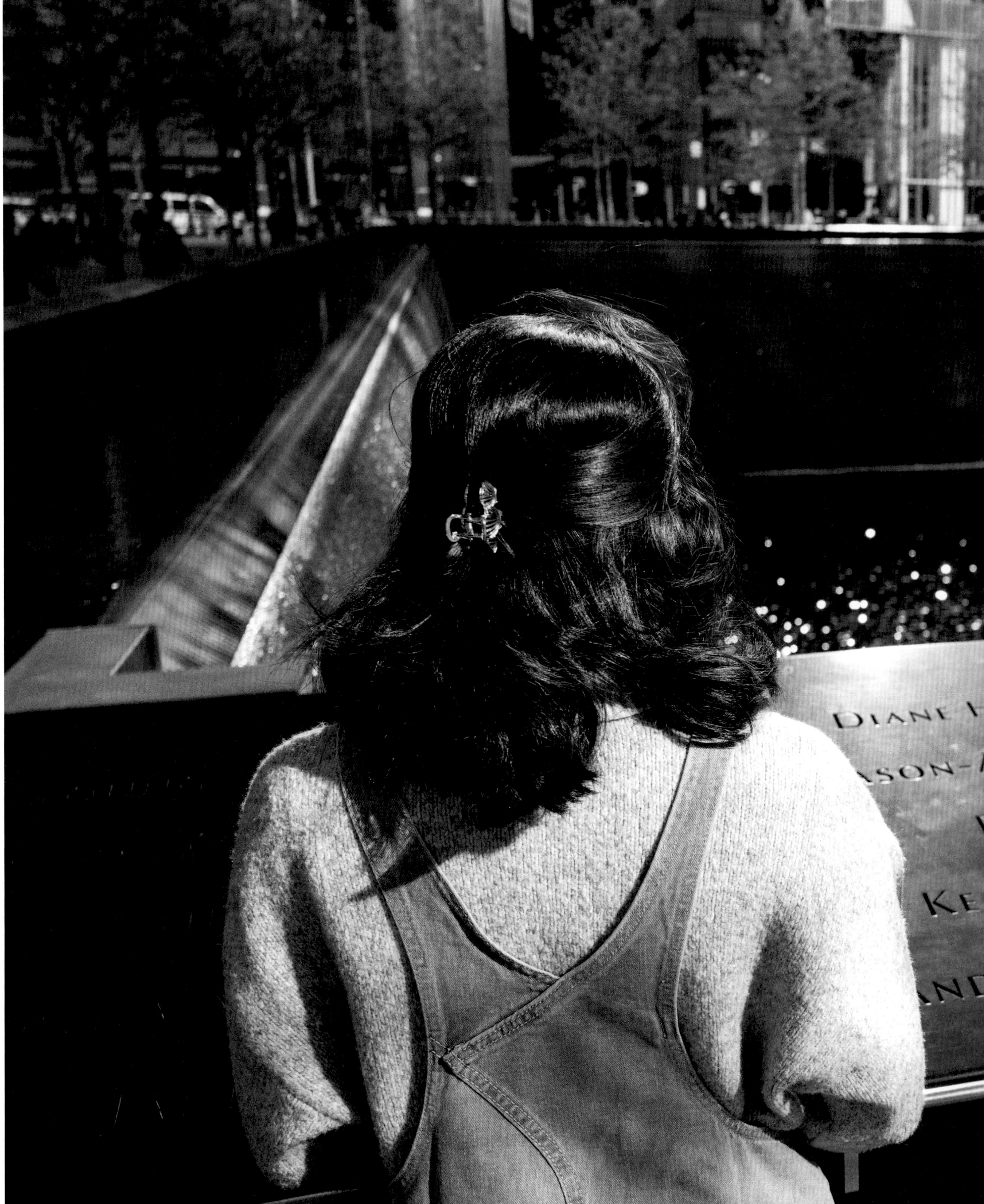
DIANE

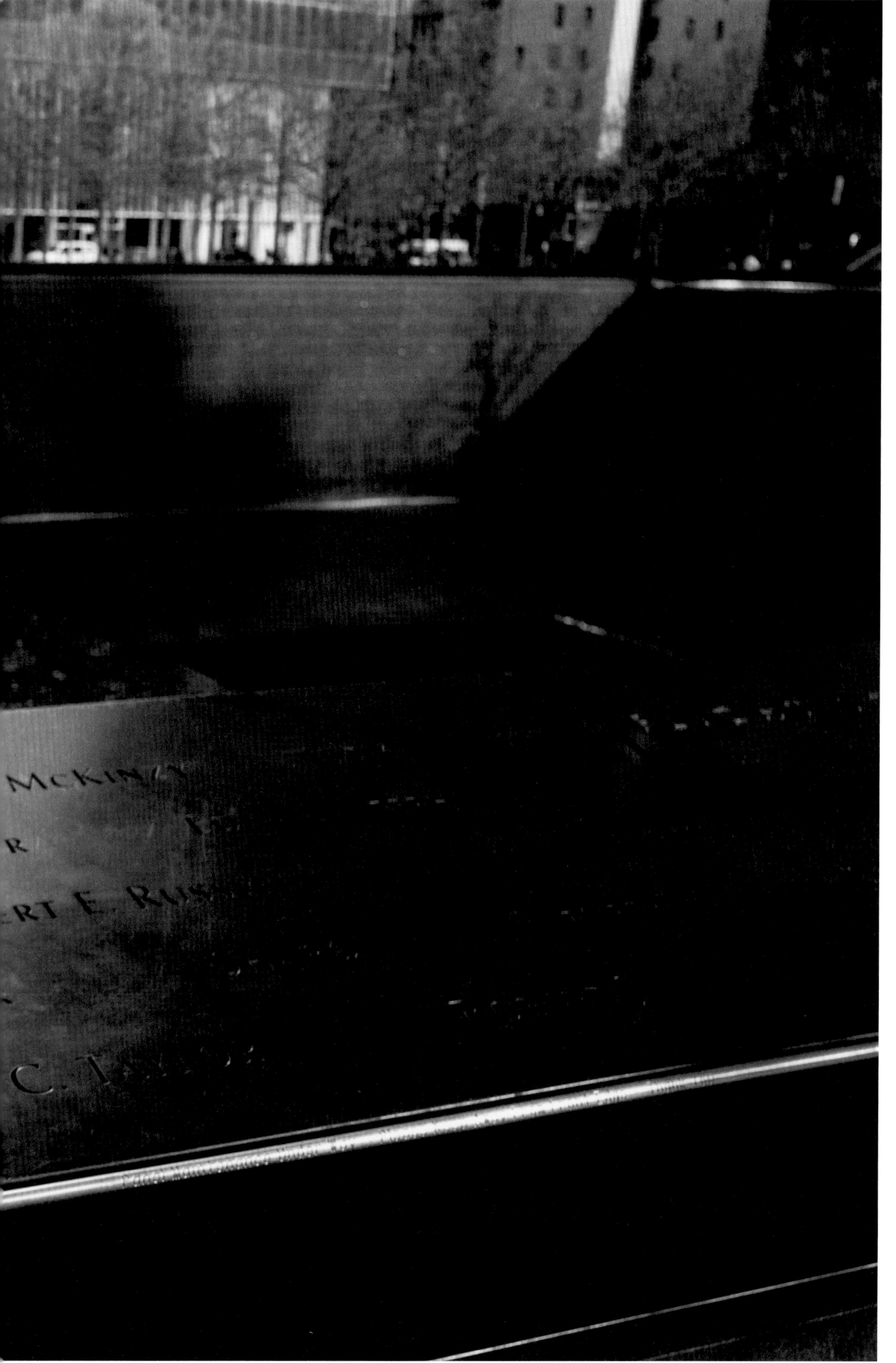
MCKIN
ERT E. RUS
C. T

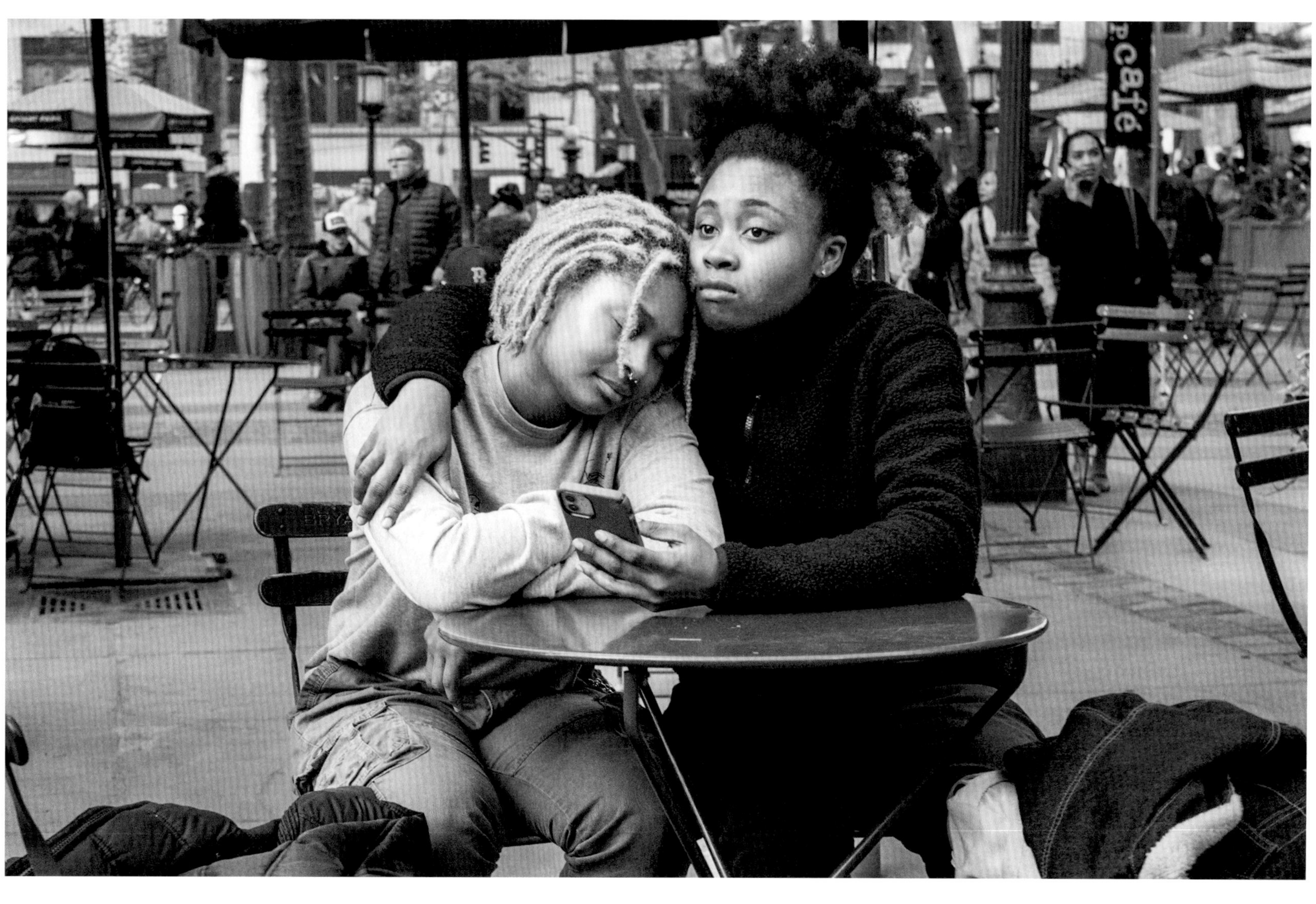
café

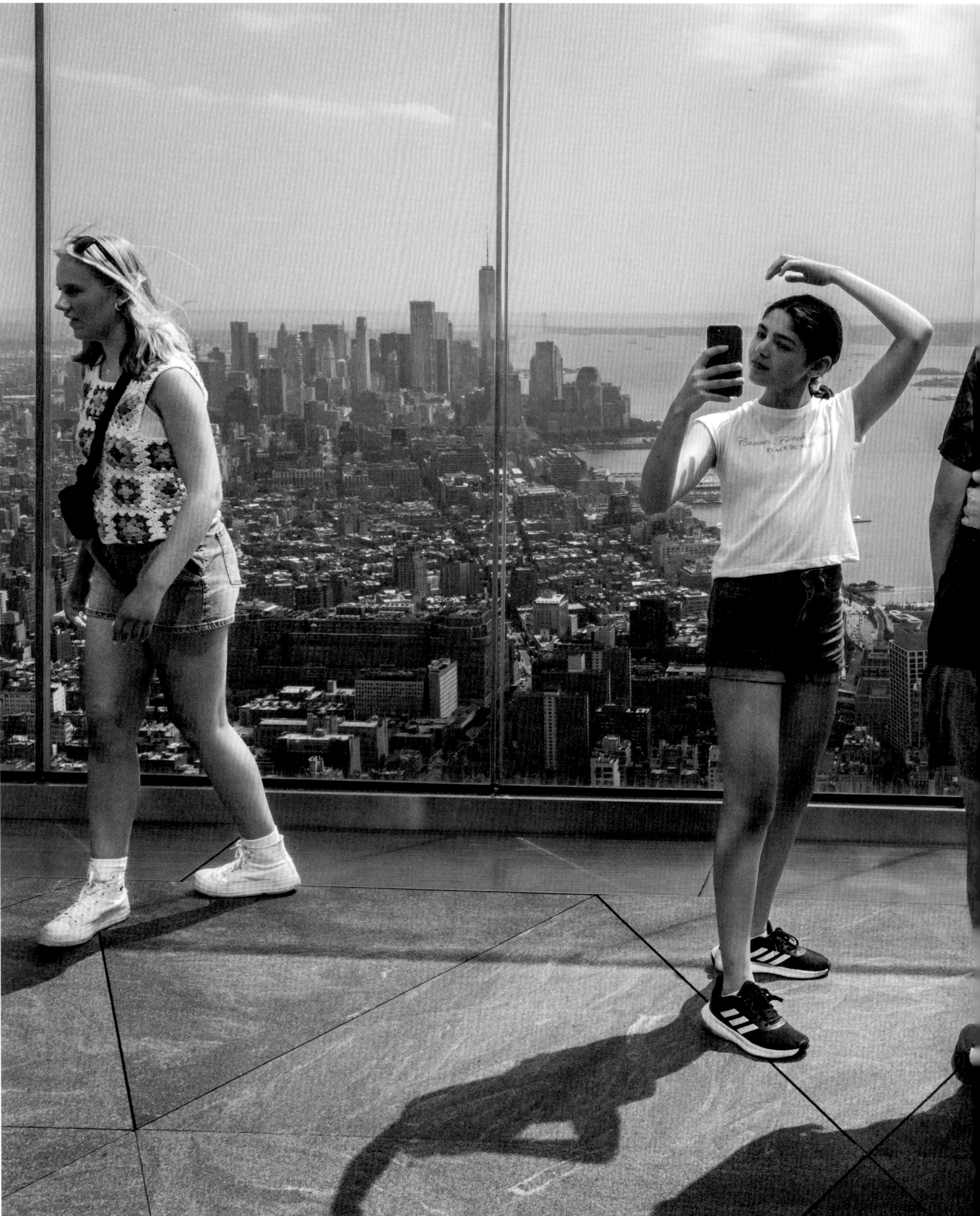

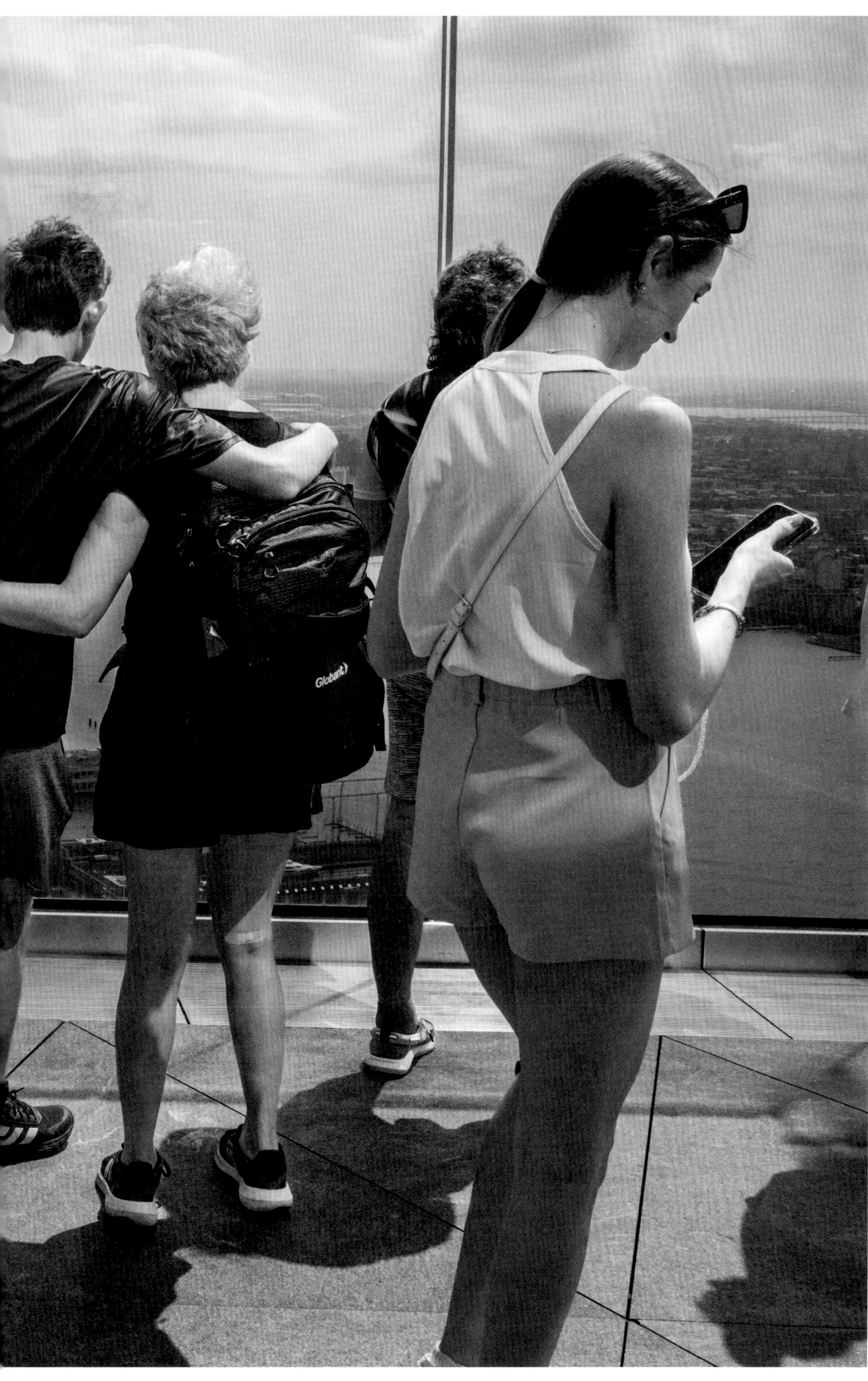
Globant

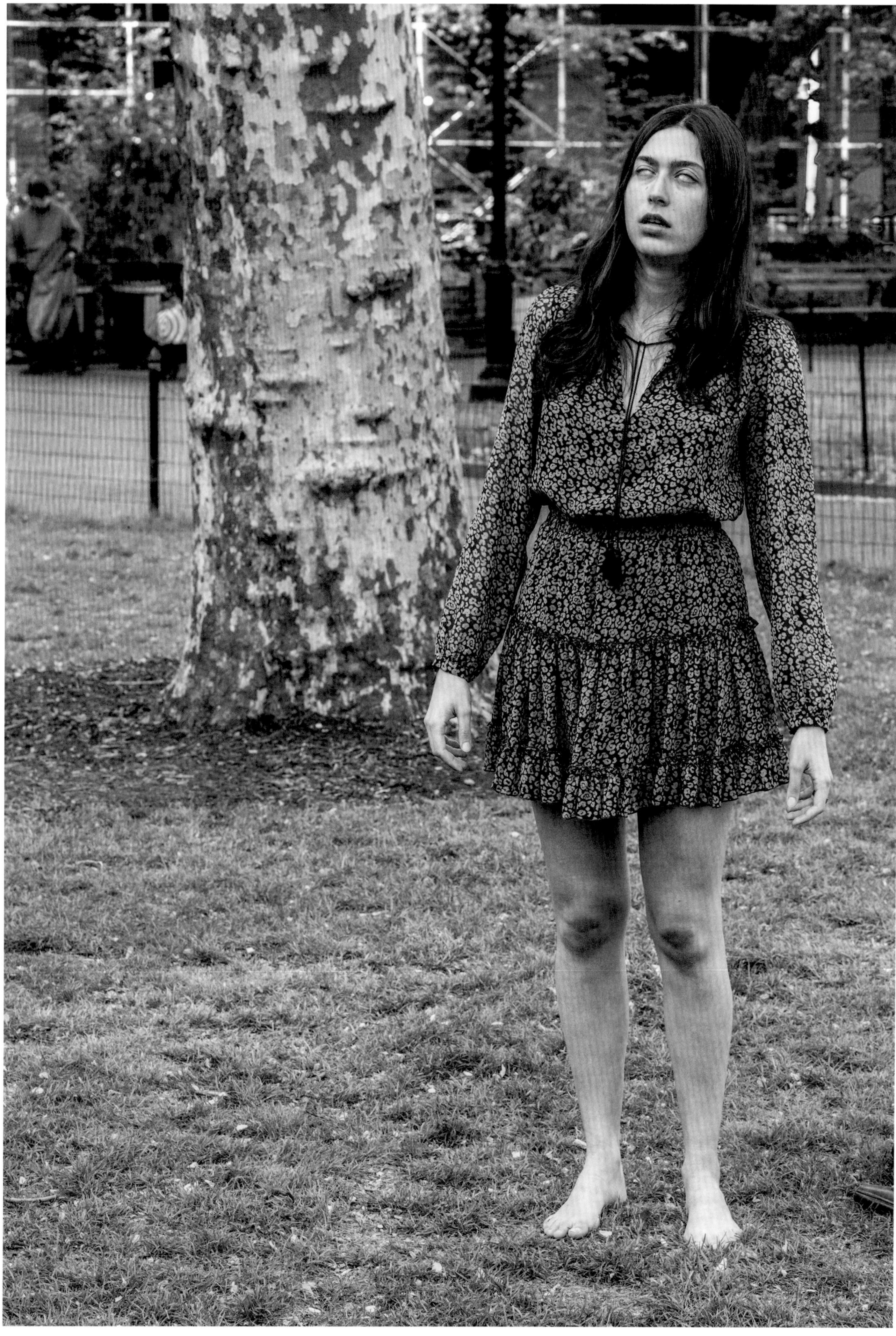

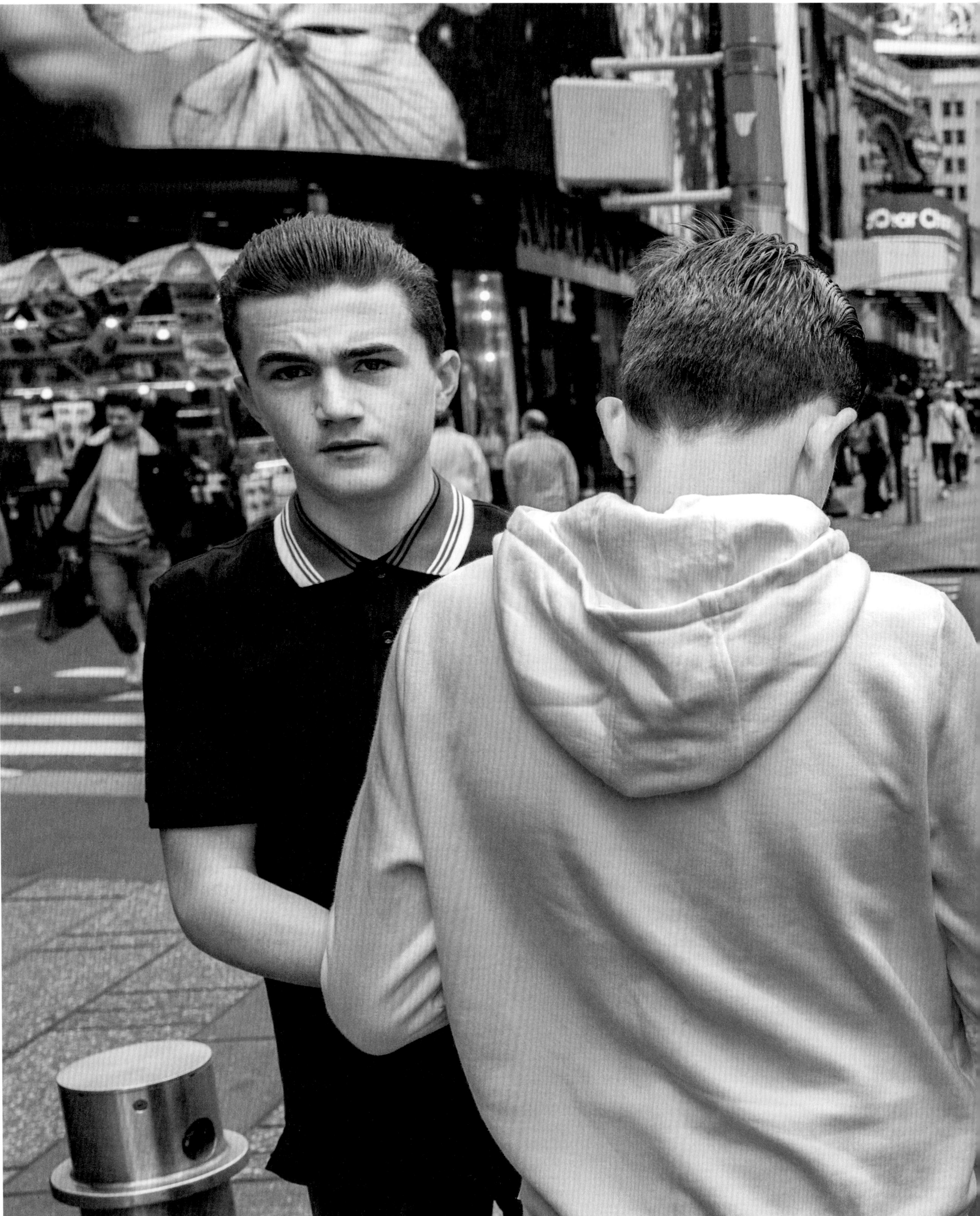

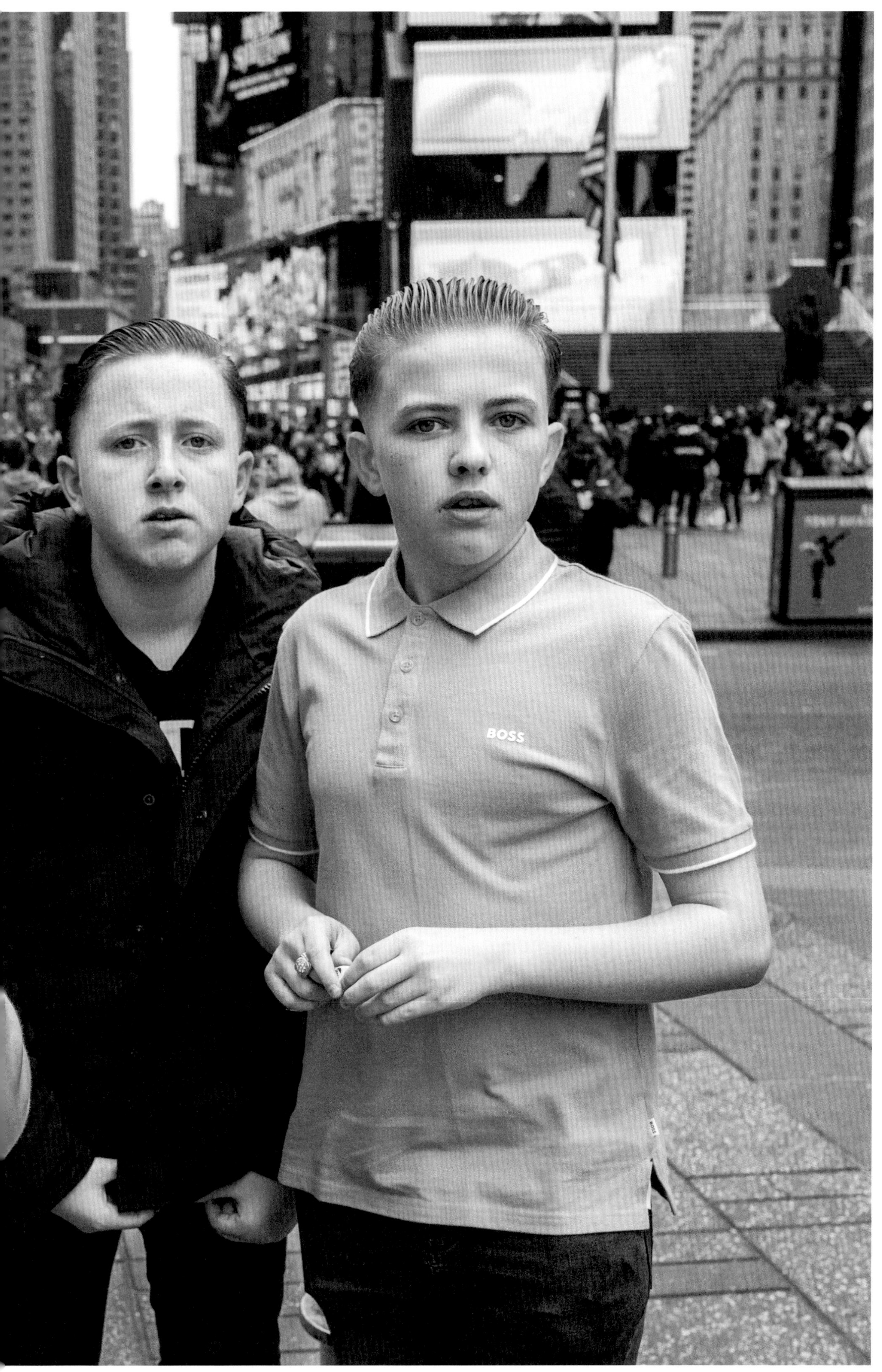
BOSS

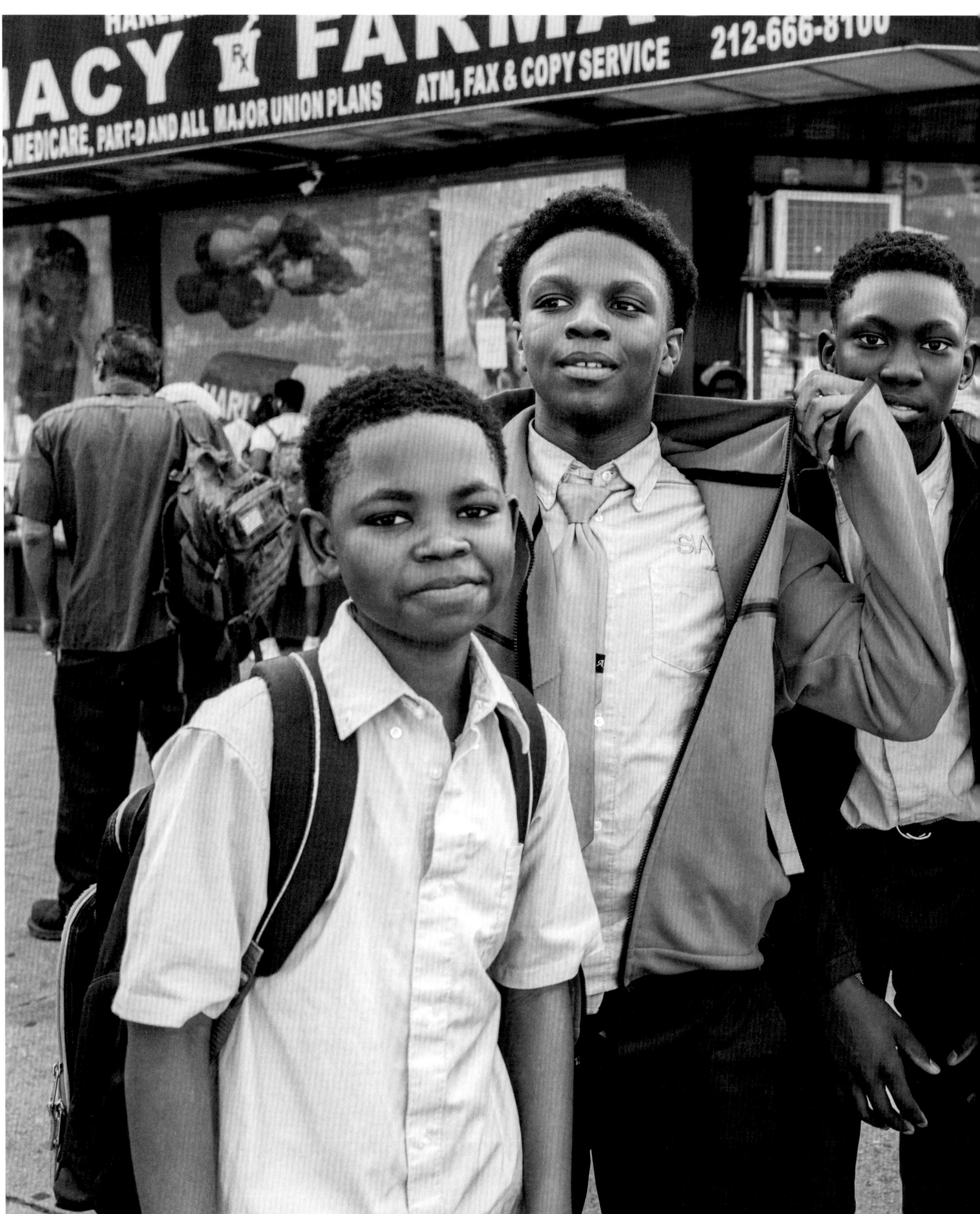
212-666-8100
ATM, FAX & COPY SERVICE
MEDICARE, PART-D AND ALL MAJOR UNION PLANS

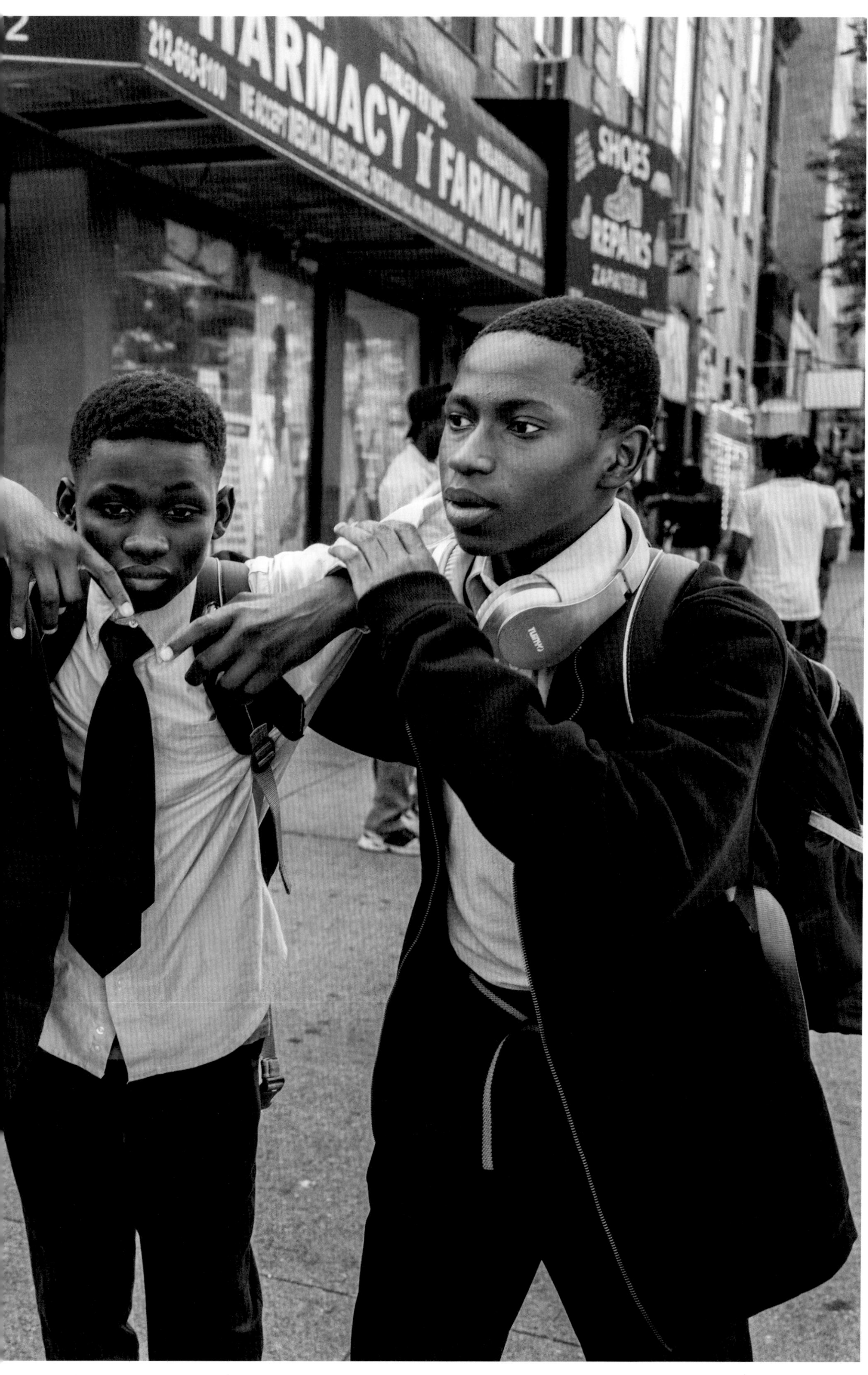
FARMACIA
SHOES
REPAIRS
ZAPATERIA

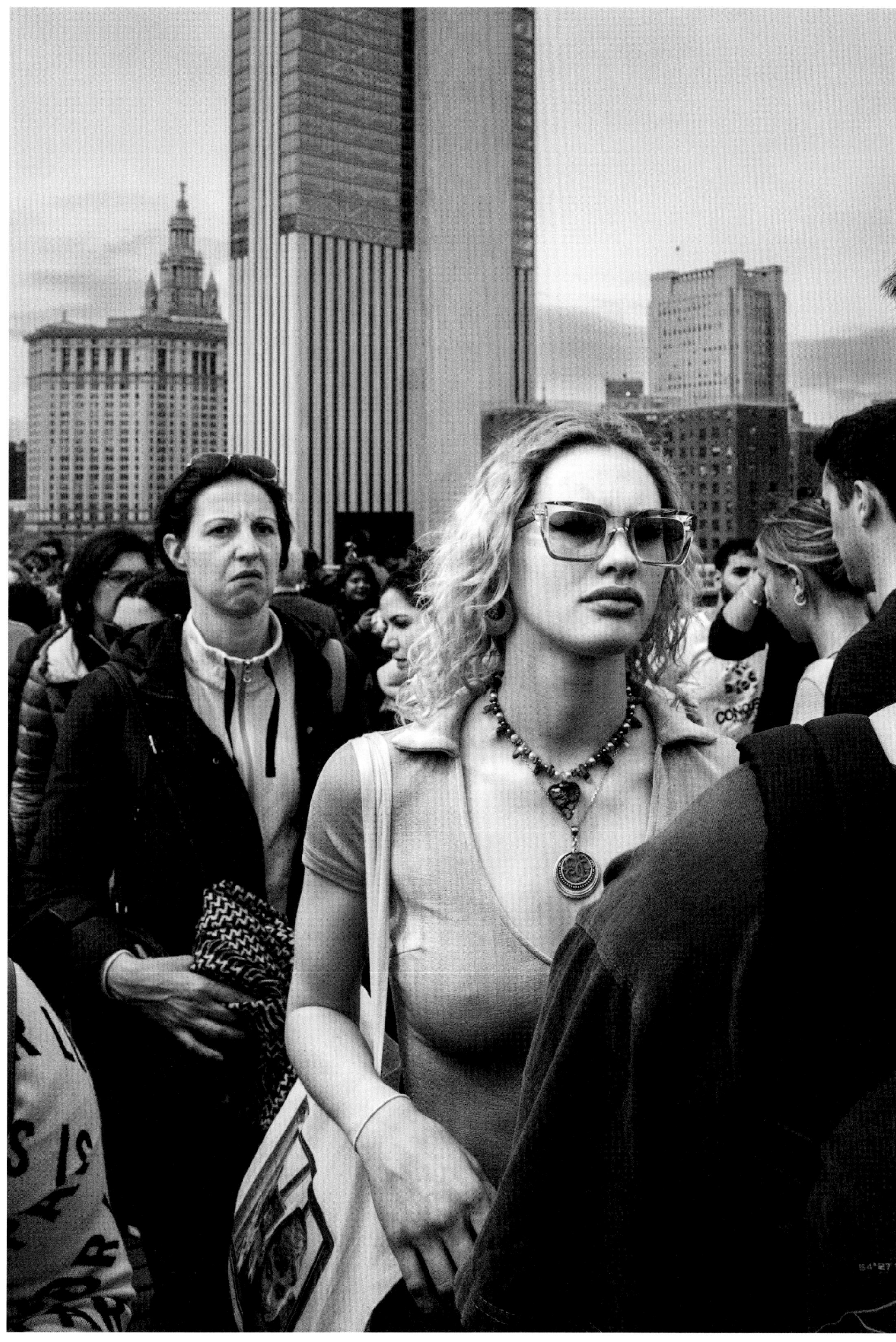

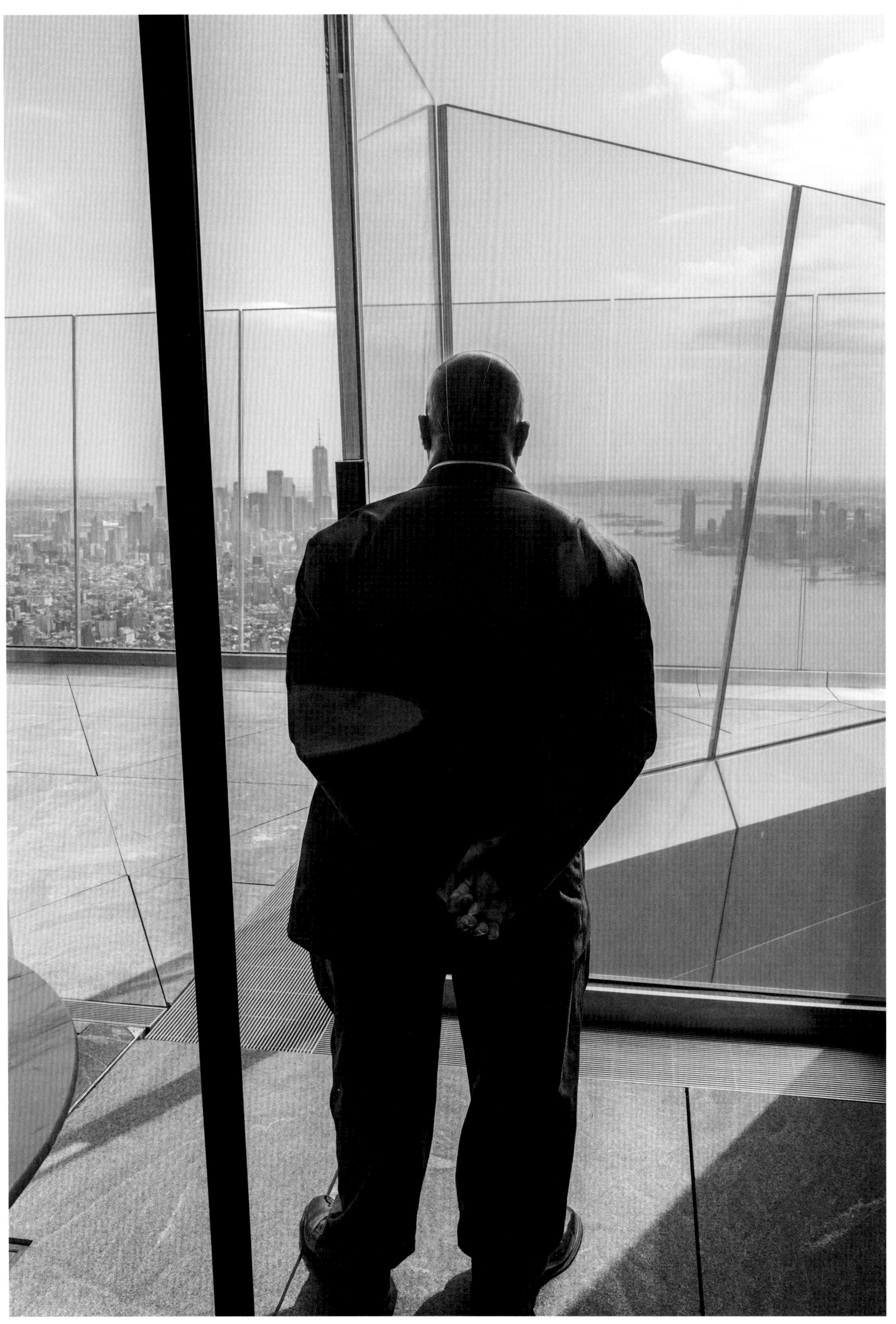

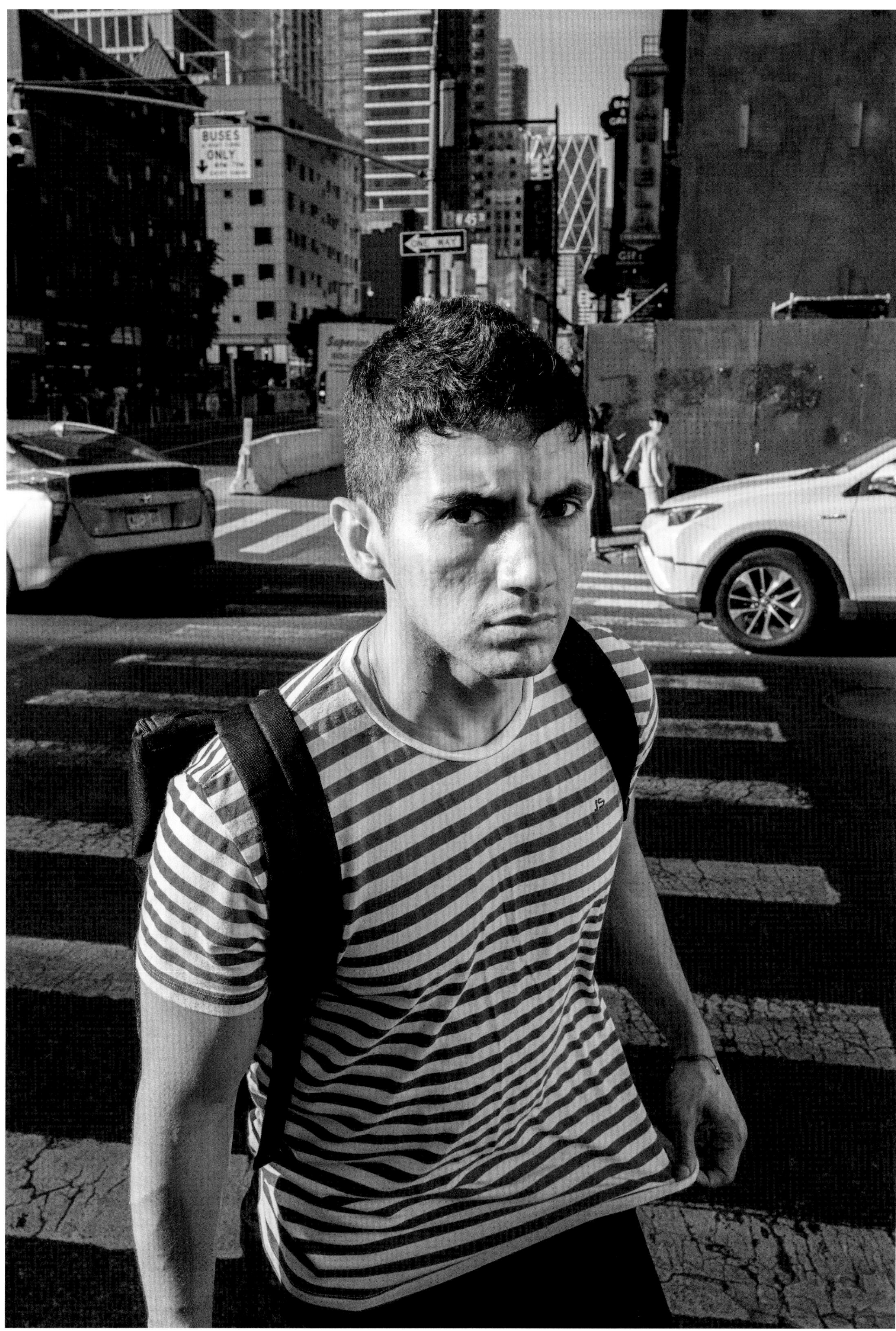
BUSES
ONLY
ONE WAY

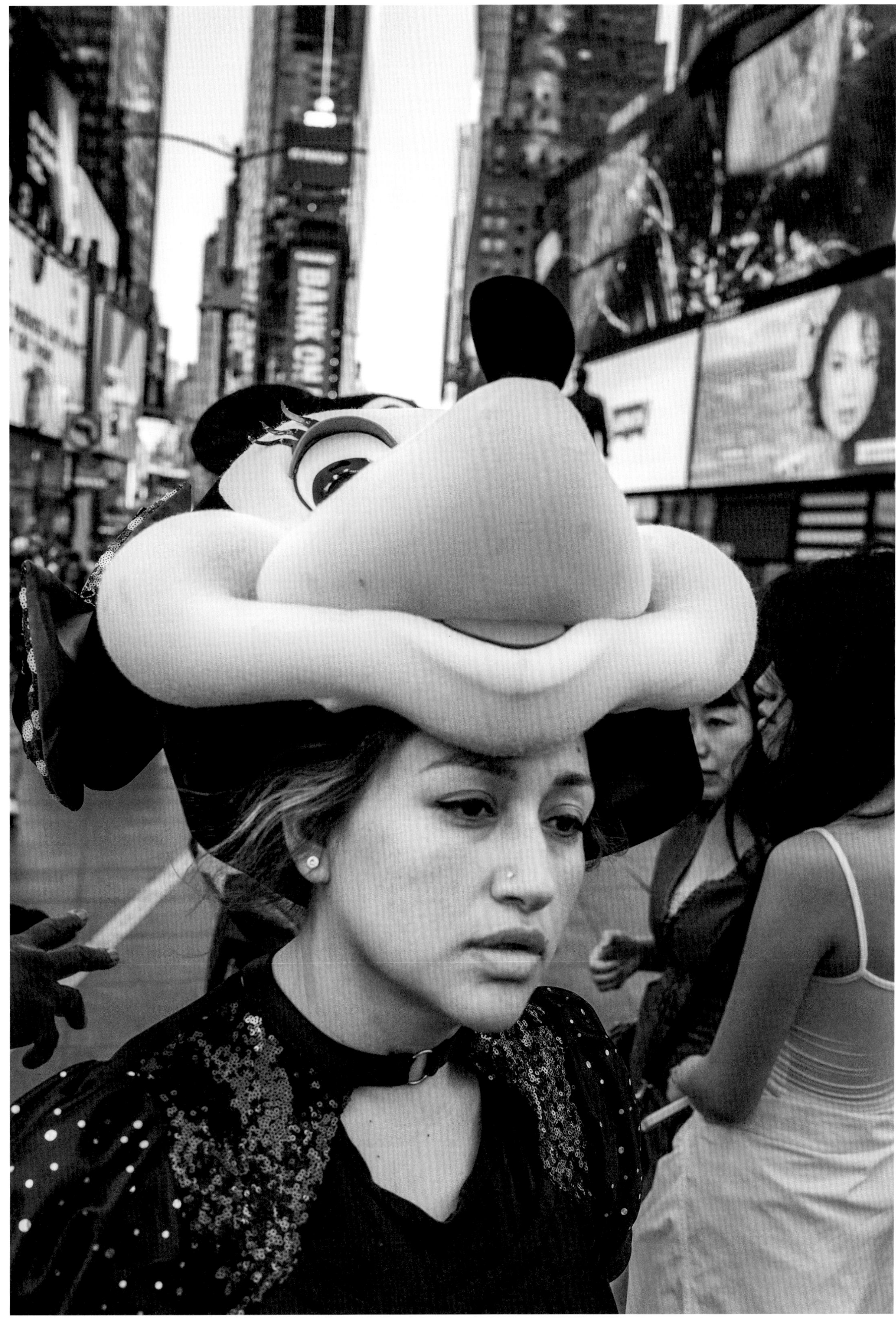
BANK

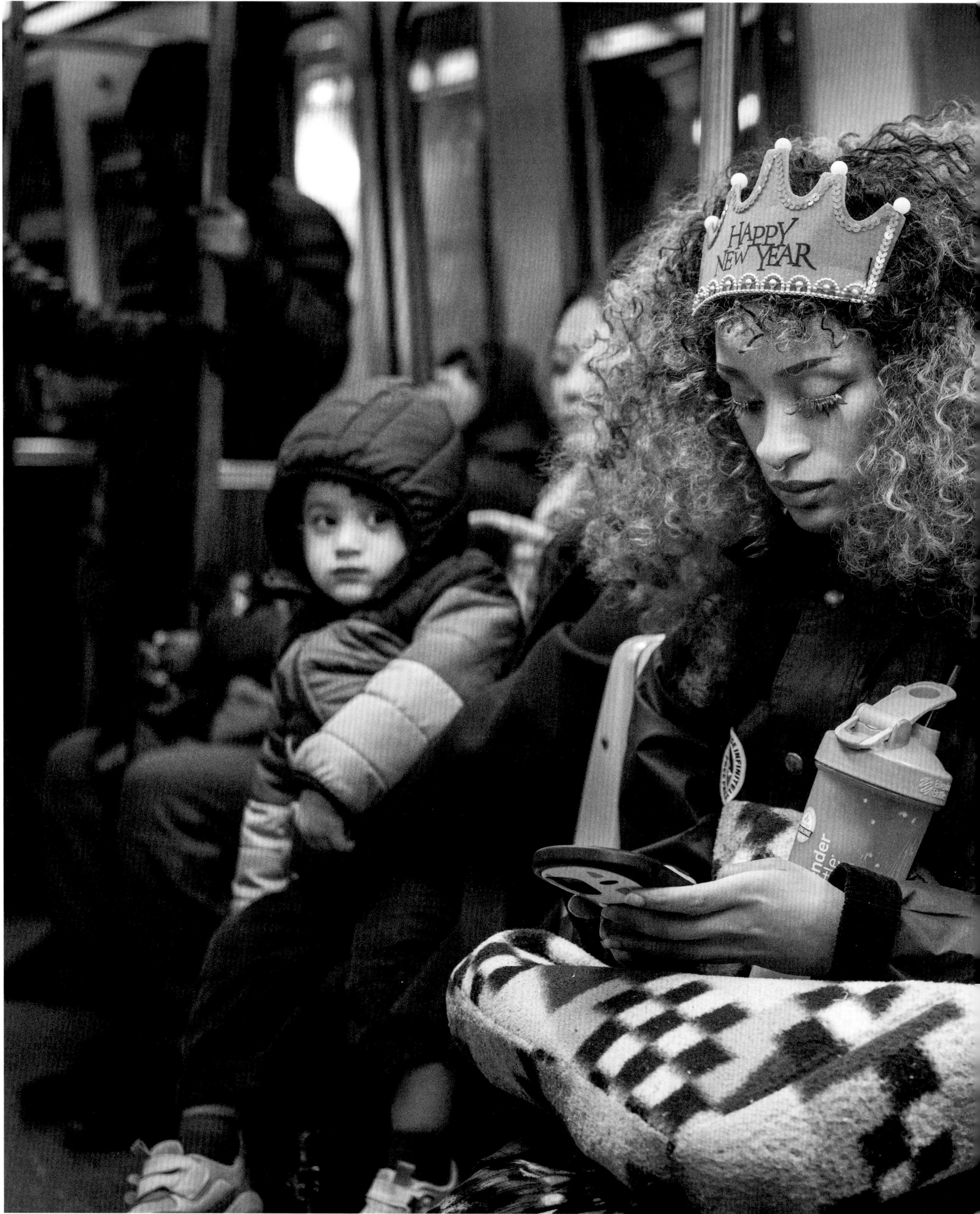
HAPPY NEW YEAR

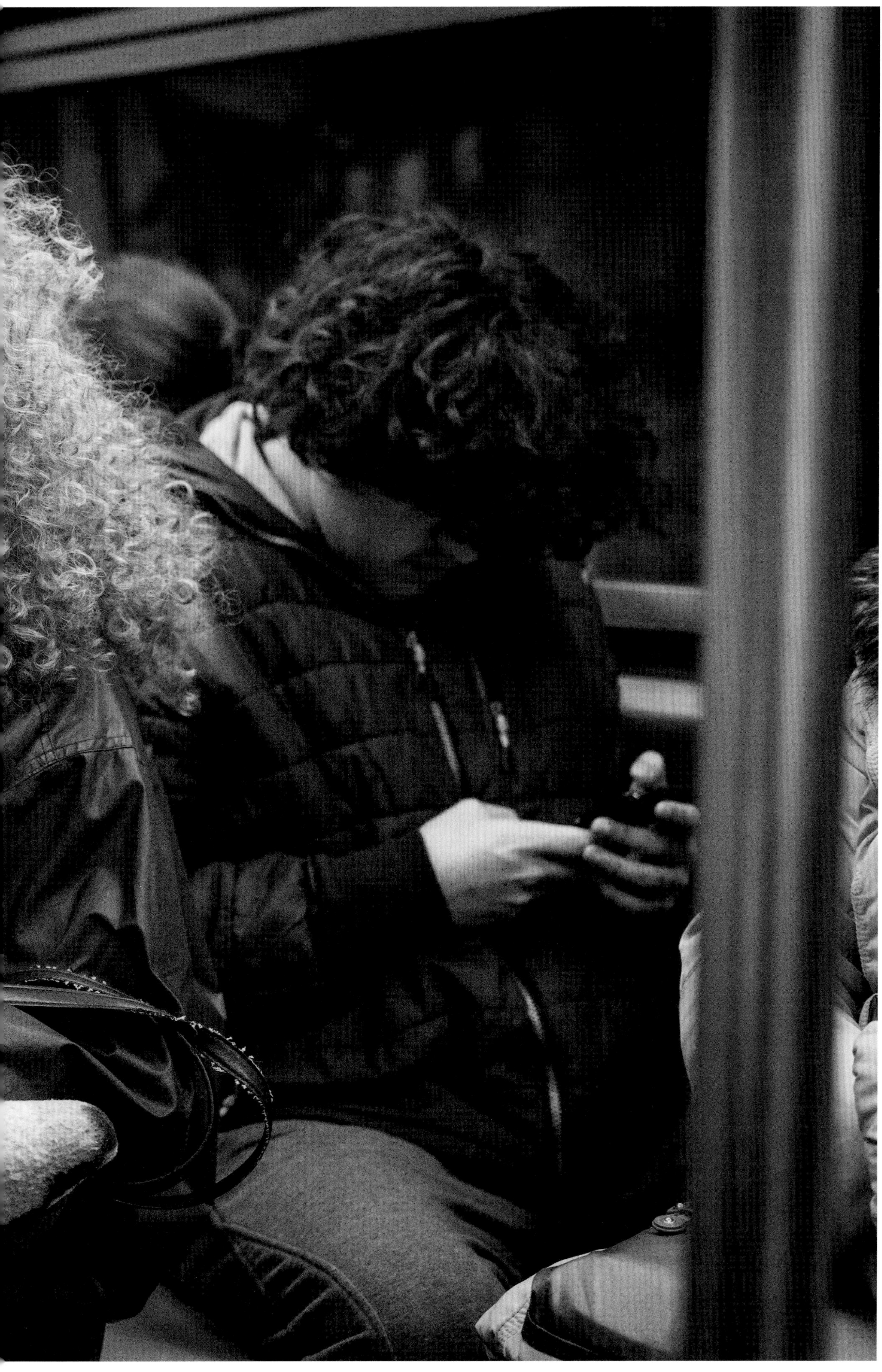

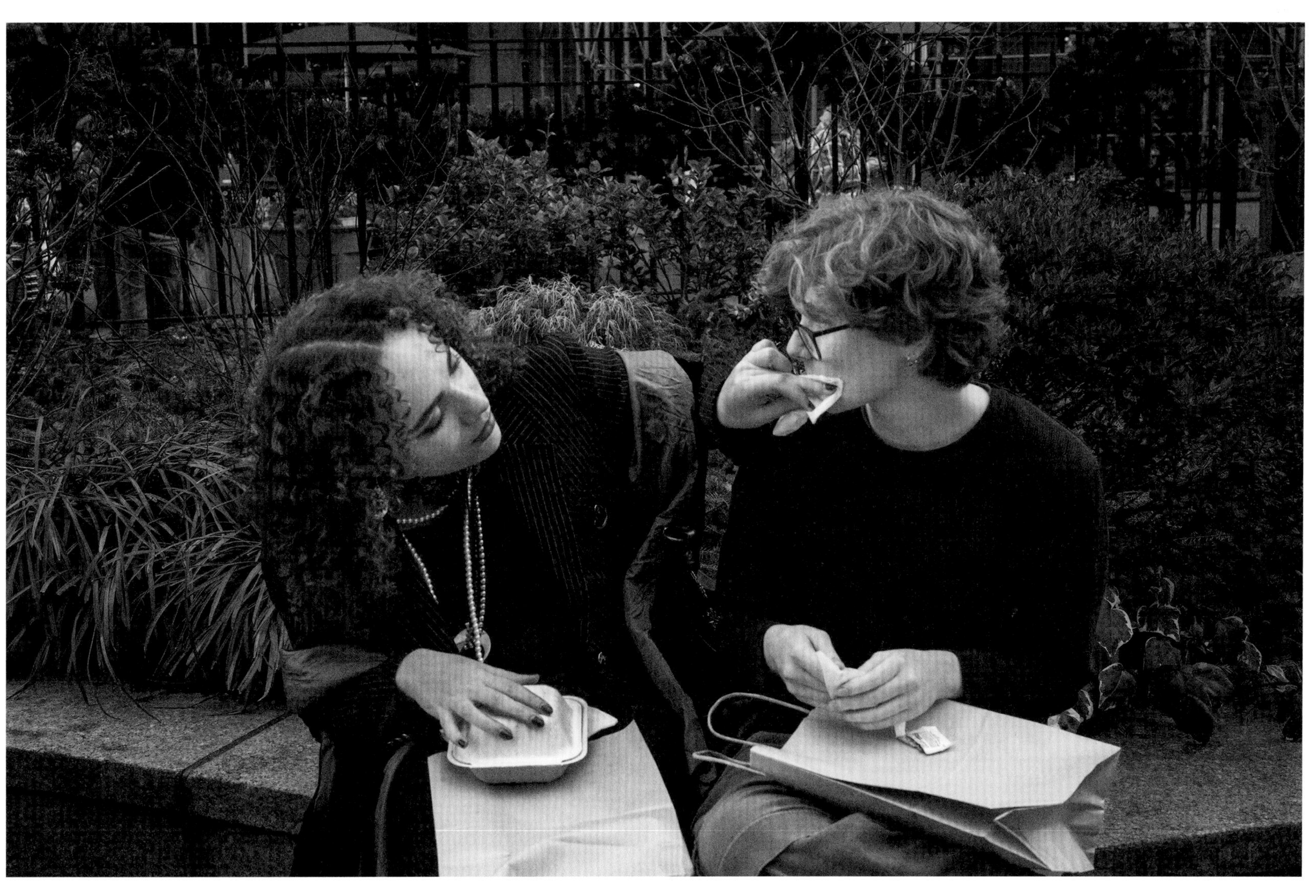

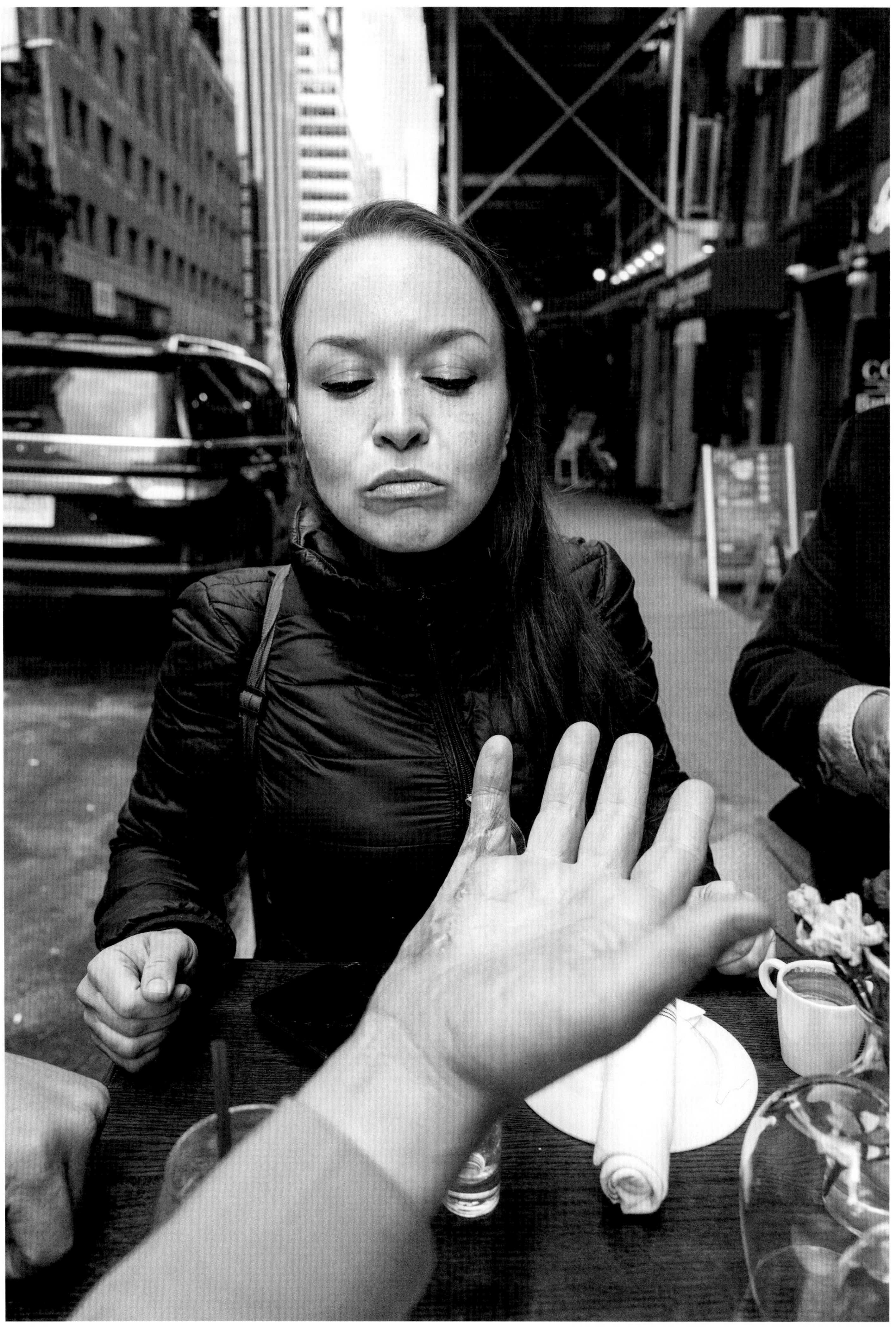

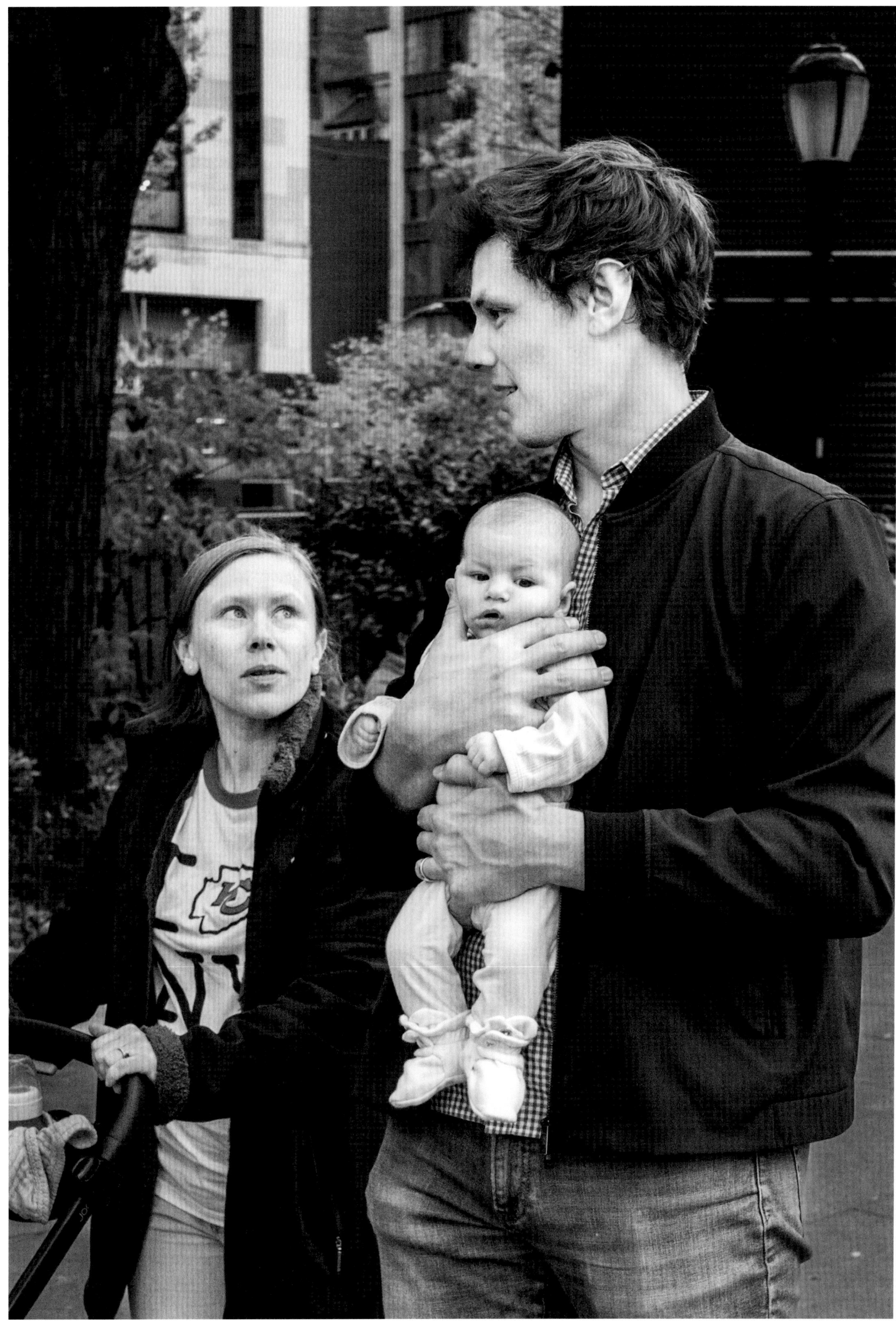

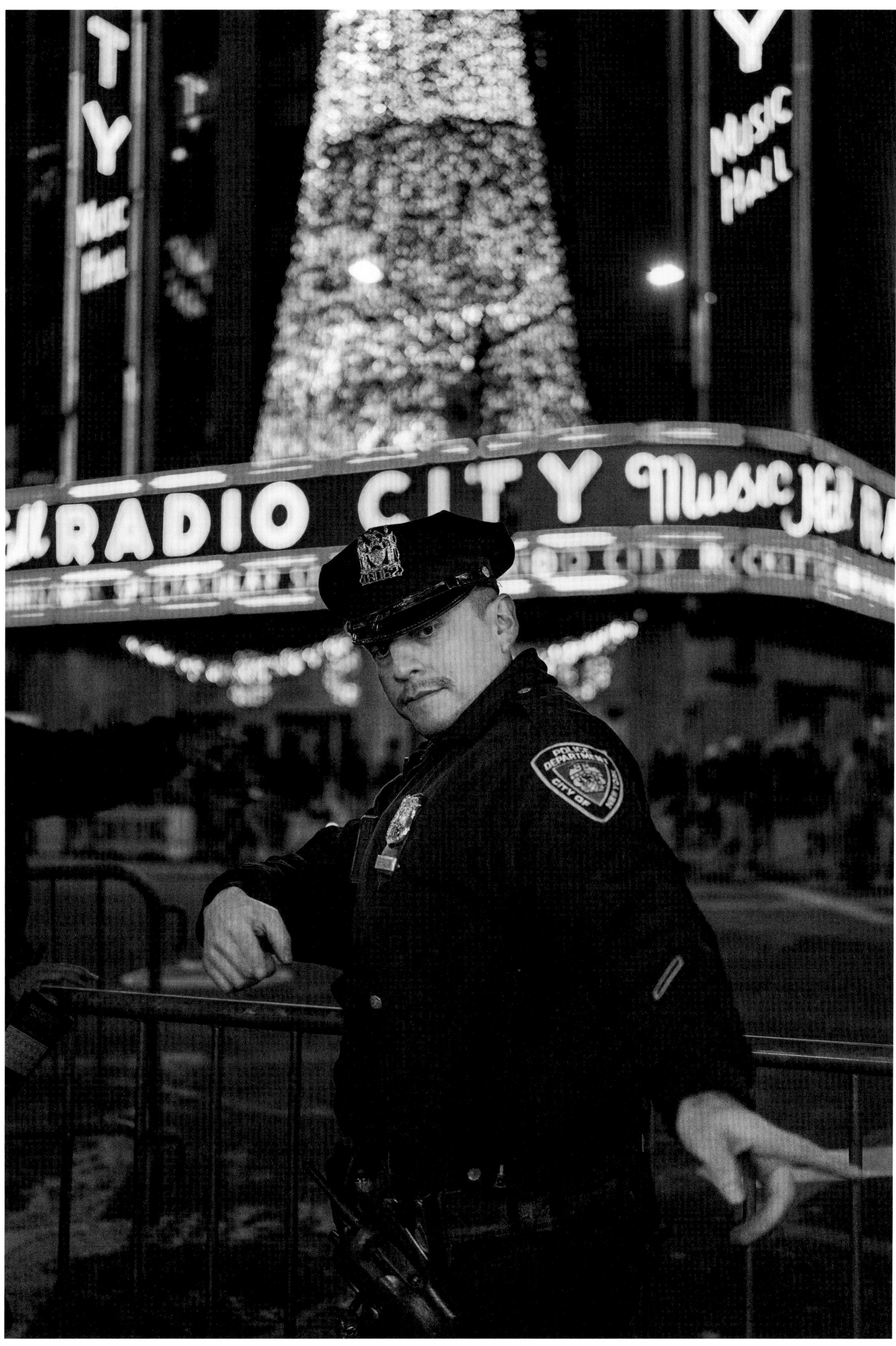
RADIO CITY
Music Hall
Music Hall
Music Hall
POLICE DEPARTMENT
CITY OF NEW YORK

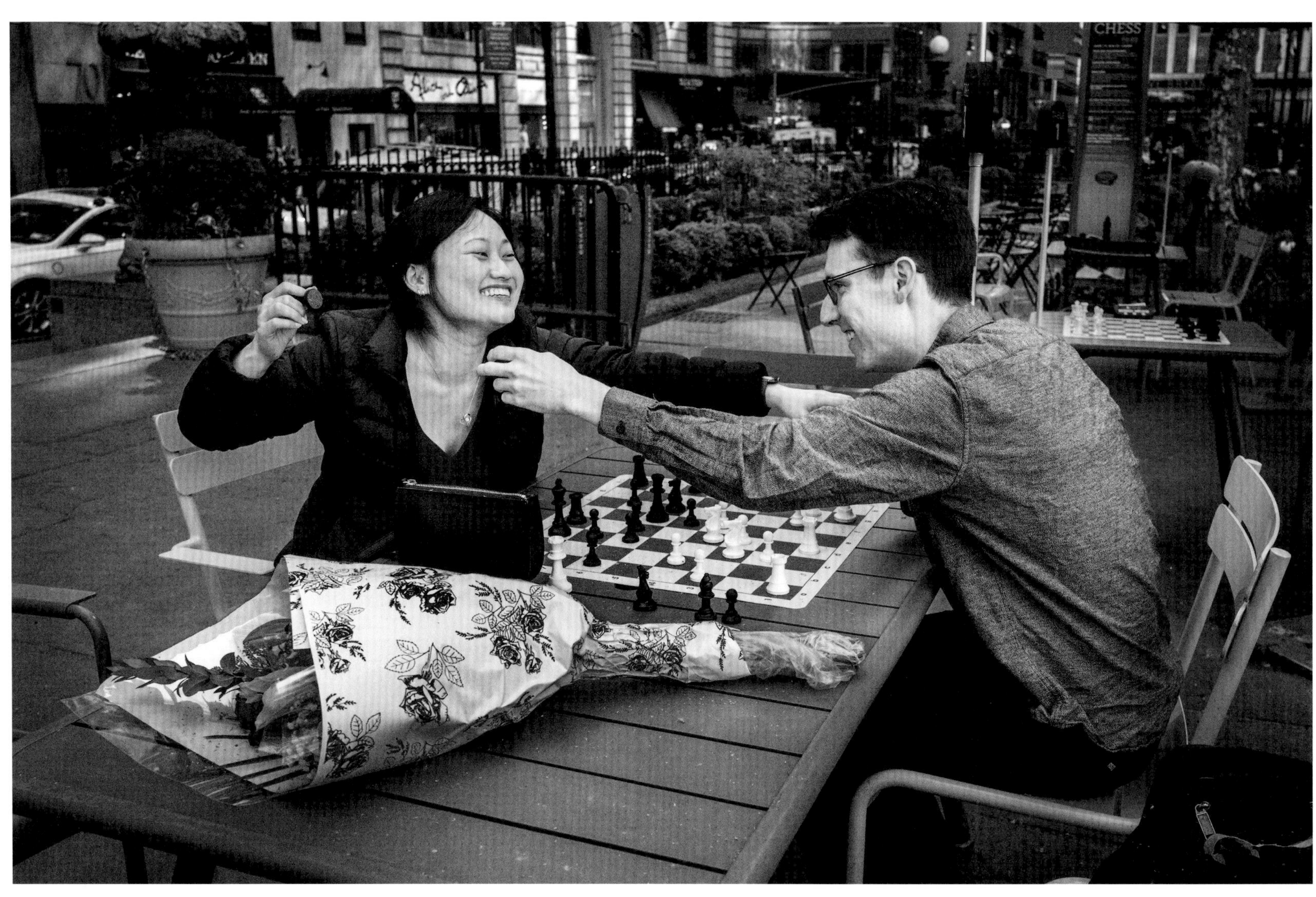
CHESS

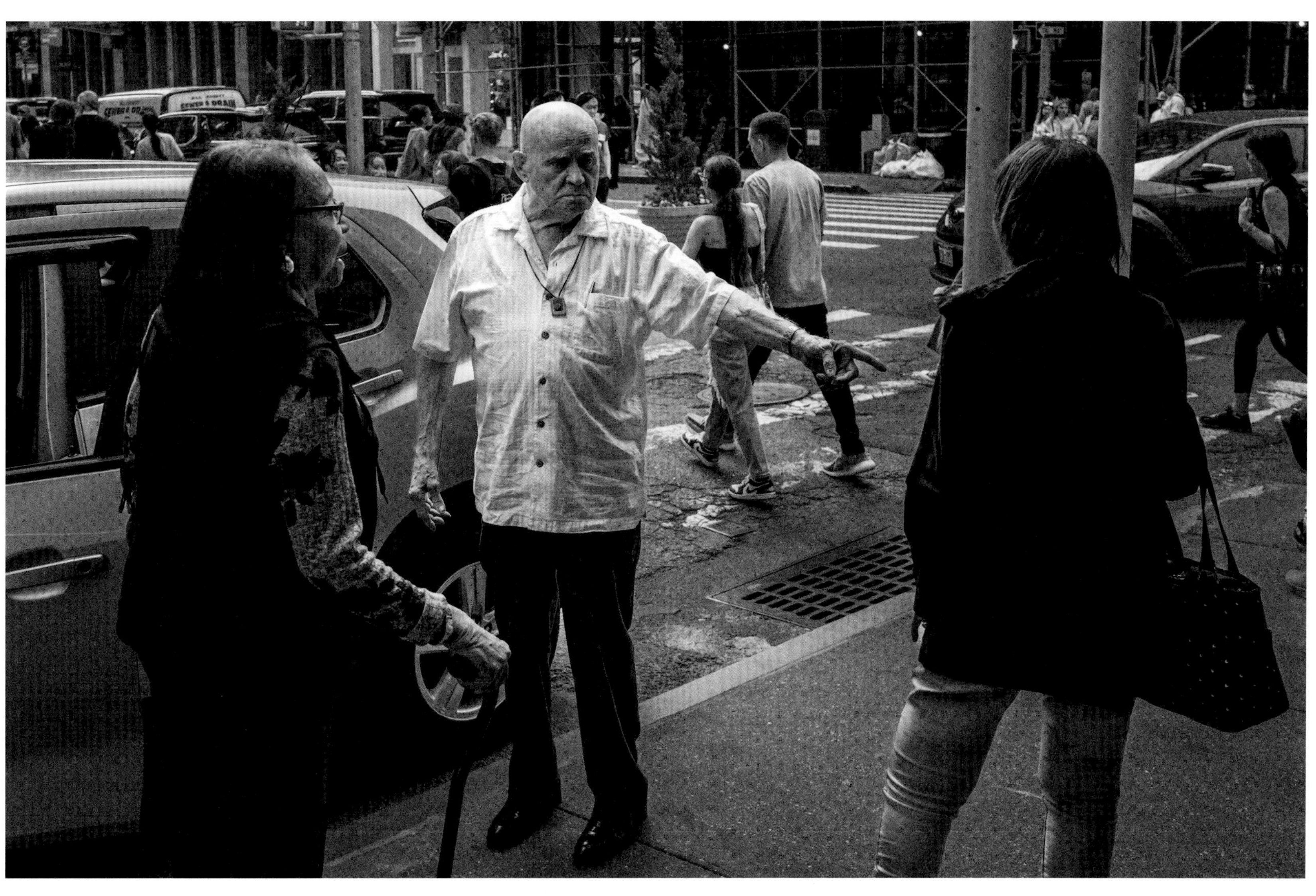
SEWER & DRAIN

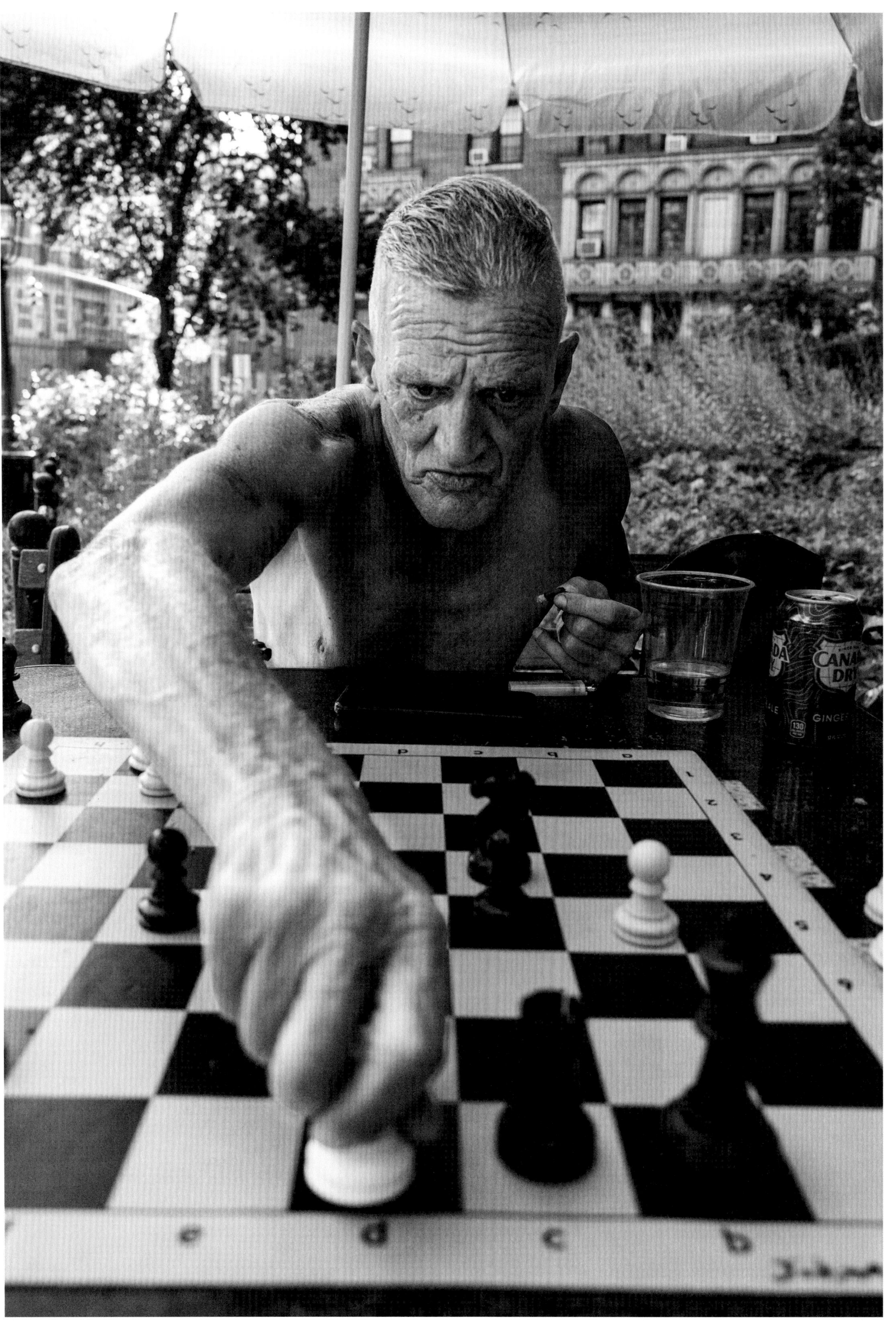

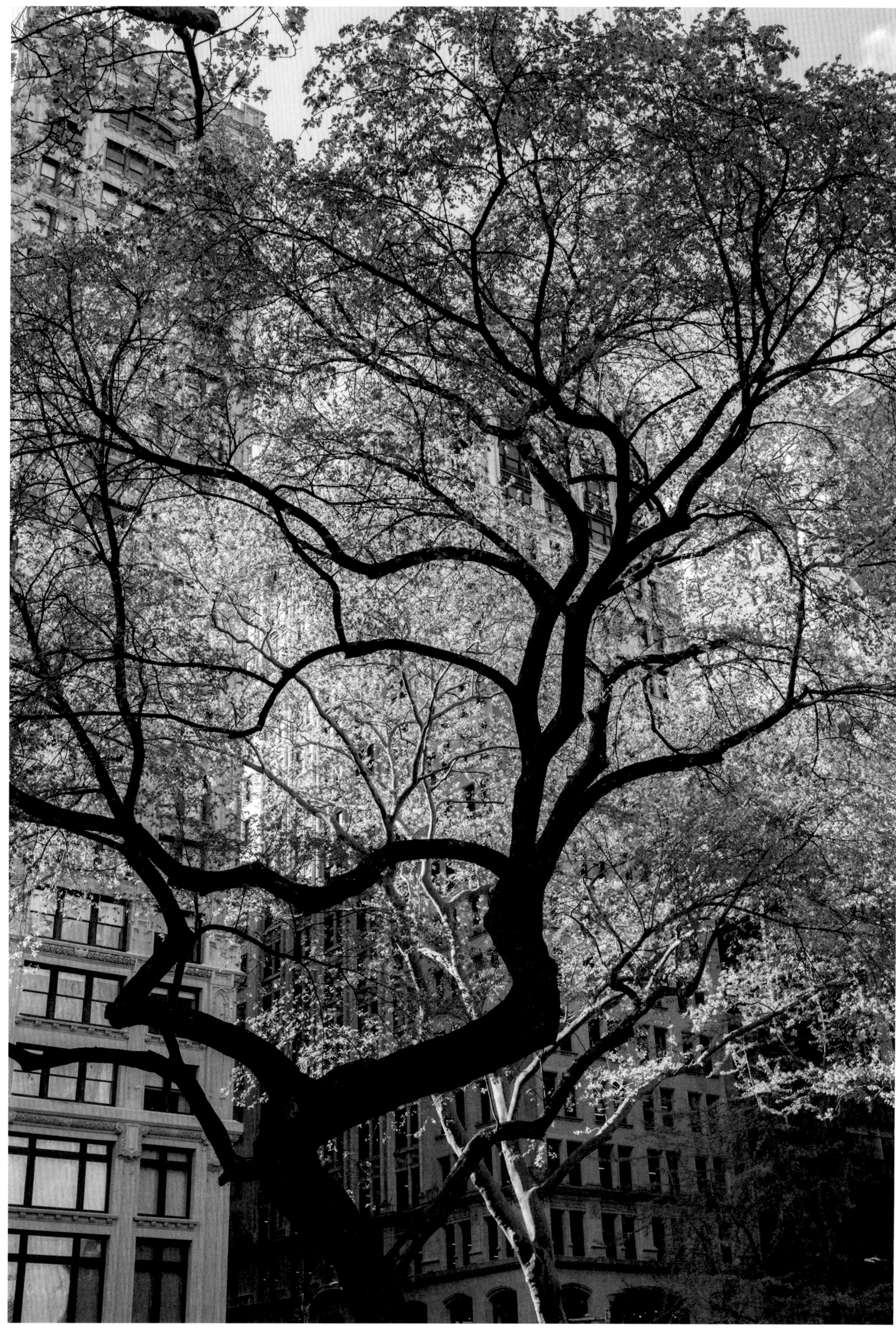

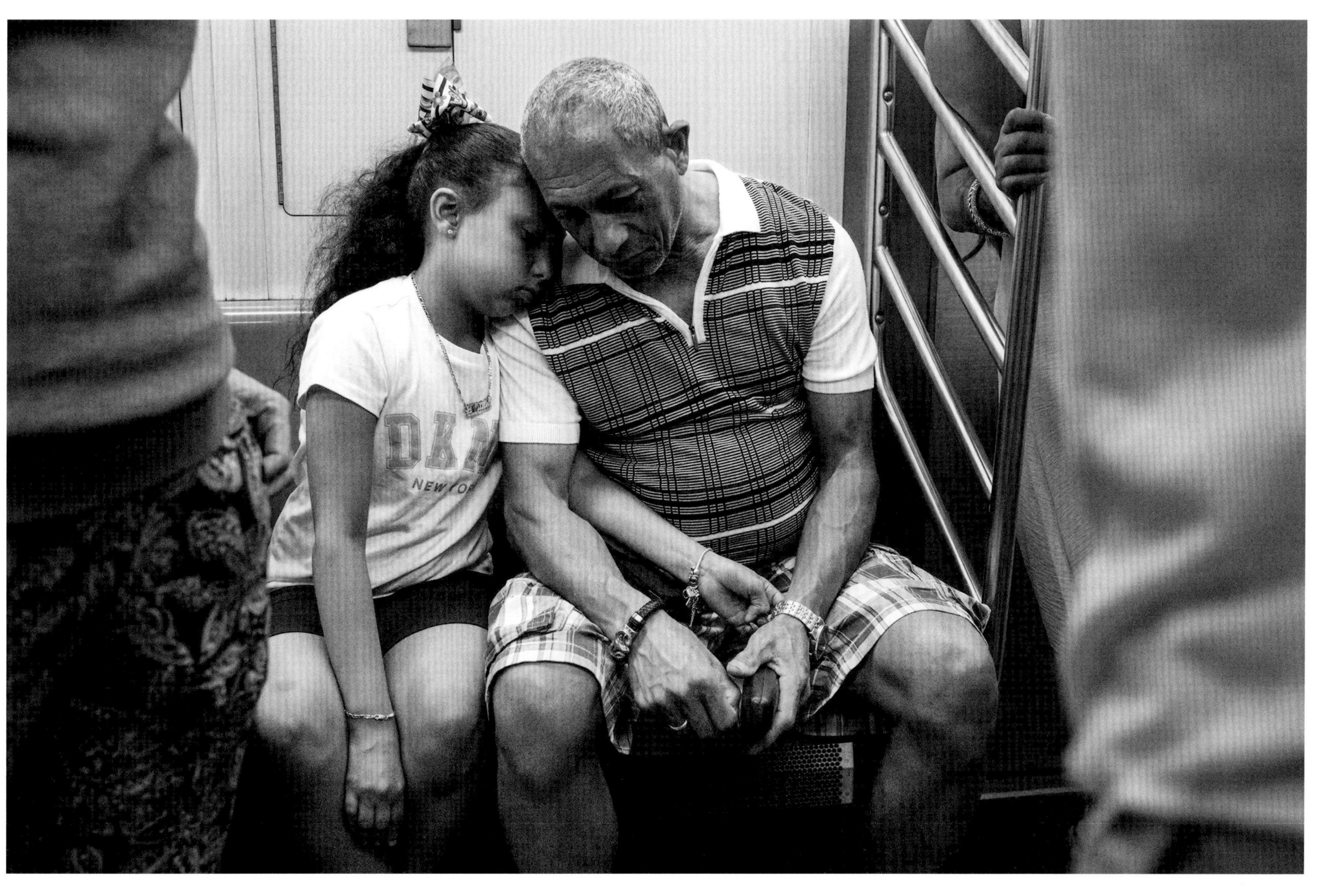

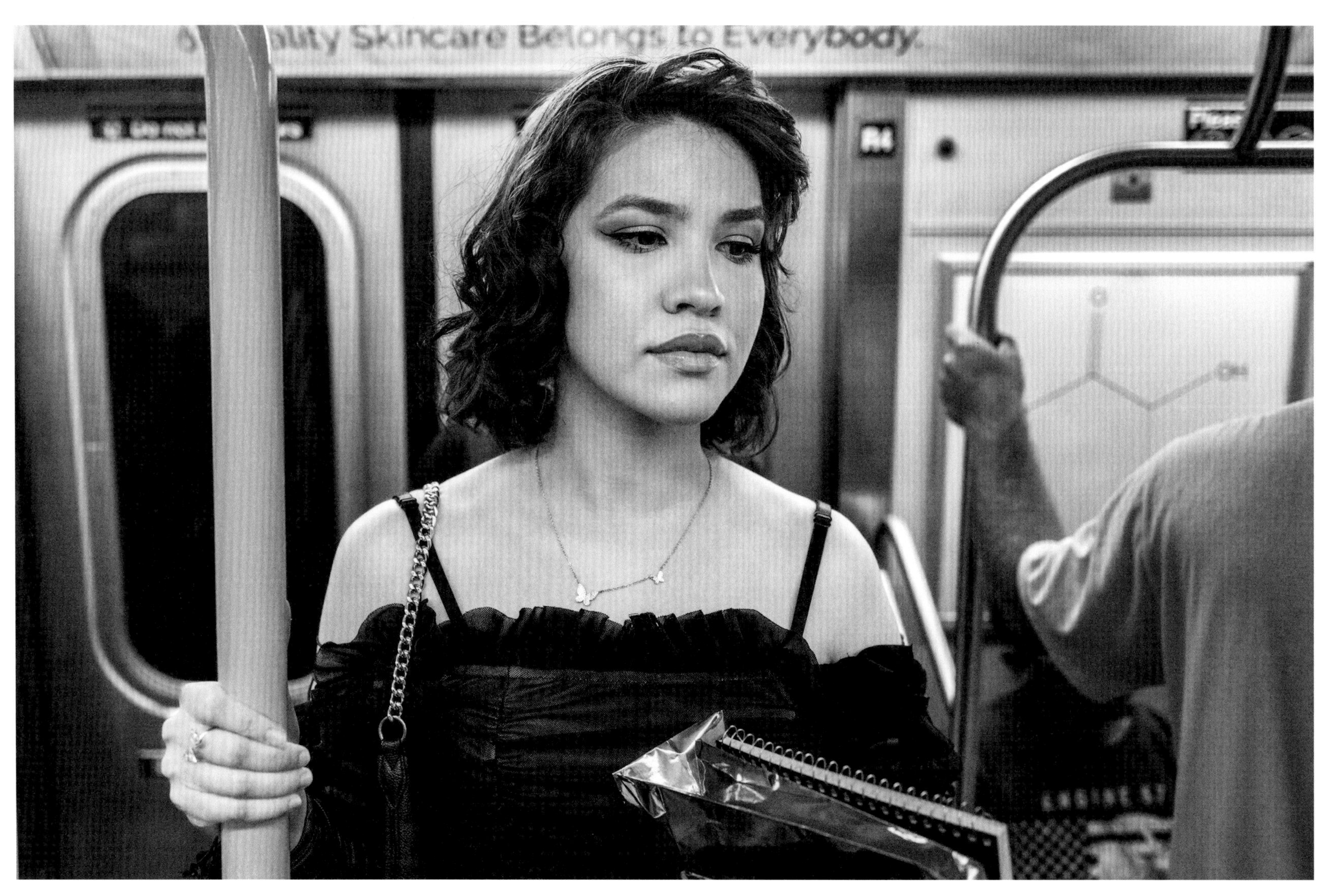
ality Skincare Belongs to Everybody.

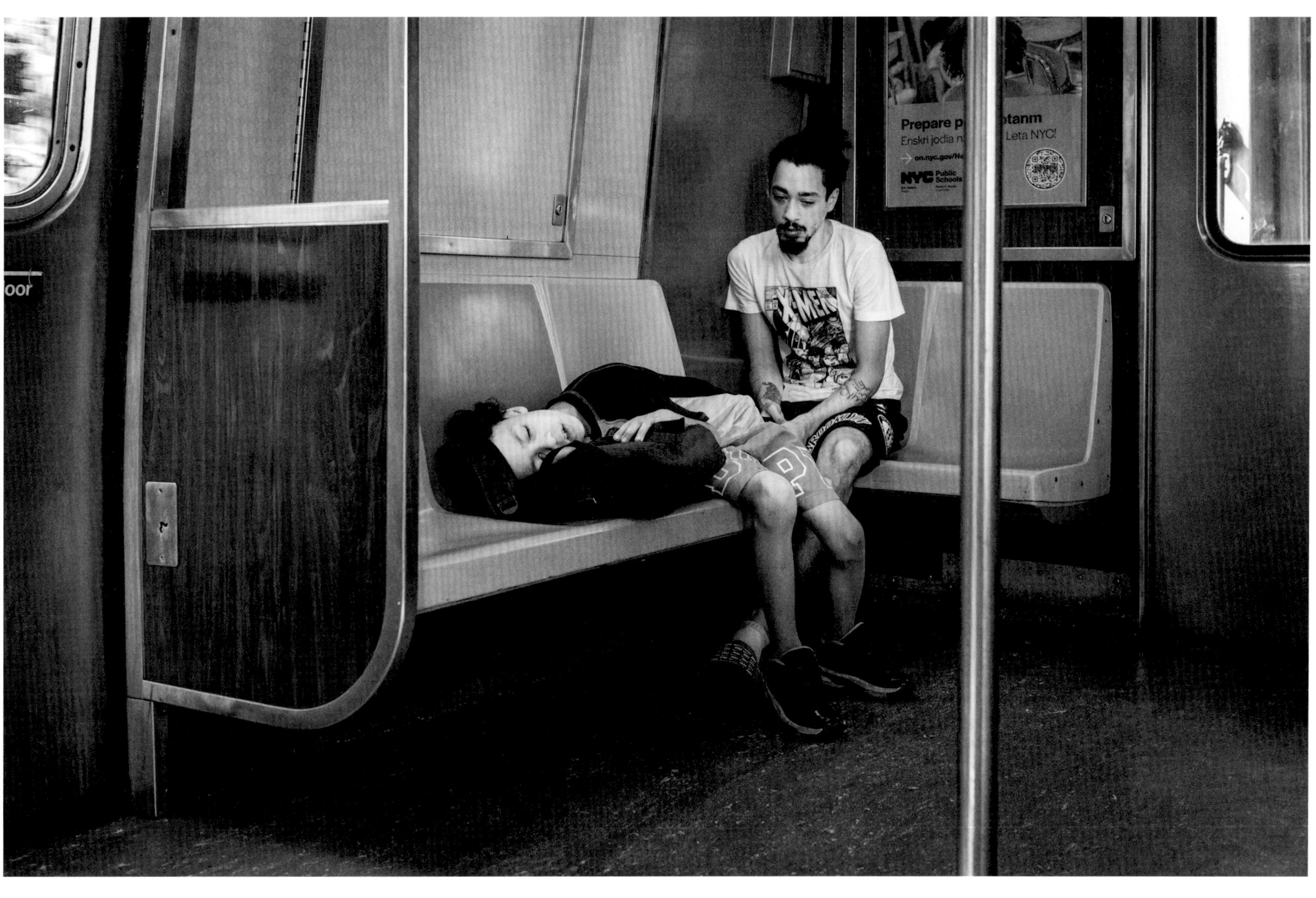
X-MEN
NYC
Public Schools

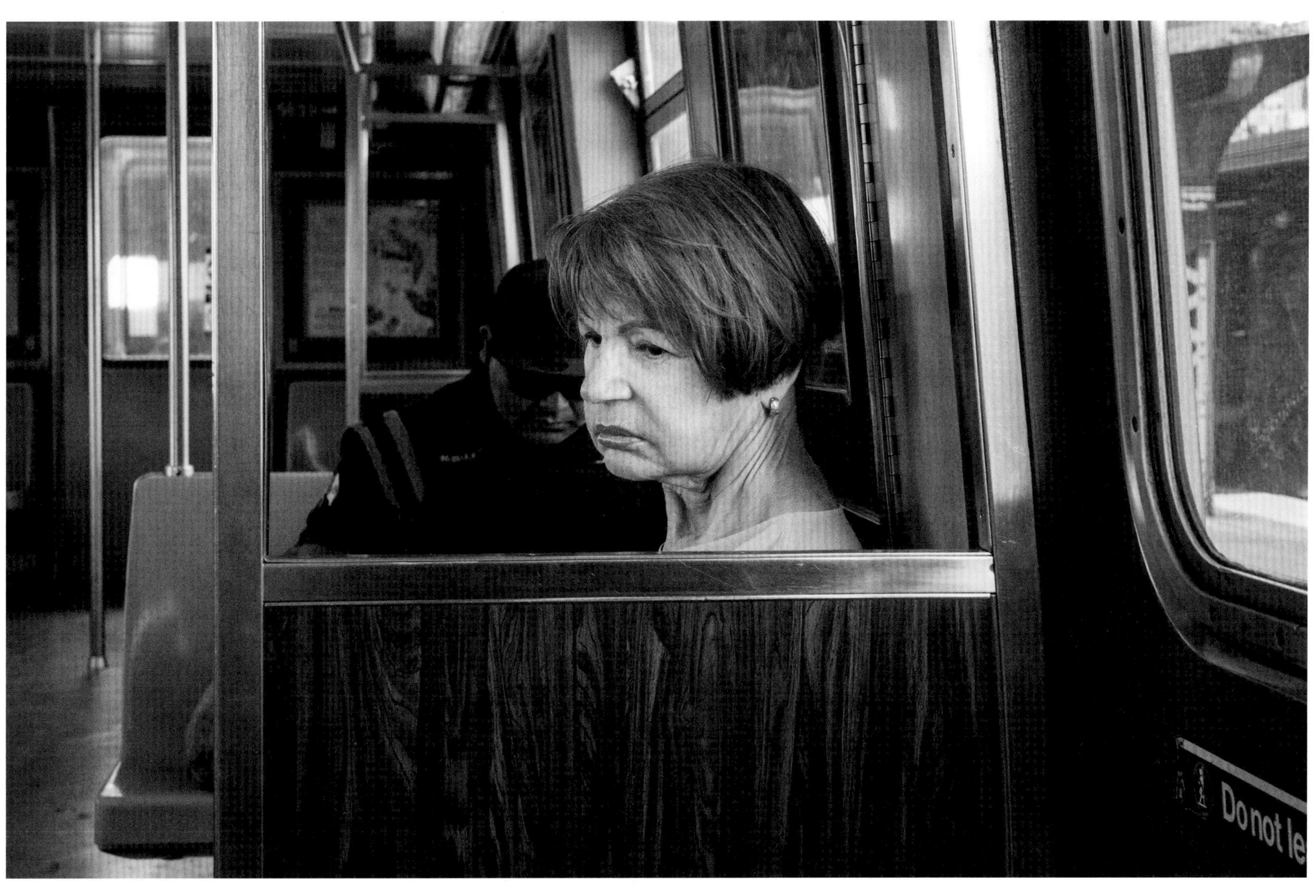
Do not le

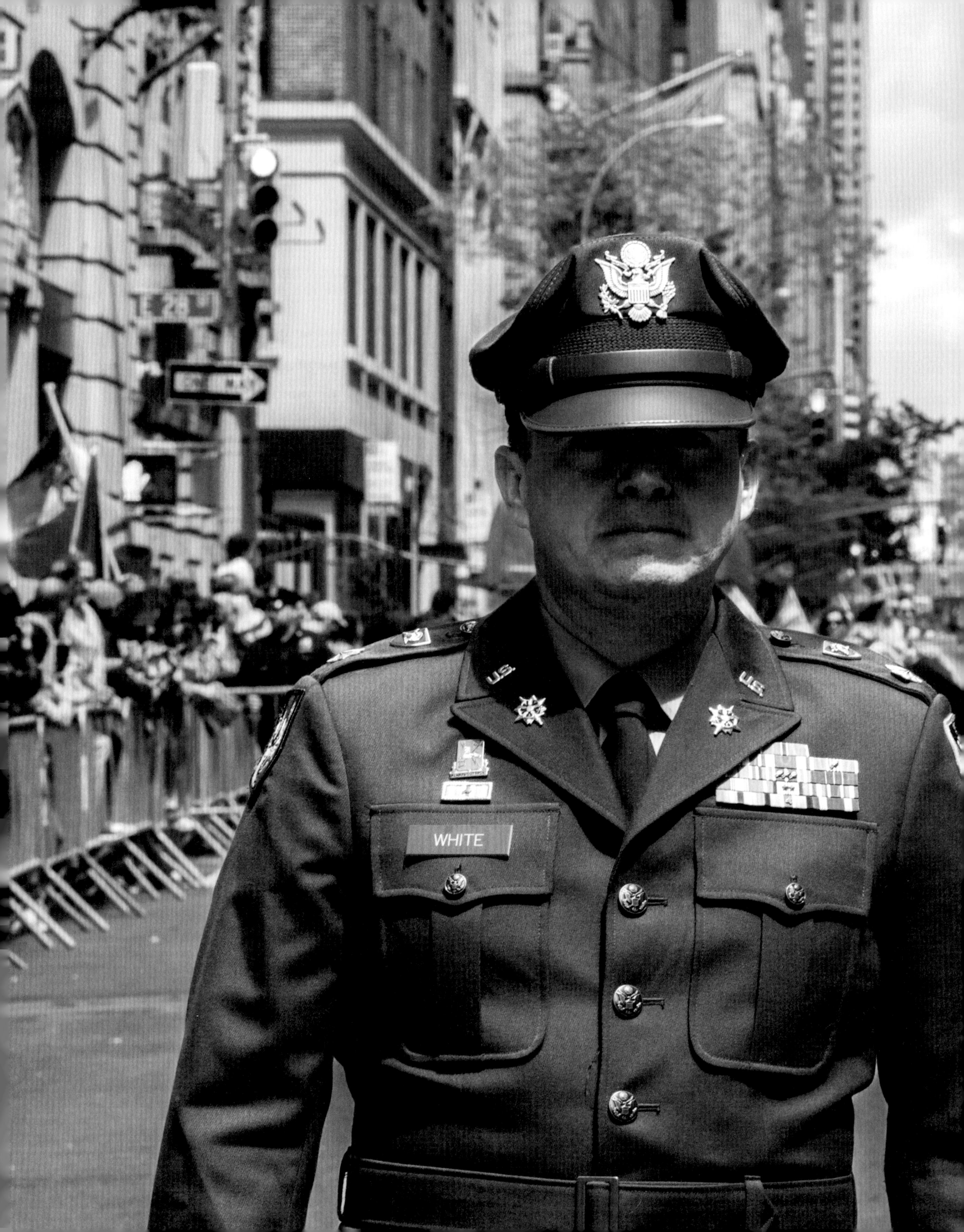
U.S.
U.S.
WHITE

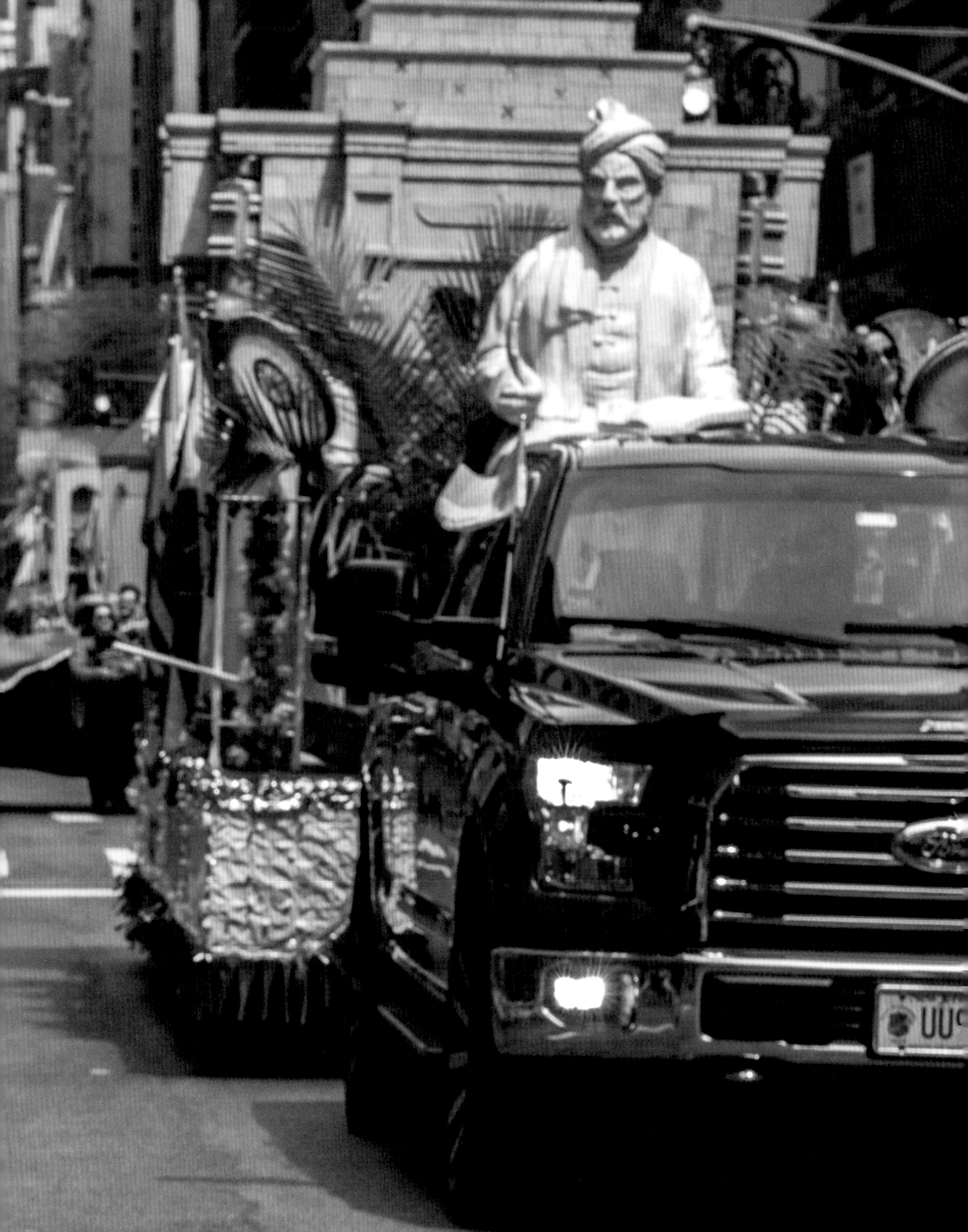

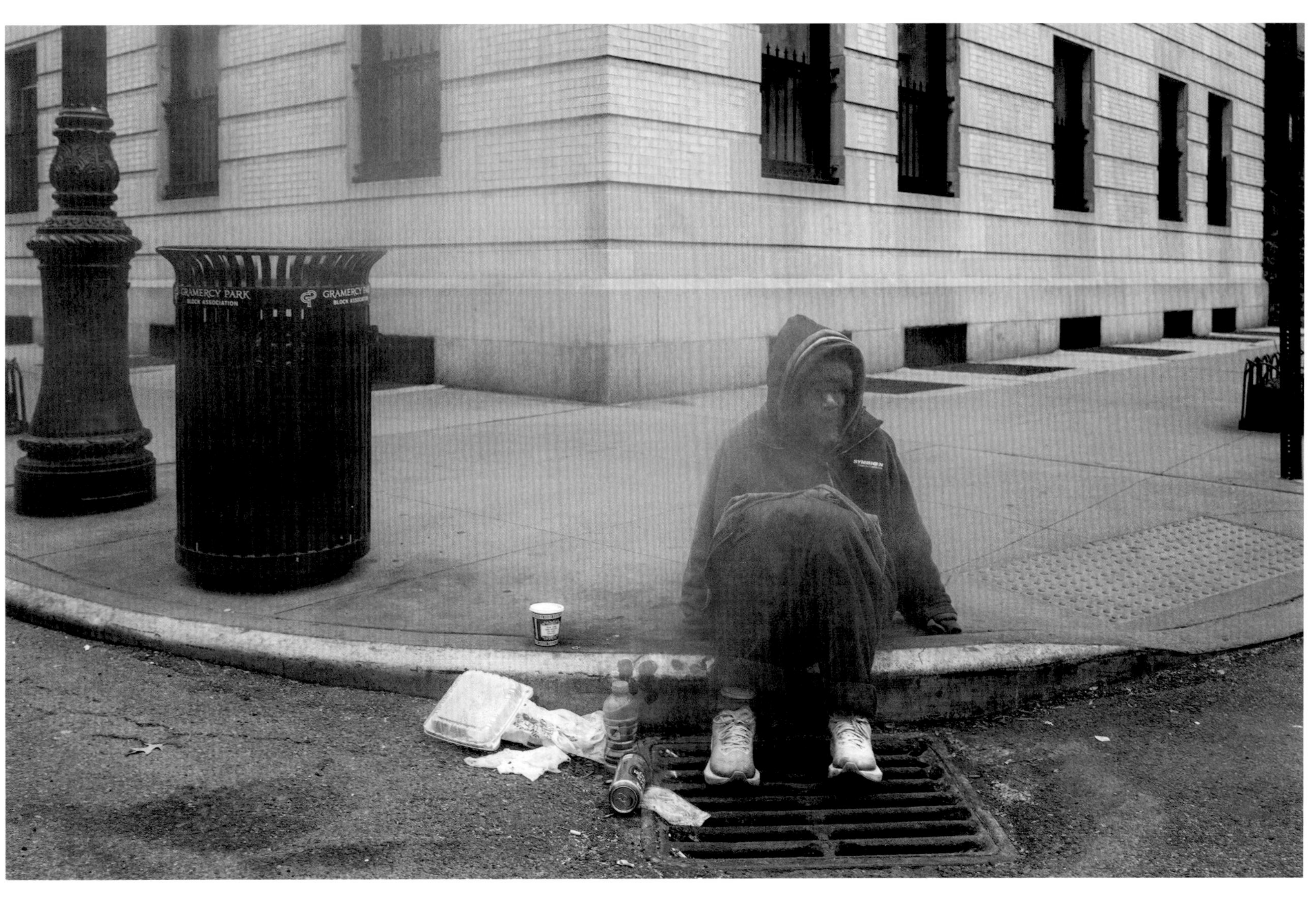
GRAMERCY PARK
BLOCK ASSOCIATION

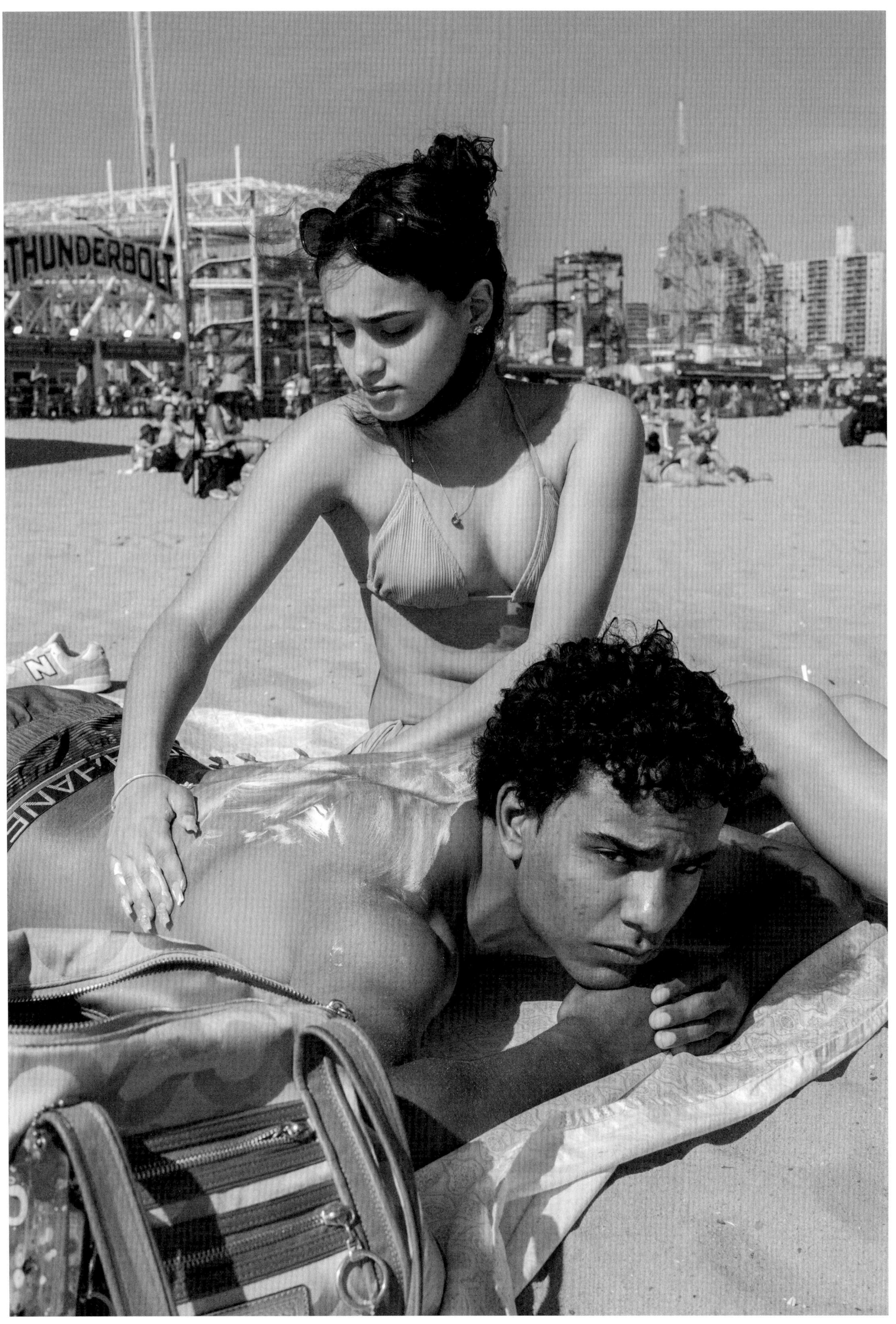
THUNDERBOLT

„Fotografieren heißt, das Leben intensiv auszukosten, jede Hundertstelsekunde." ~ MARC RIBOUD

"Taking pictures is savoring life intensely, every hundredth of a second." ~ MARC RIBOUD

Die Stadt genießen

Elin Spring

Savoring the City

Elin Spring

New York Short Stories beleuchtet intime Momente im öffentlichen Raum. Der deutsche Fotograf, Regisseur, Autor und Komponist Mario Schneider richtet wie ein Außenseiter in diesem Buch seinen Blick auf die Straßen dieser rastlosen Metropole. In der Tradition berühmter Vorgänger wie des in der Schweiz geborenen Robert Frank (*The Americans,* 1958), der aus Österreich stammenden Lisette Model (Photo League) und des gebürtigen Deutschen Alfred Eisenstaedt (*Life*) streift er durch die Parks und die Viertel der Stadt und entdeckt Momente der Verbundenheit, die jede gesprochene Sprache übersteigen. In Schneiders eindringlichen Porträts erzählen vertraute Gesten und Ausdrücke Geschichten, die genauso individuell sind wie seine Motive. Und doch ist dies kein Privileg, das allein dem Blick eines Fremden vorbehalten ist.

Dutzende berühmter amerikanischer Dokumentarfotografen wie Saul Leiter, Helen Levitt, Gordon Parks, Diane Arbus, Garry Winogrand, Vivian Maier und Joel Meyerowitz haben sich auf den Straßen New Yorks einen Namen gemacht. Als Porträtist der Straße teilt Schneider mit diesen Fotografen eine persönliche Philosophie, die eher das Verbindende und Gemeinsame als das Außergewöhnliche sucht. Diese humanistische Sichtweise verleiht Schneiders visuellen Erzählungen aufschlussreiche Emotionen und Charakter. Das zeigt sich in der privaten Verlorenheit einer jungen Frau, die in ihrem teilweise ausgezogenen Kostüm durch eine sich auflösende Parade irrt (S. 17), in den spielerischen Posen eines selbstvergessenen Paares beim Schachspiel (S. 78) und in der direkten Auseinandersetzung mit einer Gruppe neugieriger Jungen, die von der Schule nach Hause gehen (S. 62/63).

Als scharfer und einfühlsamer Beobachter wie auch als lebhafter Teilnehmer am städtischen Treiben fügt Schneider mit seinen *New York Short Stories* dem

New York Short Stories alights on intimate moments in public spaces. Within these pages, German photographer, director, writer and composer Mario Schneider brings an interloper's eye to the streets of this metropolis buzzing with constant motion. In the tradition of famous forebears like the Swiss-born Robert Frank (*The Americans,* 1958), the Austrian-born Lisette Model (Photo League), and the German-born Alfred Eisenstaedt (*Life*), he roams the city's parks and neighborhoods, encountering instants of connection that transcend any spoken language. In Schneider's evocative portraits, familiar gestures and expressions initiate narratives that are as individual as his subjects. But this is hardly a trait confined to foreign eyes.

Dozens of renowned American documentary photographers such as Saul Leiter, Helen Levitt, Gordon Parks, Diane Arbus, Garry Winogrand, Vivien Maier, and Joel Meyerowitz earned their reputations on the streets of New York City. As a street portraitist, Schneider shares with these photographers a personal philosophy that seeks connection and commonality, rather than exceptionalism. This humanistic viewpoint endows Schneider's visual narratives with insightful emotions and inklings of character. We observe it in the private reverie of a young woman wandering amidst a parade's dissipating crowd in her partially shed costume (page 17), in an oblivious couple's playful antics over their contested chess game (page 78), and in the direct engagement with a group of inquisitive boys returning home after school (page 62/63).

At once a keen and empathetic observer as well as a lively participant in the bustle of city life, Schneider's *New York Short Stories* updates the canon of street photography from a distinctly contemporary perspective. His image of a pedestrian's steady gaze also divulges today's urban street scene (page 170/171), two

Kanon der Street Photography ein neues Kapitel aus einer dezidiert zeitgenössischen Perspektive hinzu. So verweist seine Aufnahme vom starren Blick eines Passanten auf die heutige Realität einer urbanen Straßenszene (S. 170/171), während die Fotografie zweier Freundinnen auf einem sonnigen Bürgersteig aktuelle Modetrends zeigt (S. 48/49) und das Bild eines Mädchens, das die atemberaubende Skyline New Yorks durch ihr Telefon erlebt, von der Allgegenwart mobiler Geräte zeugt (S. 56/57). In Fotografien wie diesen übernimmt Schneider die Rolle eines Anthropologen, der unserer Gegenwart einen Zeitstempel aufdrückt.

Dauerhafte Fotografien sind zugleich zeitlos. Diese Dauerhaftigkeit erreicht Schneider mit Bildern, die unabhängig von Zeit und Ort Emotionen ausdrücken. Wir sehen sie in den überraschten Gesichtern von Frauen in einem vorbeifahrenden Auto (S. 100/101), in der Freude eines Kindes in den Armen seiner Eltern (S. 44/45) und in der liebevollen Hingabe eines Mannes an seinen Hund (S. 148/149). Wir sehen die heftige Empörung eines mit dem Finger zeigenden Mannes (S. 79), das Mitgefühl für eine leidende Freundin (S. 55) und die Verzweiflung einer obdachlosen Frau (S. 51). Auf seinen leidenschaftlichen Streifzügen hat Schneider ein breites Spektrum an Stimmungen dieser Stadtbewohner eingefangen. Aber warum New York?

Die USA werden dafür gefeiert, ein kultureller, politischer und wirtschaftlicher Schmelztiegel zu sein: Die Freiheitsstatue am Eingang des New Yorker Hafens steht für das Bekenntnis des Landes zu dieser Eigenschaft. Als größte Stadt der USA ist New York ein faszinierendes Symbol für die Kakofonie menschlicher Träume und Bestrebungen in diesem Land. Die Anziehungskraft ihrer großen Vielfalt erweist sich seit Langem als unwiderstehlich. Mario Schneiders faszinierende dokumentarische Porträts spiegeln die Seele dieser Metropole wider – einzigartig und universell, trendig und zeitlos zugleich. Die lebendigen Einblicke seiner *New York Short Stories* treffen den Nerv der Zeit.

companions on a sunny sidewalk broadcast current styles in fashion (page 48/49), and a charming girl experiencing New York City's stunning skyline through her phone attests to the ubiquity of handheld devices (page 56/57). In photographs like these, Schneider assumes the role of an anthropologist placing a time stamp on our era.

Enduring photographs are also timeless. Schneider achieves this lasting quality in images that express emotions independently of either period or place. We see it in the surprised faces of women passing by in a car (page 100/101), in the joy of a child in its parent's arms (page 44/45), and in the loving devotion of a man for his dog (page 148/149). We recognize, too, the stern indignation of a pointing man (page 79), the compassion for a suffering friend (page 55), and the desolation of a homeless woman (page 51). In his ardent wanderings, Schneider has assembled a resonant spectrum of moods in these urbanites. But why New York City?

The United States is celebrated for being a melting pot, culturally, politically and economically. Standing at the entrance to New York Harbor, the Statue of Liberty proclaims the country's allegiance to that defining trait. As the country's largest city, New York is the grand, enthralling symbol of the country's cacophony of human dreams and endeavors. The allure of its dense diversity has long proven irresistible. Mario Schneider's enticing documentary portraits reflect the soul of this metropolis, at once unique and universal, trendy and ageless. His lively inquiries tap its pulse in *New York Short Stories*.

Hungriger Mann

Sergio Purtell

Wenn man an Street Photography denkt, ist New York oft der erste Ort, der einem in den Sinn kommt. Für Mario Schneider, der in Ostdeutschland aufwuchs, war New York jedoch ein unerreichbarer Ort – einer, den er wahrscheinlich niemals sehen würde. „New York war für mich ein Sehnsuchtsort, so wie die Ringe des Saturn", sagt er.

Es ist diese Anziehungskraft, die ihn schließlich im Jahr 2000 auf Einladung seiner damaligen Freundin zum ersten Mal in die Stadt führt. Nachdem er als Tourist bereits durch ganz Europa gereist war, überkam ihn bei seiner Ankunft ein völlig neues Gefühl: Es war, als wäre er zu Hause.

Während seines Aufenthalts in New York lernte er durch den neuen Freund seiner Ex-Freundin den wohlhabenderen Teil der Stadt, die High Society, kennen. Er saugte die Stadtansichten in den Stretchlimousinen auf, die Lichter spiegelten sich in den Fenstern – er fühlte sich high, es war wie in den Filmen, die er als Kind gesehen hatte. Gleichzeitig erlebte er die andere Seite der Stadt, Bettler und Armut – alles an ein und demselben Ort. Dieses Nebeneinander empfand er als schockierend und abstoßend, zugleich spürte er eine große Distanz. Er machte zwar ein paar Fotos, jedoch keines von Menschen, denn er war noch nicht so weit. Nach einer Woche saß er im Flugzeug zurück nach Deutschland und hatte bereits Heimweh nach New York. „Das ist mir geblieben", sagte er zu mir.

Jahre später kehrte er zurück und unternahm vier Reisen in zwei Jahren (2023 und 2024). Die Bilder, die er in dieser Zeit machte, sind aufgeladen mit athletischer Kraft und Körperlichkeit. Endlich hatte er seine künstlerische Heimat gefunden und sich in sie verliebt. Er hat gelernt, dass die Welt selbst eine Künstlerin von unvergleichlichem Einfallsreichtum ist und dass er belohnt wird, wenn er ganz im Hier und Jetzt ist. Daraus ist dieses Buch entstanden.

Mario vergleicht diese Erfahrung mit der eines visuell hungrigen Menschen: Er fotografierte von

Starving Man

Sergio Purtell

When one thinks of street photography, New York is often the first place that comes to mind. For Mario Schneider, who grew up in East Germany, New York was however an unattainable place. It seemed a fact that he would never see it. As he says, "it was a place of longing for me, just as I would have loved to see the Rings of Saturn."

This sort of gravitational pull is what finally led him to the city for the first time in 2000, on the invitation of his former girlfriend. Having travelled throughout Europe at this point as a tourist, he was struck by a novel feeling on arrival: he felt at home.

While in New York he experienced the wealthier part of the city, high society, through his ex-girlfriend's new boyfriend. He absorbed the city views in stretch limos, the lights reflected on the windows, he felt high, it was like in the movies he had seen as a child. At the same time he saw the other side of the city, beggars and poverty—all in the same place. He found this juxtaposition shocking and repellent, and he felt the distance keenly. He took a few pictures, none were of people. He wasn't ready yet. After a week he was sat in the plane back to Germany, already homesick for New York. "That is what remained," he said to me.

Years later he returned, making four trips in two years (2023 and 2024). The pictures he made during these trips are charged with athletic strength and physicality. He had finally found his artistic home and he remains in love with it. He has learned that the world in itself is an artist of incomparable inventiveness, and that by being present and in the moment, he will be rewarded. The result is this book.

Mario equates this experience to that of a visually starving man. He would shoot from dawn to dusk. He did nothing but eat, sleep, and make pictures. He says that no one forced him to fall into this behavior, that he just knew he had to do it, and that it was like falling into an enchanted place, where staying alive meant being out in the world making pictures.

morgens bis abends. Er tat nichts anderes als essen, schlafen und fotografieren. Niemand habe ihn zu diesem Verhalten gezwungen, es war eine Notwendigkeit für ihn. Als sei er an einem verzauberten Ort gelandet, an dem am Leben zu sein bedeutet, auf die Straße zu gehen und Bilder zu machen.

Seine Fotografien zeugen von Klarheit, Kohärenz und einem unverwechselbaren Blick. Sie sind das Ergebnis von Wissen, Können und Sensibilität. Das Leben ist Chaos, und deshalb gibt es die Form: Sie hilft, das Herz zu heilen, indem sie uns eine Struktur gibt, in die wir die Fäden unserer verschiedenen Lebenserfahrungen einweben können.

Folglich liegt die Stärke seiner Fotografien in dem, was sie andeuten, und nicht in dem, was sie unmittelbar zeigen. Denn die Wahrheit offenbart sich immer in Grautönen.

His photographs reveal clarity, coherence, and a distinctive point of view. They are the product of knowledge, skill, and sensibility. Life is chaos, and that is why we have form. It helps to heal the heart by giving us a structure through which we can weave the threads of our disparate life experiences.

The strength of his photographs is what they suggest, not what they literally show. The truth always comes in shades of grey.

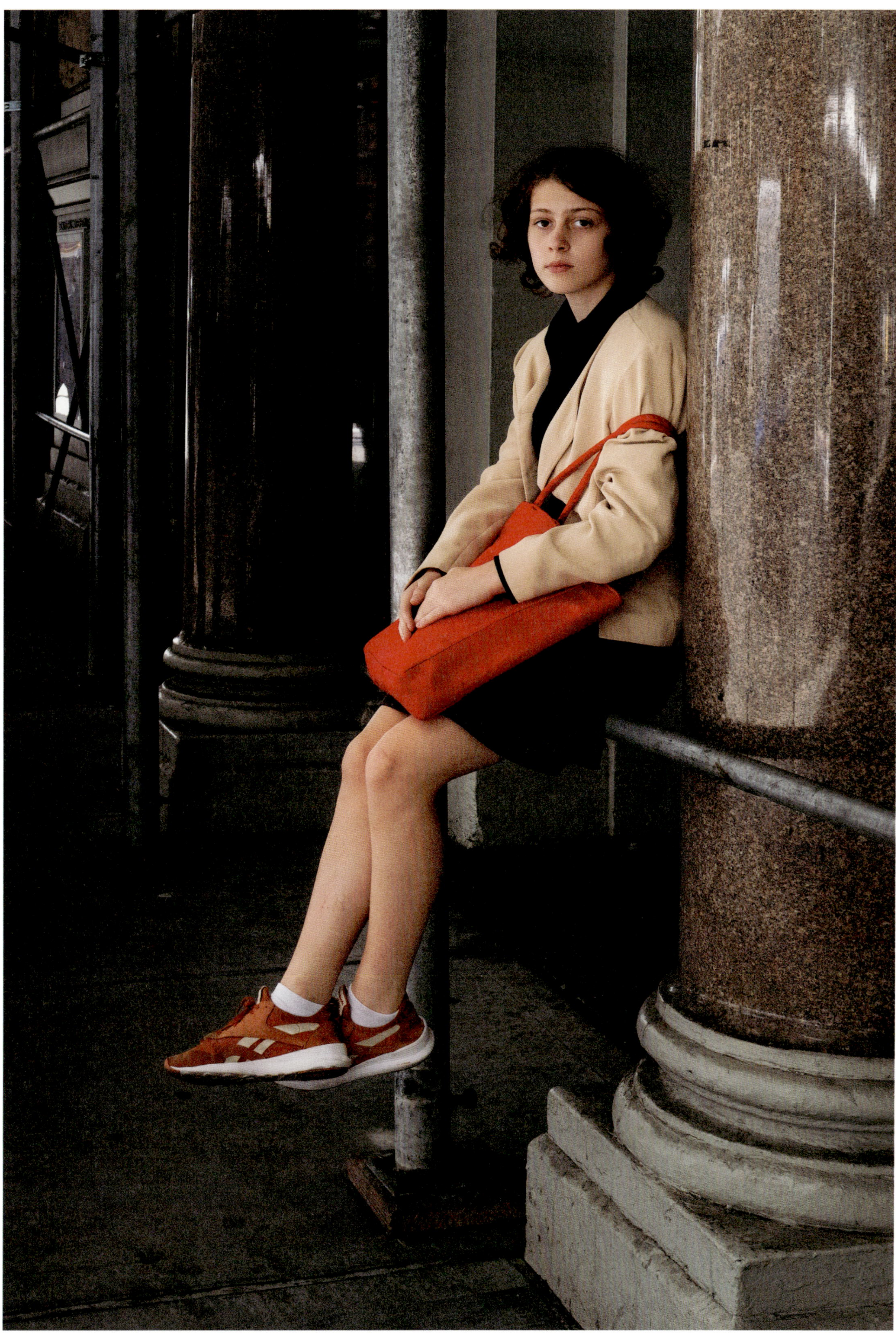

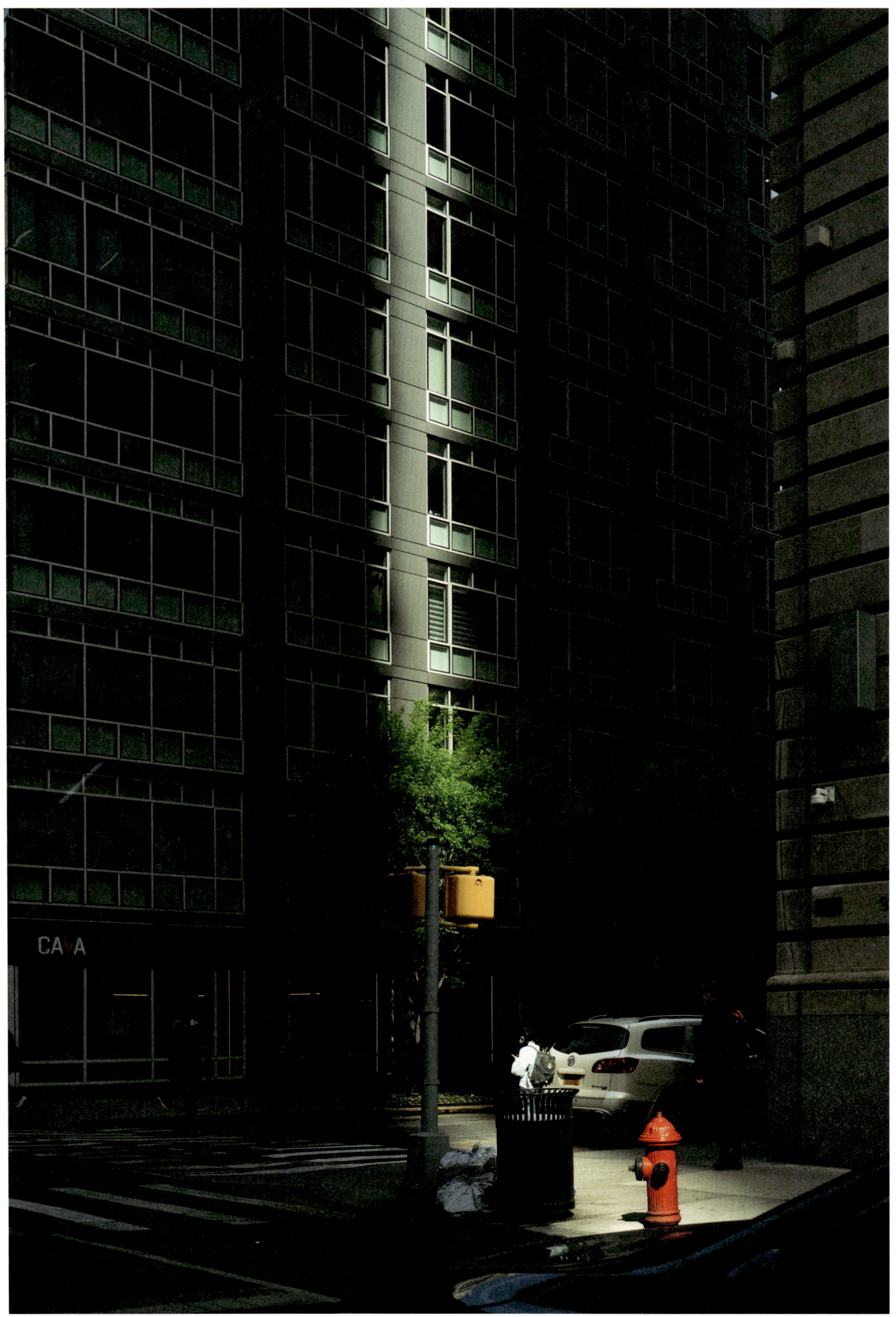
CAVA

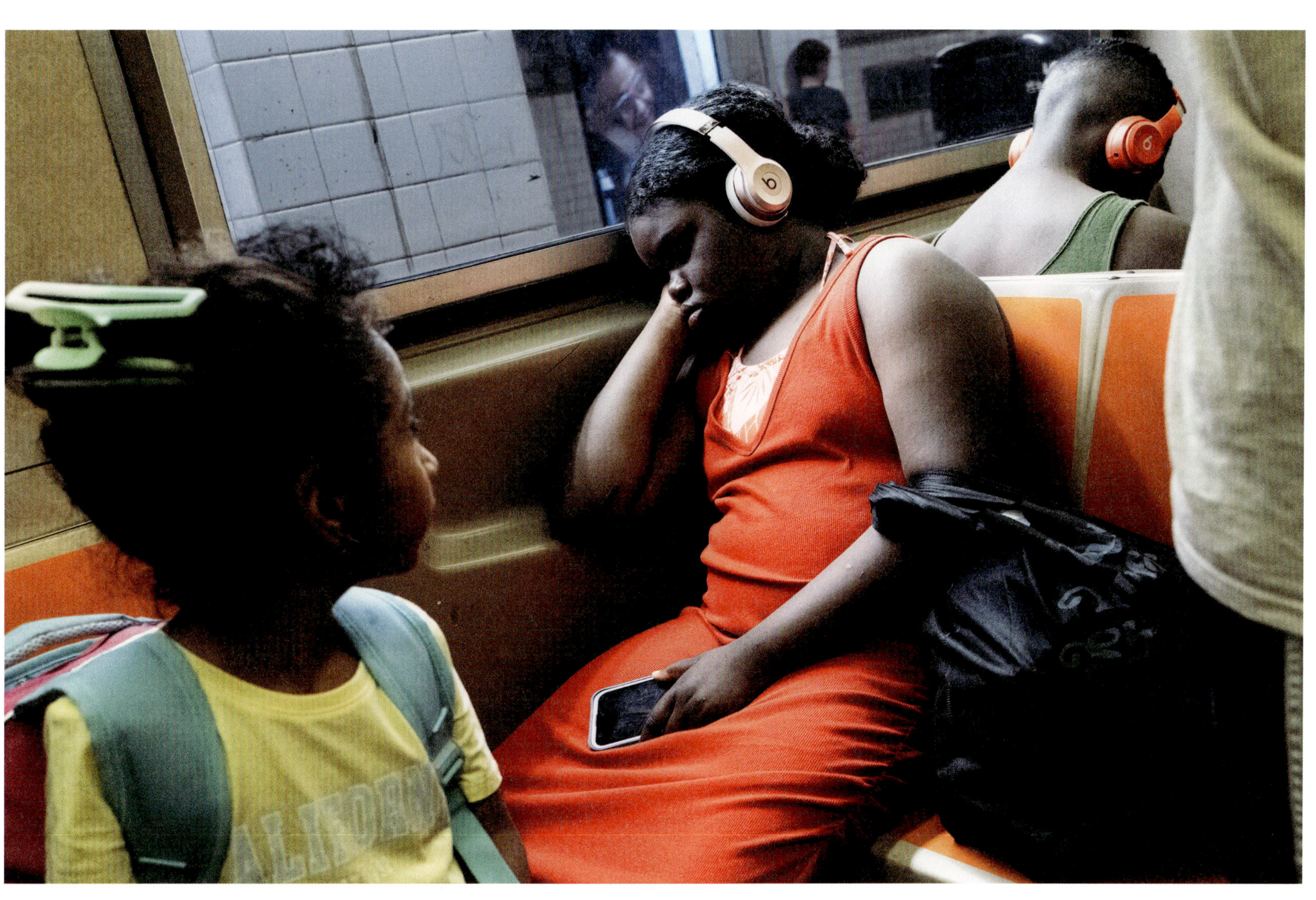

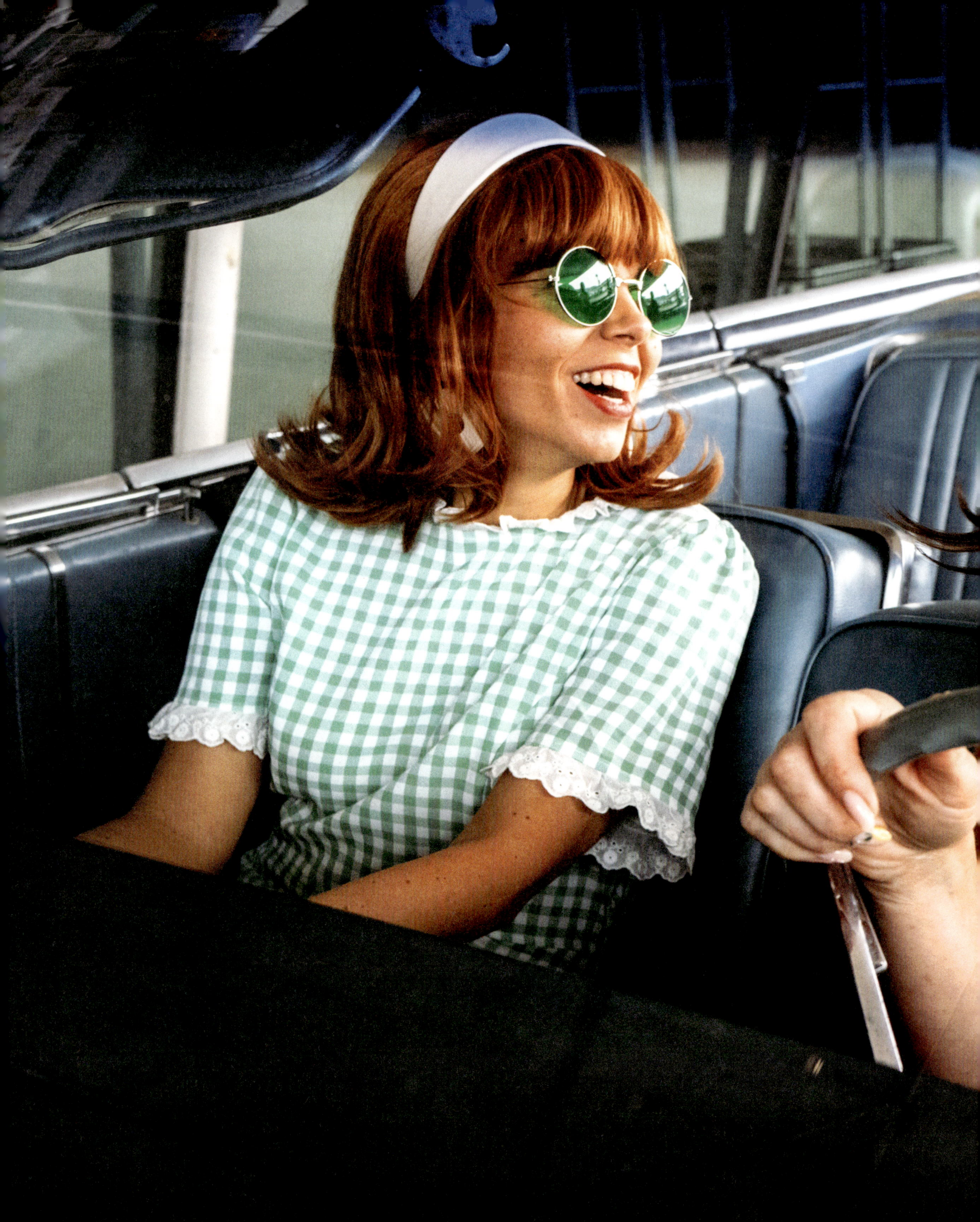

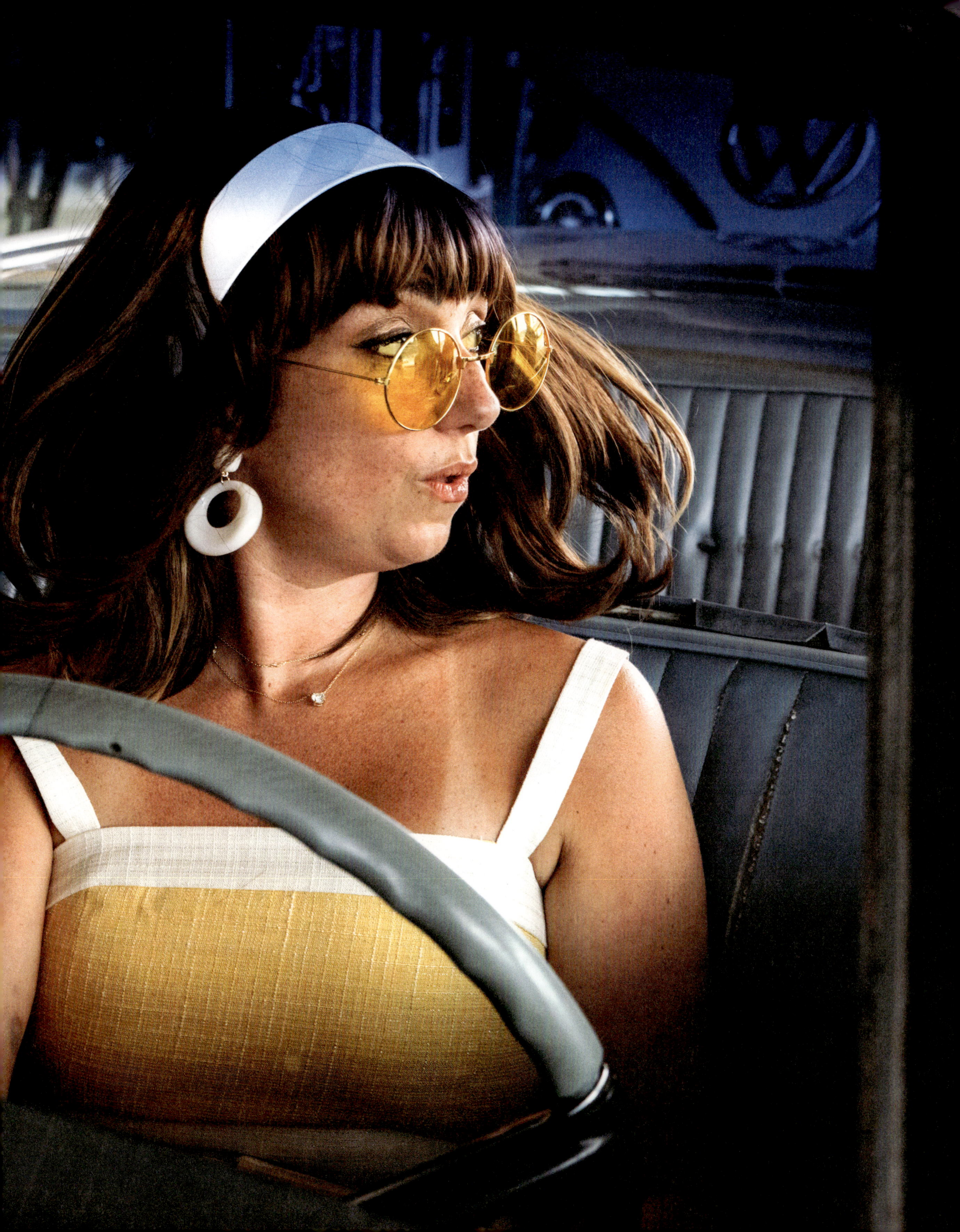

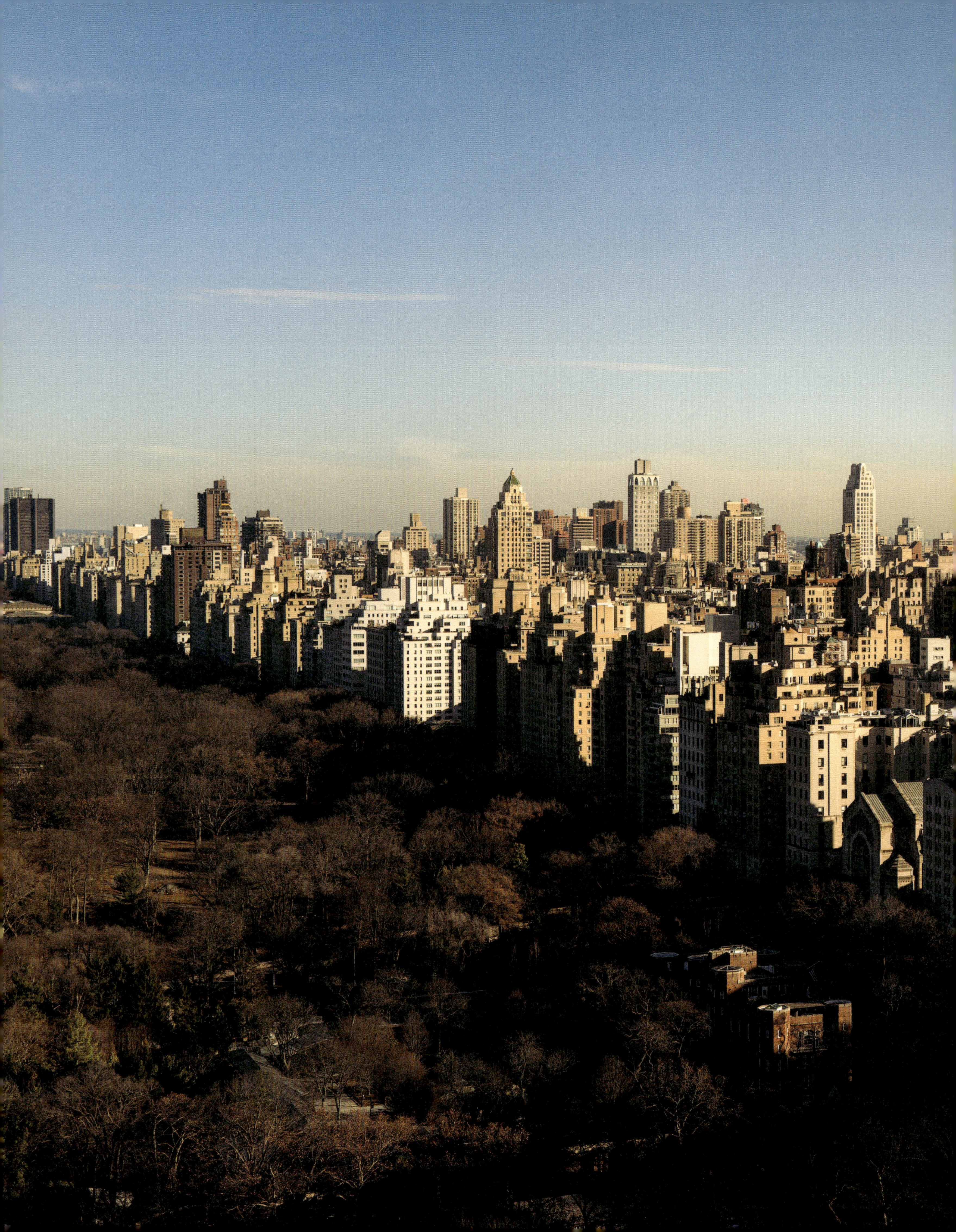

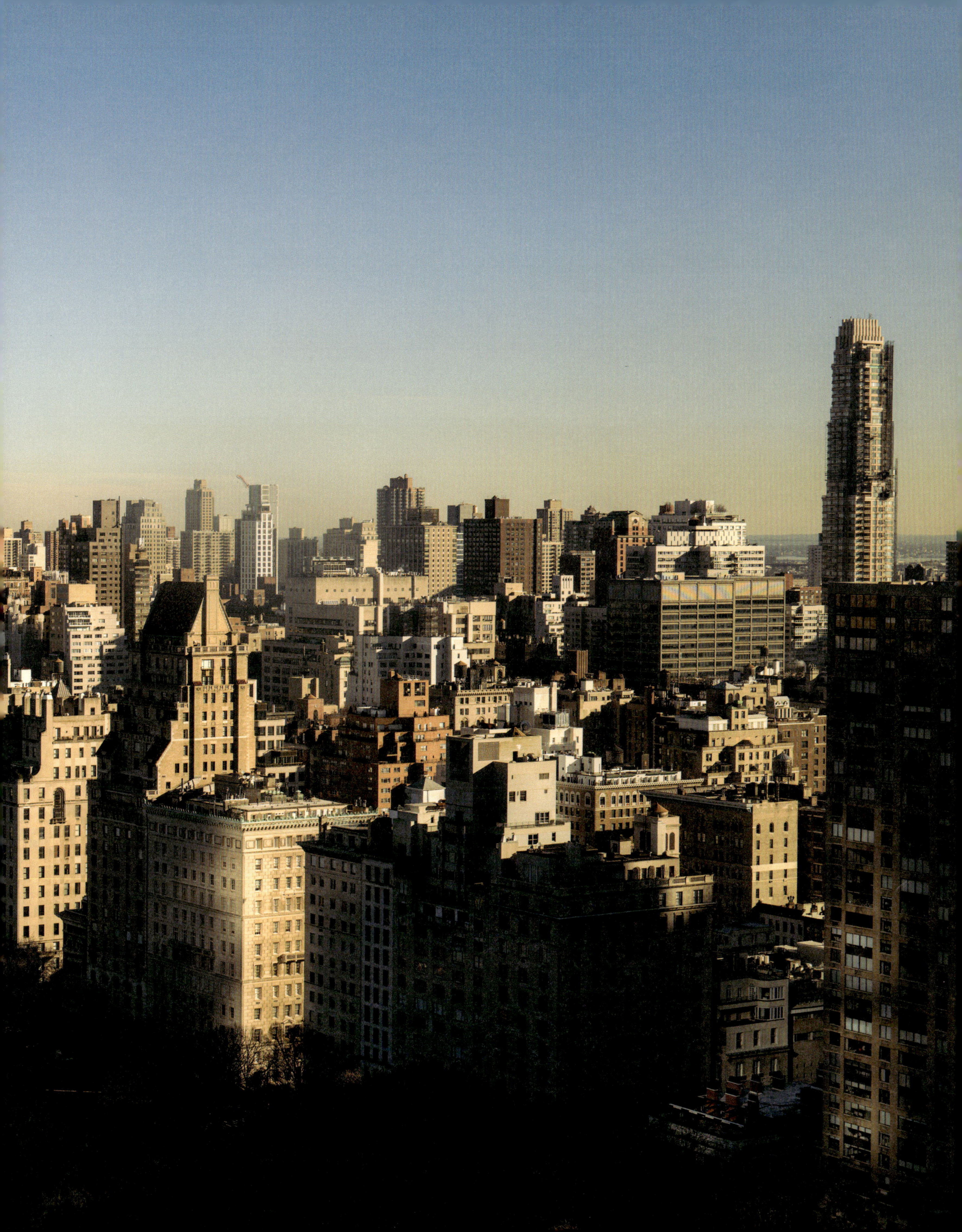

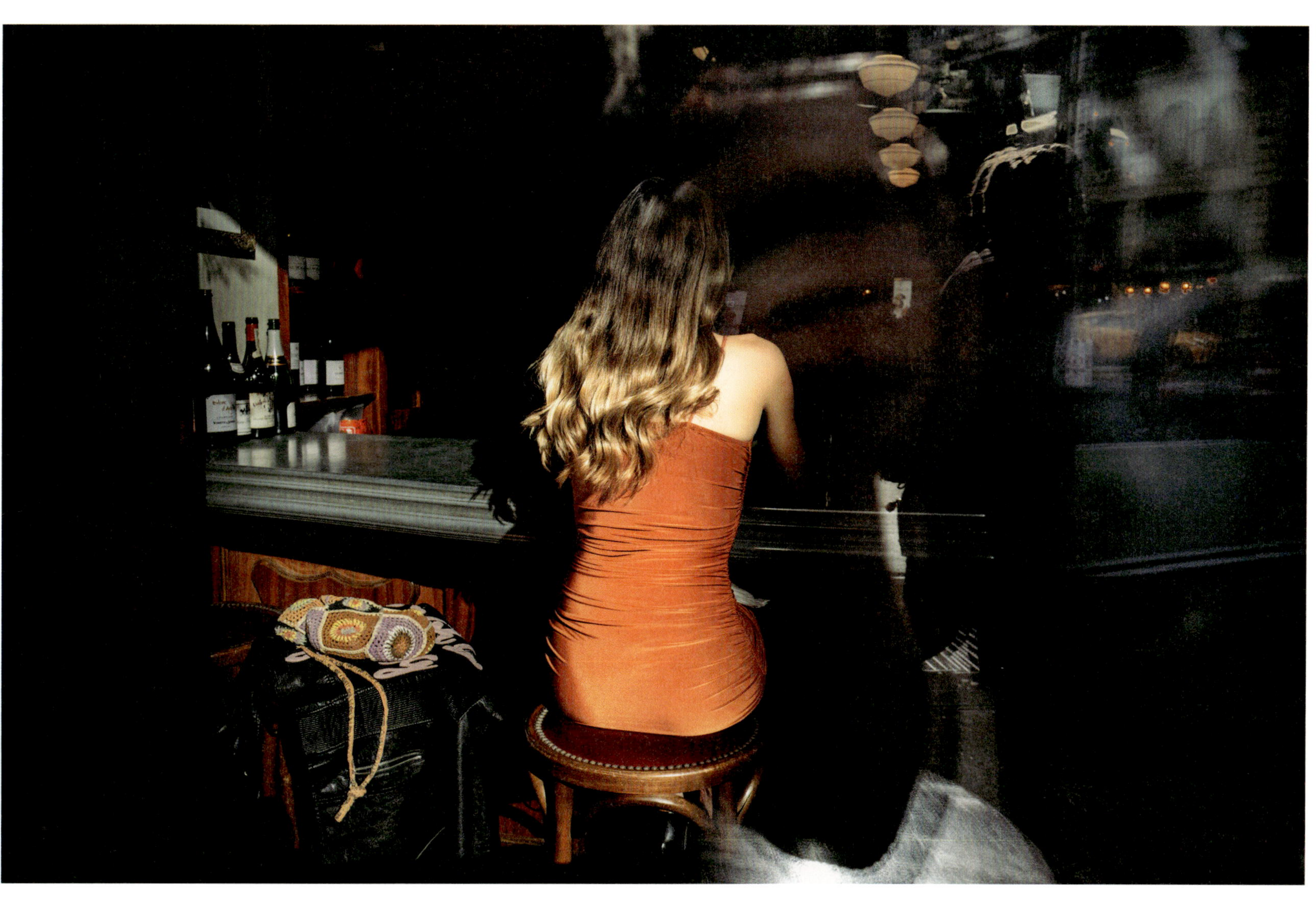

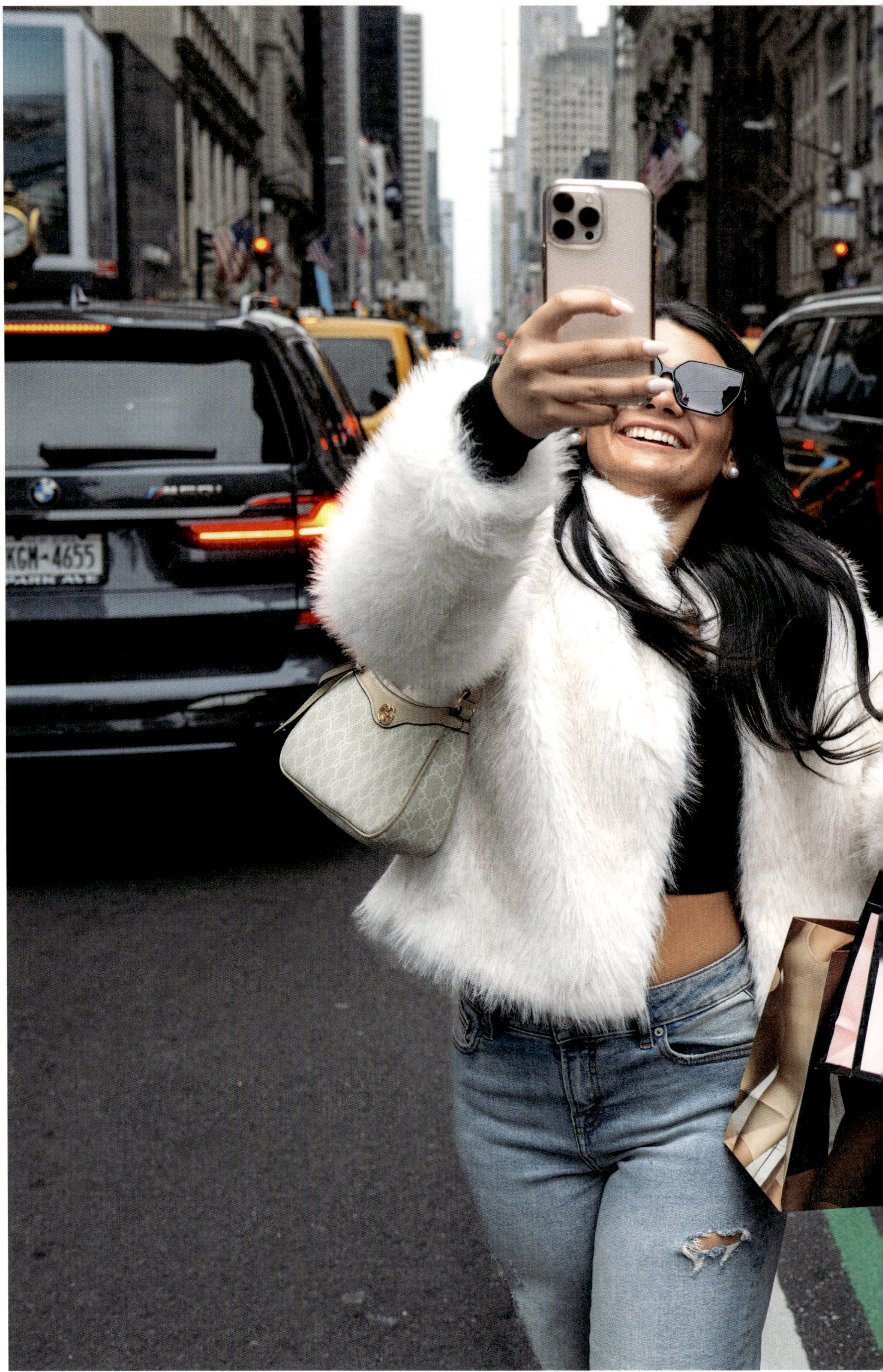
KGM-4655

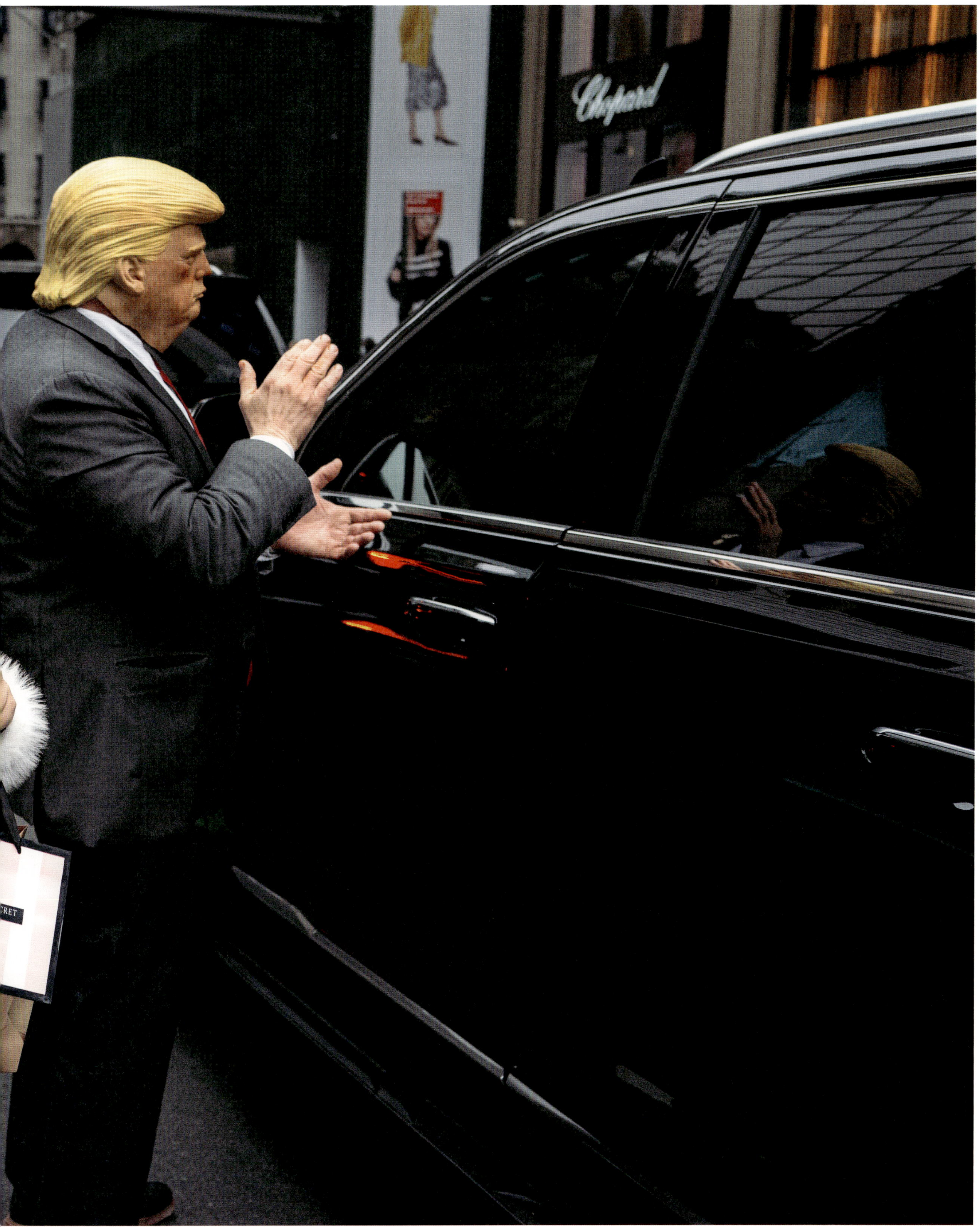

Chopard
CRET

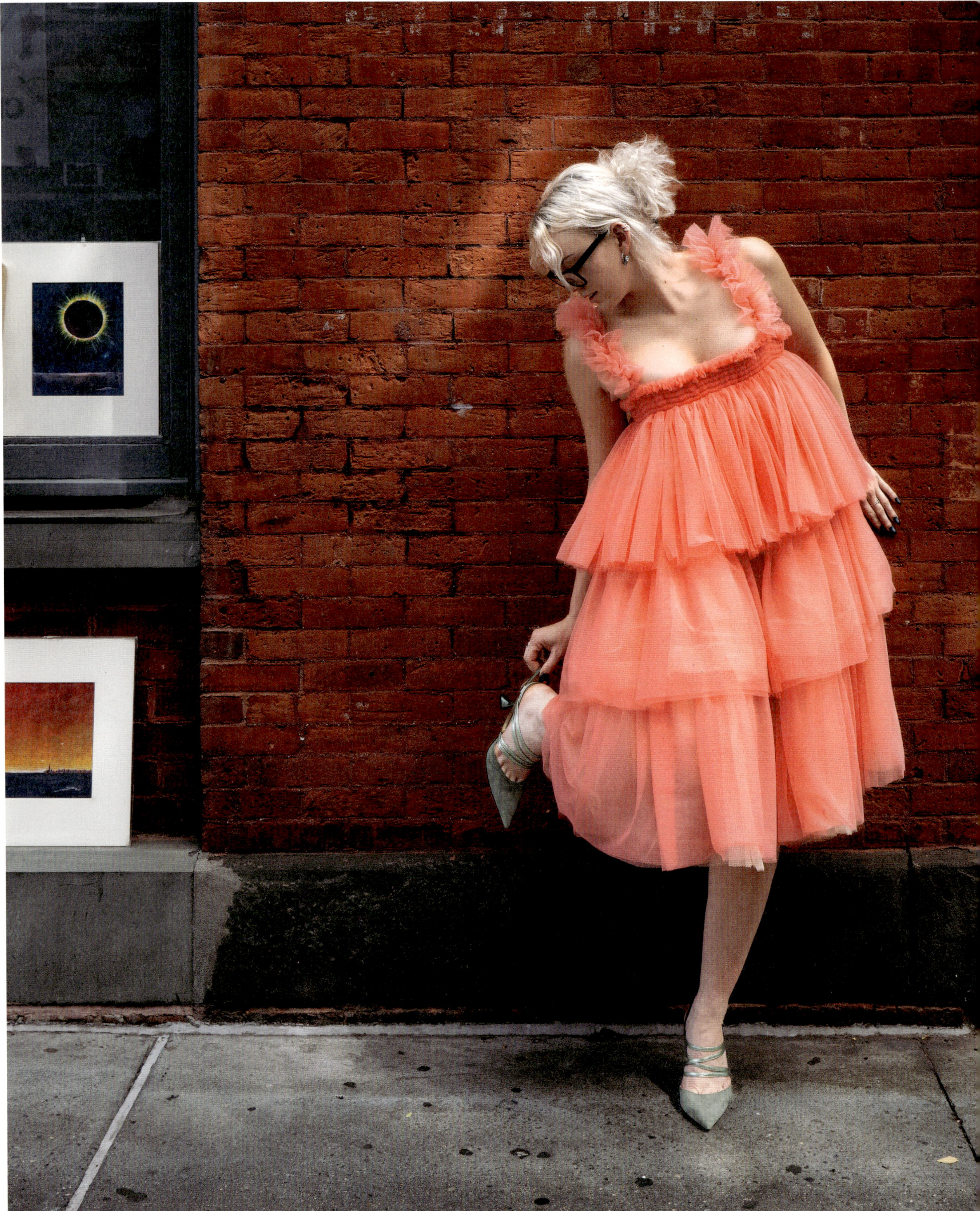

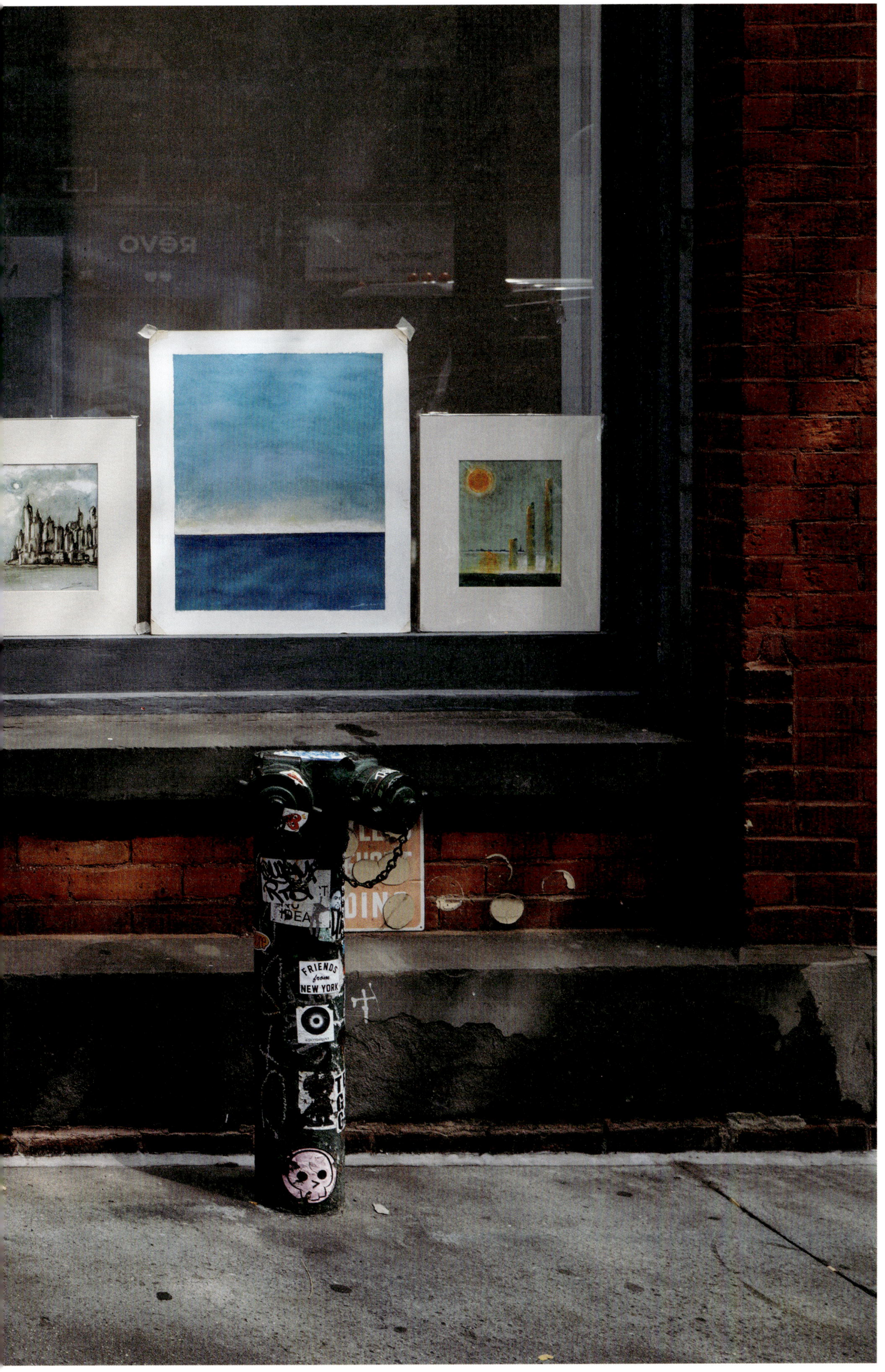
FRIENDS
from
NEW YORK

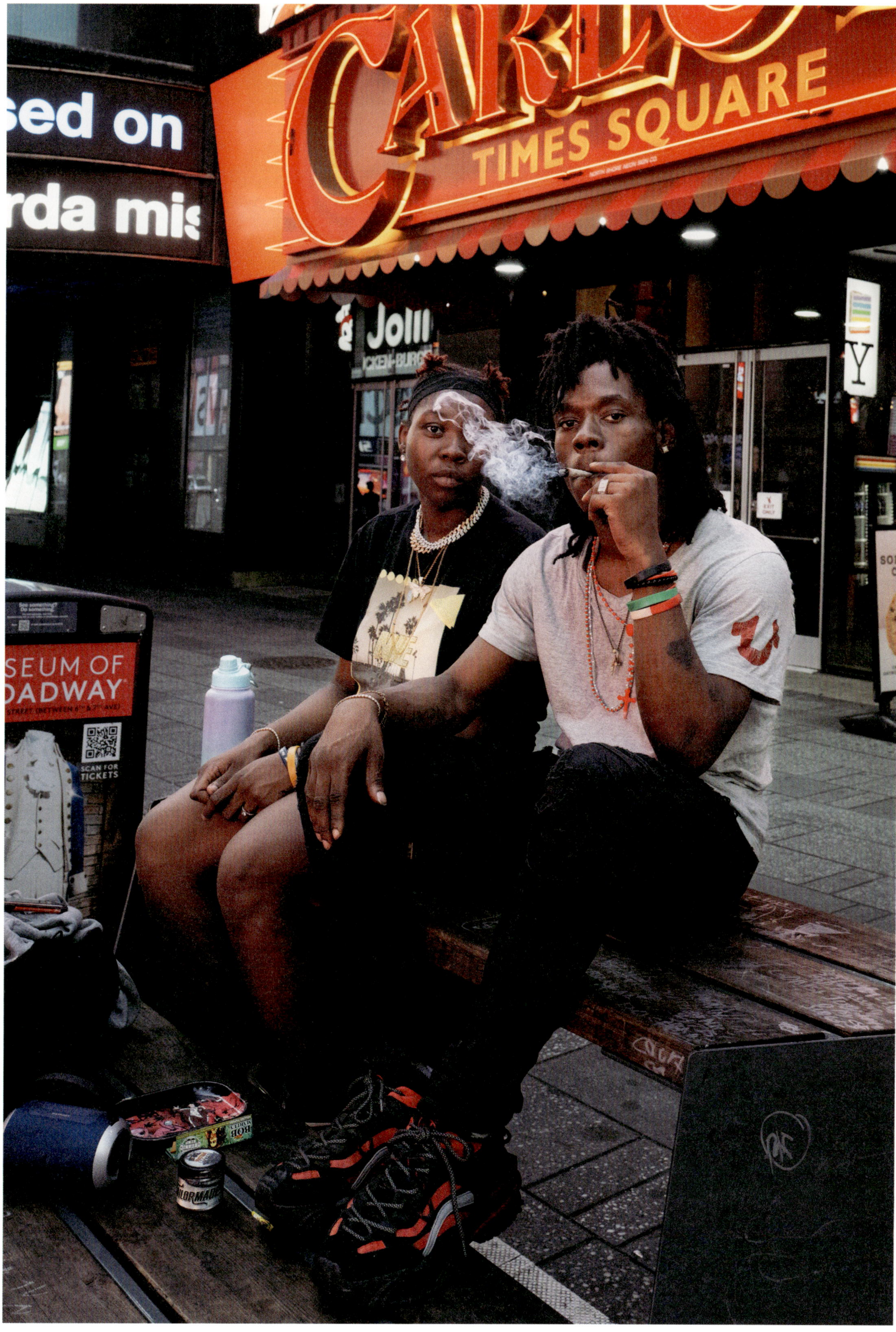
sed on
rda mis
CARLO'S
TIMES SQUARE
Jolli
SEUM OF
DADWAY
SCAN FOR
TICKETS

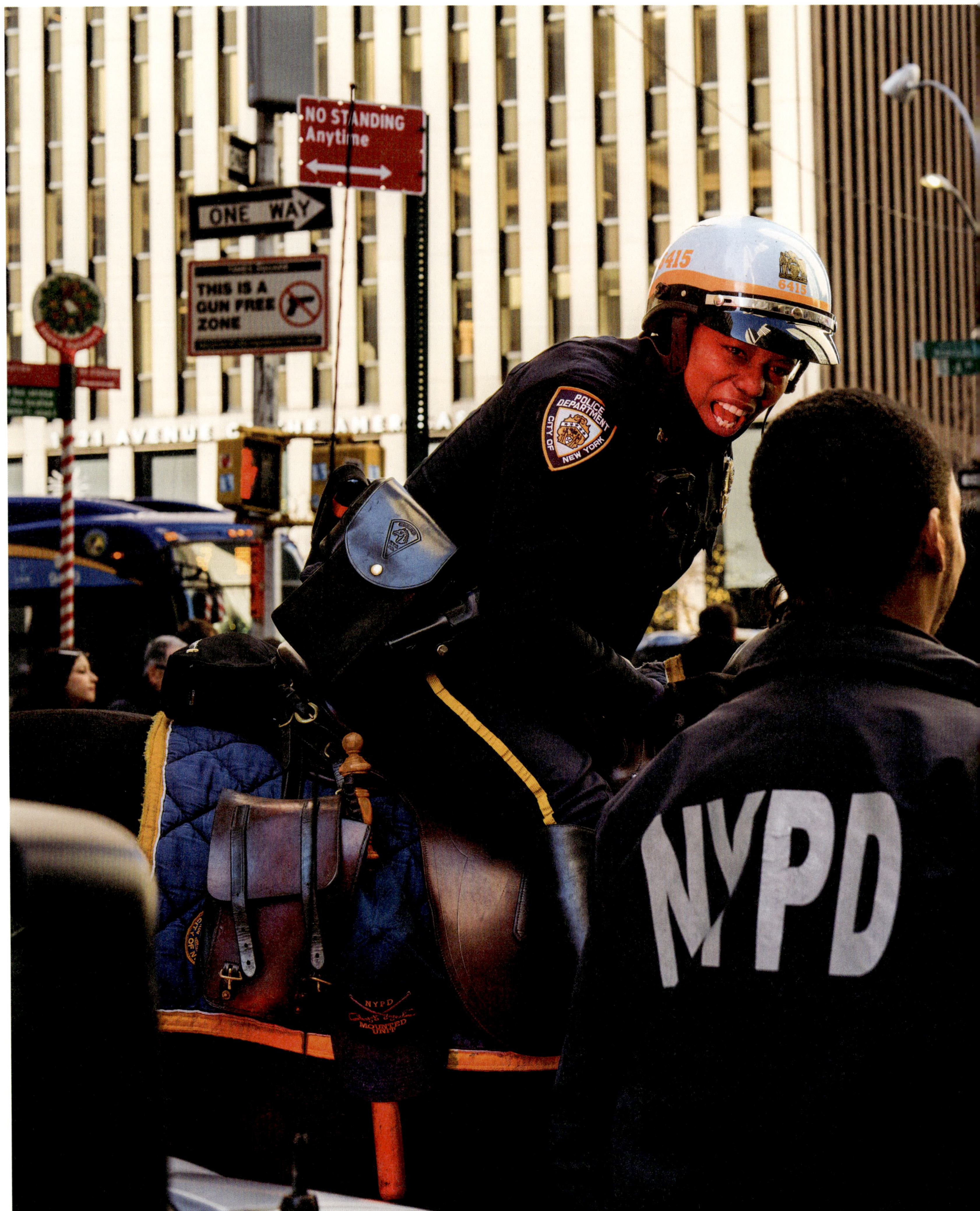
NO STANDING
Anytime
ONE WAY
THIS IS A
GUN FREE
ZONE
6415
POLICE
DEPARTMENT
CITY OF NEW YORK
NYPD
MOUNTED
UNIT
NYPD

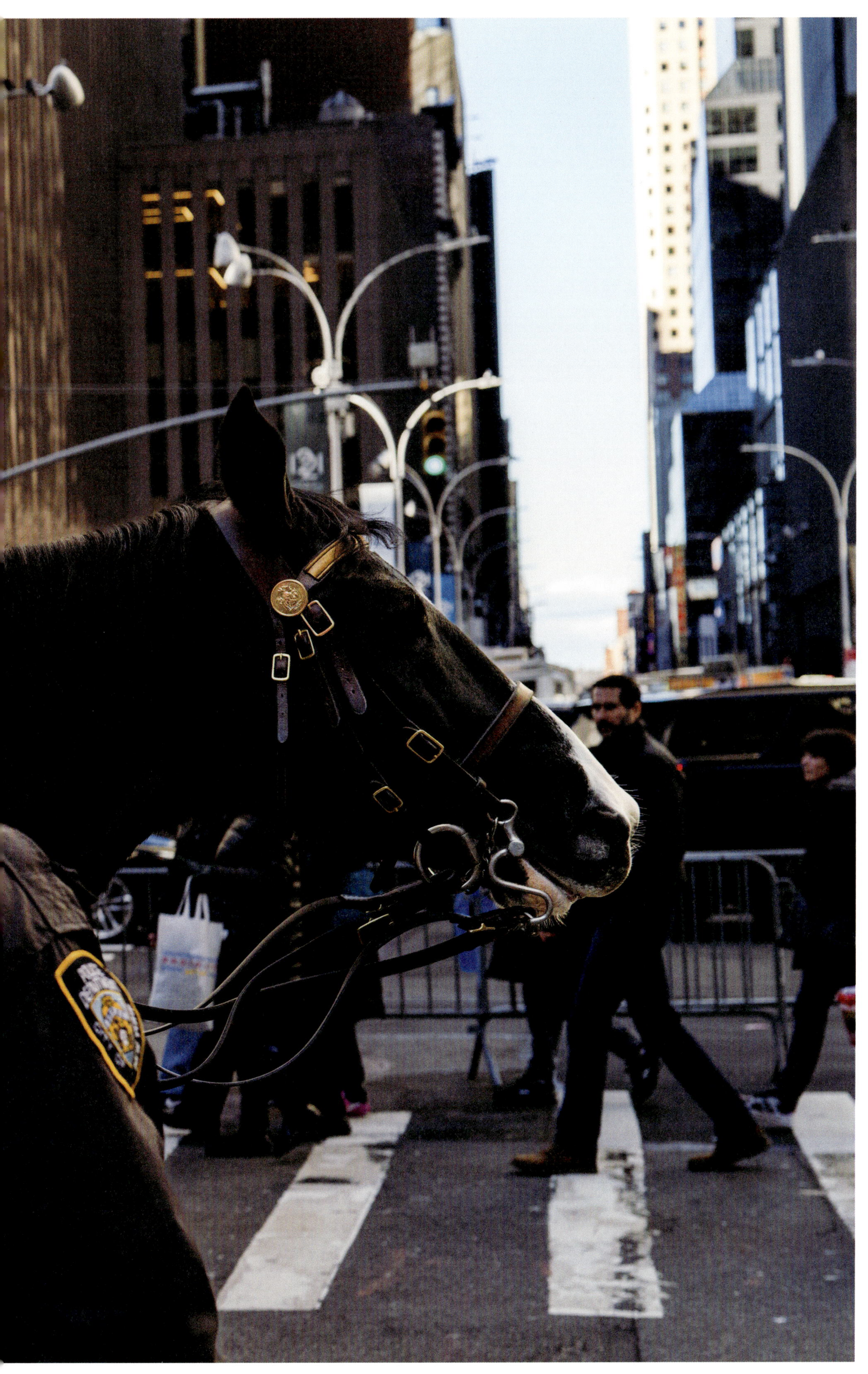

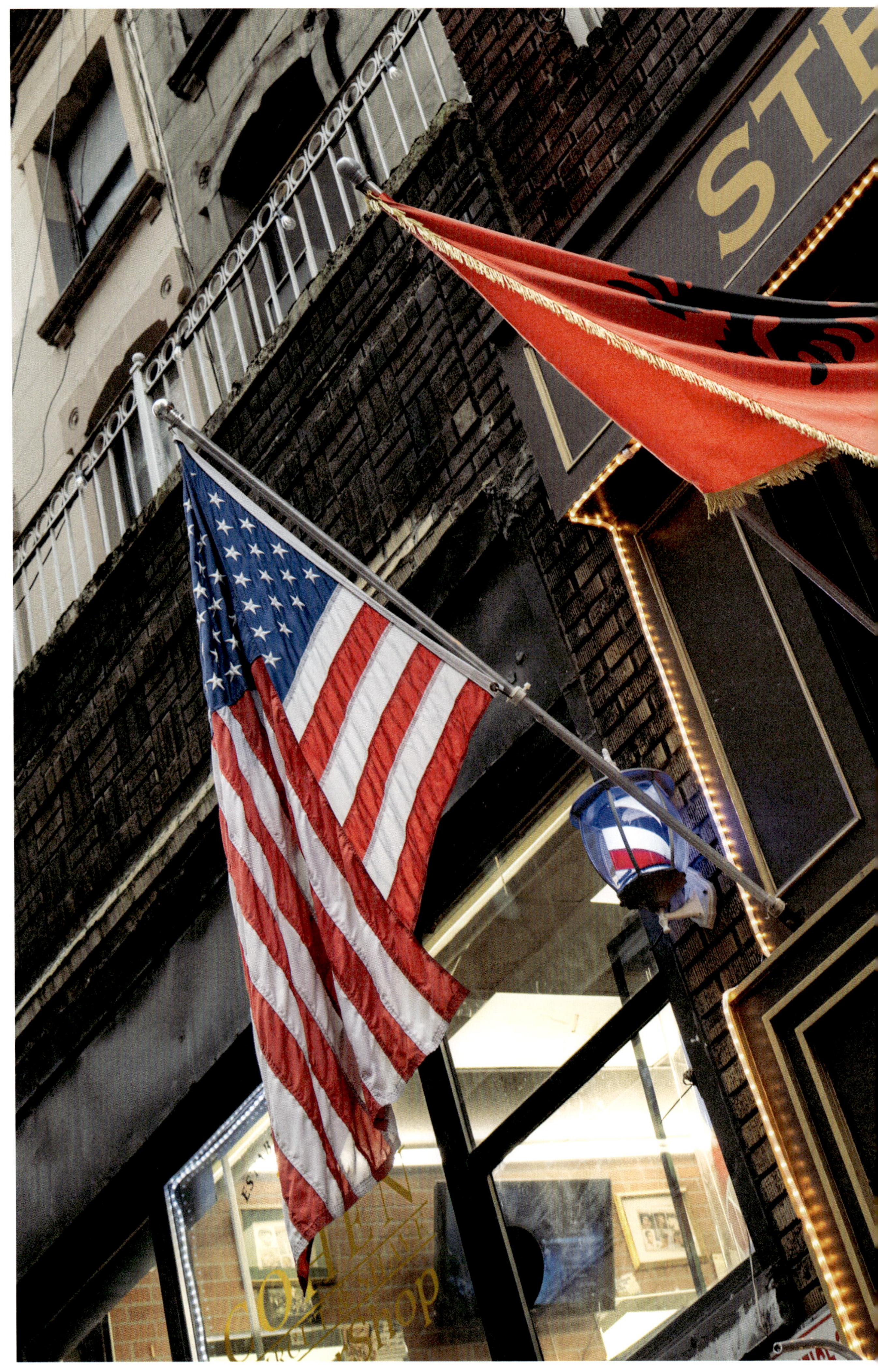
Shop

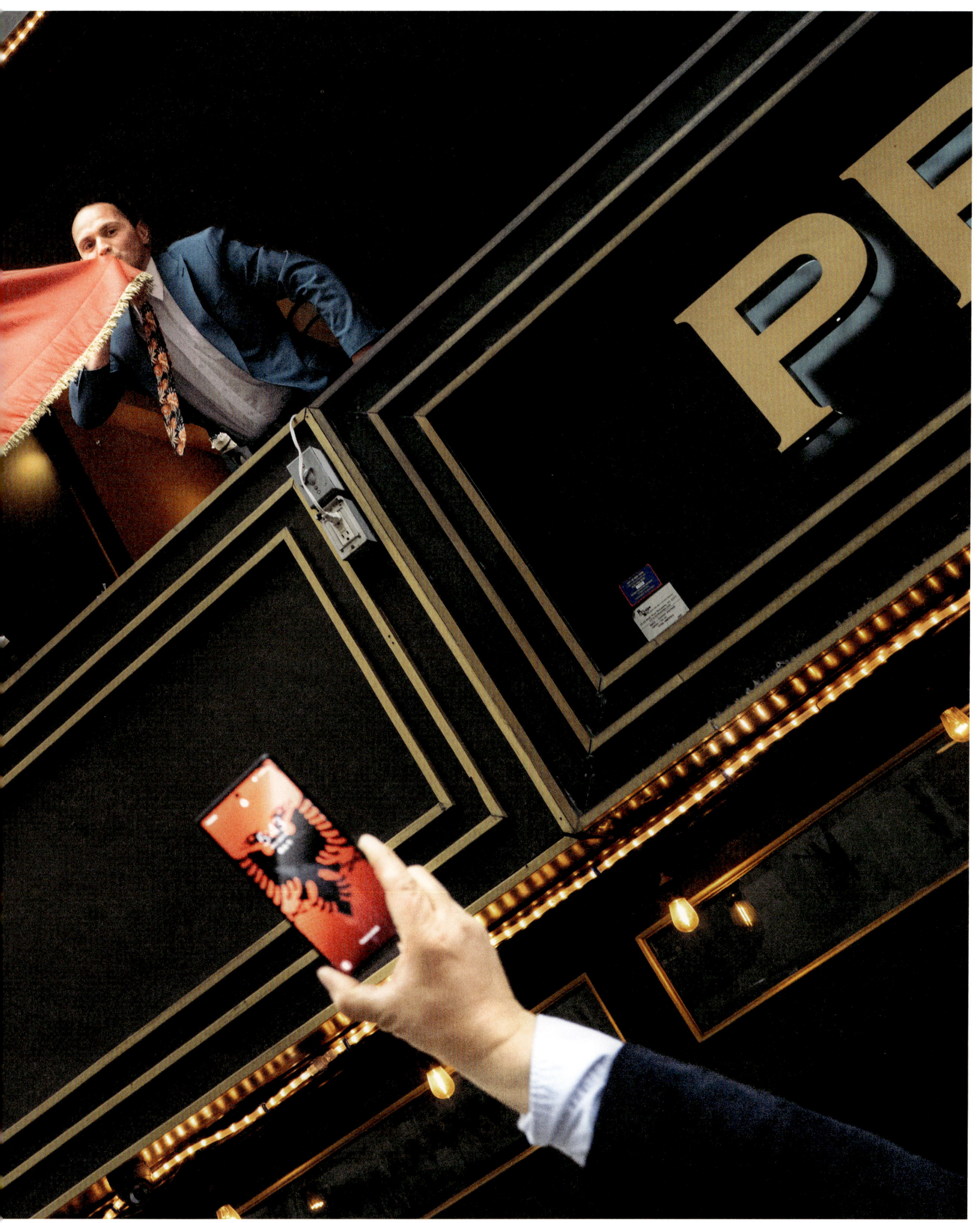

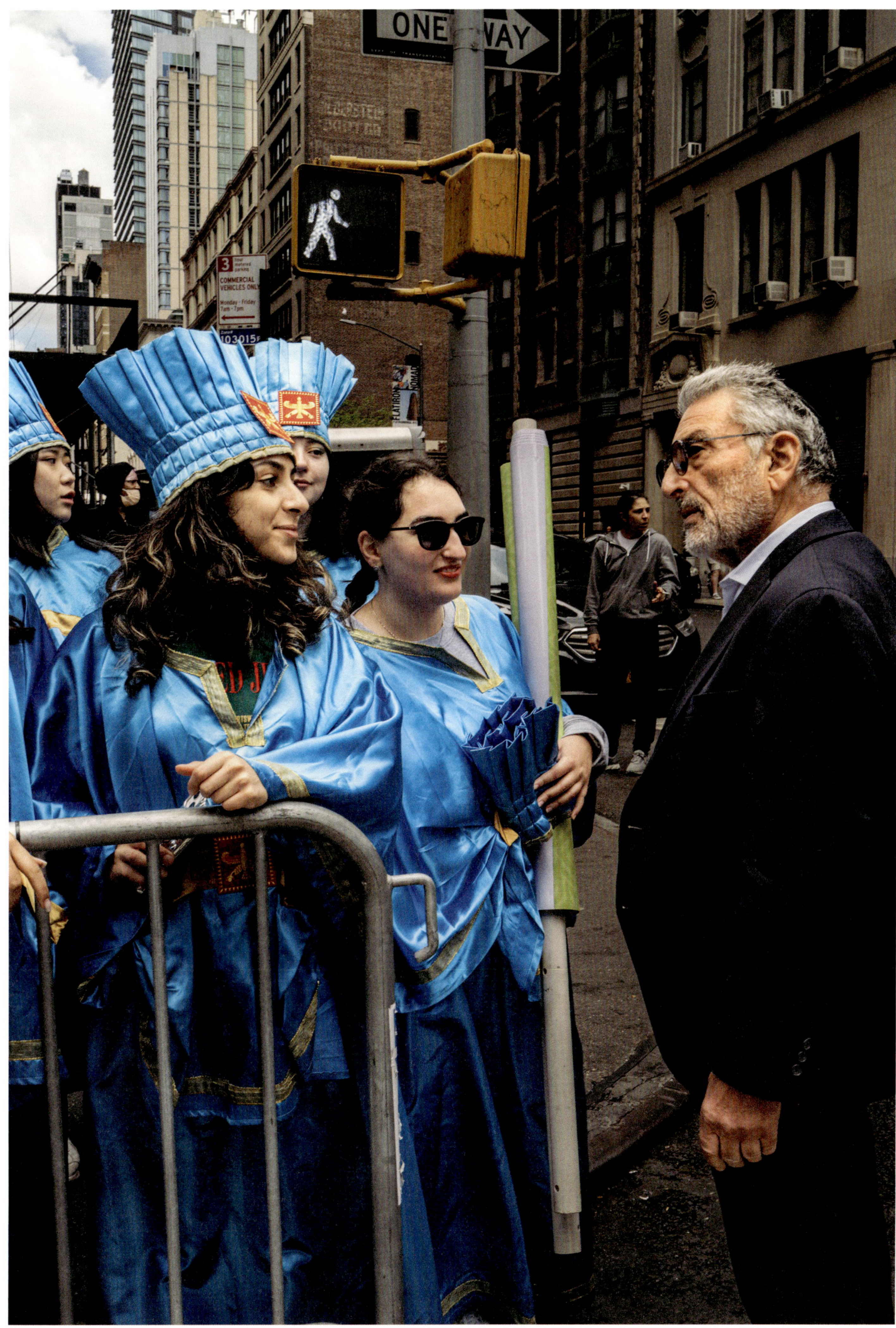
ONE
WAY
3
COMMERCIAL
VEHICLES ONLY
103015F

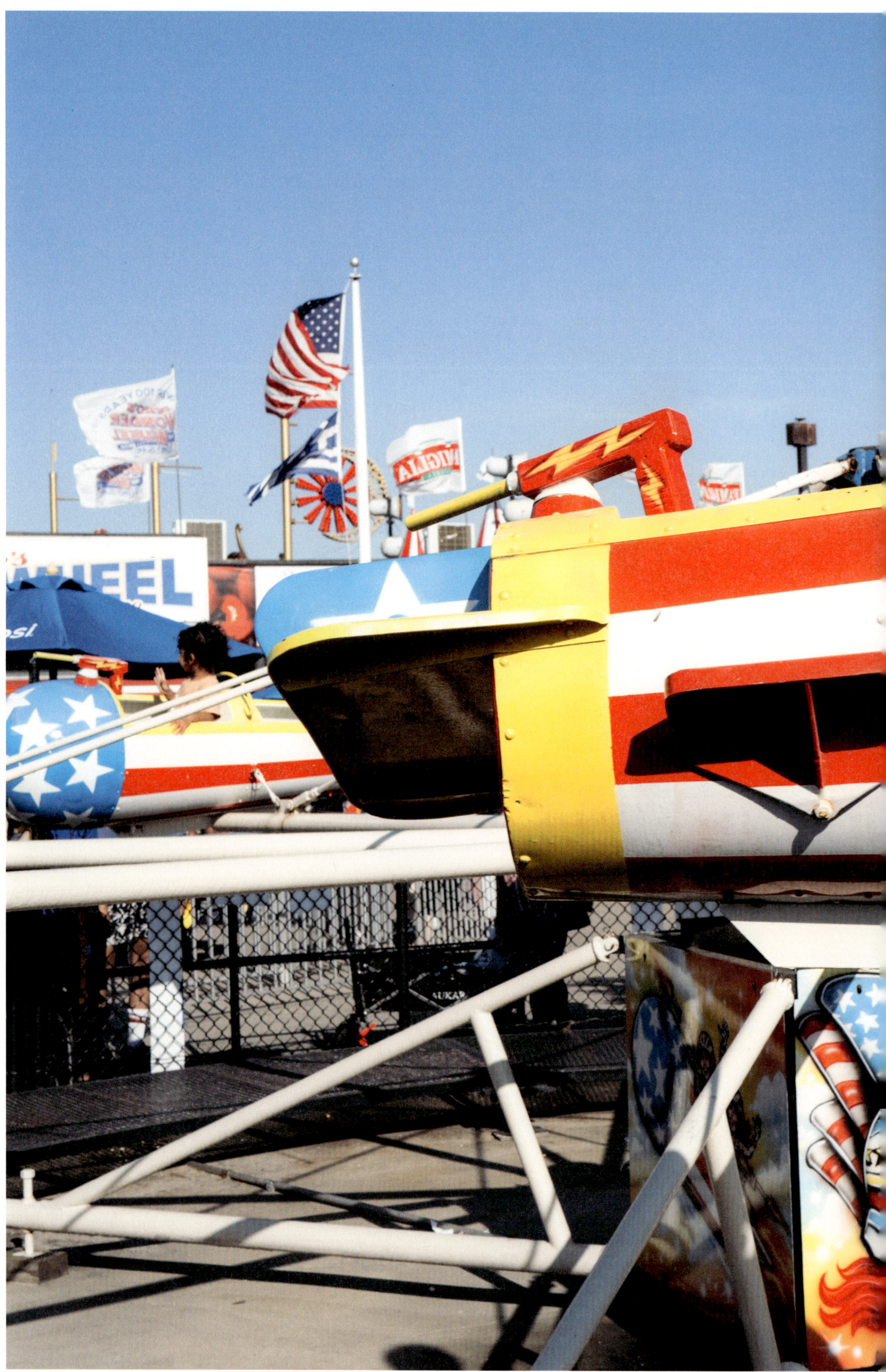
WHEEL

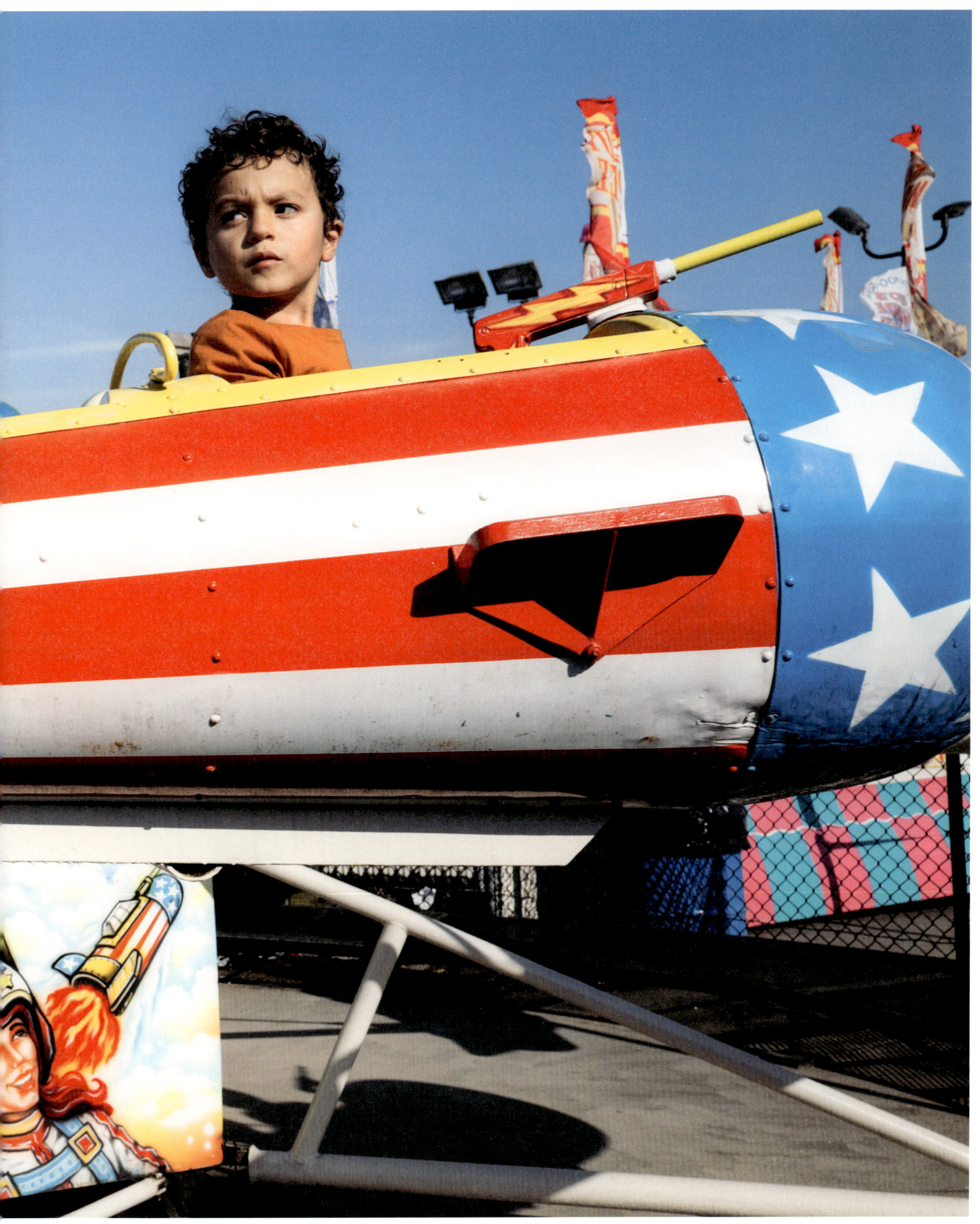

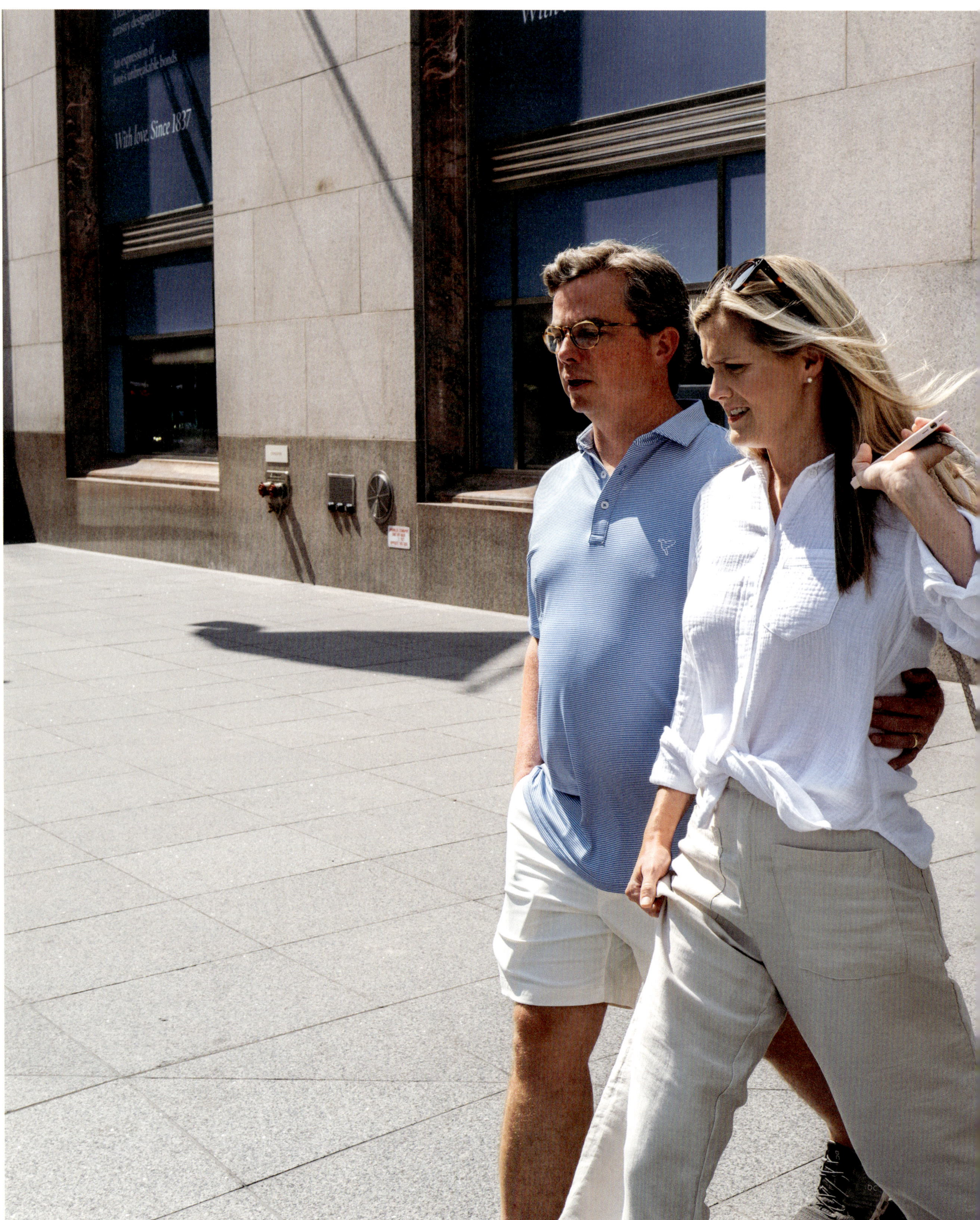
With love, Since 1837

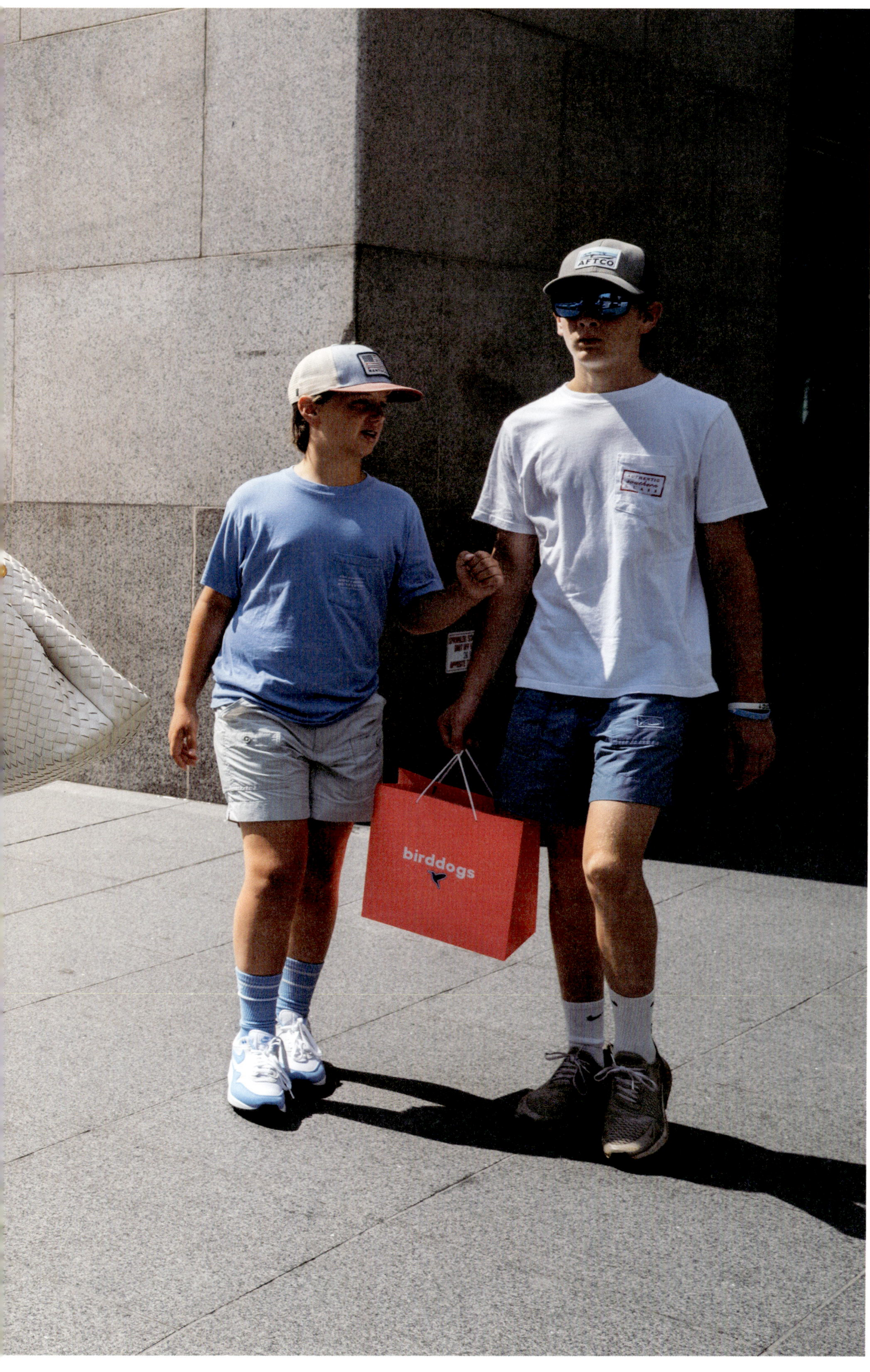
AFTCO
birddogs

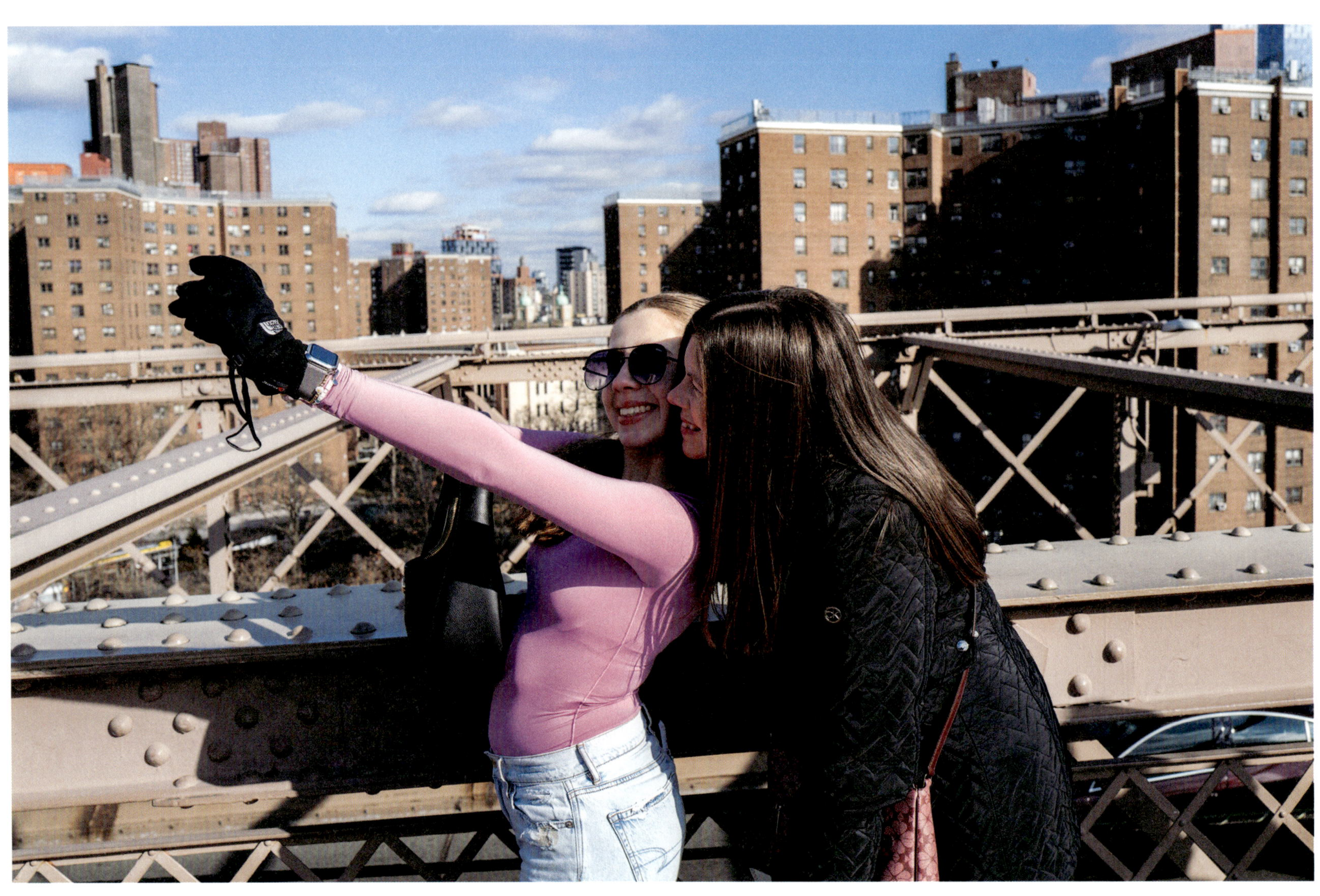

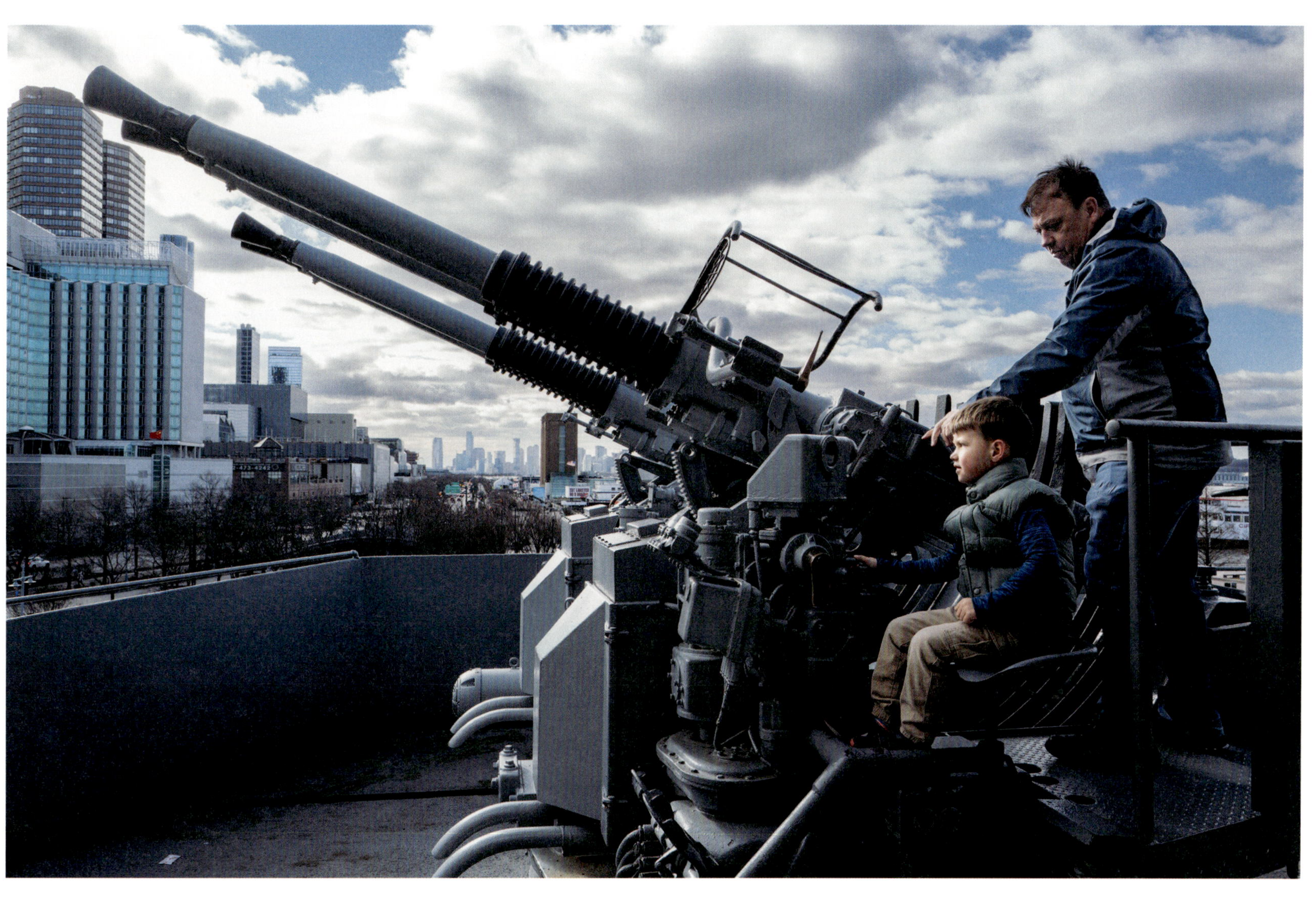

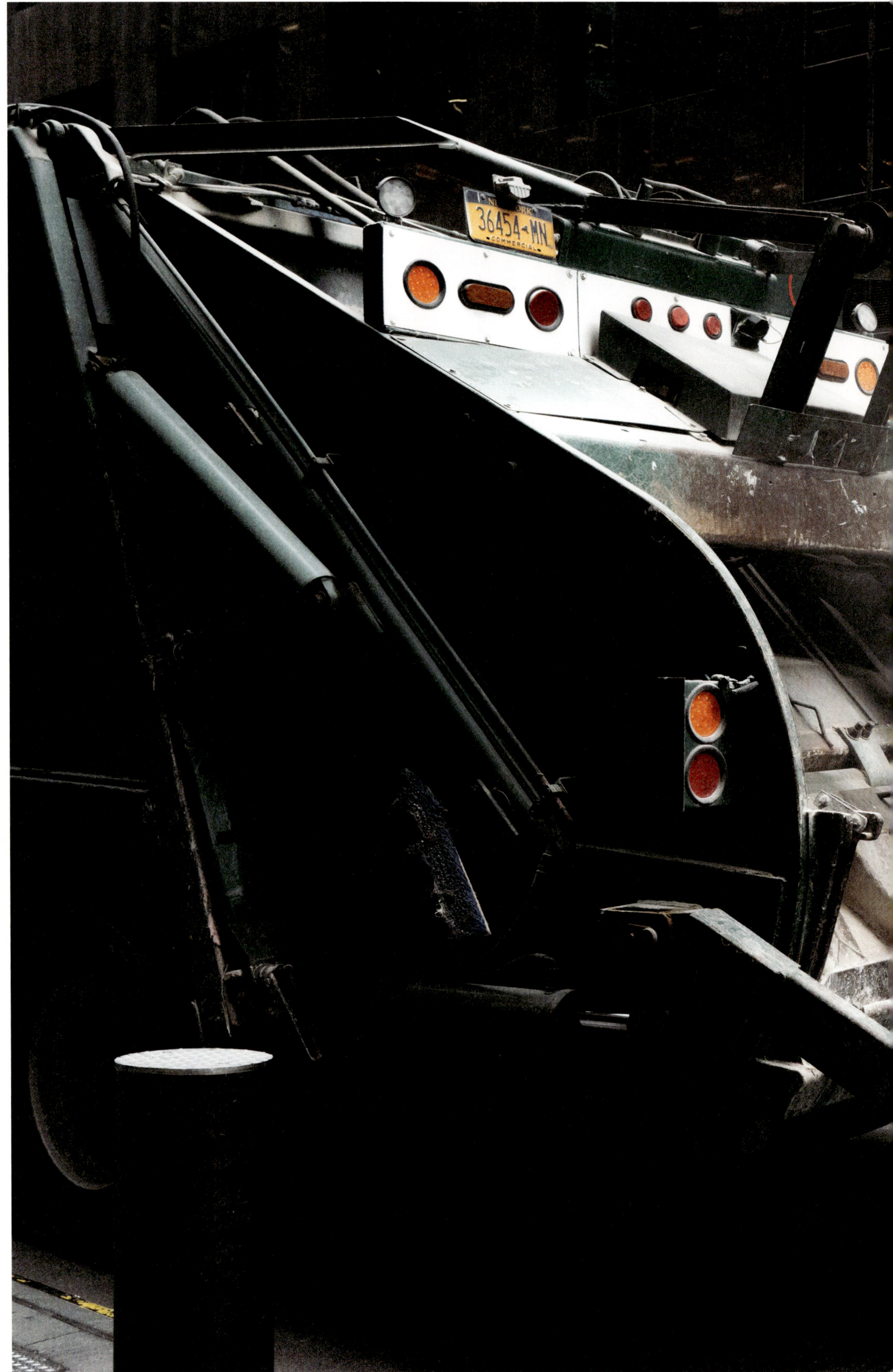
36454 MN
COMMERCIAL

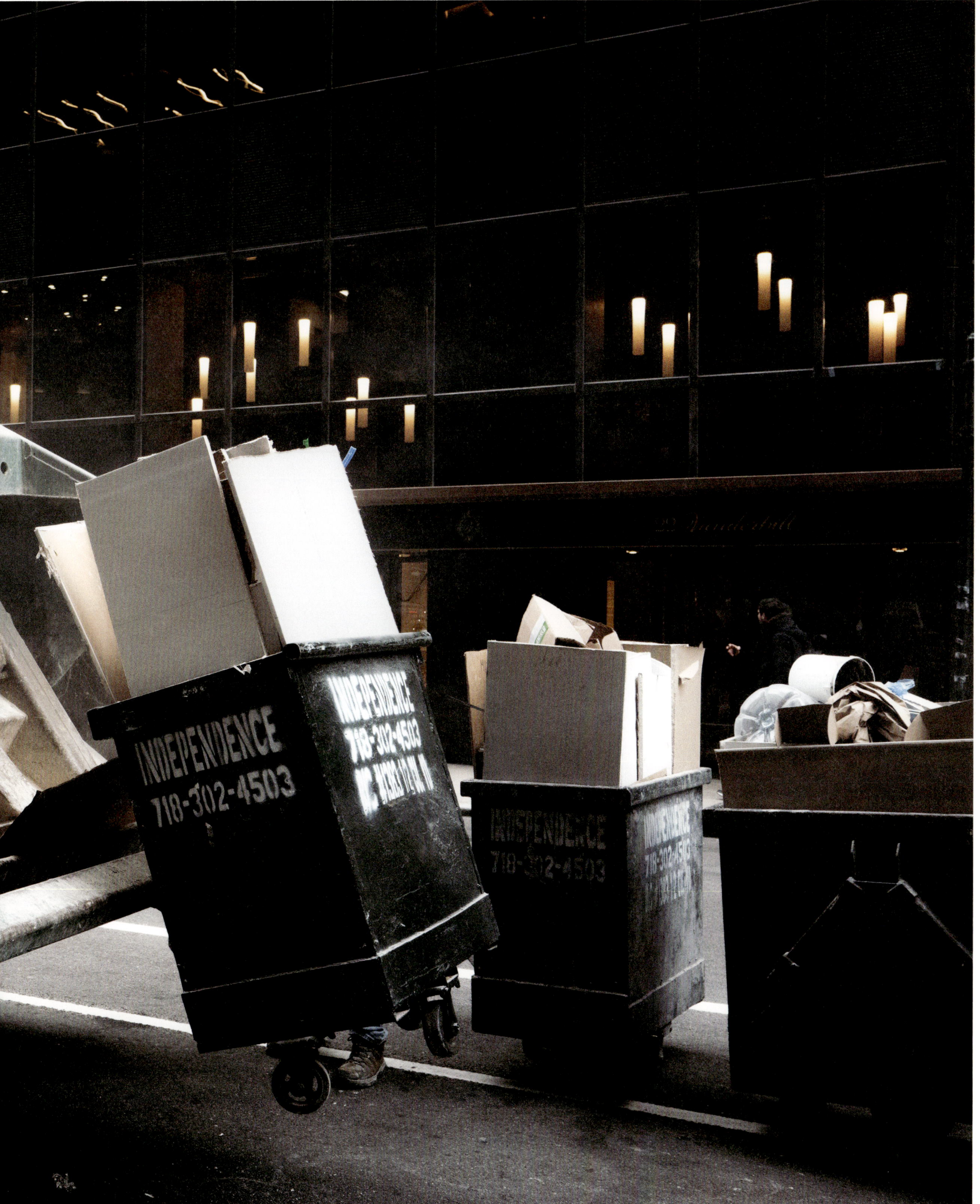
INDEPENDENCE
718-302-4503
INDEPENDENCE
718-302-4503
INDEPENDENCE
718-302-4503

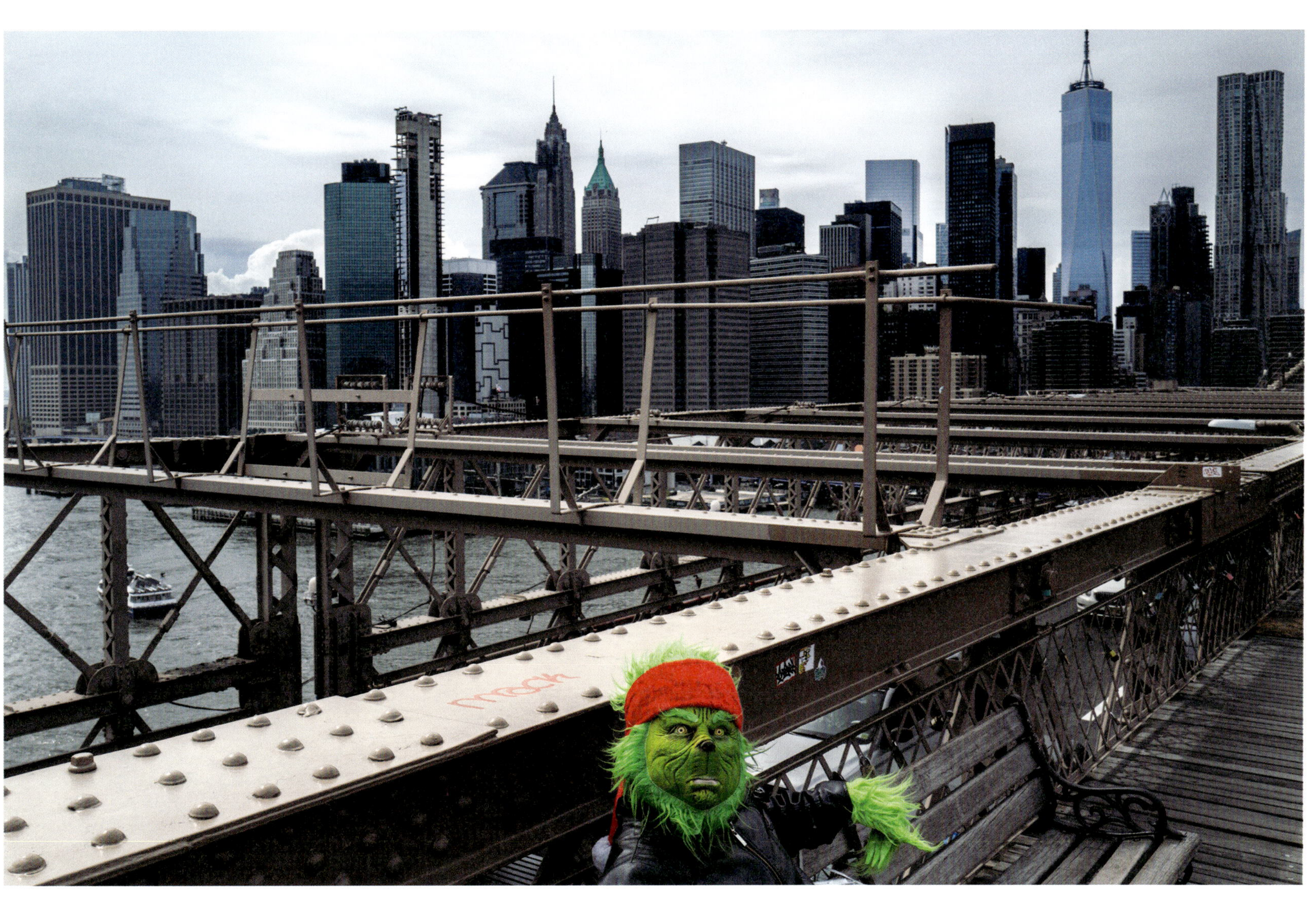

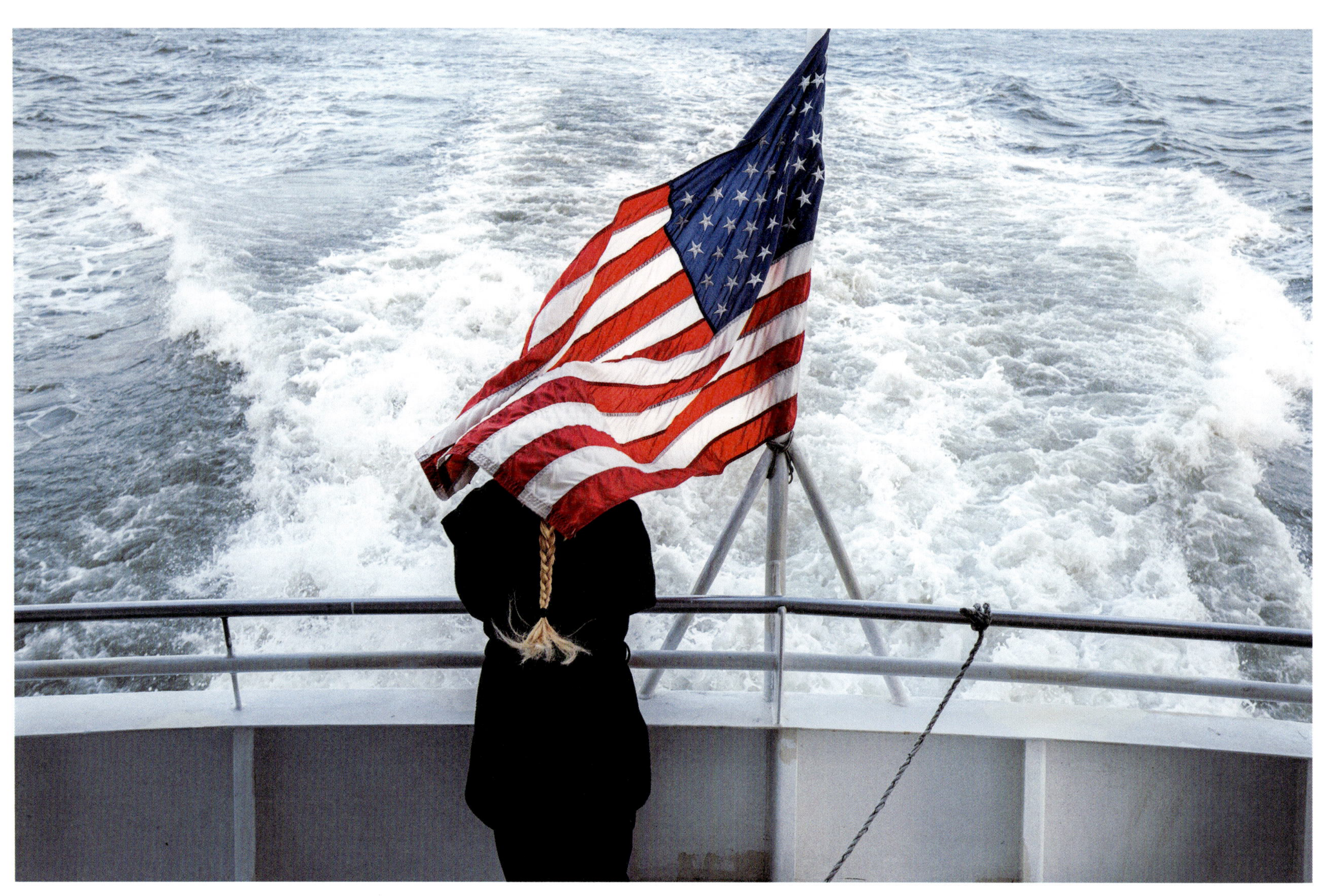

Brief von Andreas Reimann

Lieber Mario,

wie schon angedeutet, fühle ich mich nun doch außerstande, dir wie versprochen einen Beitrag zu deinem Bildband zu formulieren.

Ich hätte nämlich, um Etwas über deine Arbeiten sagen zu können, zunächst über andere, ältere Bilder – bewegte und unbewegte, geschriebene und gesungene – reden müssen: jene Bilder, die mich, den Vielreisenden, bis zum heutigen Tage davon abgehalten haben, ein Flugticket nach New York zu erwerben.

Denn: Am Anfang war das Bild.
Das Vor-Bild. Das Vor-Gesehene.
Mitsamt dem daraus erwachsenden Vor-Urteil.

New York – das ist für mich Fritz Langs *Metropolis*, Bertolt Brechts Gedicht *Verschollener Ruhm der Riesenstadt New York* inklusive einer Fotografie, auf der B. B., halb verschattet von einem anscheinend monströsen Gebäude, unentschlossen in die Höhe blickt; das sind Bilder aus den Ghettos und Slums oder Dokumentarfilme über ausgewanderte Einwanderer, die bangfreudig einer überdimensionalen Nippesfigur entgegenfahren, oder von polizeieifrig zusammengeprügelten Demonstrationen; das ist der Song von der Stadt, die niemals schläft, also *New York, New York* in der Interpretation von Frank Sinatra, der selbst schon wieder mein Bild vom leibhaftigen Amerikaner mitgeprägt hat.

Und sehr weit oben, und höher und höher, immer und ewig: King Kong!

Nein, auch die krakeelend bunten Hollywood-Filmchen konnten nicht davon ablenken: Alle diese Bilder waren schwarz-weiß!

Aber auch die meisten deiner Fotografien sind ja schwarz-weiß!
Etwas zu deinem Buch schreibend, hätte ich also nicht nur behaupten müssen, du habest bei ihnen mit Künstler-eigener Hinterlist auf das Monochrome als das ästhetisch Verführerische, weil unserem Augenschein eigentlich Ungewohnte bzw. Fremde, gesetzt. Ich wäre vor allem nicht um die Mutmaßung herumgekommen, es wäre dir bei der Entscheidung zugunsten des Schwarz-Weiß darauf angekommen, direkt an oben erwähnte Bilder eines durchkäferten Steinehaufs namens New York anzuknüpfen, um damit den von dir ins Bild gebrachten Moment in ein geschichtliches Kontinuum einzufügen.

Alles eben nur Vermutungen meinerseits; fragende Überlegungen darüber, was deine Darstellungen von „echten" Dokumentaraufnahmen unterscheidet, die sich als Feststellungen verkleidet haben, zum Beispiel die: Ein Dokumentarfotograf versucht das Wesen der Situation genau zu erfassen; der Fotograf dieser Sammlung hingegen die Situation der Wesen.

In einem Beitrag zum Buch hätte ich dies zumindest – aber wie? – weniger pathetisch formulieren müssen …
Obwohl unterkühlt ja auch nicht gerade deine Sache ist.
Schon erstaunlich, wie du auch intimere Momente dem Betrachter quasi aus der Sicht eines Mitbetroffenen mitteilst.
Und es ist vermutlich deine freundliche, bisweilen zärtliche Haltung zu den von dir ins Bild Geladenen, die dich befähigt hat, den Versuchungen des Voyeurismus mit Gelassenheit zu widerstehen.

Und wenn ich sehe, wie viele Personen dir bei der Arbeit direkt in die Augen schauen und eben nicht in die Kamera, also in ihrer erstaunlichen Unterschiedlichkeit erstaunlich selbstverständlich und auffällig unverstellt agieren, schließe ich daraus, dass sie dir gerade eine jener Geschichten erzählen, die auch ich durch dich erfahren durfte und von denen ich meinte, ich müsse sie zum Leser weitertragen.
Was für eine Torheit! Die Geschichten, die deine Bilder und/oder die in strahlendem Schwarz-Weiß Erscheinenden jedem einzelnen Betrachter – und erfreulicherweise jedem anders! – erzählen möchten: Wo blieben dann diese wunderreichen Geschichten?

Lieber Mario,
wenn meine bild-geprägte Scheu vor New York der Neugier den Platz räumen muss, hast du bei mir zwar 'n dankenswertes Um-Fühlen bewirkt, aber auch diese Feststellung ist doch eher privater Natur.
Und von den Leuten, die dein Buch in Erinnerung an ihren touristischen Ausflug nach New York in die Hand nehmen, werden etliche – die absoluten Metropolis-Besucher – es enttäuscht beiseiteschieben, und einige sagen: So habe ich das noch gar nicht gesehen!

Und letzterer, mehrdeutiger Satz ist dir zugedacht; und ich sage ihn in fröhlichem Staunen zu mir selbst.
Aber ein Vor-, Zwischen- oder Nachwort deinem New-York-Bildband bei-schreiben?

Wie schon angedeutet: Ich vermag es nicht.

Herzlich
Dein
A. R.

Dear Mario,

As already hinted, I now don't feel capable of formulating an article for your illustrated book as promised.

In order to be able to say something about your works, I would namely first have had to talk about other, older images—moving and still, written and sung: those images that have stopped me, the frequent traveller, from purchasing an airline ticket to New York even to the present day.

Because: in the beginning was the image.
The before-image. The before-seen.
Including the pre-judice resulting from this.

New York—for me that is Fritz Lang's *Metropolis*, Bertolt Brecht's poem *Verschollener Ruhm der Riesenstadt New York* (The Late Lamented Fame of the Giant City of New York), including a photograph in which B. B. looks upwards indecisively, half in the shadows of a seemingly monstrous building. It is images from the ghettos and slums or from documentary films about emigrated immigrants who travel in cheerful trepidation toward an oversized knick-knack, or of demonstrations smashed by zealous police. It is the song of the city that never sleeps, *New York, New York,* as interpreted by Frank Sinatra, who also partly defined my image of the American in the flesh.

And extremely high up, higher and higher, always and forever: King Kong!

No, even the roistering, colourful little Hollywood films couldn't distract from this: all these images were in black and white!

But most of your photographs are also black and white!
If I were to write something about your book, I would have had to claim that you trusted in the monochrome as the aesthetically seductive force for these with the guile inherent to artists, because it is actually as unusual or strange as it appears to us.
I would especially not have avoided to mention that it was of primary importance to you when deciding in favour of black and white to create a direct link to the above-mentioned images of a thoroughly beetle-ridden heap of stone known as New York, in order to in this way insert the moment you created as an image into a historical continuum.

All of this is simply presumption on my part; questioning considerations of what distinguishes your representations from "real" documentary recordings, which have disguised themselves as statements of fact. For example, a documentary photographer attempts to precisely capture the nature of the situation, while the photographer of this collection instead attempts to capture the situation of the nature.

In an article for the book, I would at least have had to formulate this with somewhat less pathos—but how?
Although "hypothermic" is also not really your specialty. It's astonishing how you also inform the viewer of more intimate moments from the perspective of a co-affected person, so to speak. It is your presumably friendly, tender attitude toward those you have included in the image that has made it possible for you to easily resist the traps of voyeurism.

When I see how many people look directly into your eyes when working with you, rather than at the camera, thus acting in an astonishingly natural and conspicuously normal way in their astonishing diversity, I conclude from this that they are telling you one of those stories that I have also been able to experience through you, and which I believed I had to pass on to the reader of this publication.
What idiocy! The stories that your images and/or those appearing to each individual viewer in radiant black and white—and happily differently to each one!—hope to tell: Where would these wonderful stories be then?

Dear Mario,
If my dread of New York—defined by its images—has been forced to make way for curiosity, you must have had a commendable re-feeling impact on me, but this realization is also more of a private nature. And of the people who pick up your book in memory of their tourist trip to New York, quite a few—the absolute Metropolis visitors—will push it aside in disappointment, and some will say: "I've never seen it like that!"

The previous, ambivalent, sentence is meant for you; I say it to myself in cheerful astonishment.
However, to co-write a foreword, afterword, or other contribution to your New York photo book?

As already suggested: I simply can't do it.

With warmest regards,
Yours,
A. R.

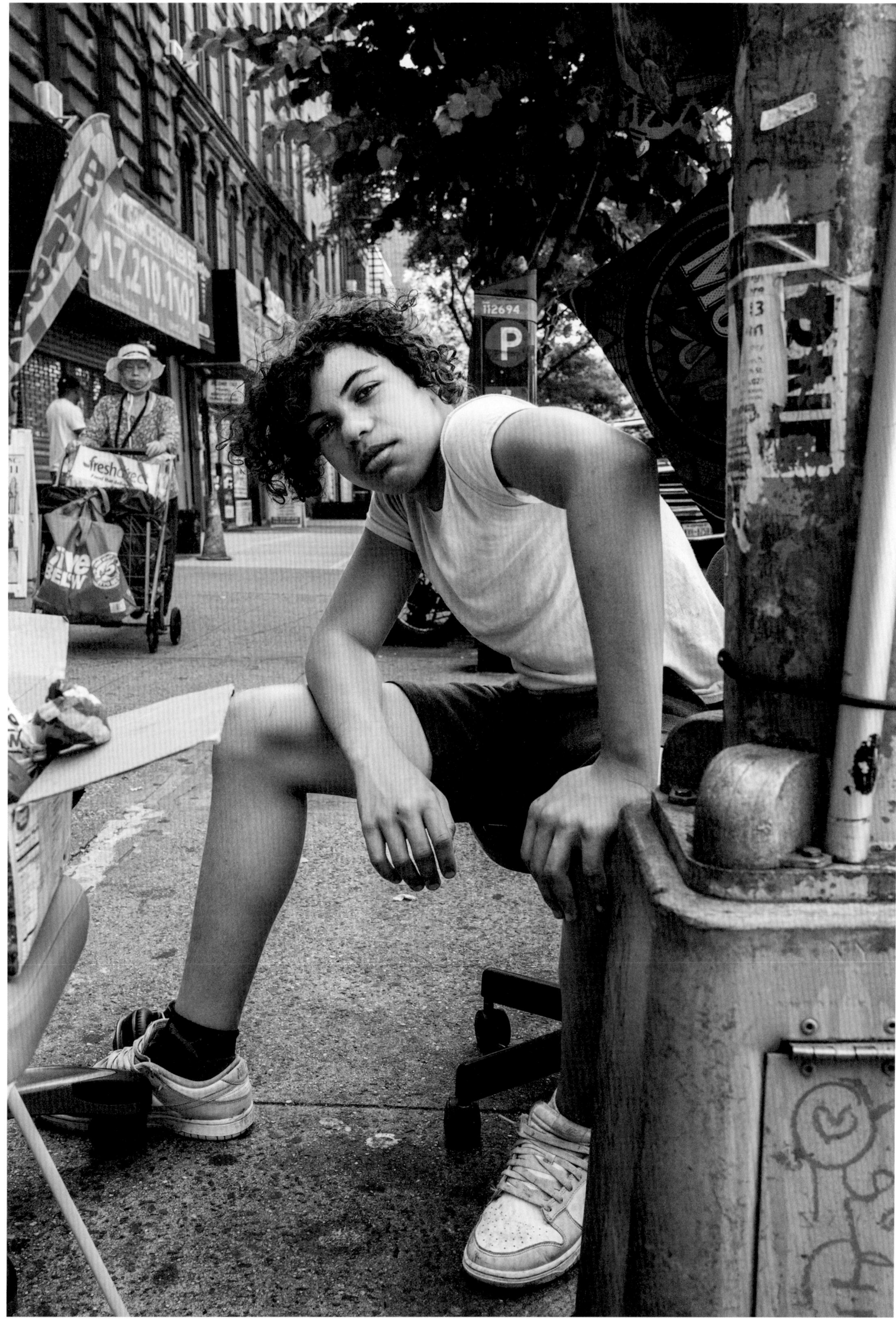
112694
P

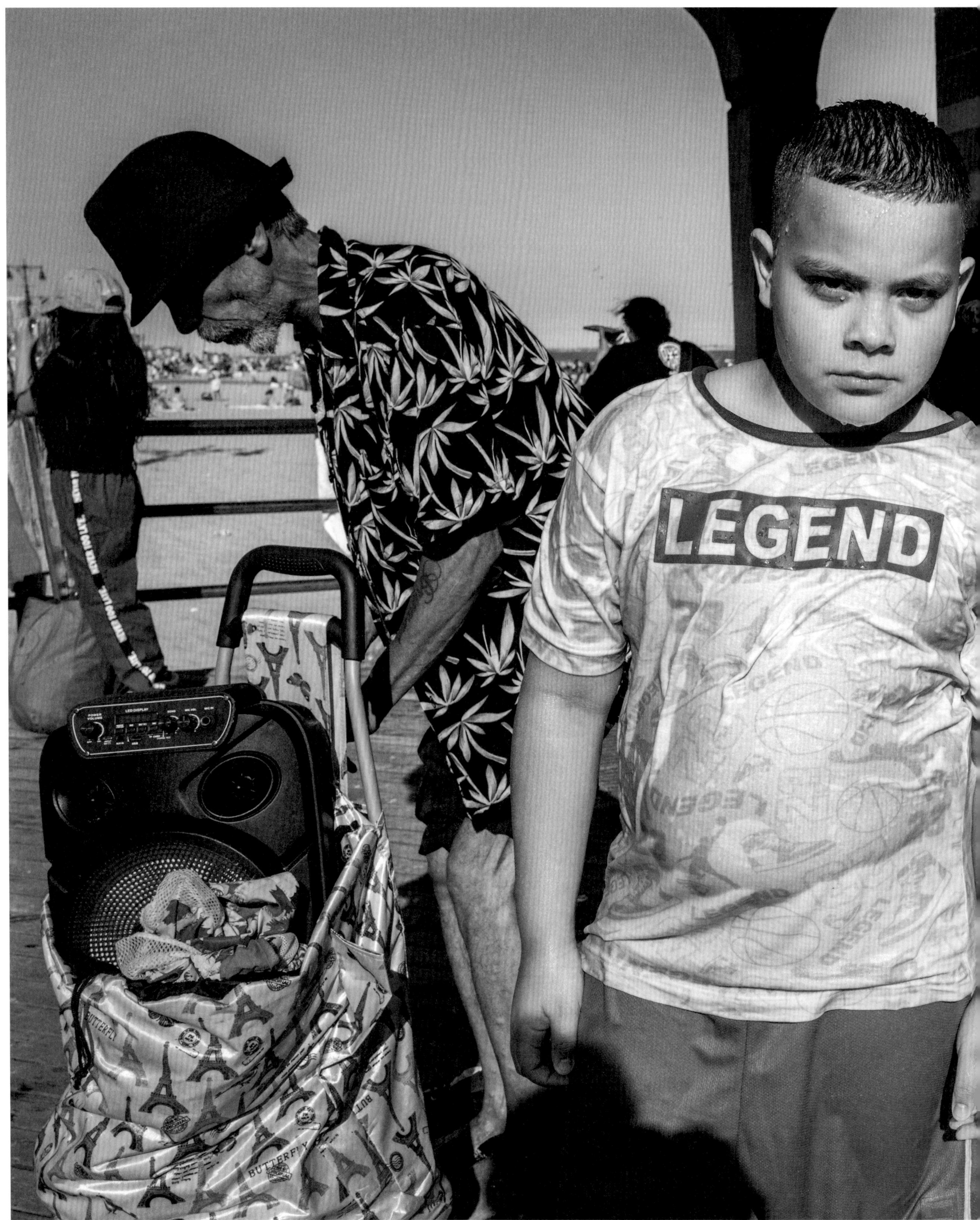
LEGEND
BUTTERFLY

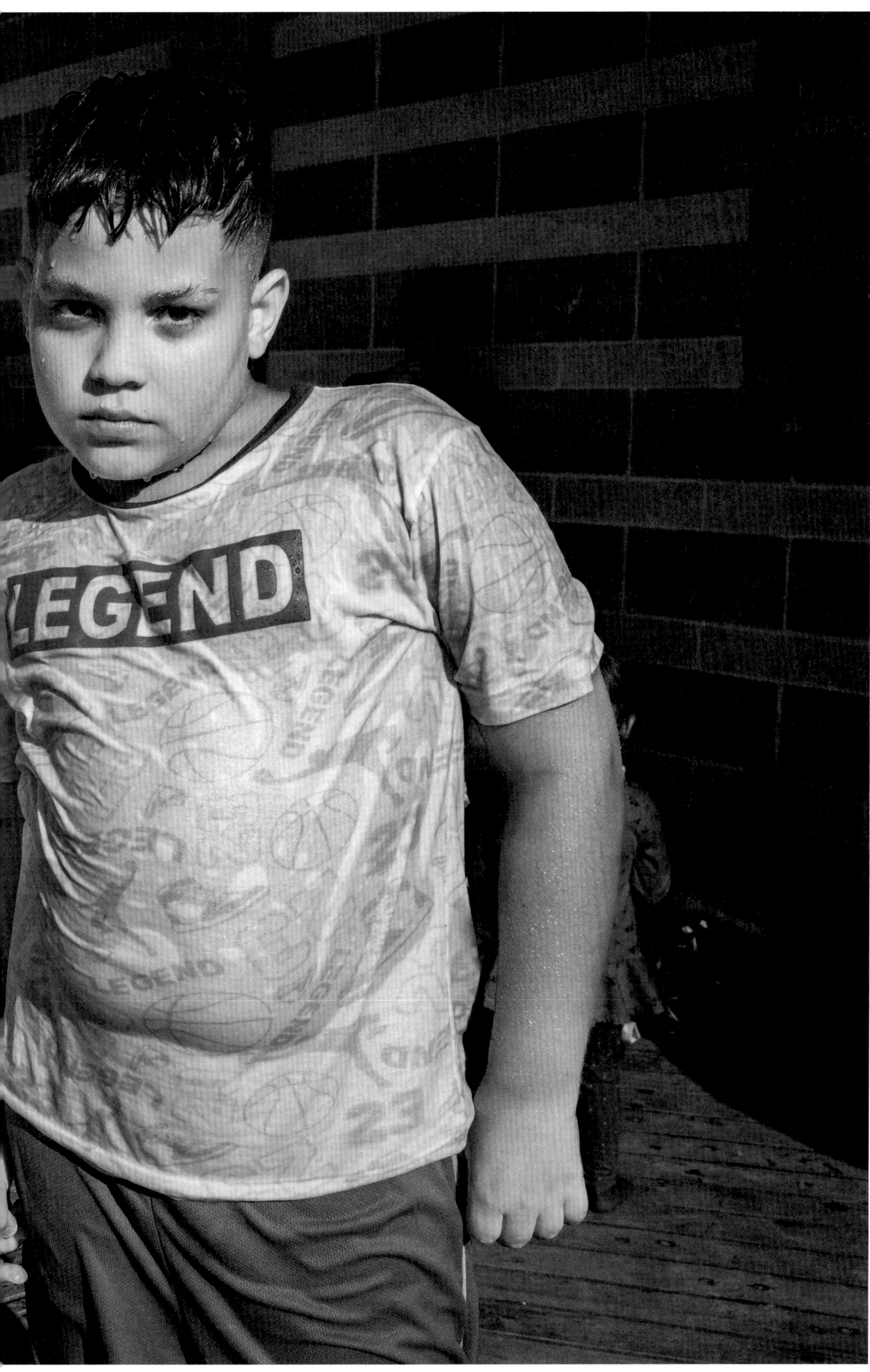
LEGEND

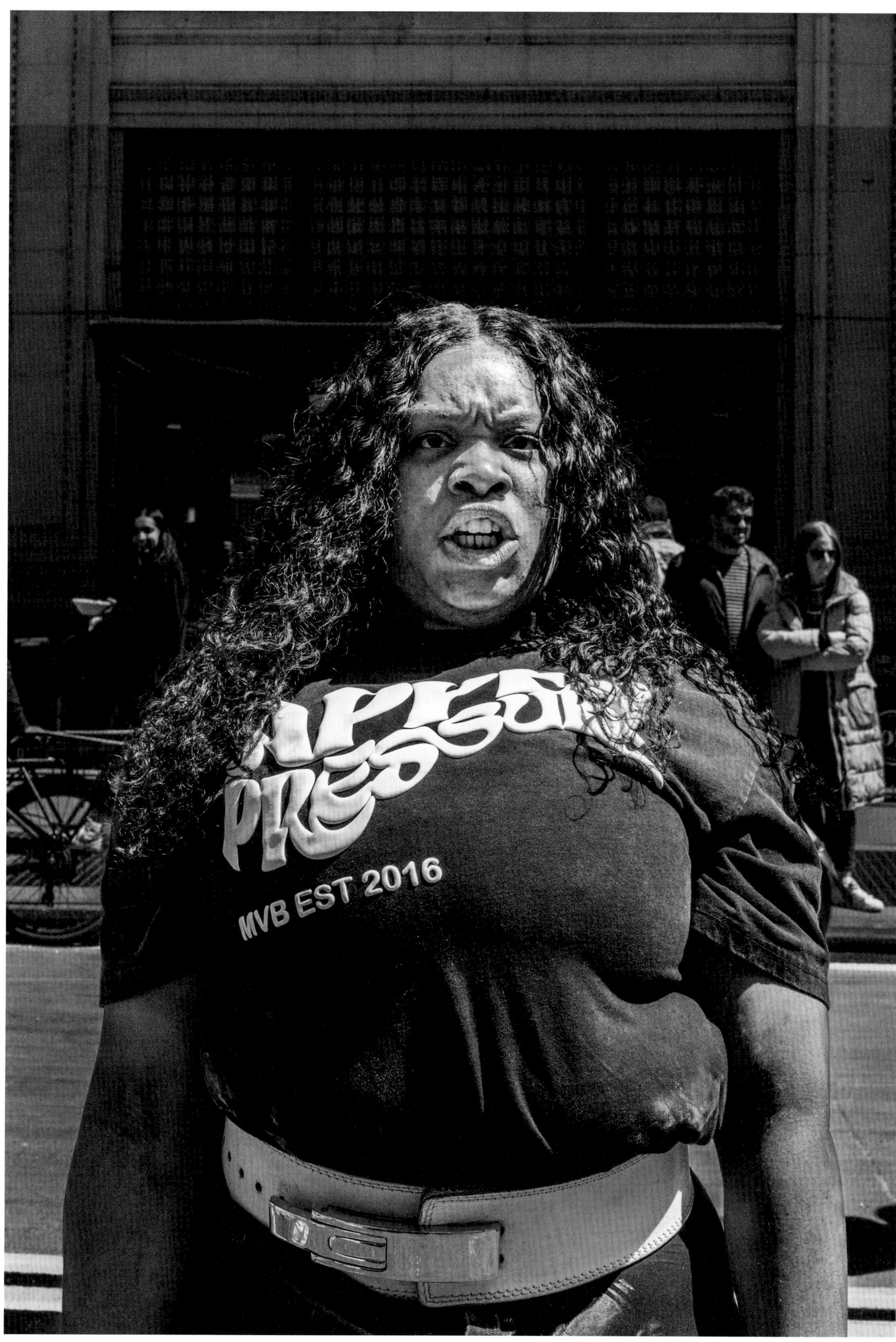
MVB EST 2016

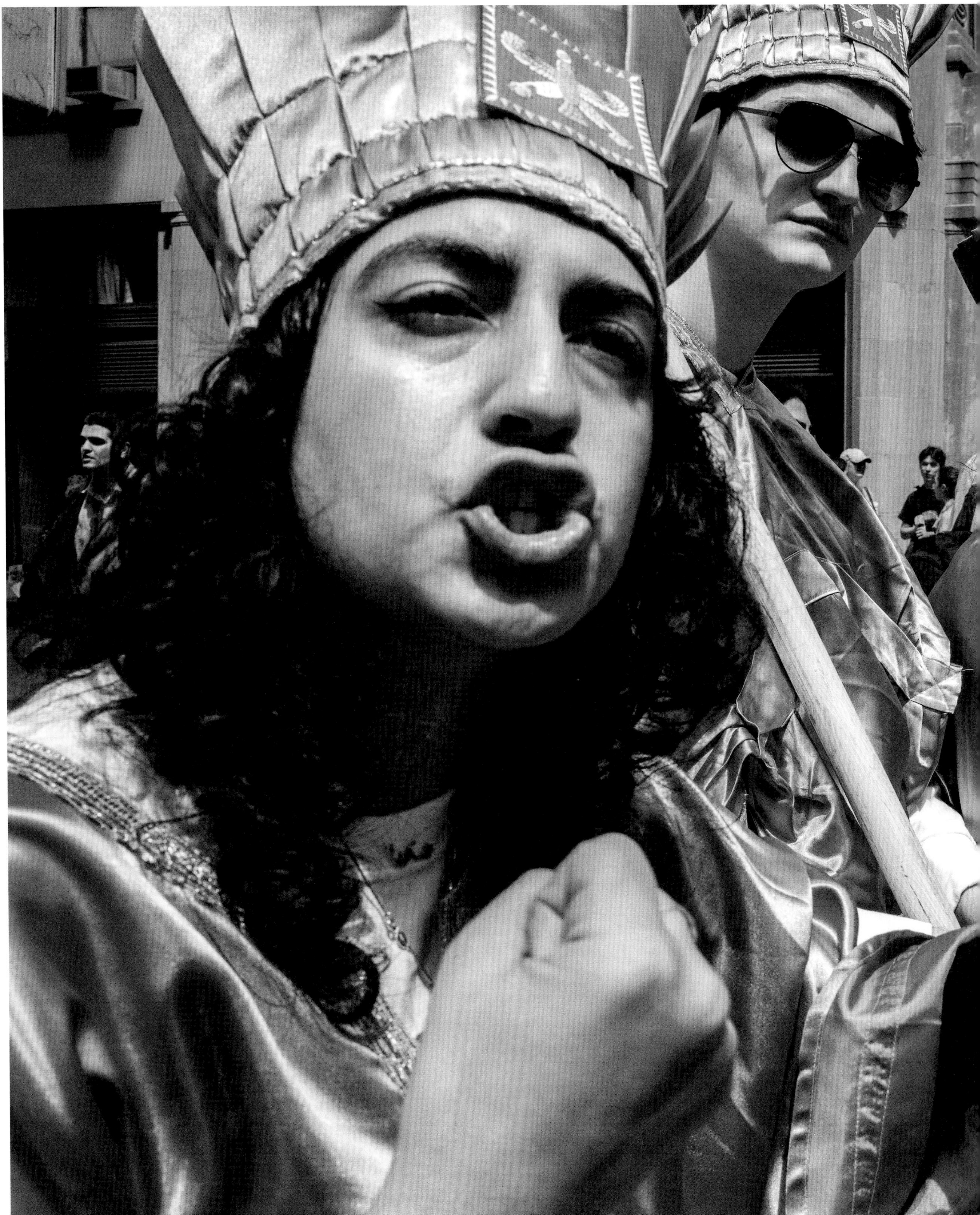

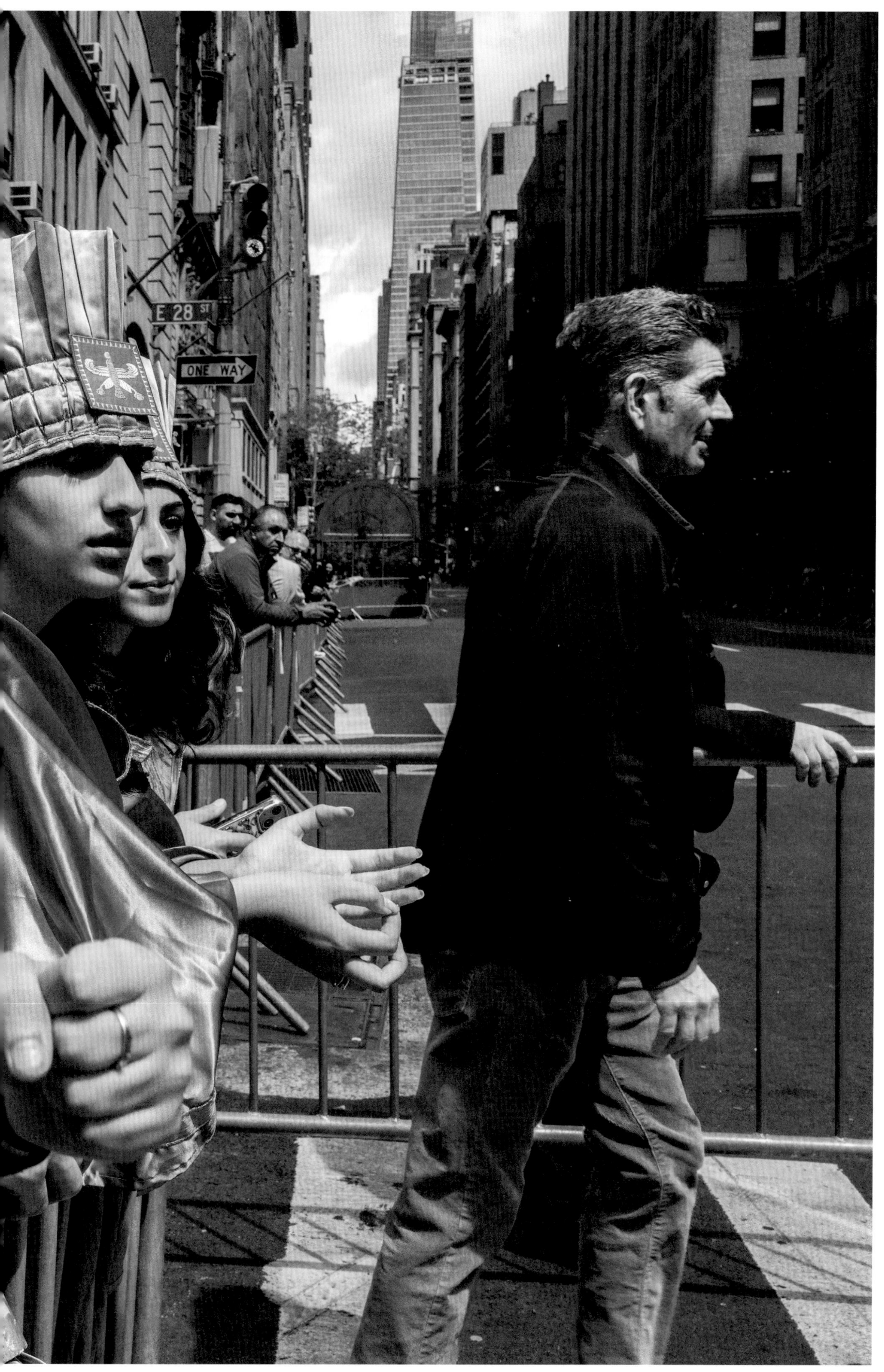
E 28 ST
ONE WAY

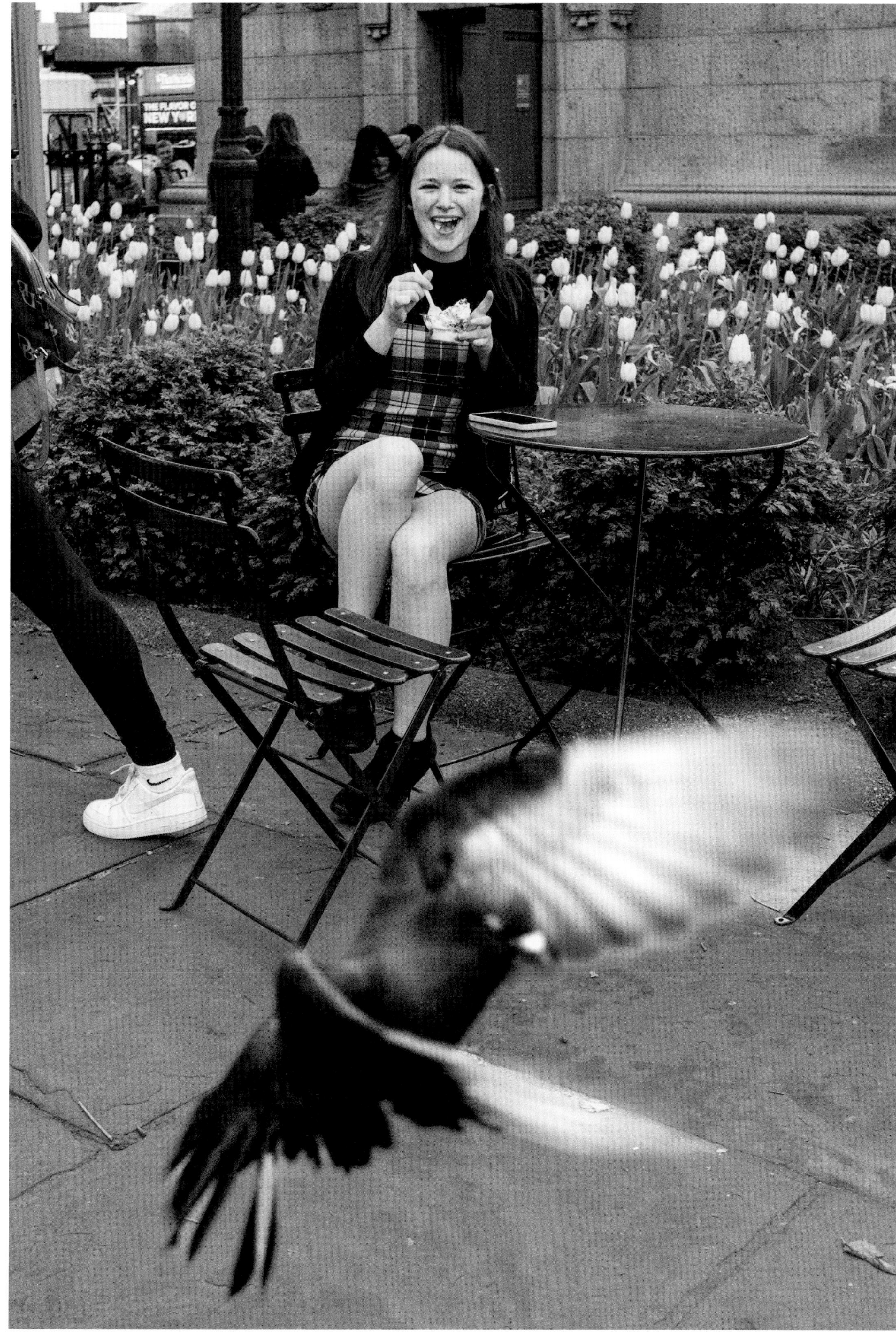

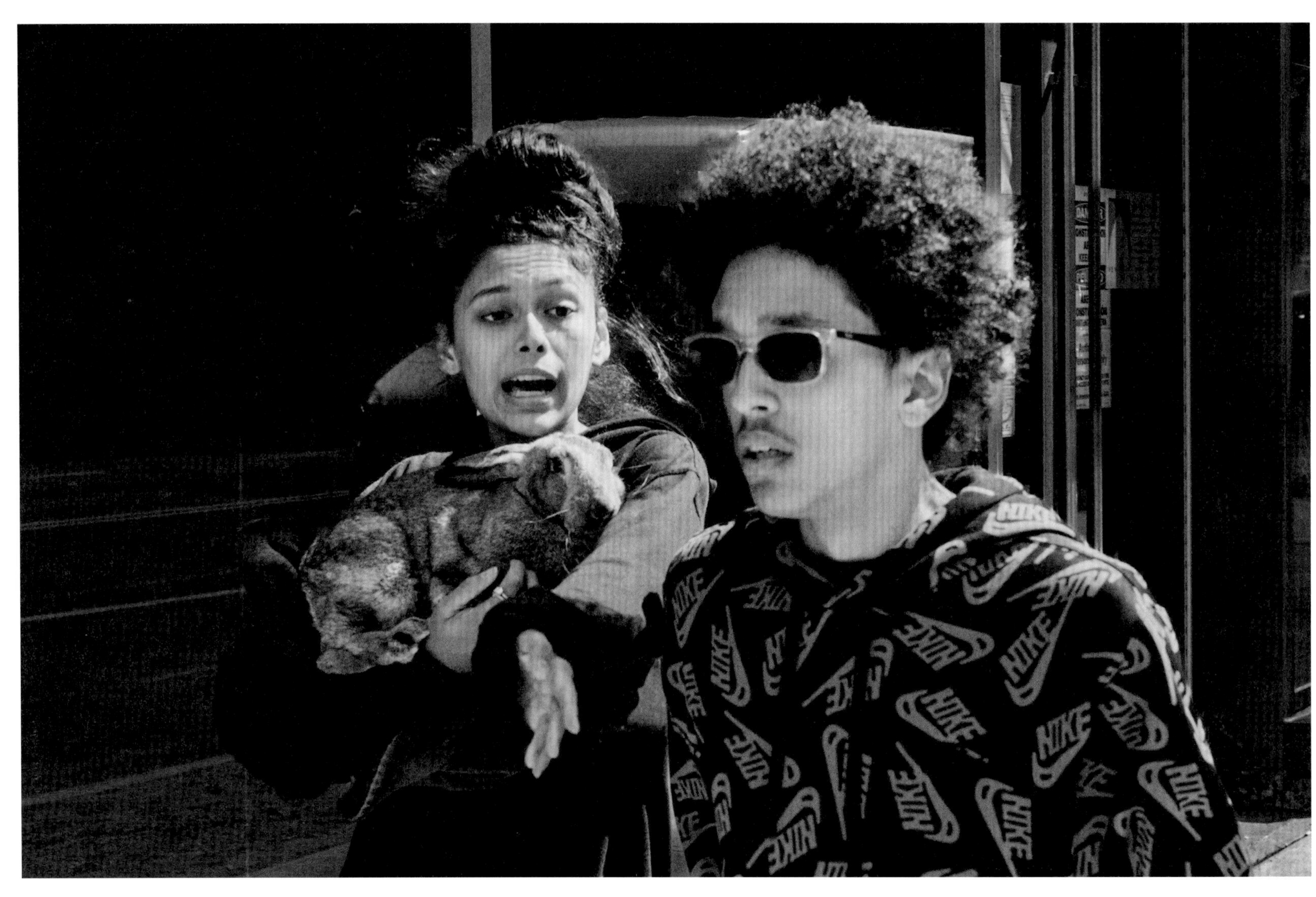
NIKE

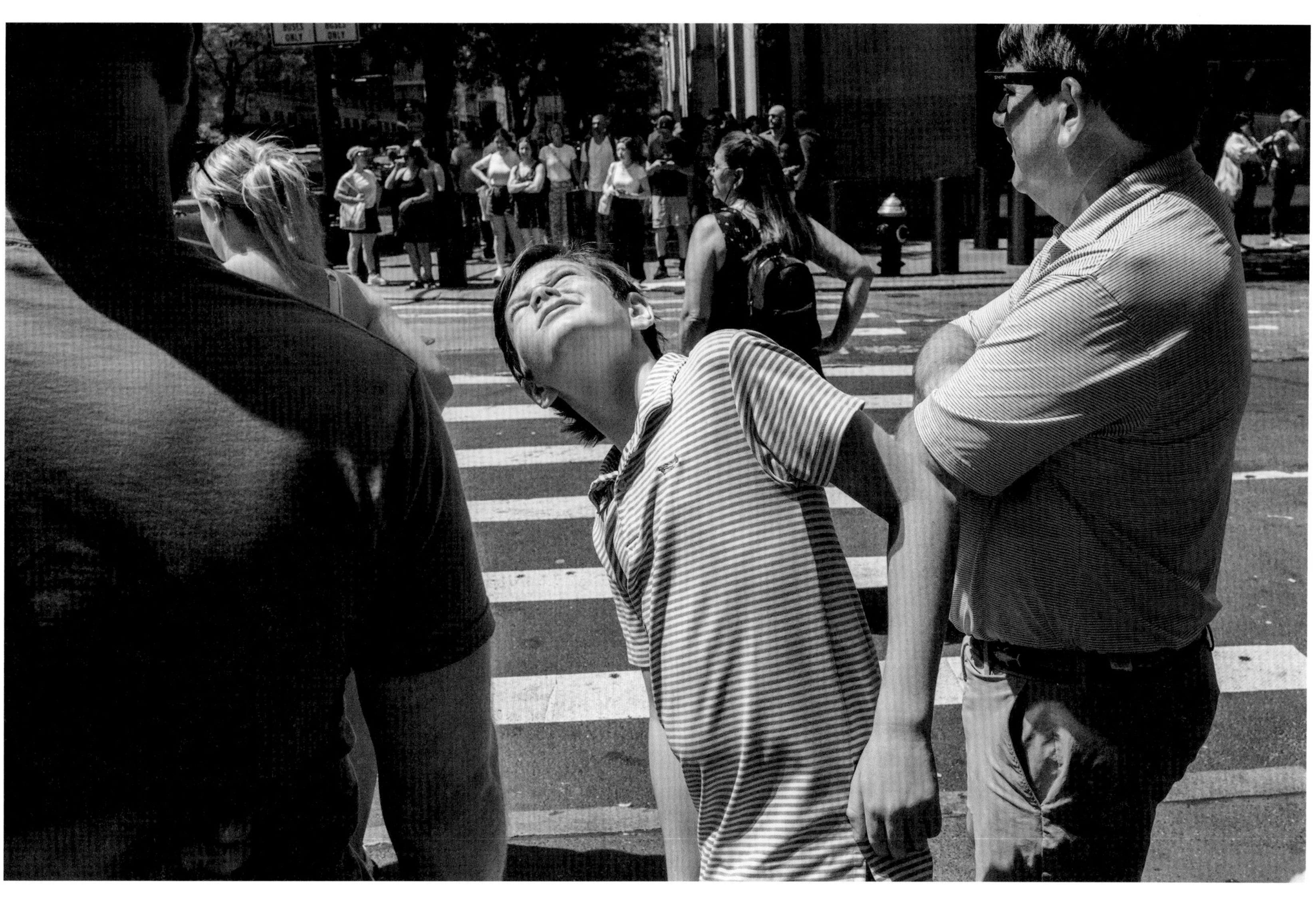

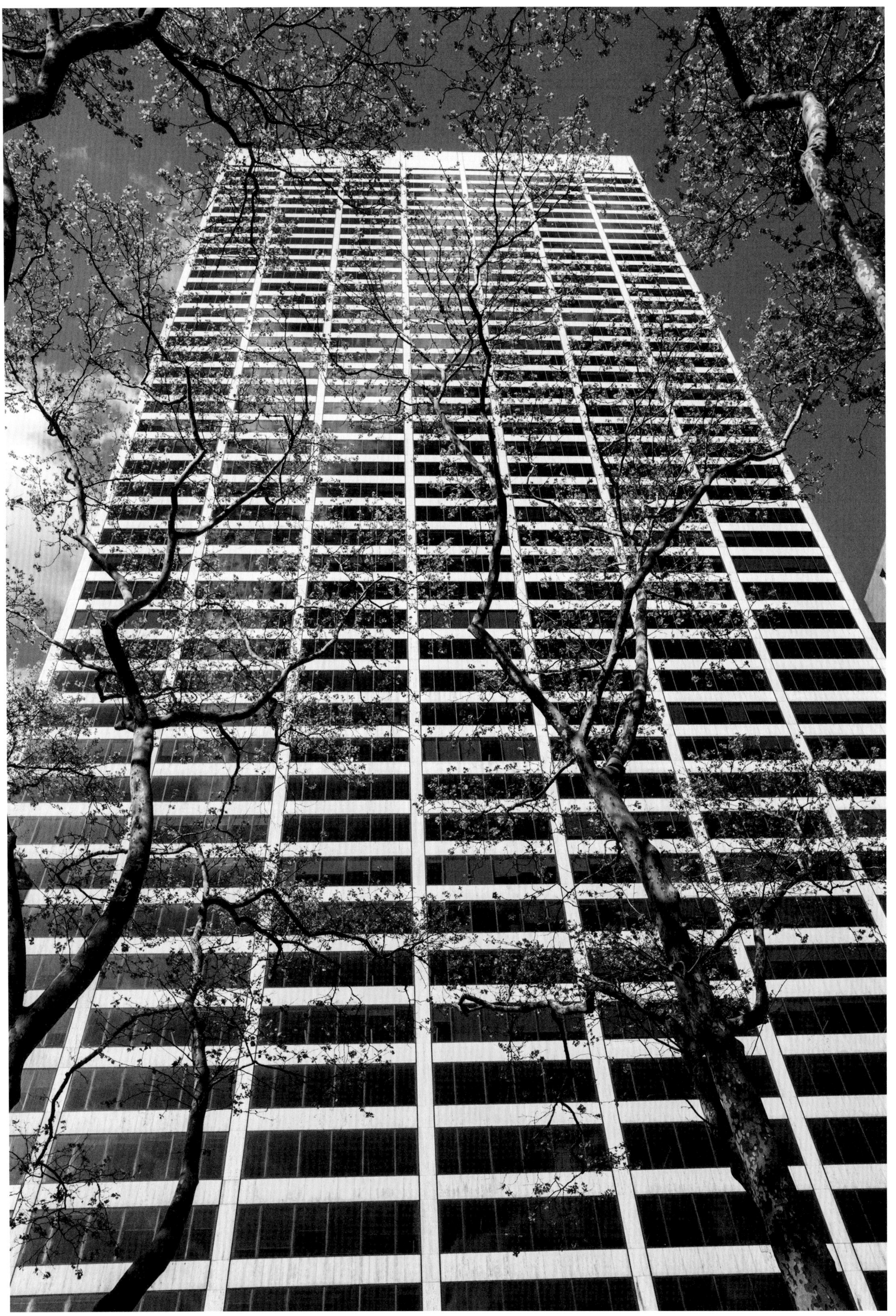

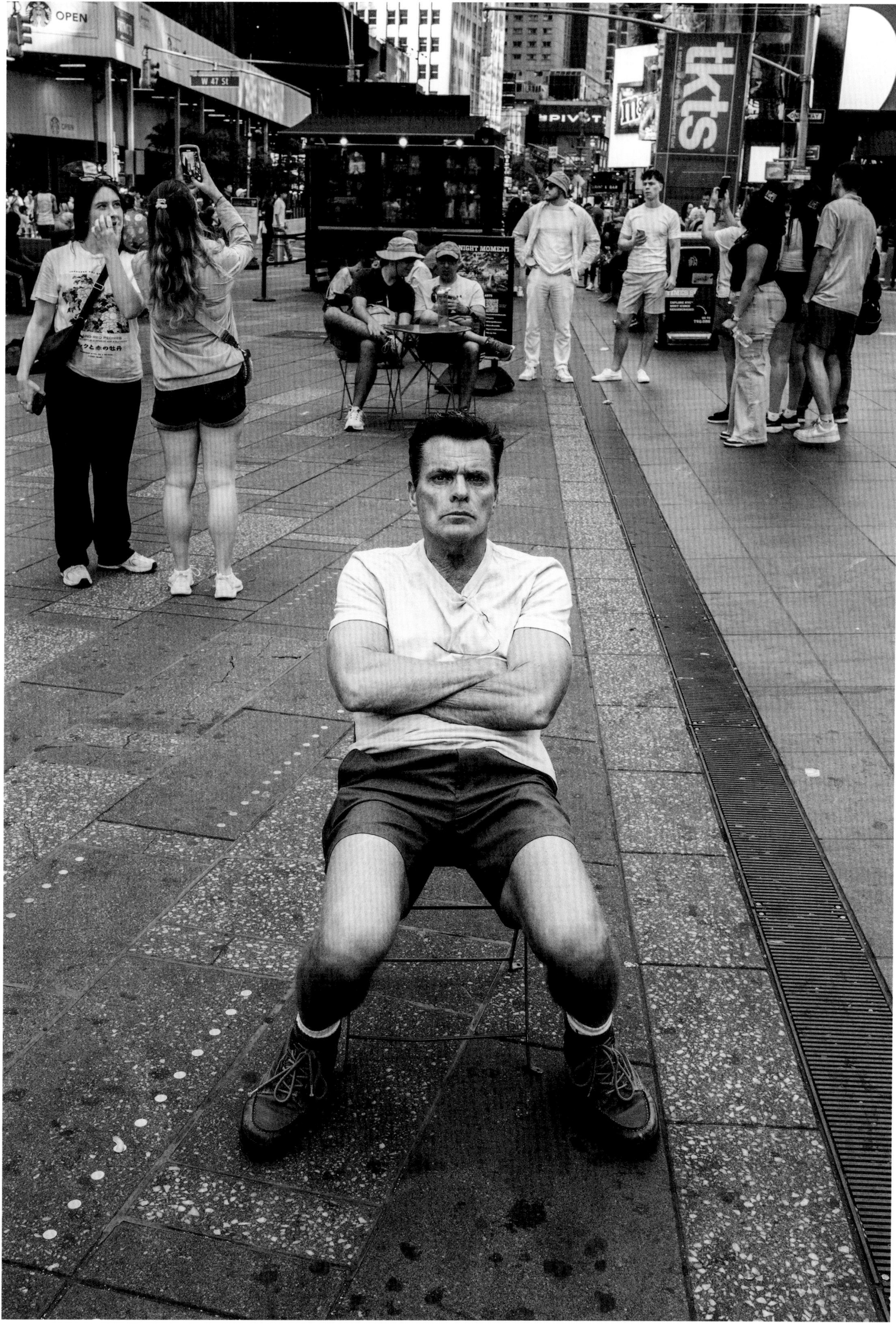
OPEN
W 47 St
PIVOT
tkts

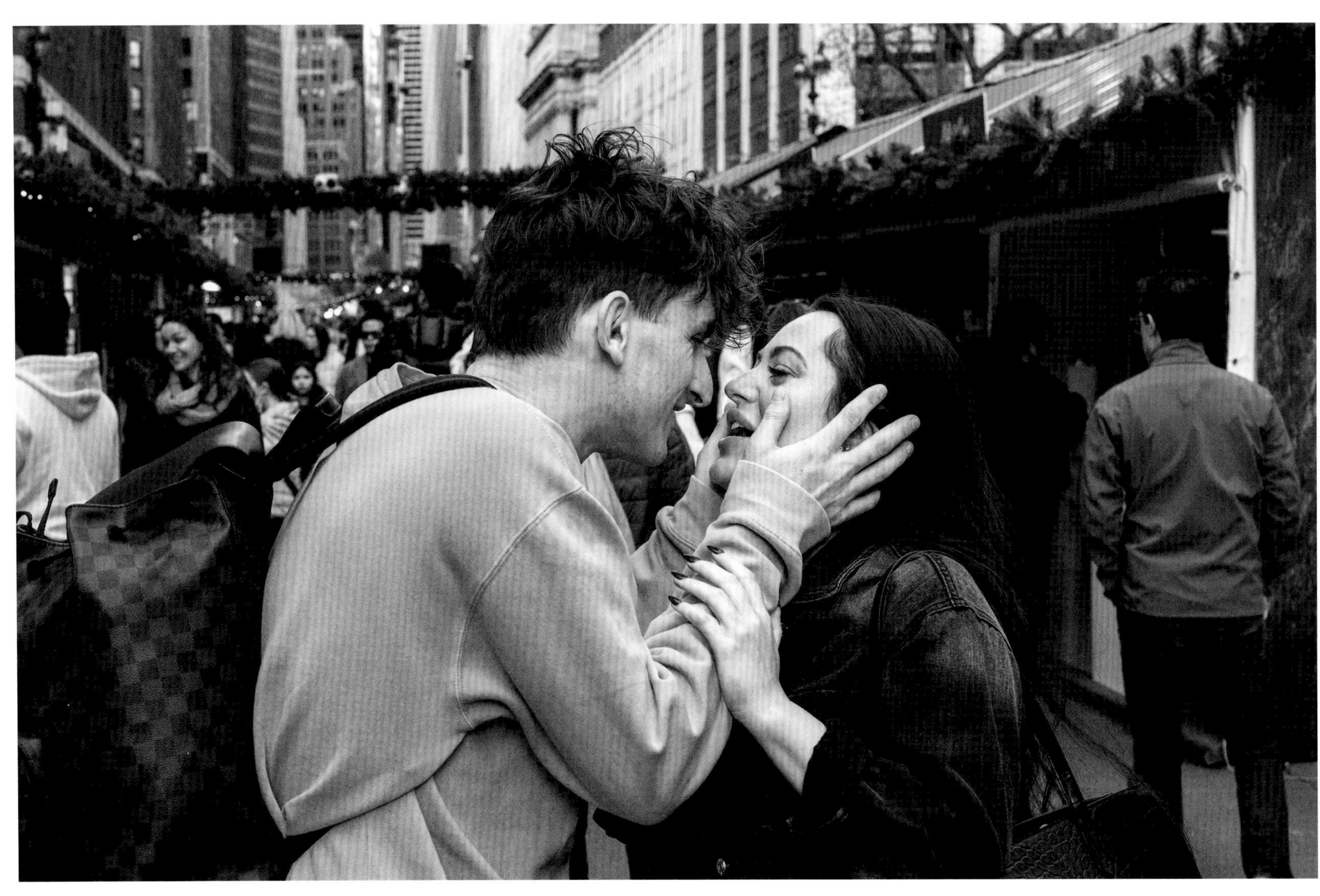

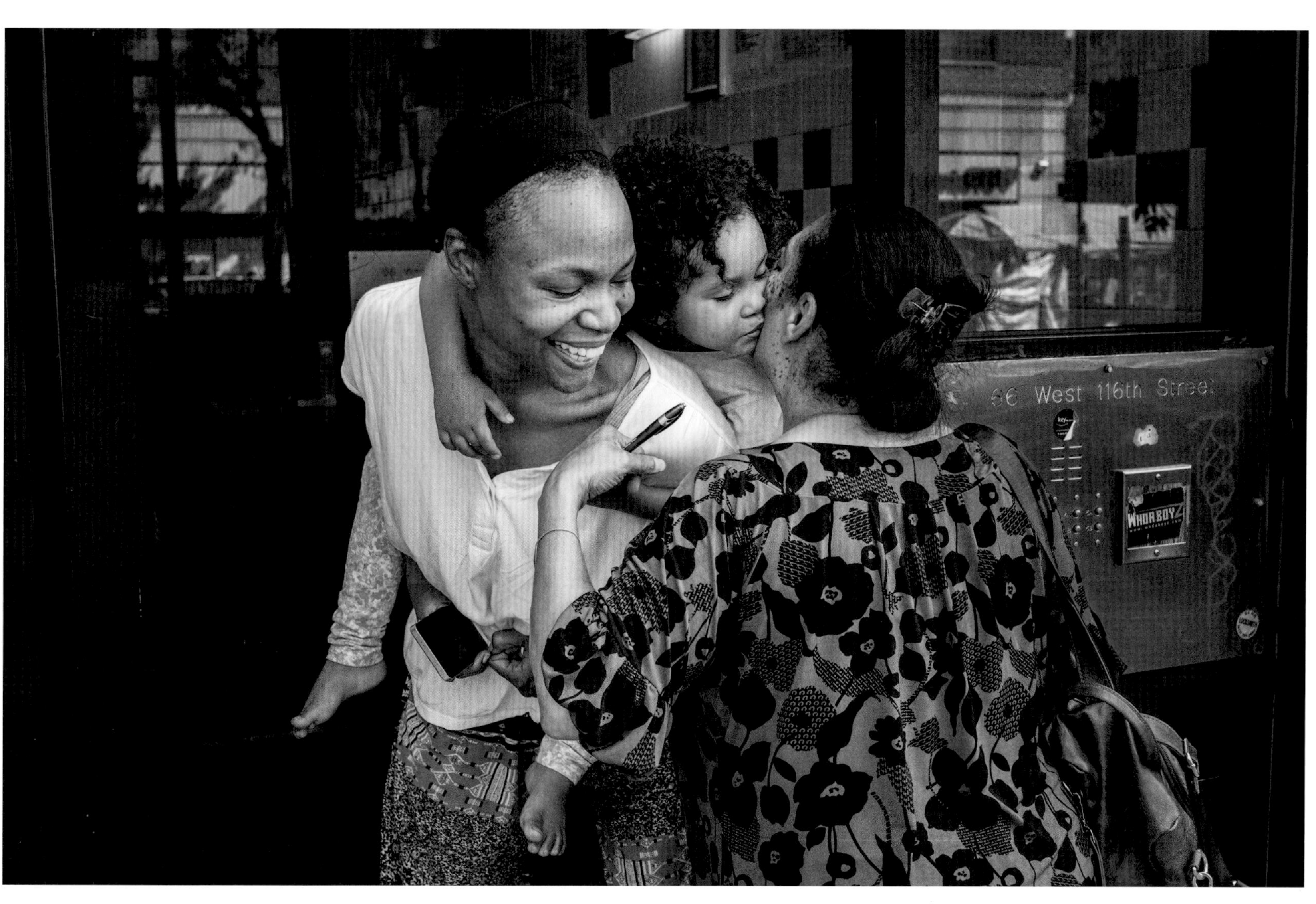
66 West 116th Street
WHOA BOYZ

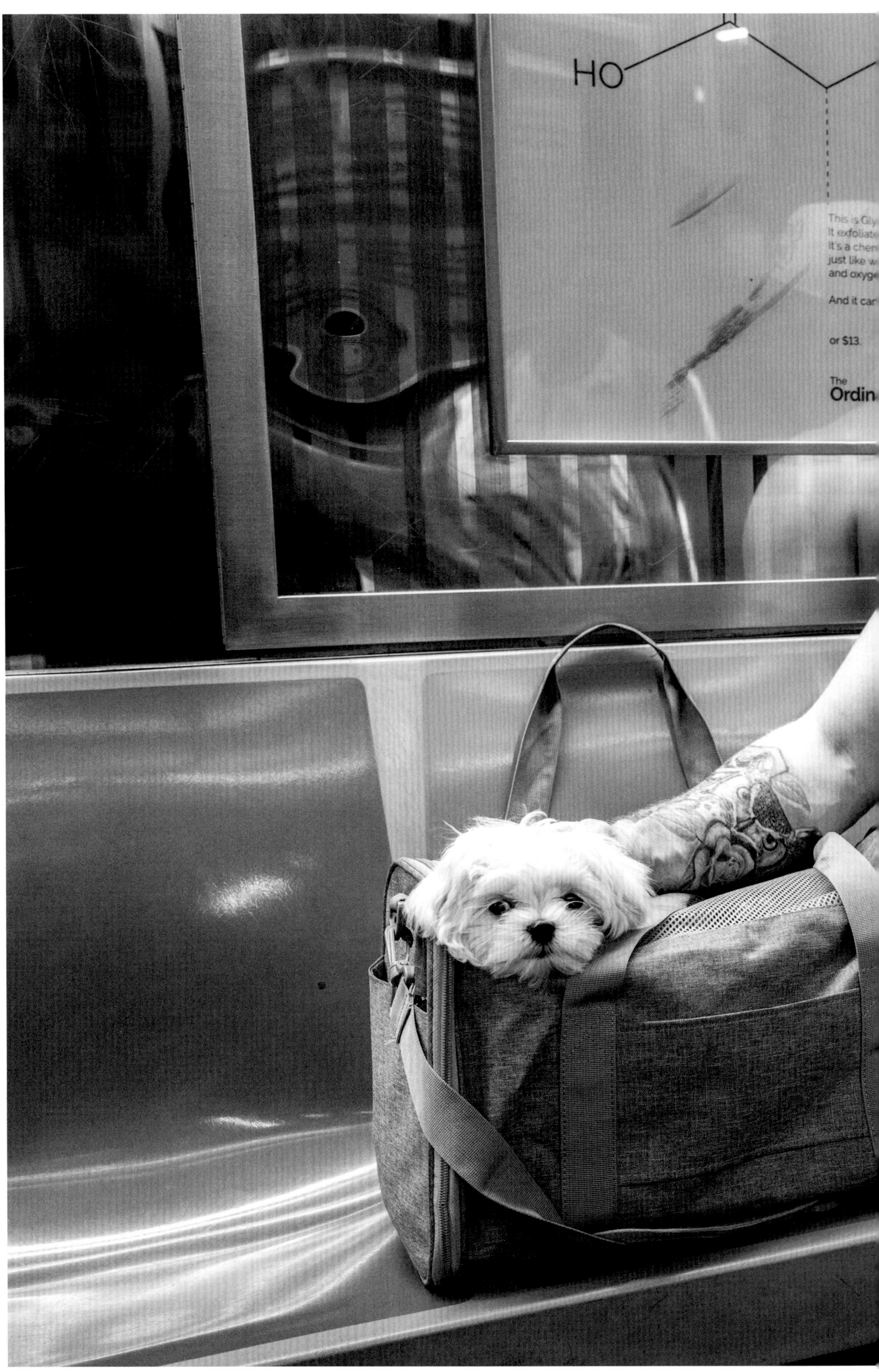
HO
or $13.

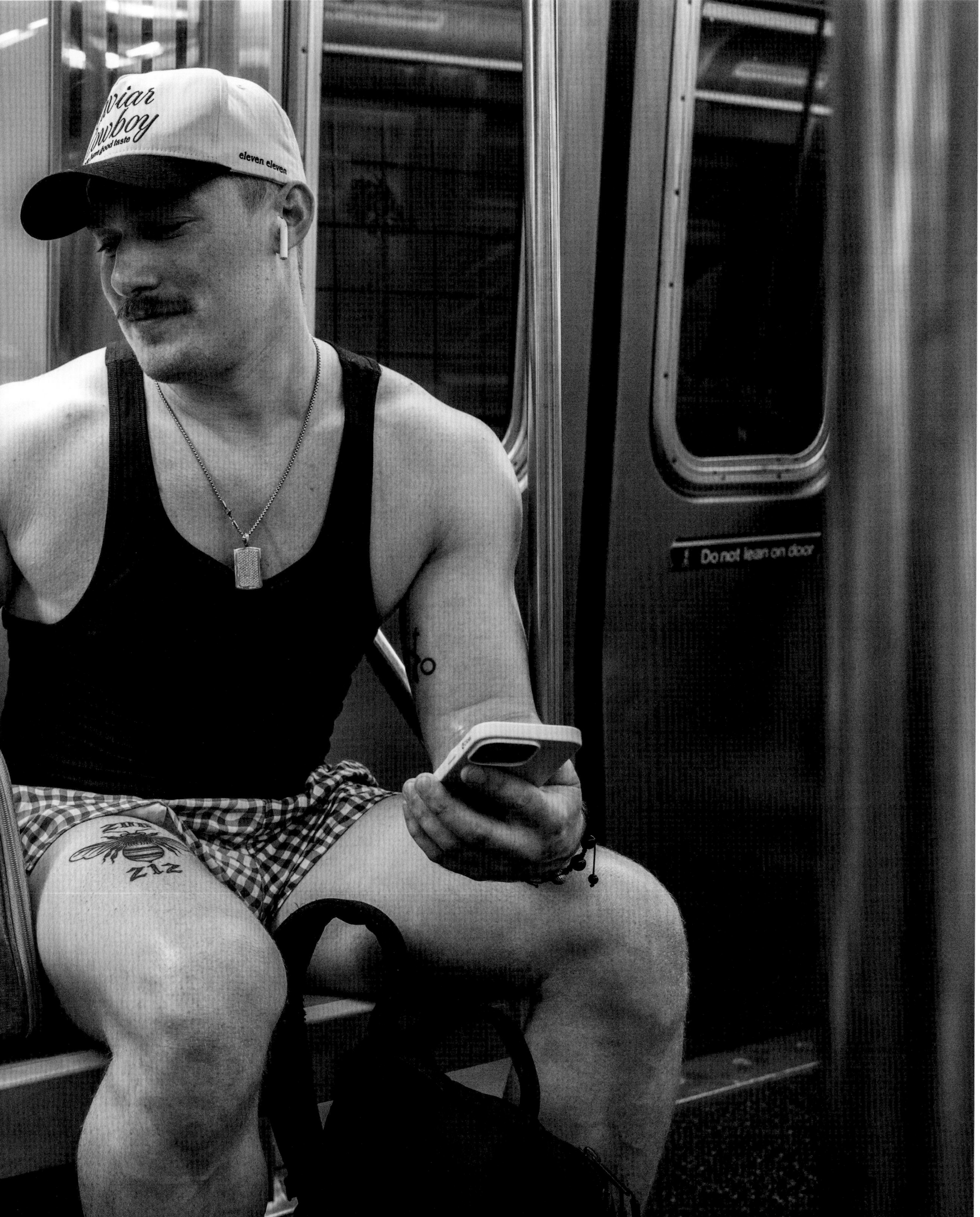
eleven eleven
Do not lean on door

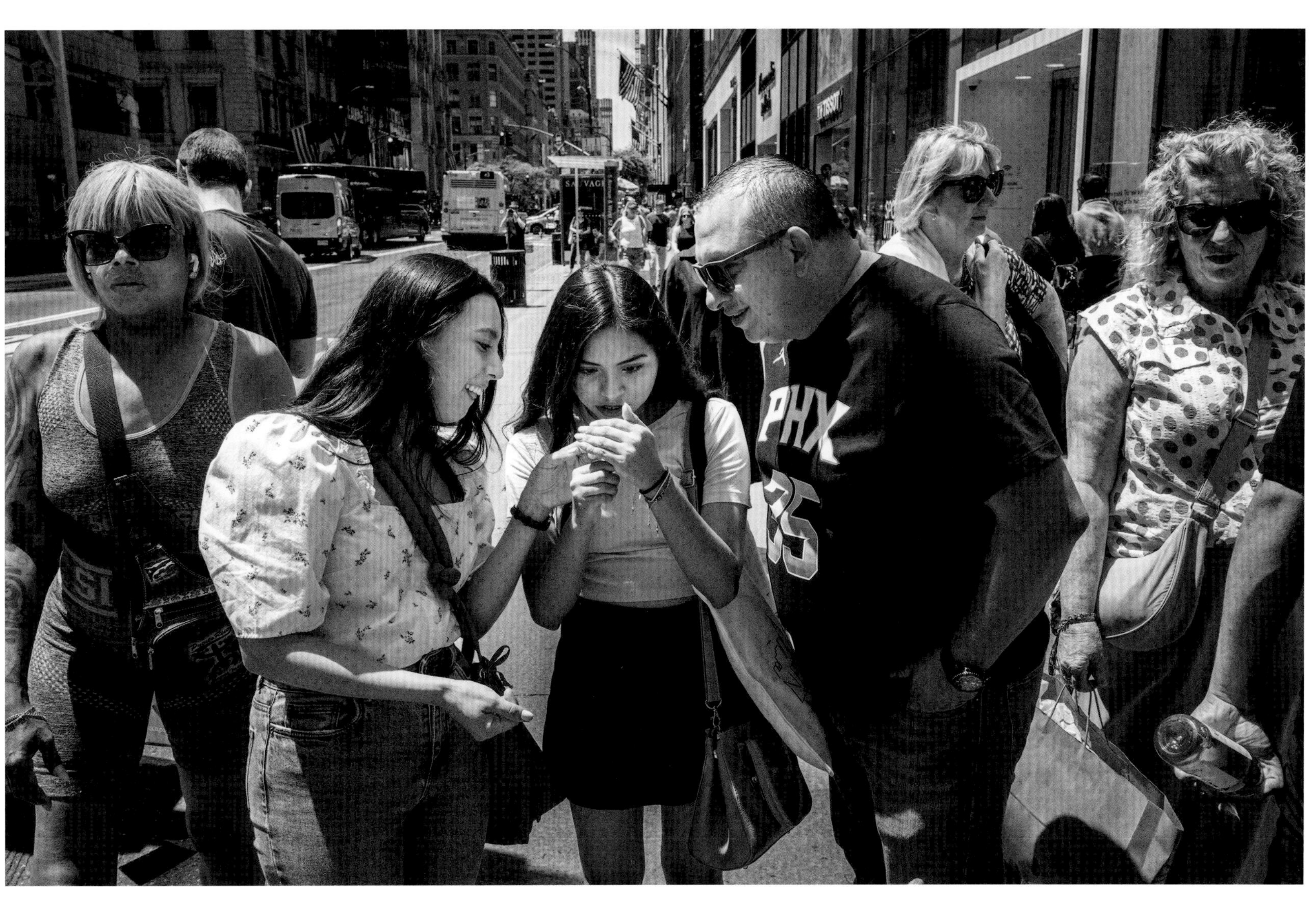
PHX
35

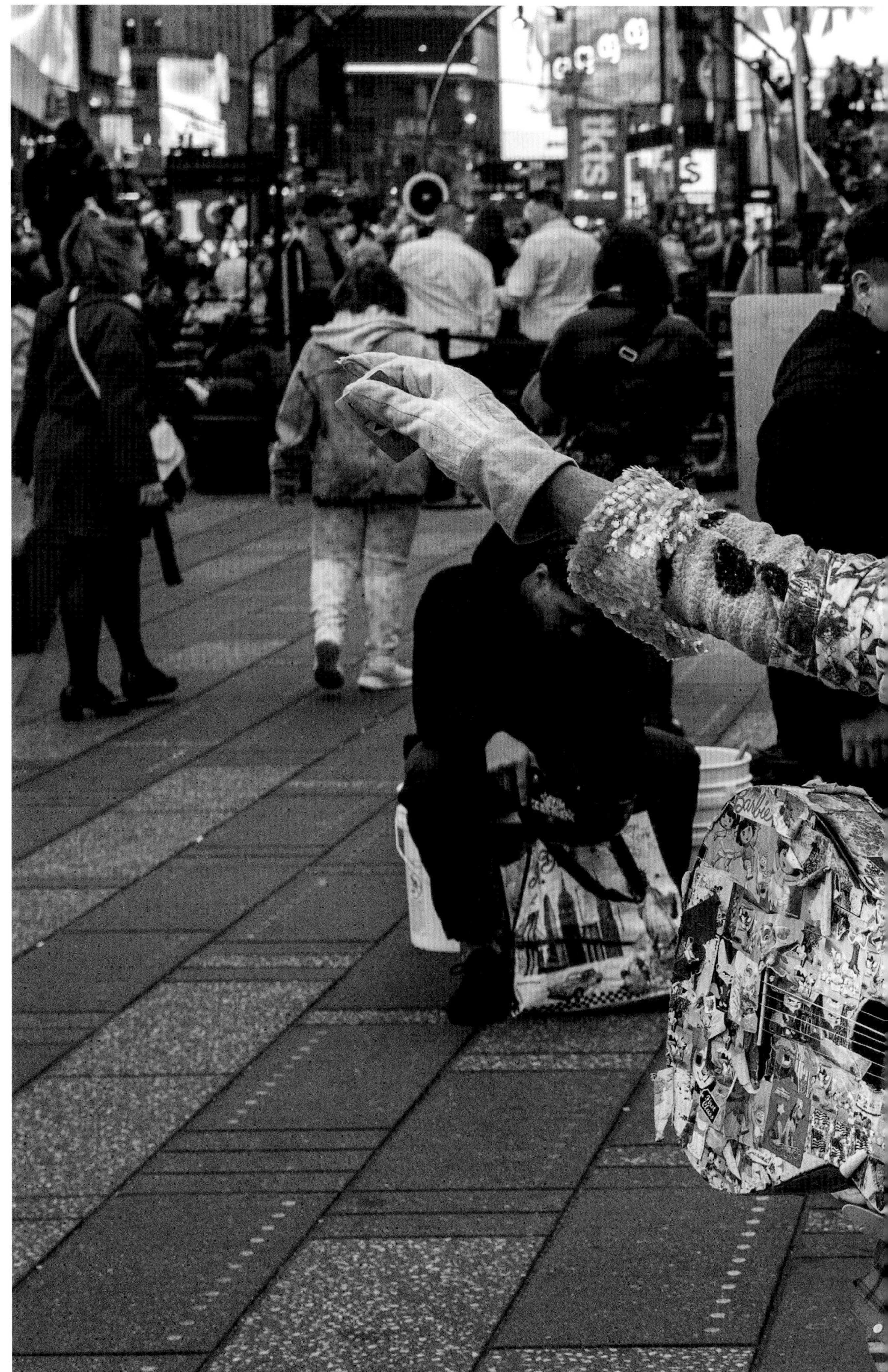
tkts
Barbie

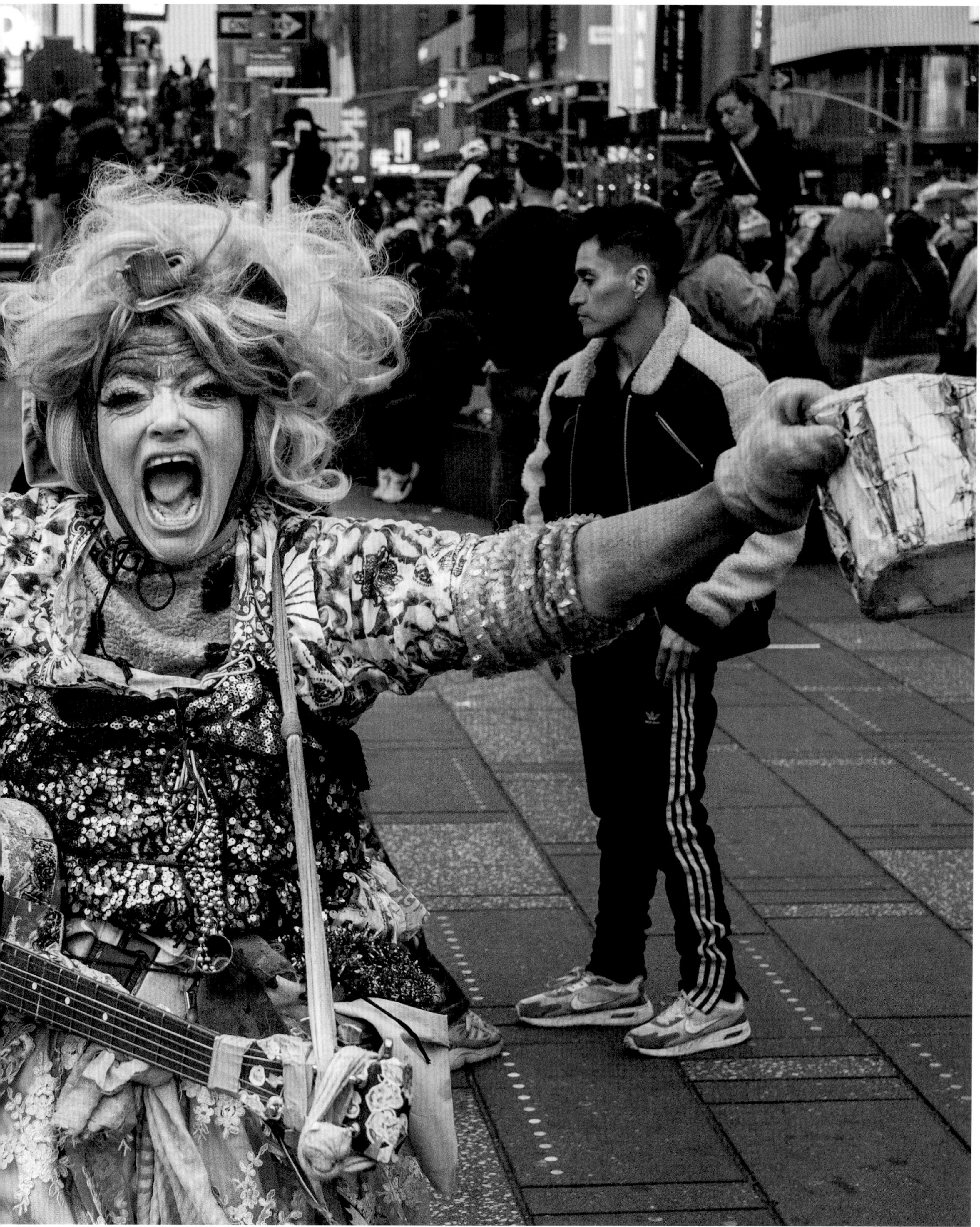

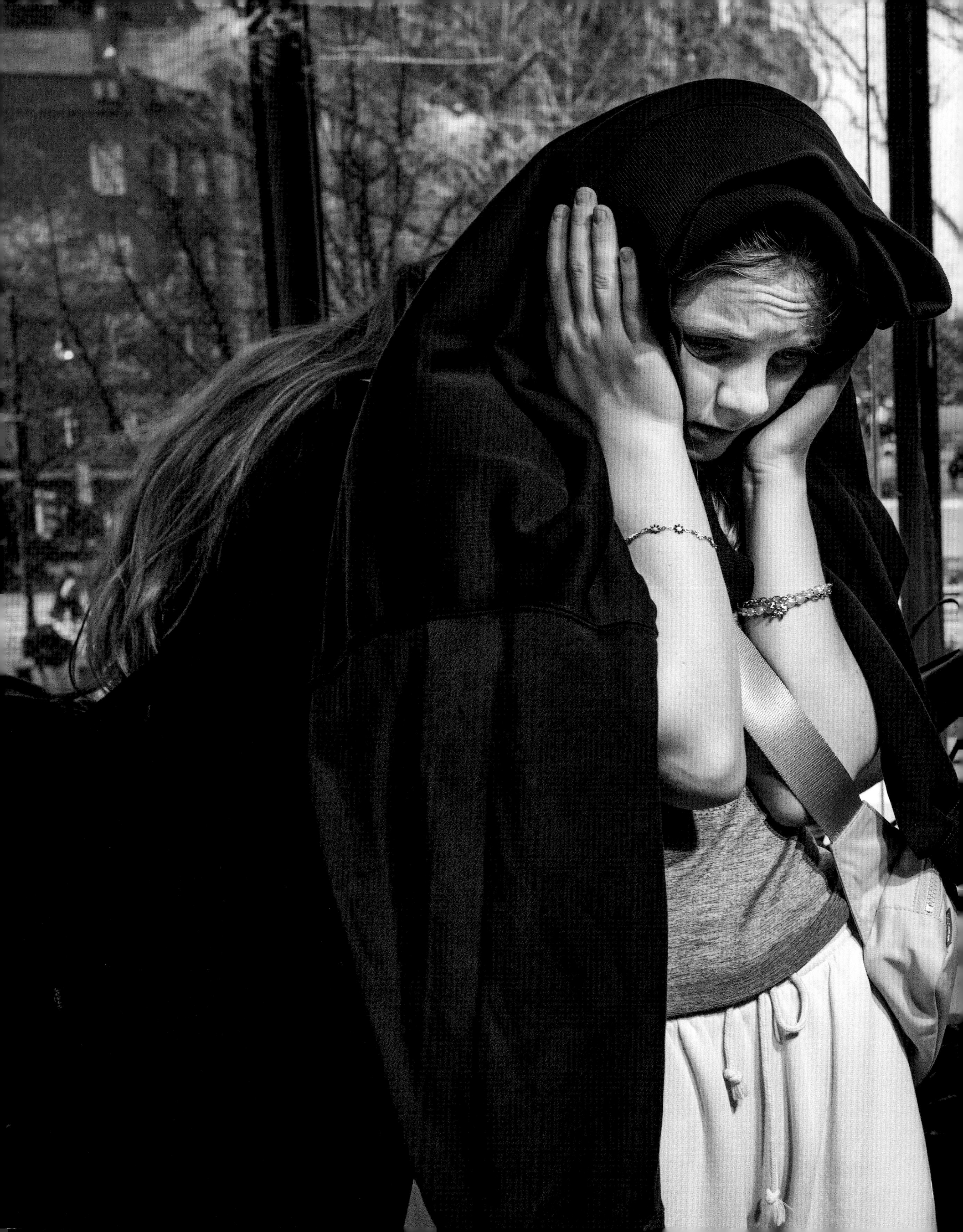

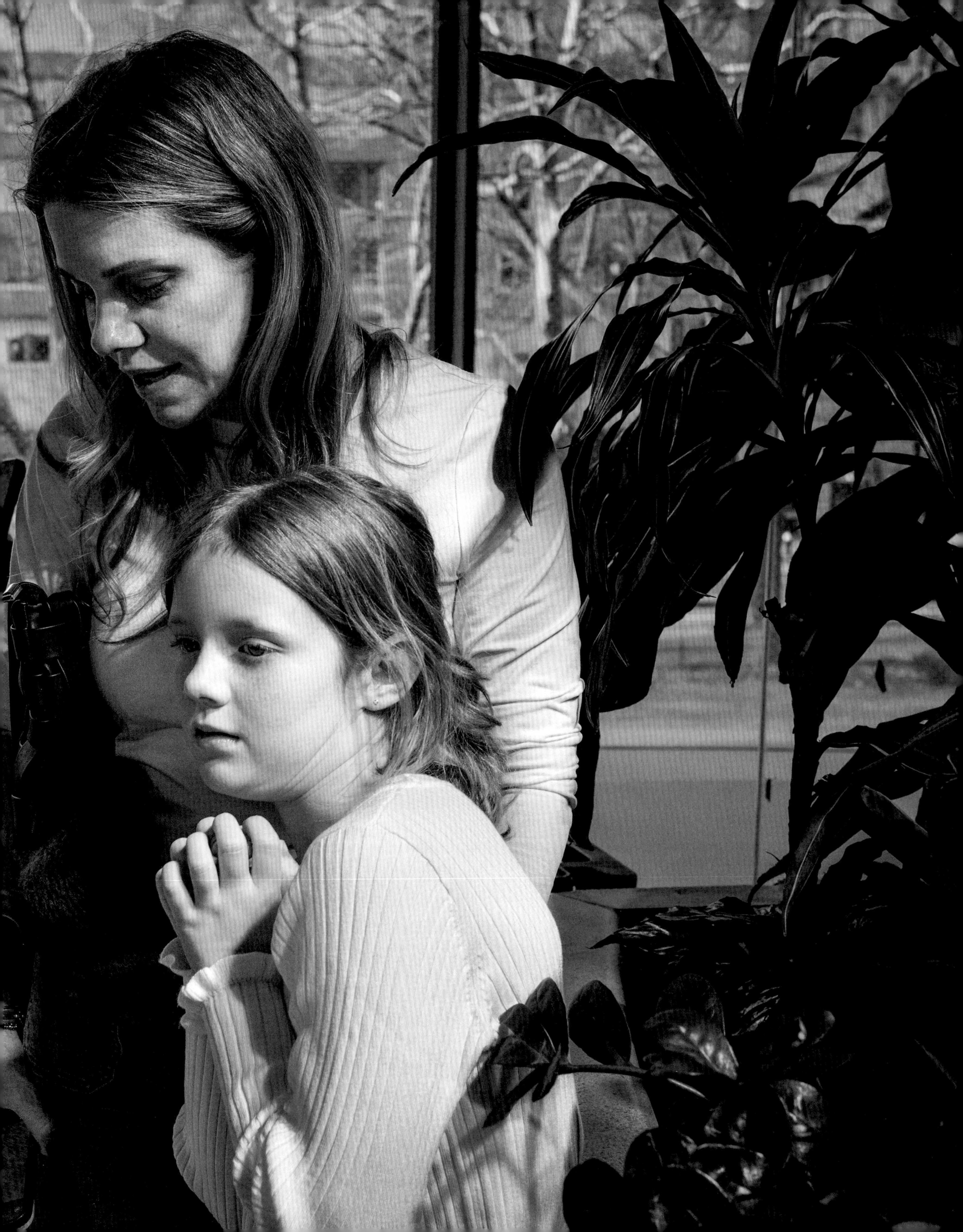

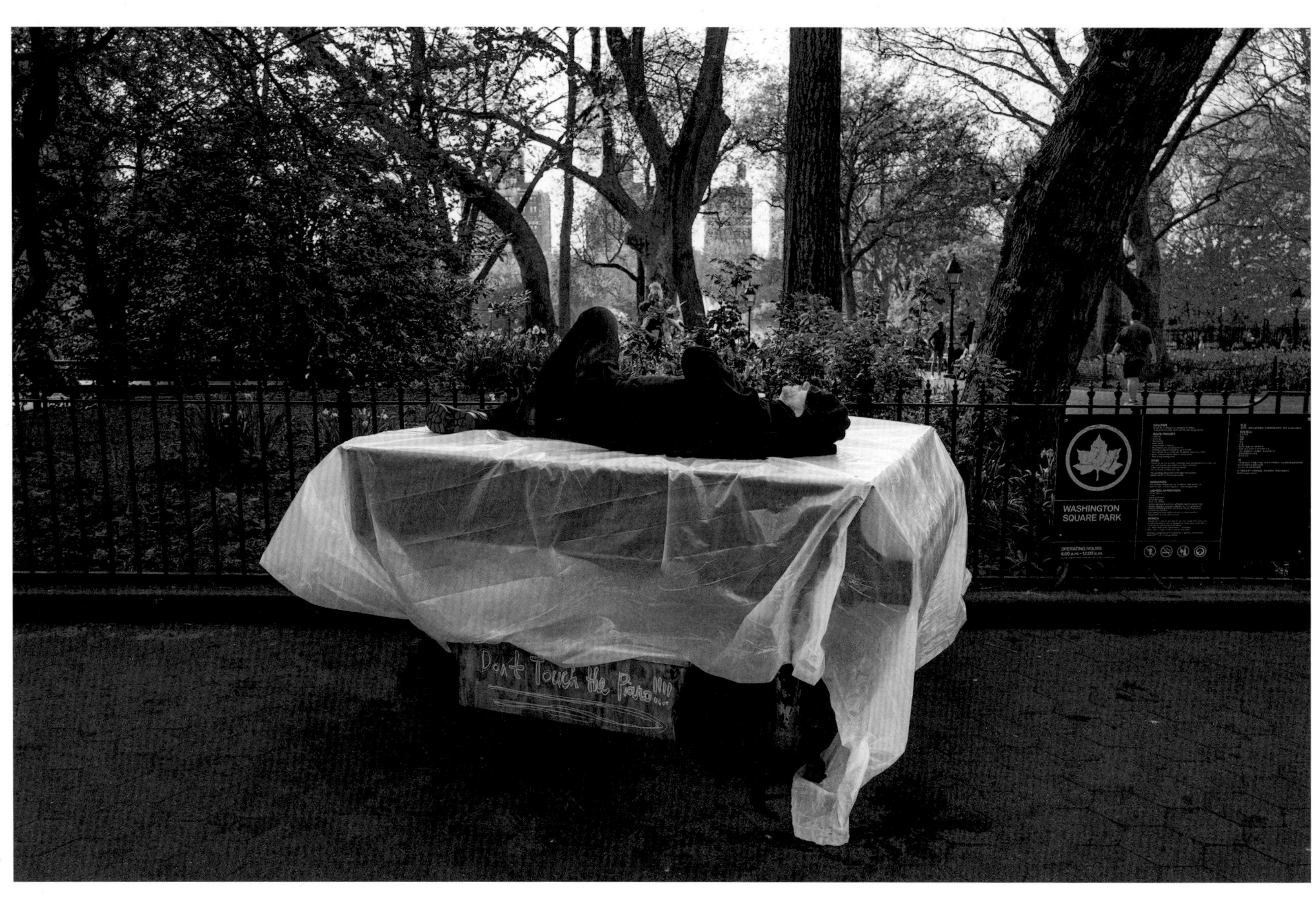
Don't Touch the Piano!!!!
WASHINGTON
SQUARE PARK
OPERATING HOURS
6:00 a.m.–12:00 a.m.

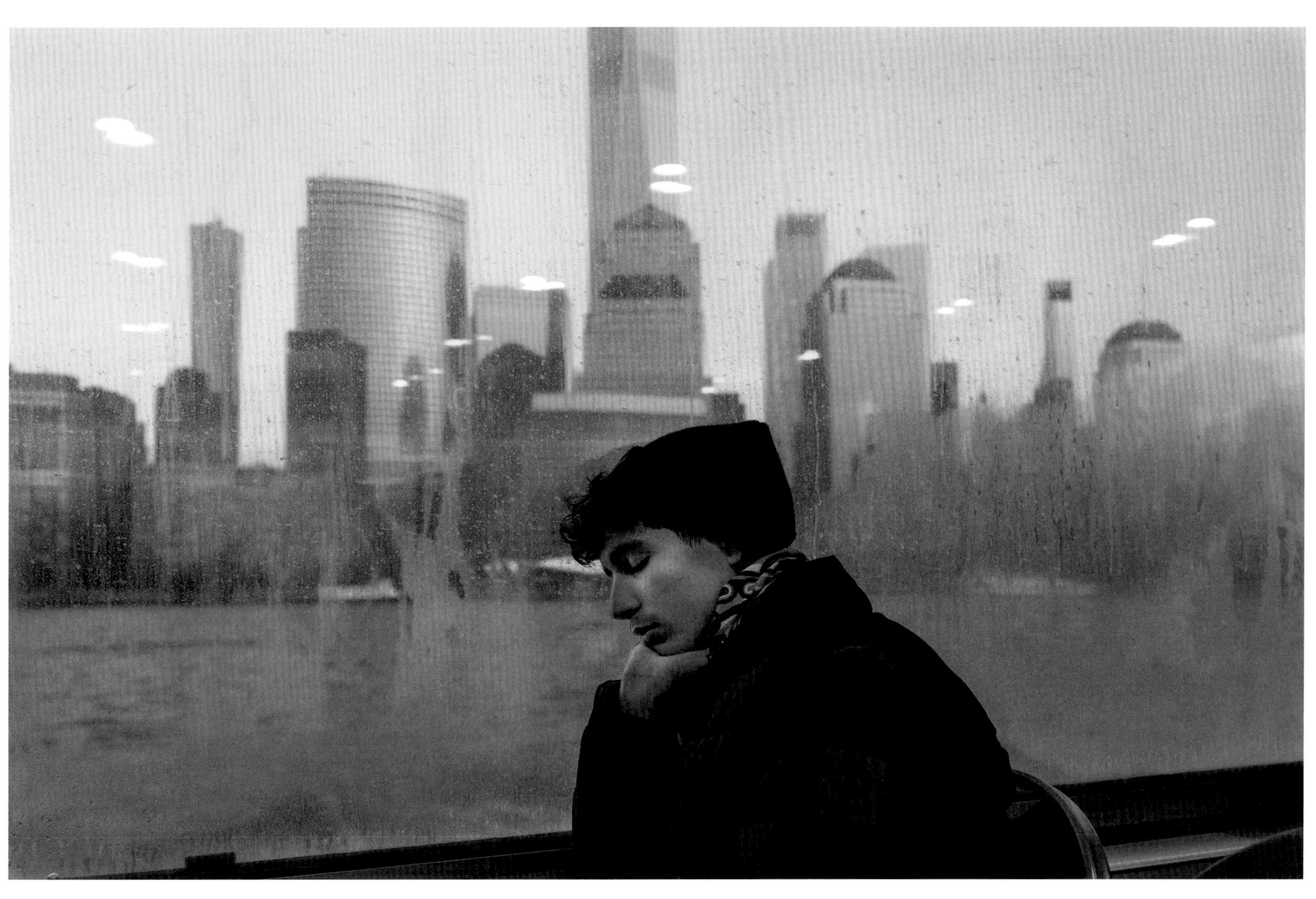

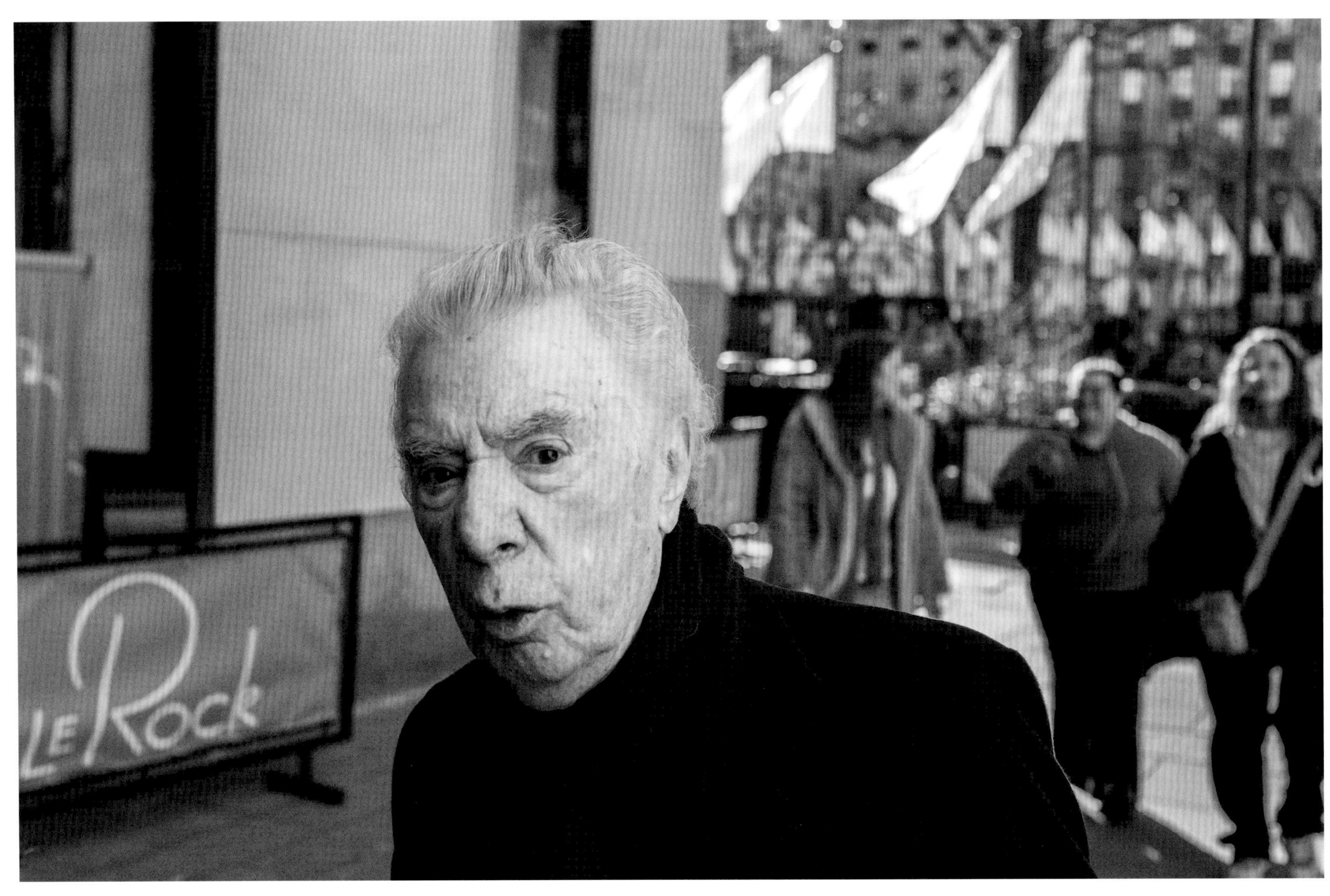
Le Rock

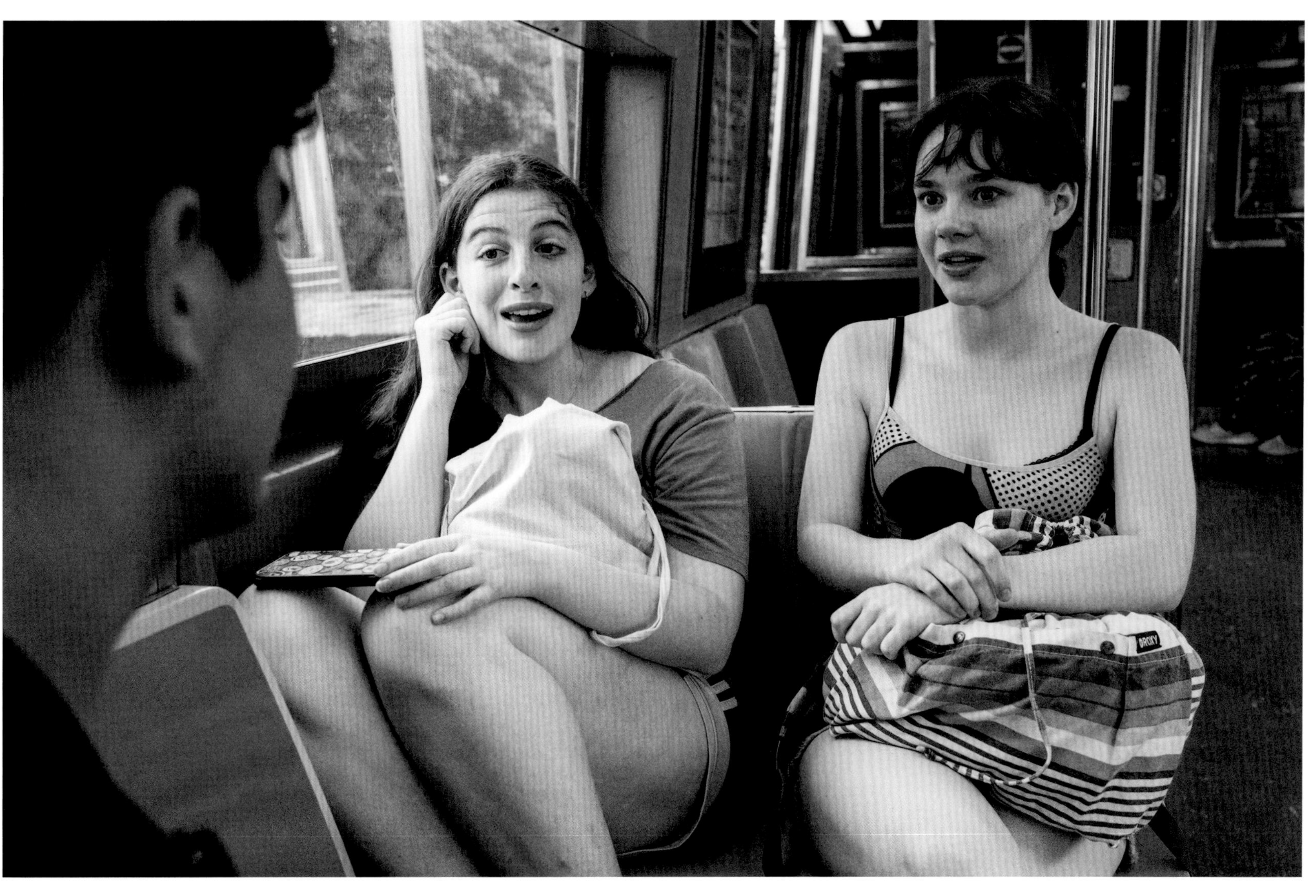

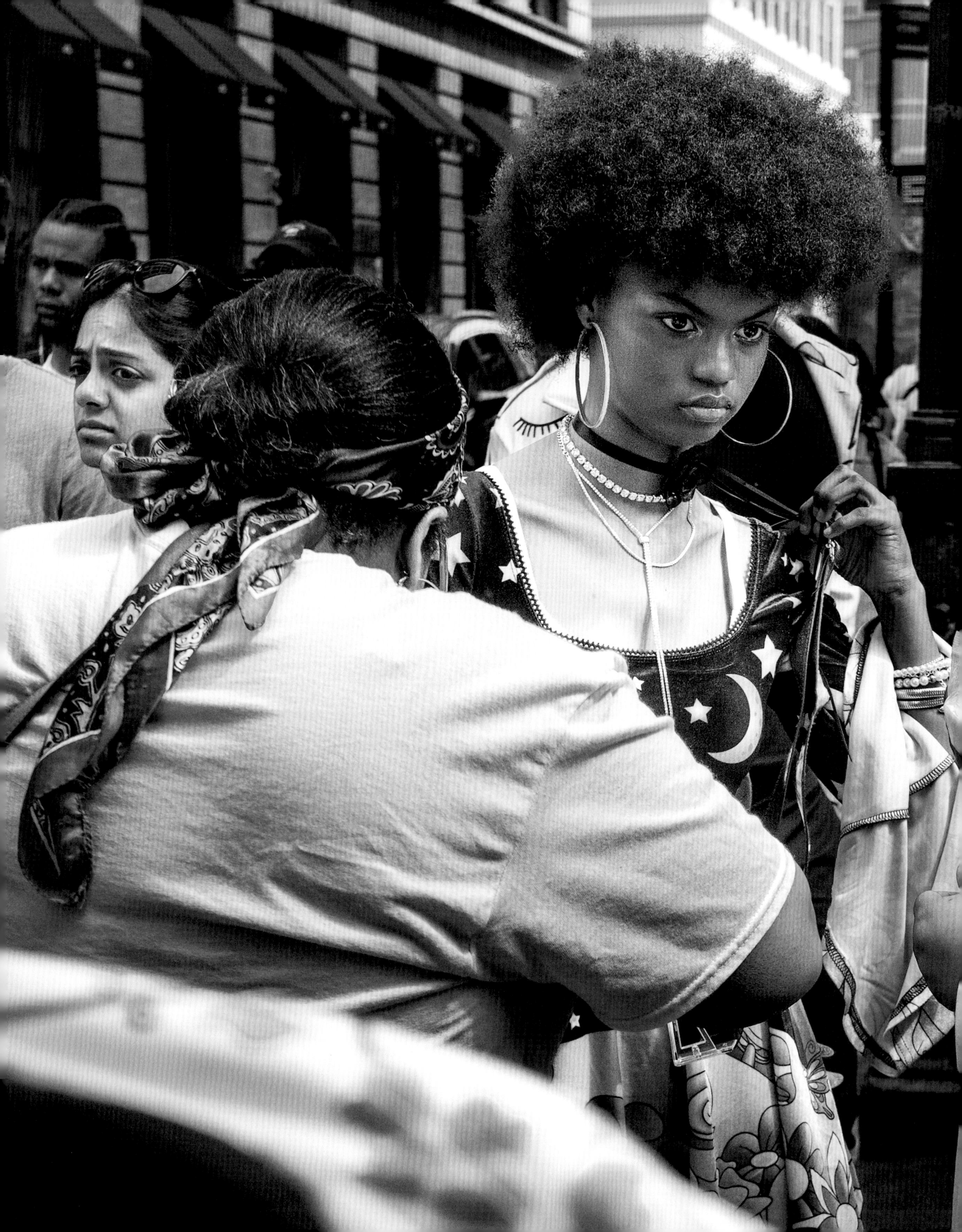

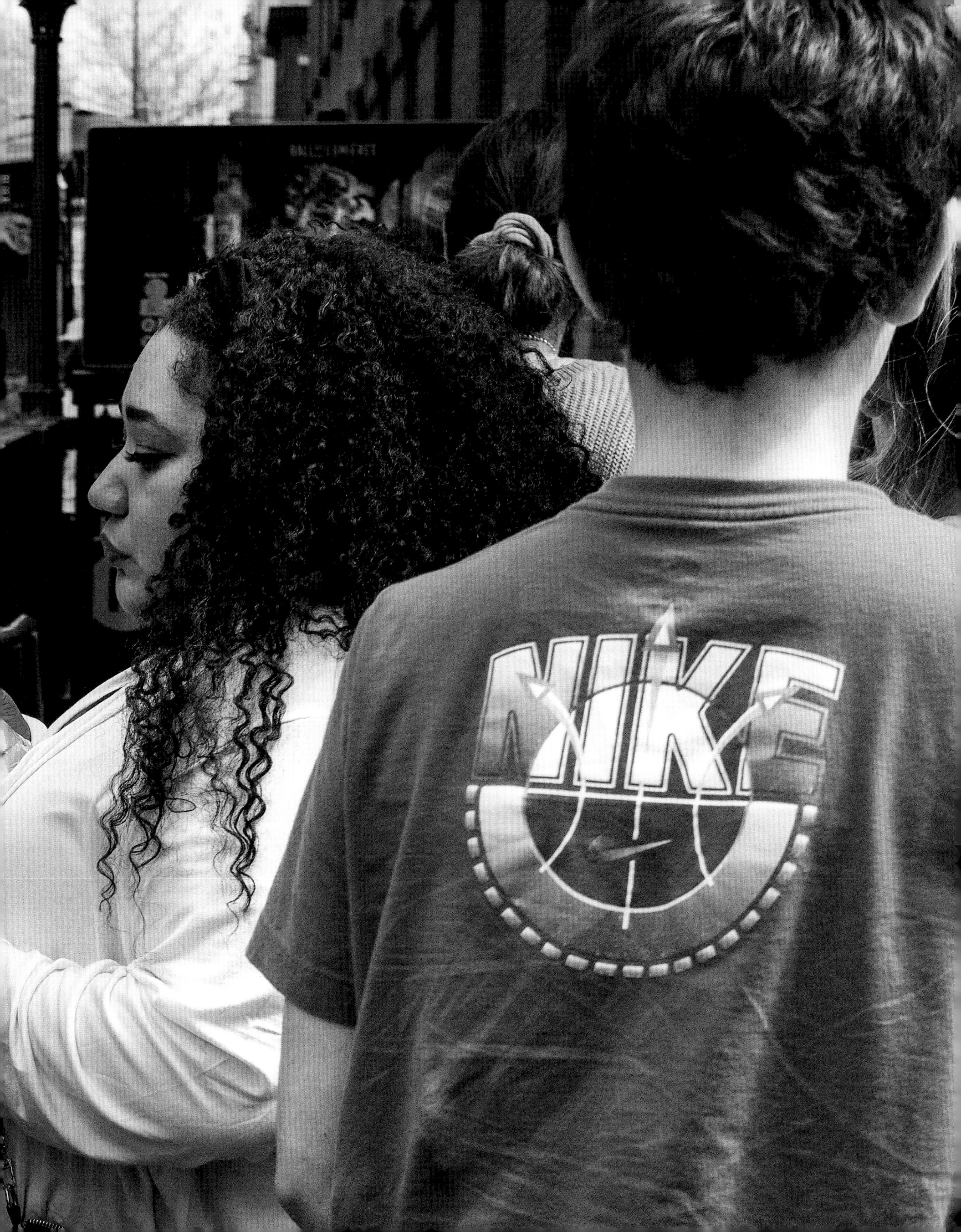
NIKE

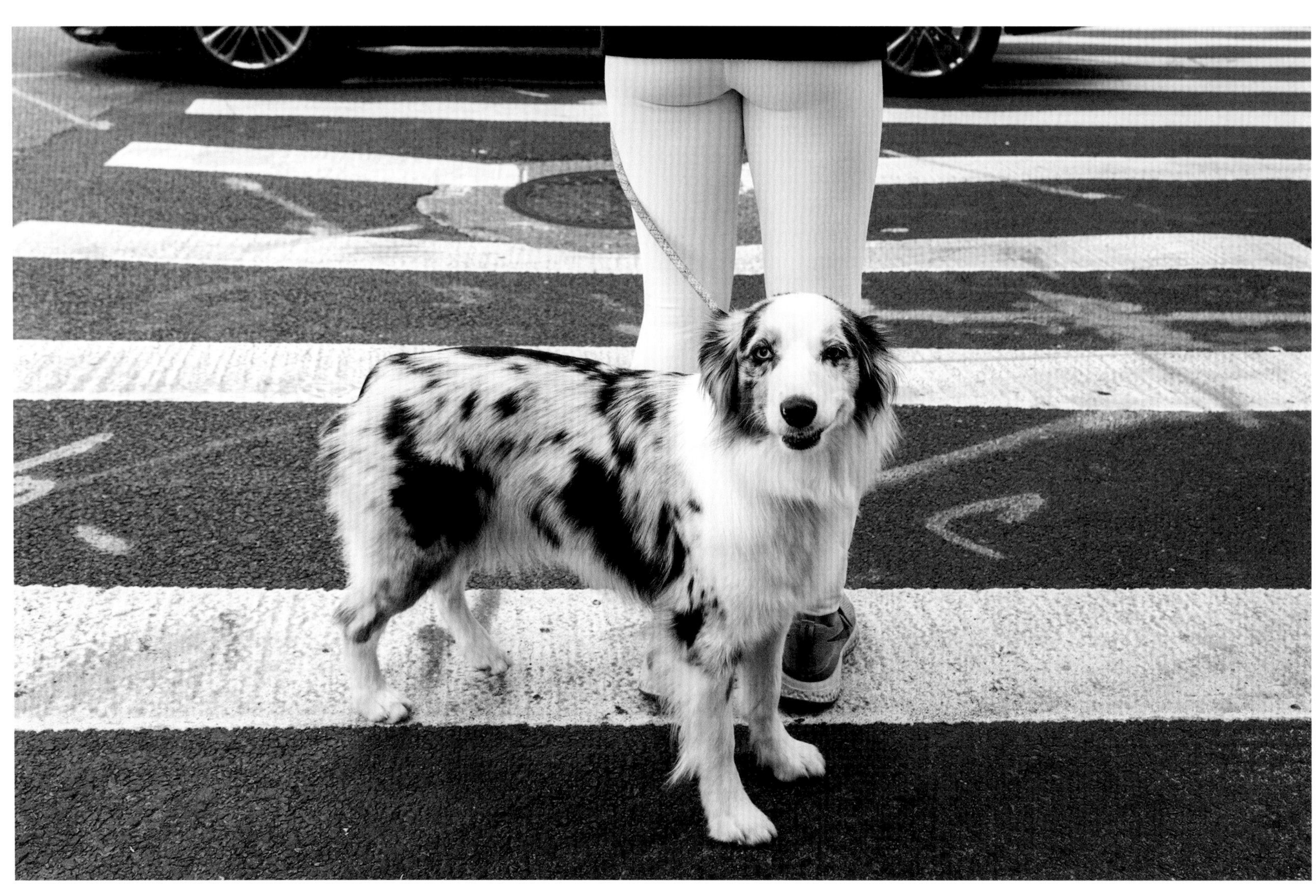

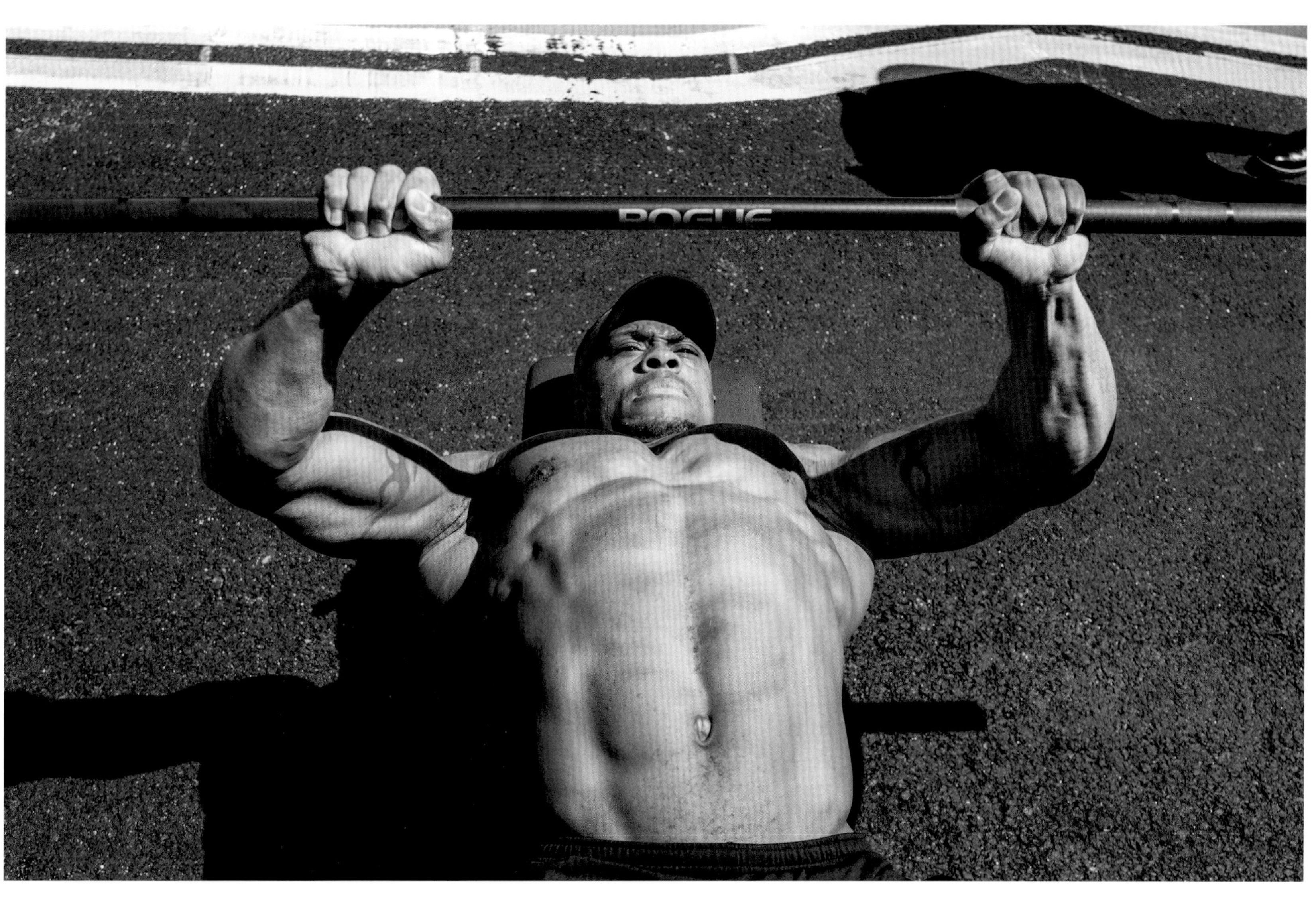
ROGUE

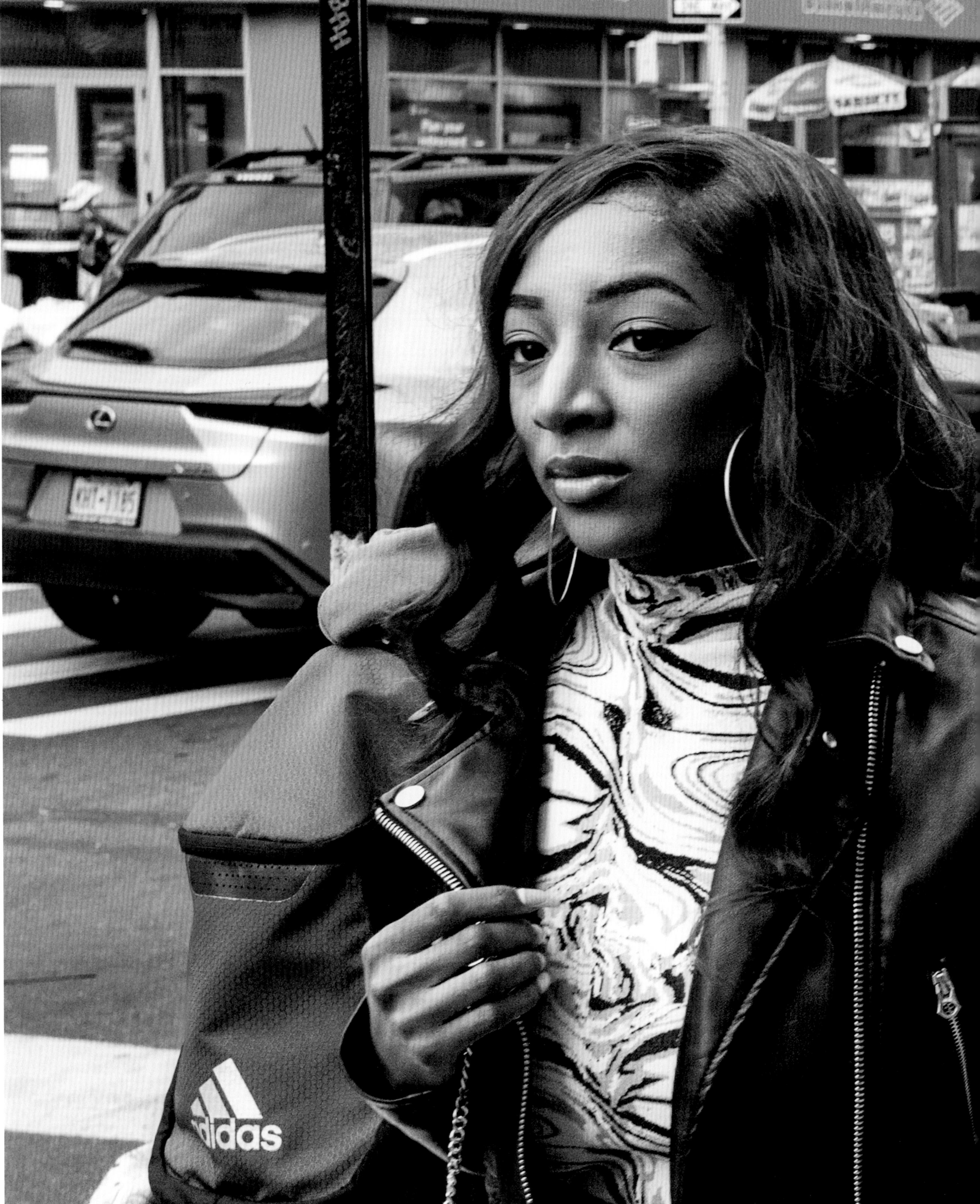

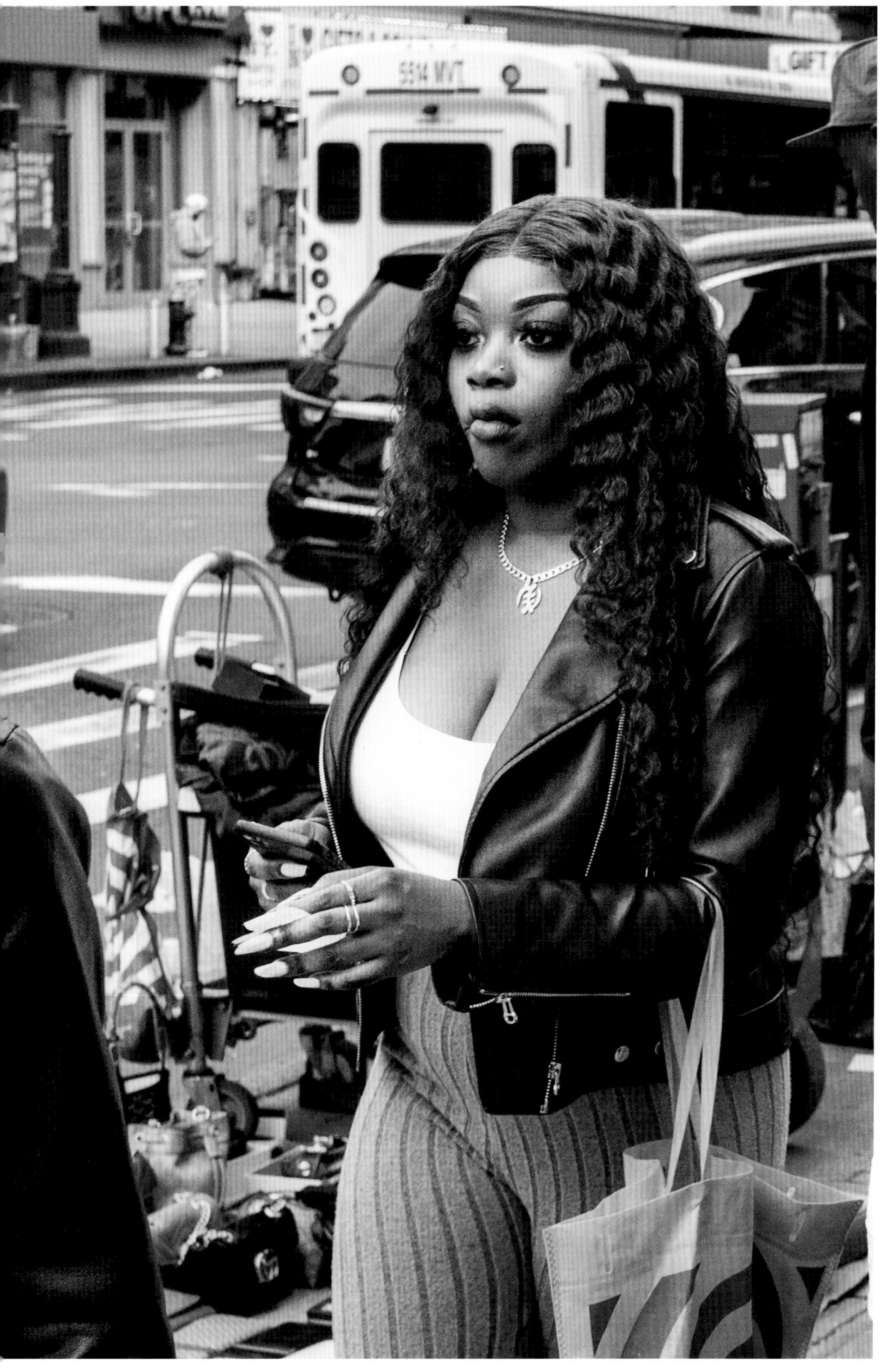
5514 MVT
GIFT

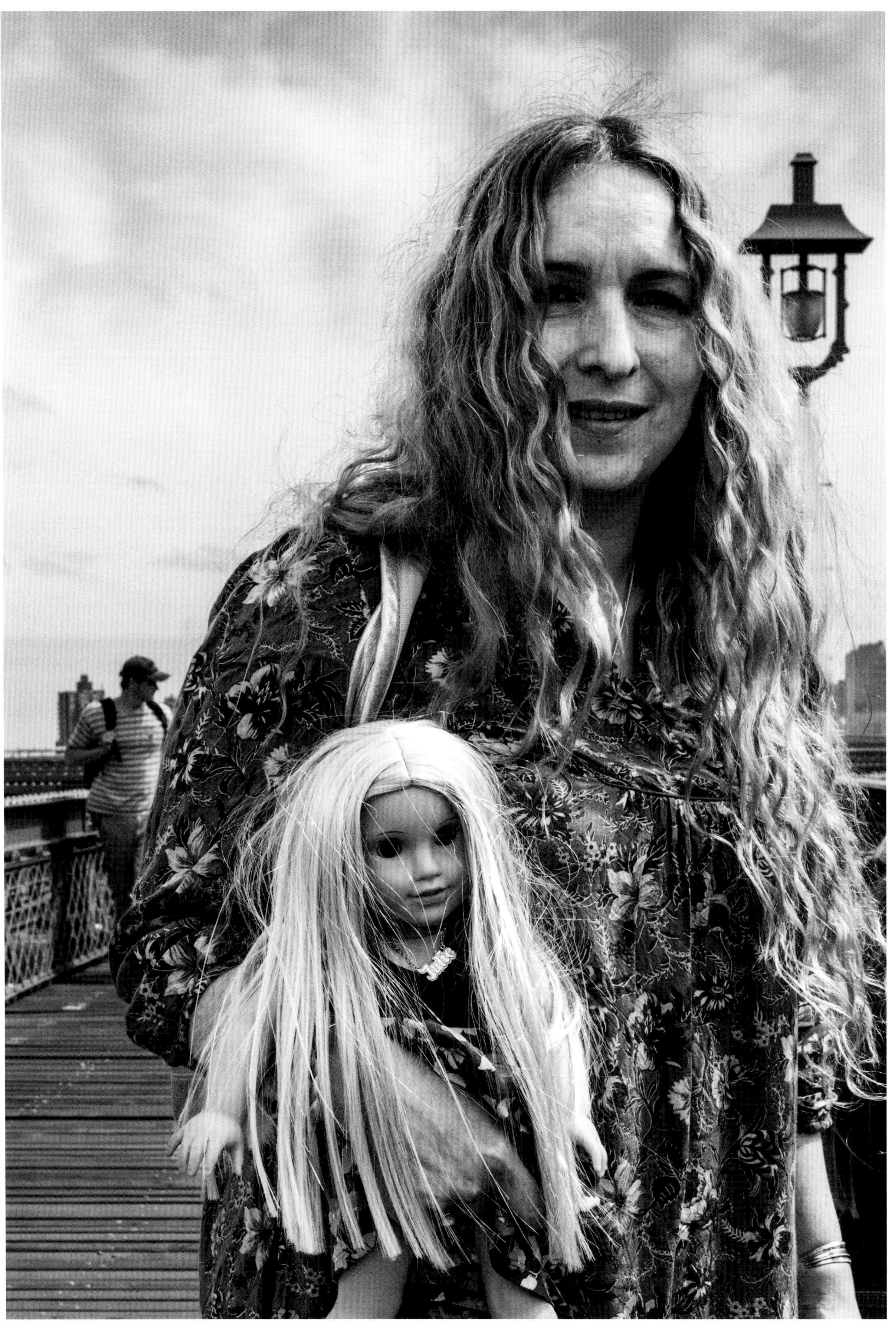
Julie

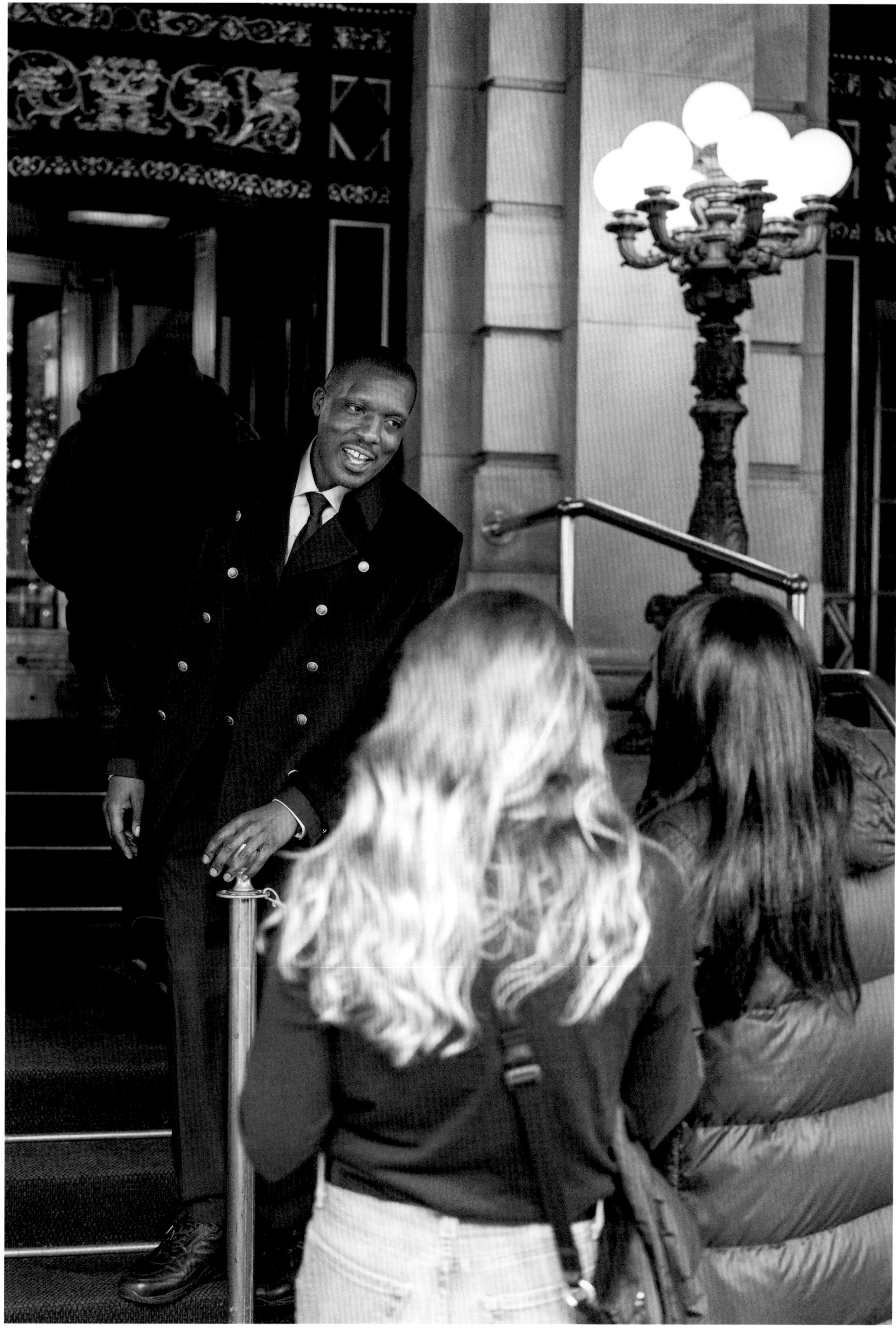

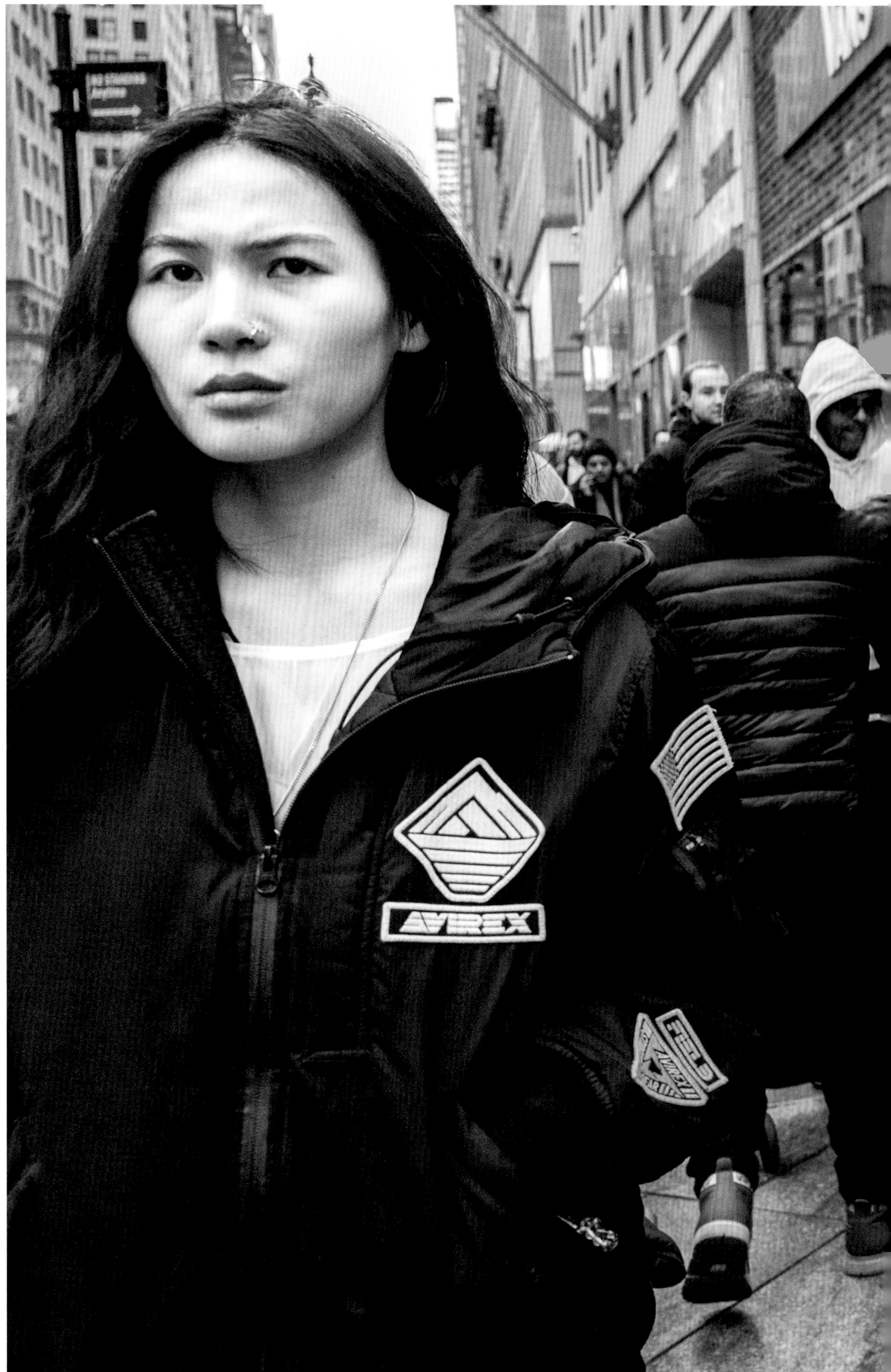
AVIREX

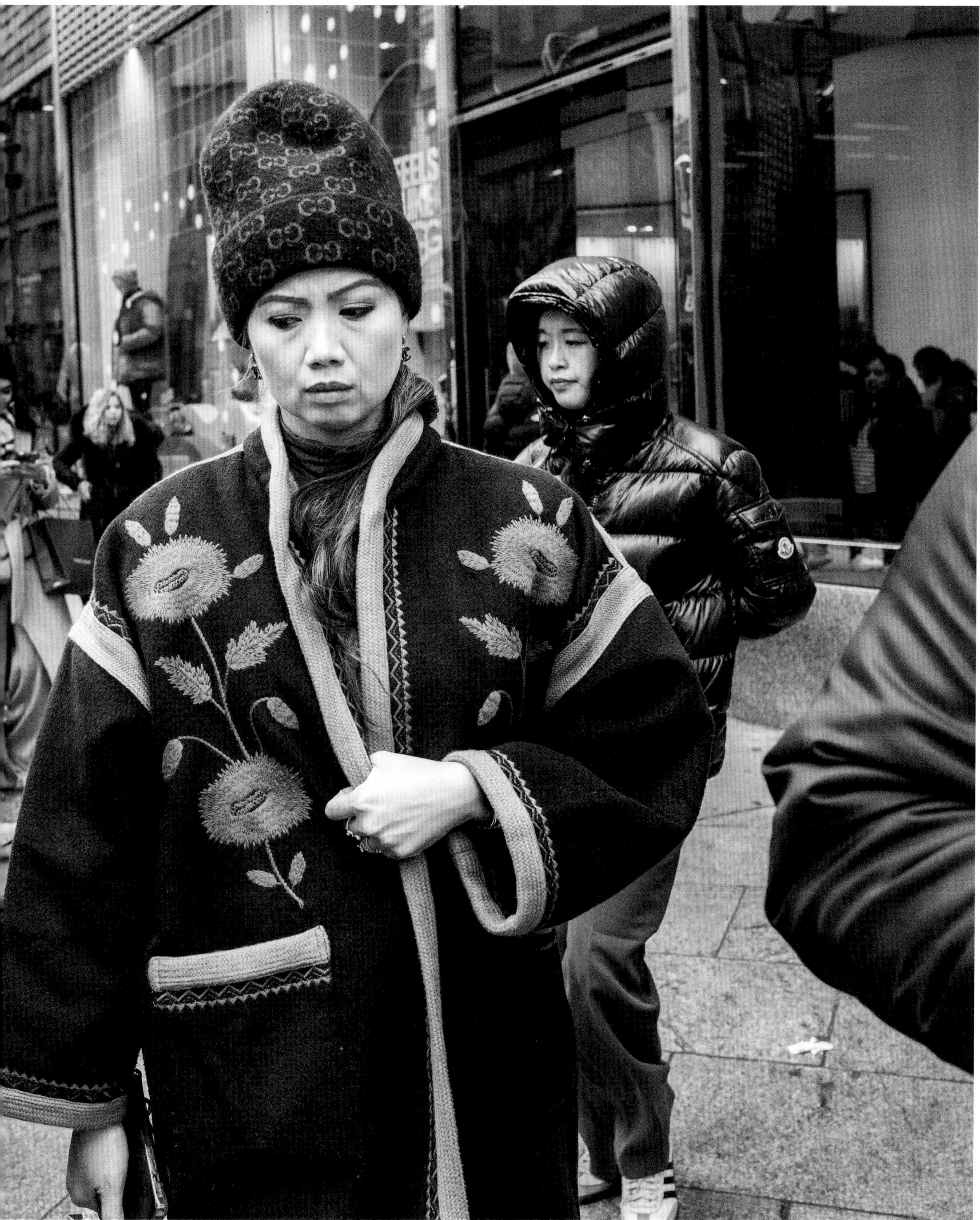

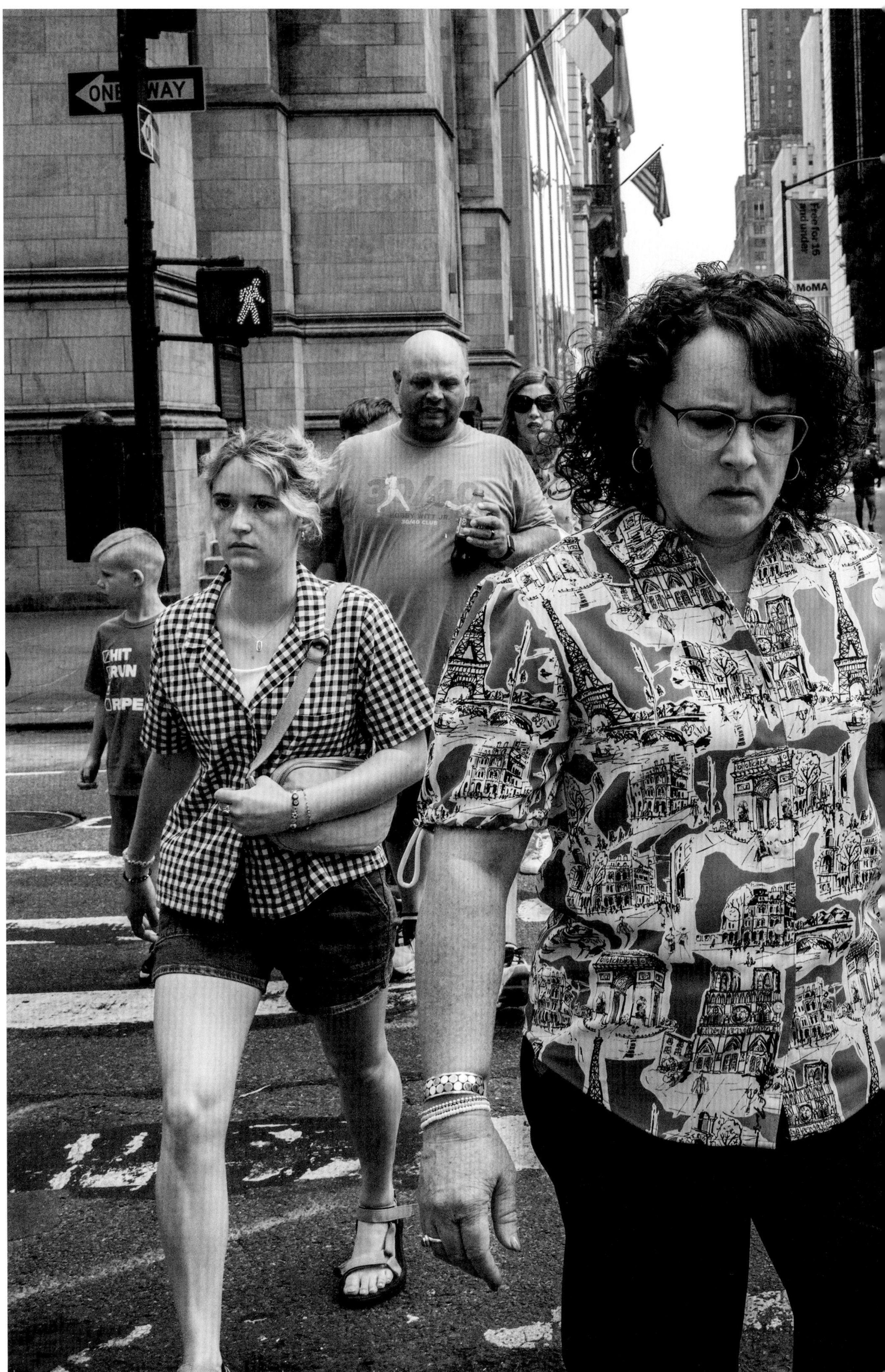
ONE WAY
MoMA

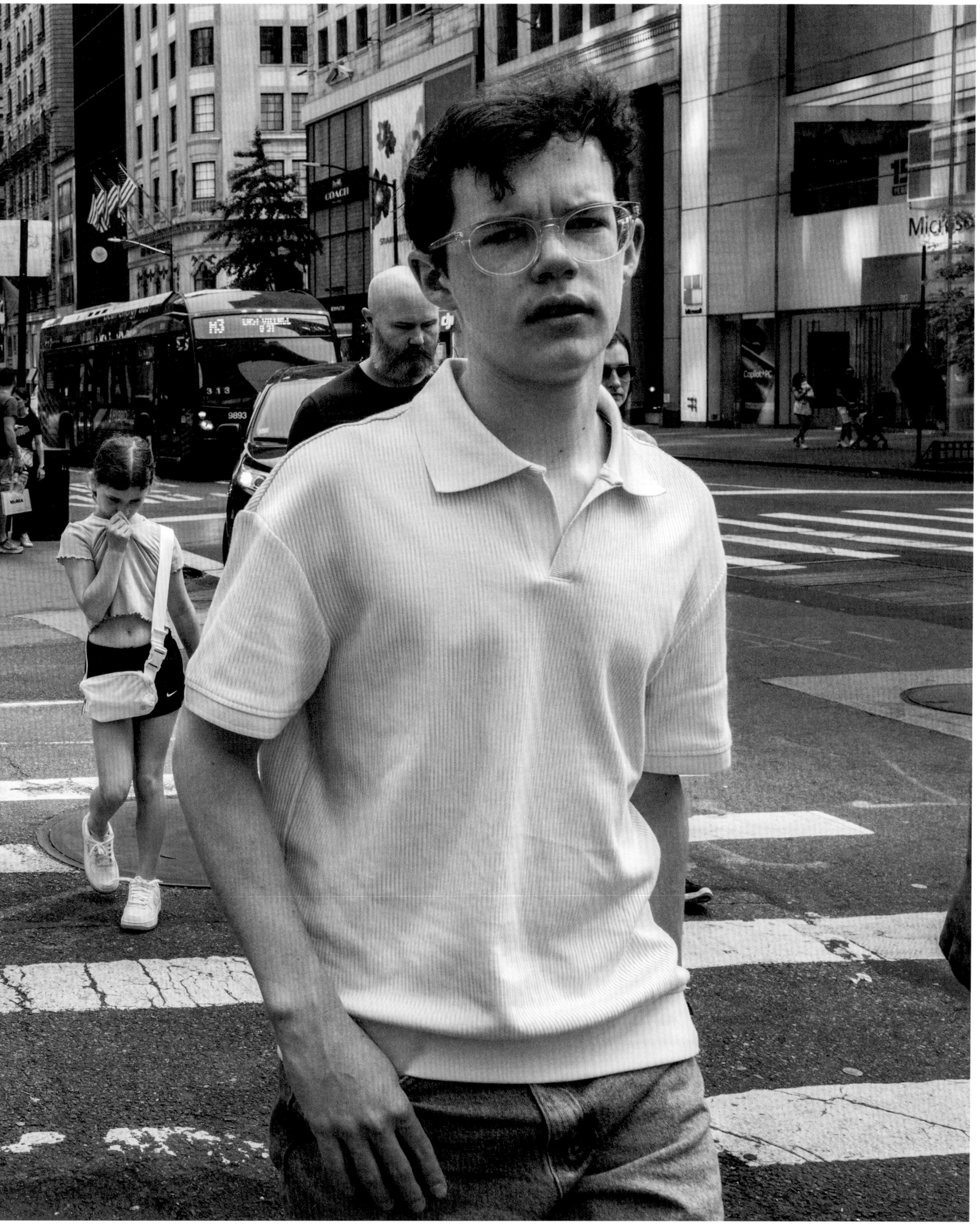
COACH
M3
313
9893

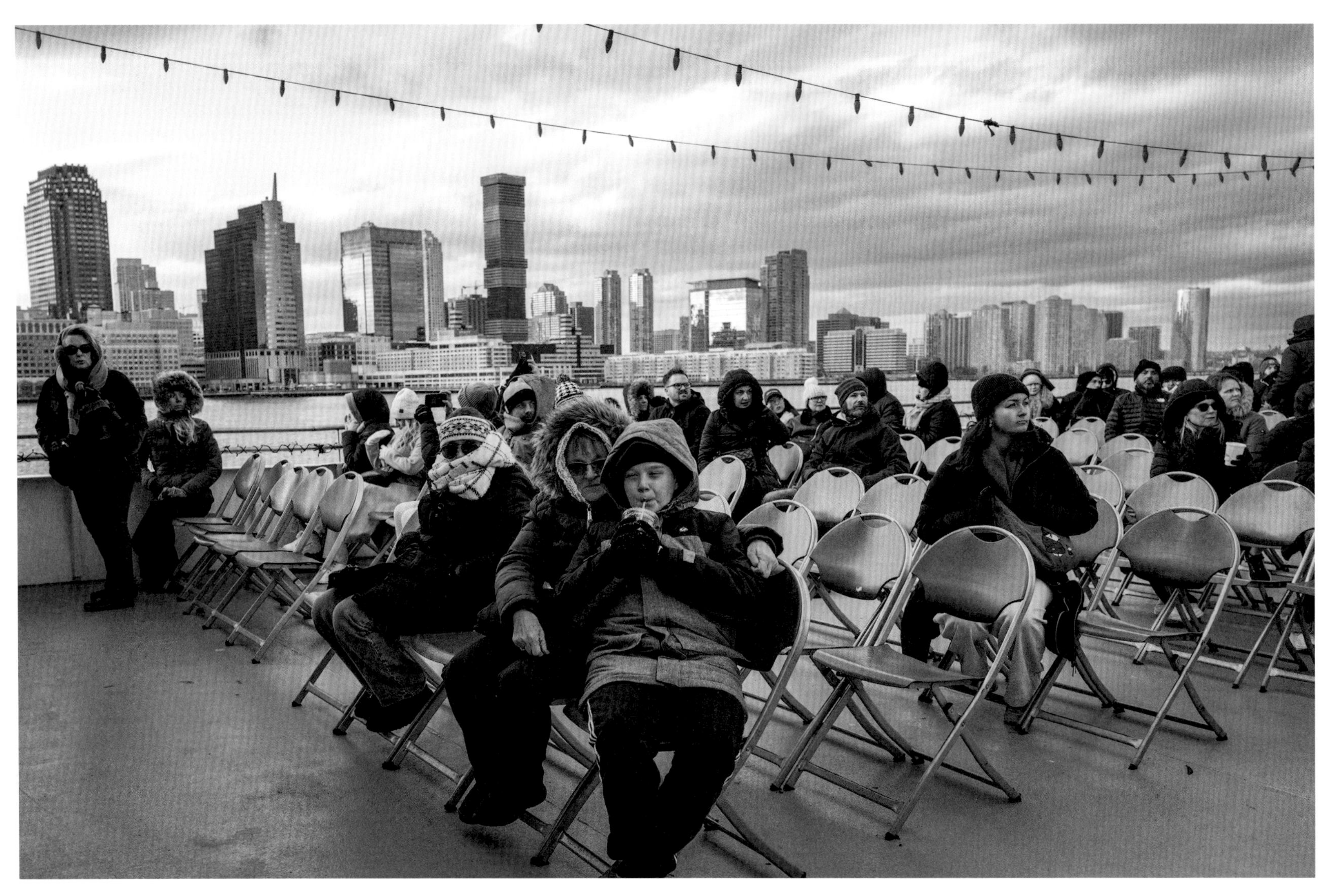

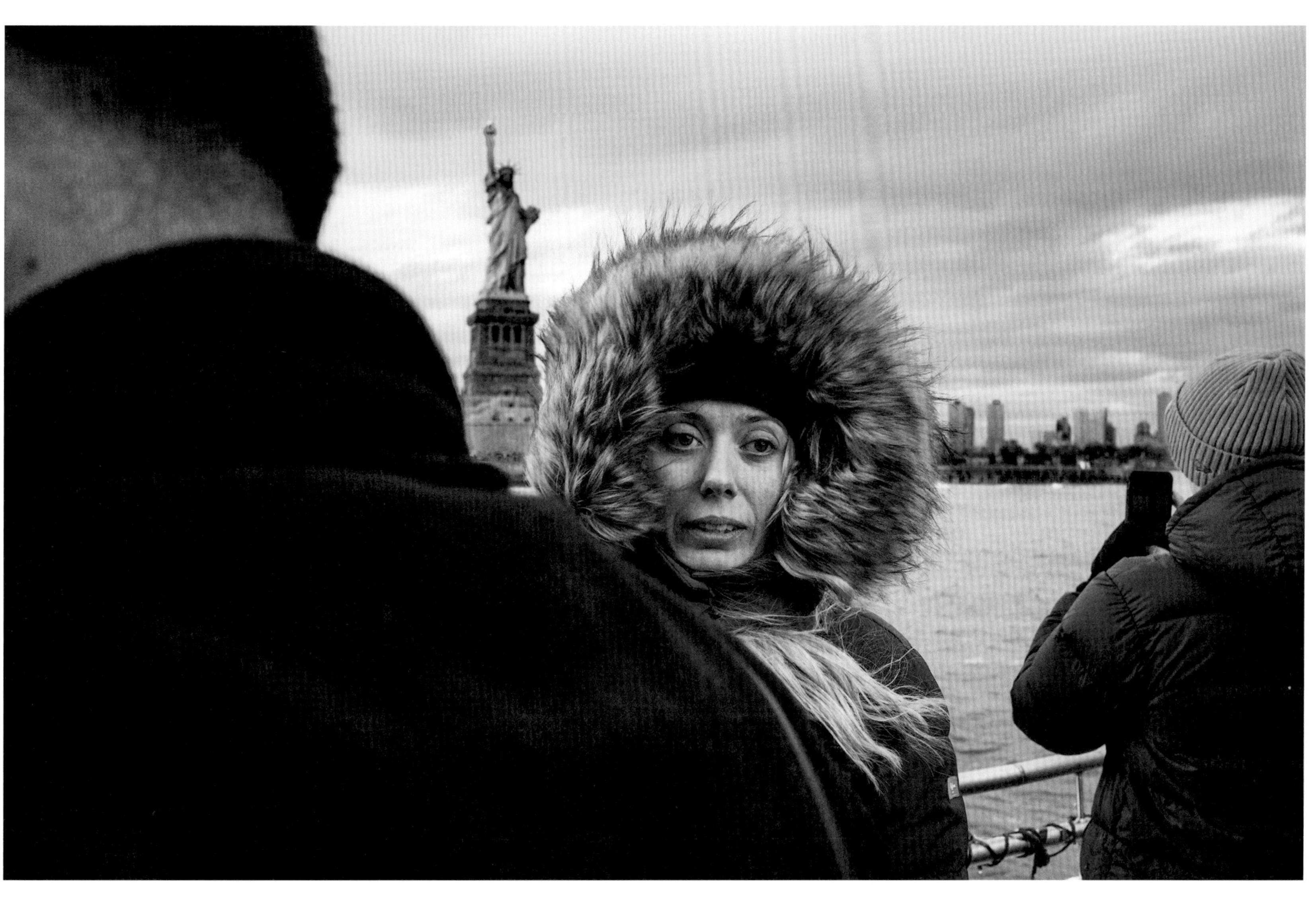

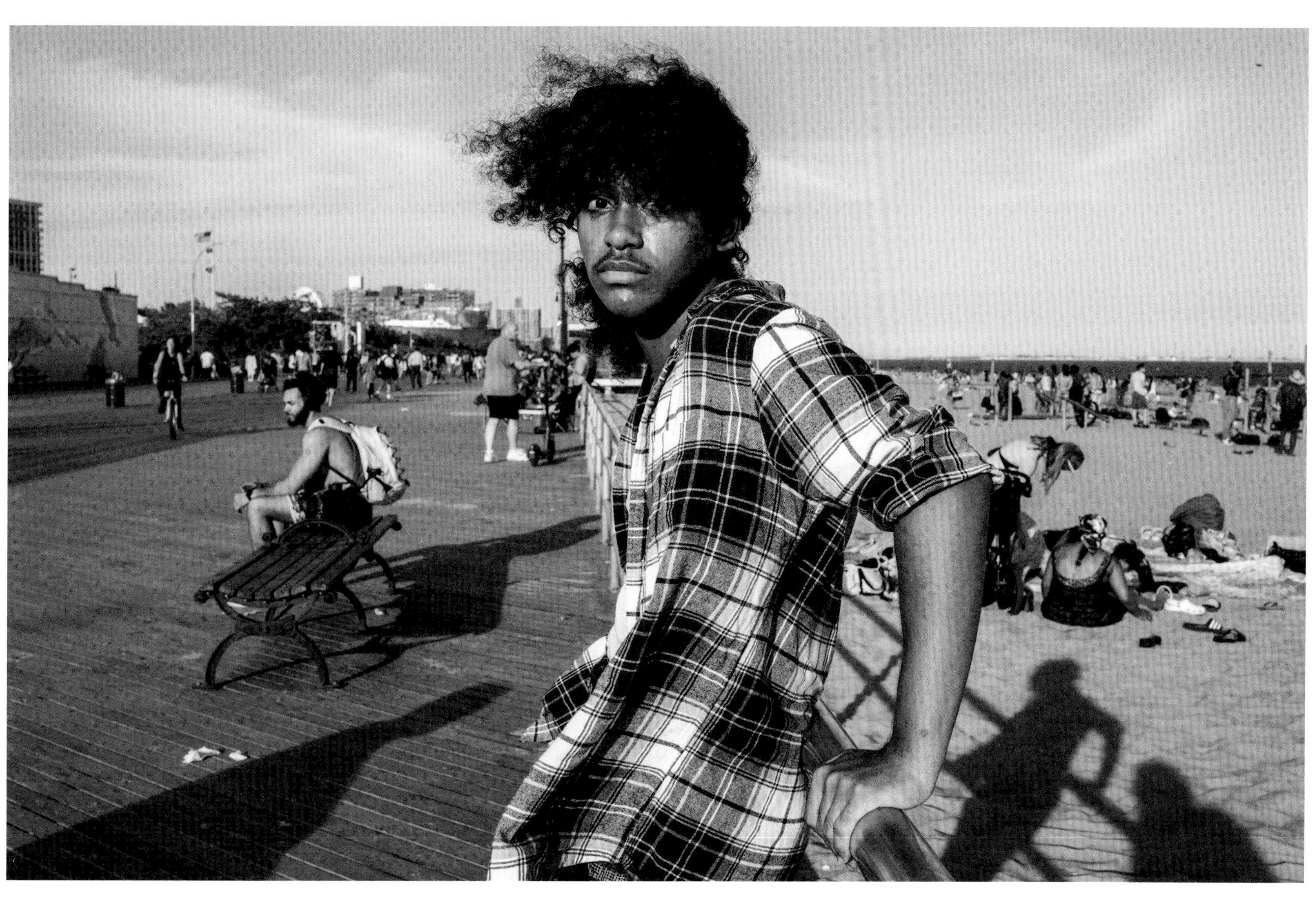

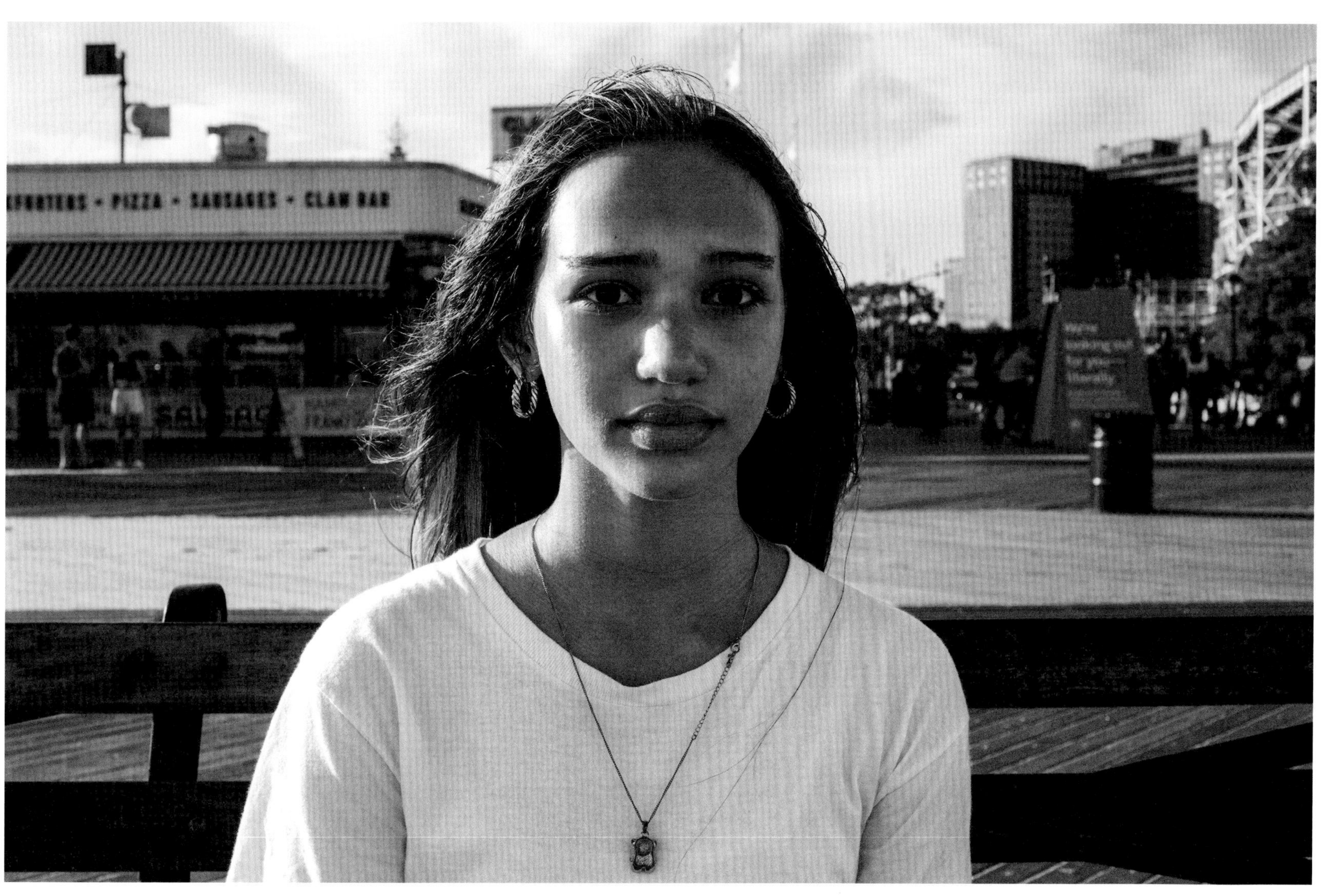
PIZZA • SAUSAGES • CLAM BAR

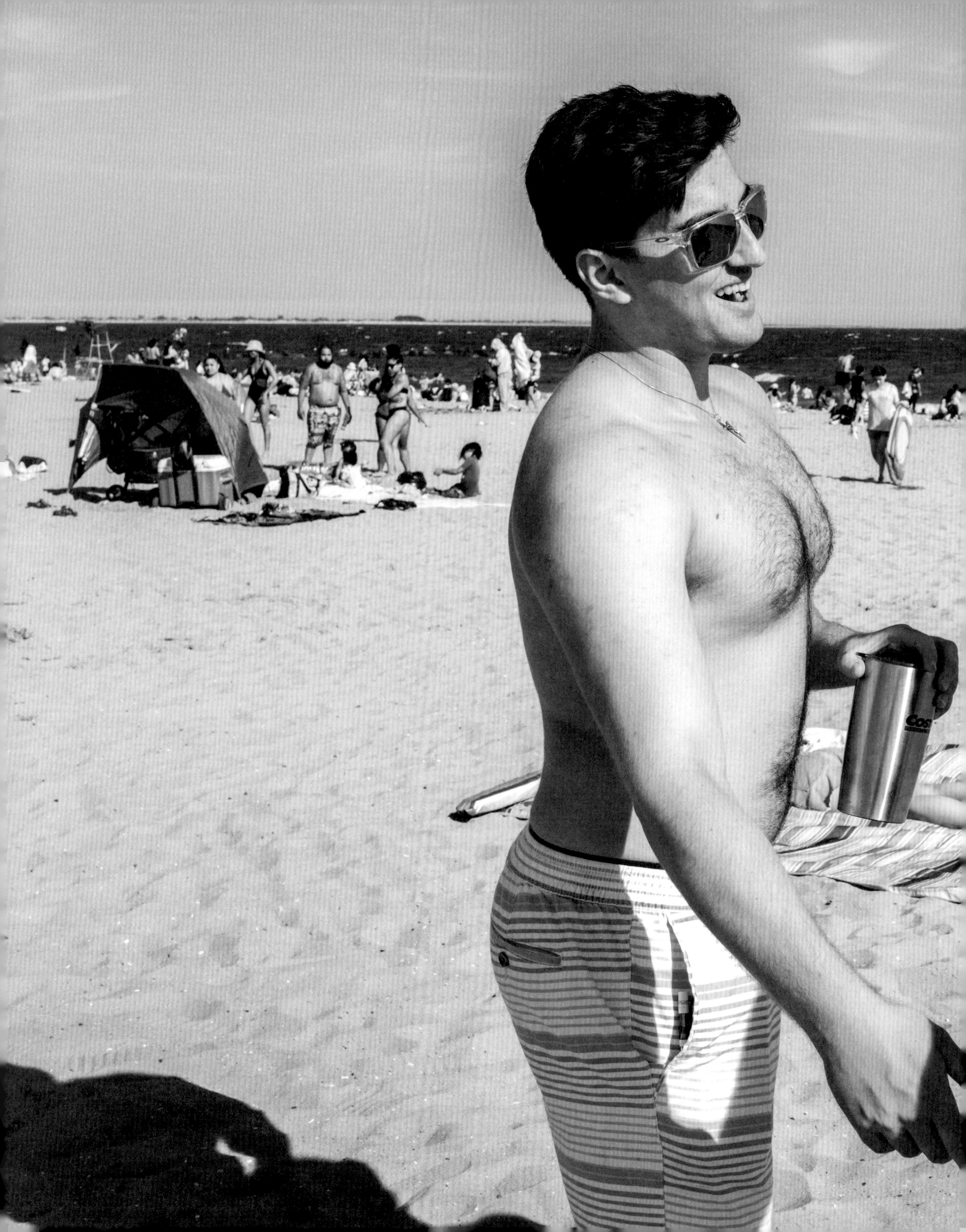

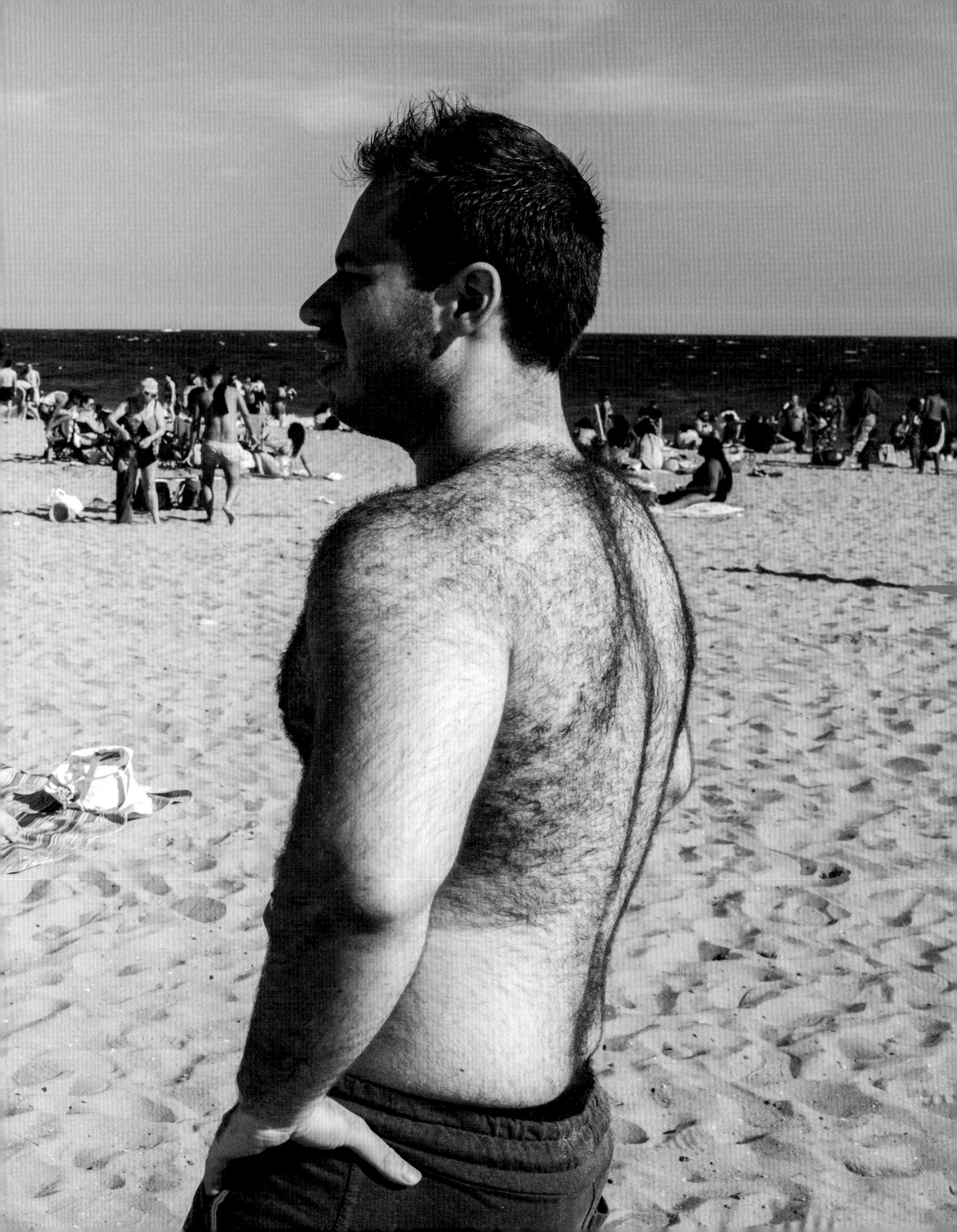

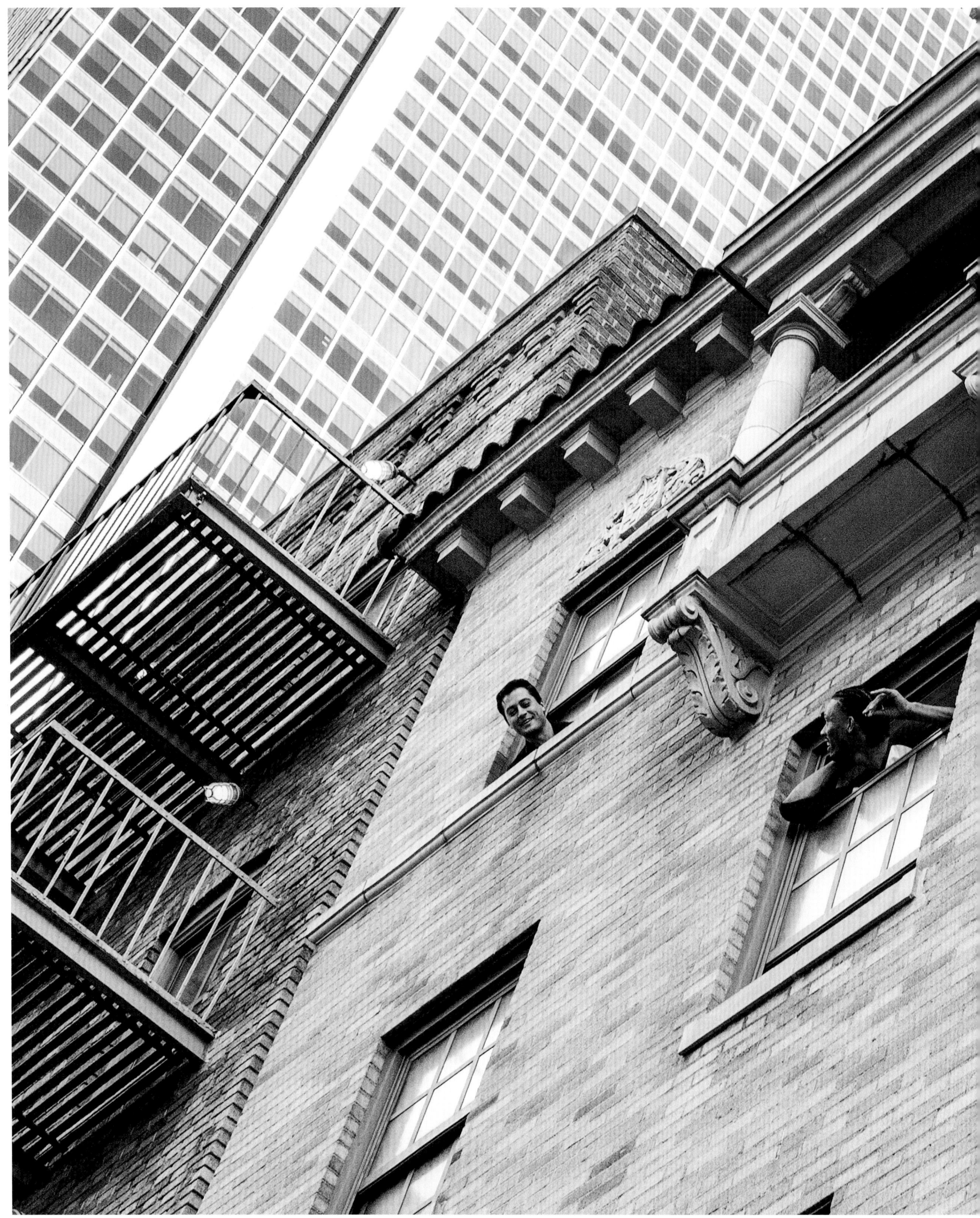

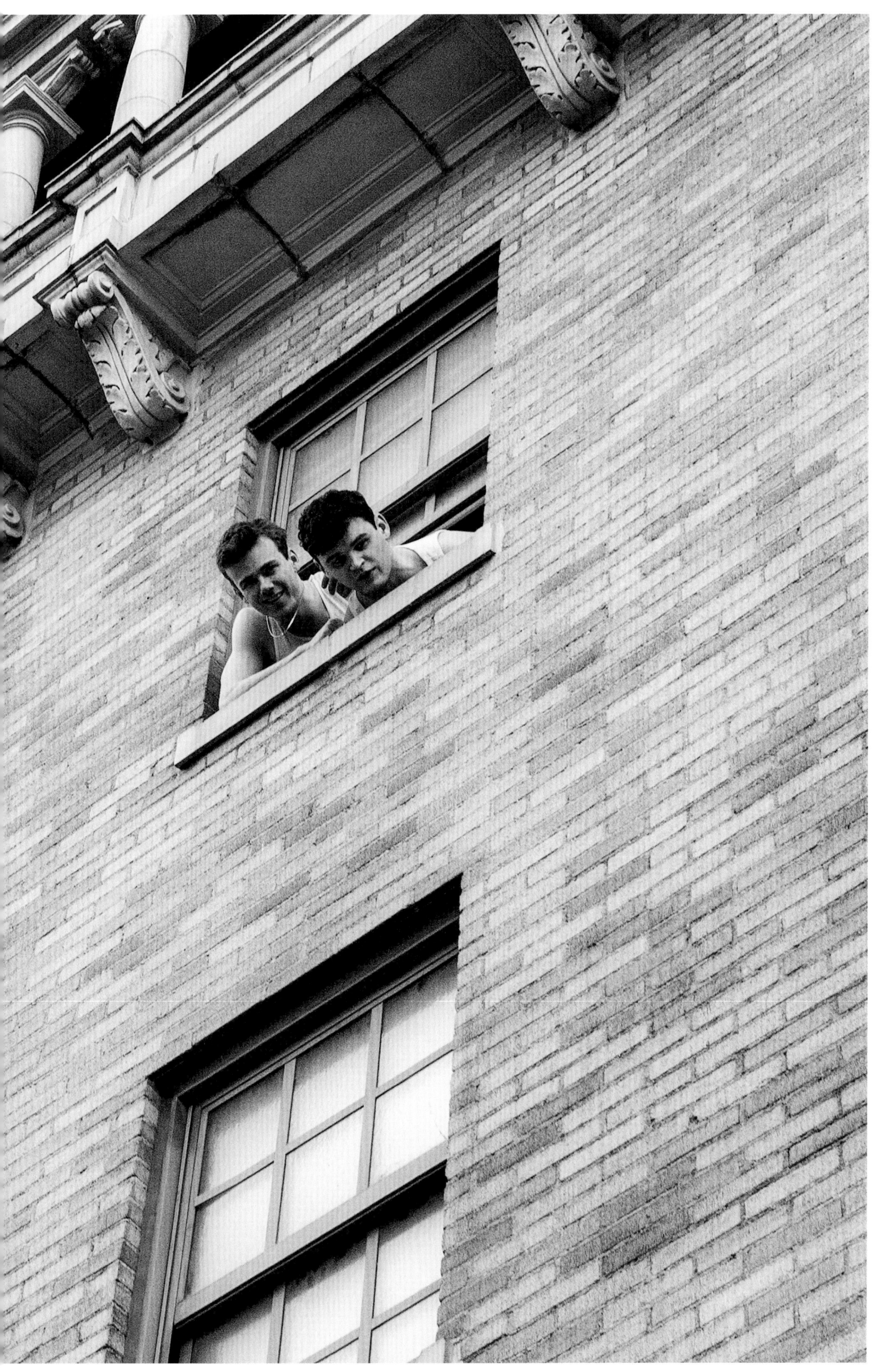

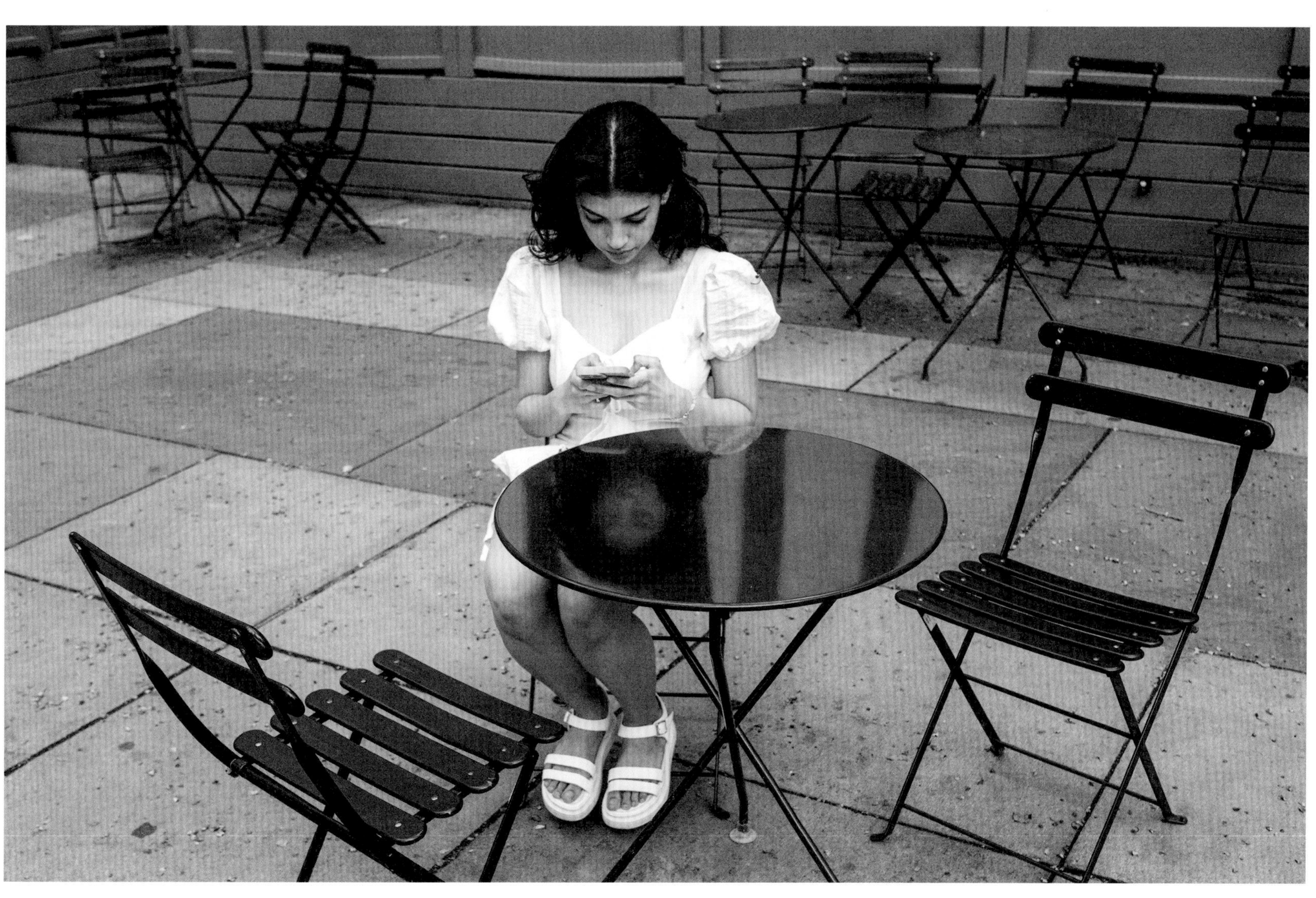

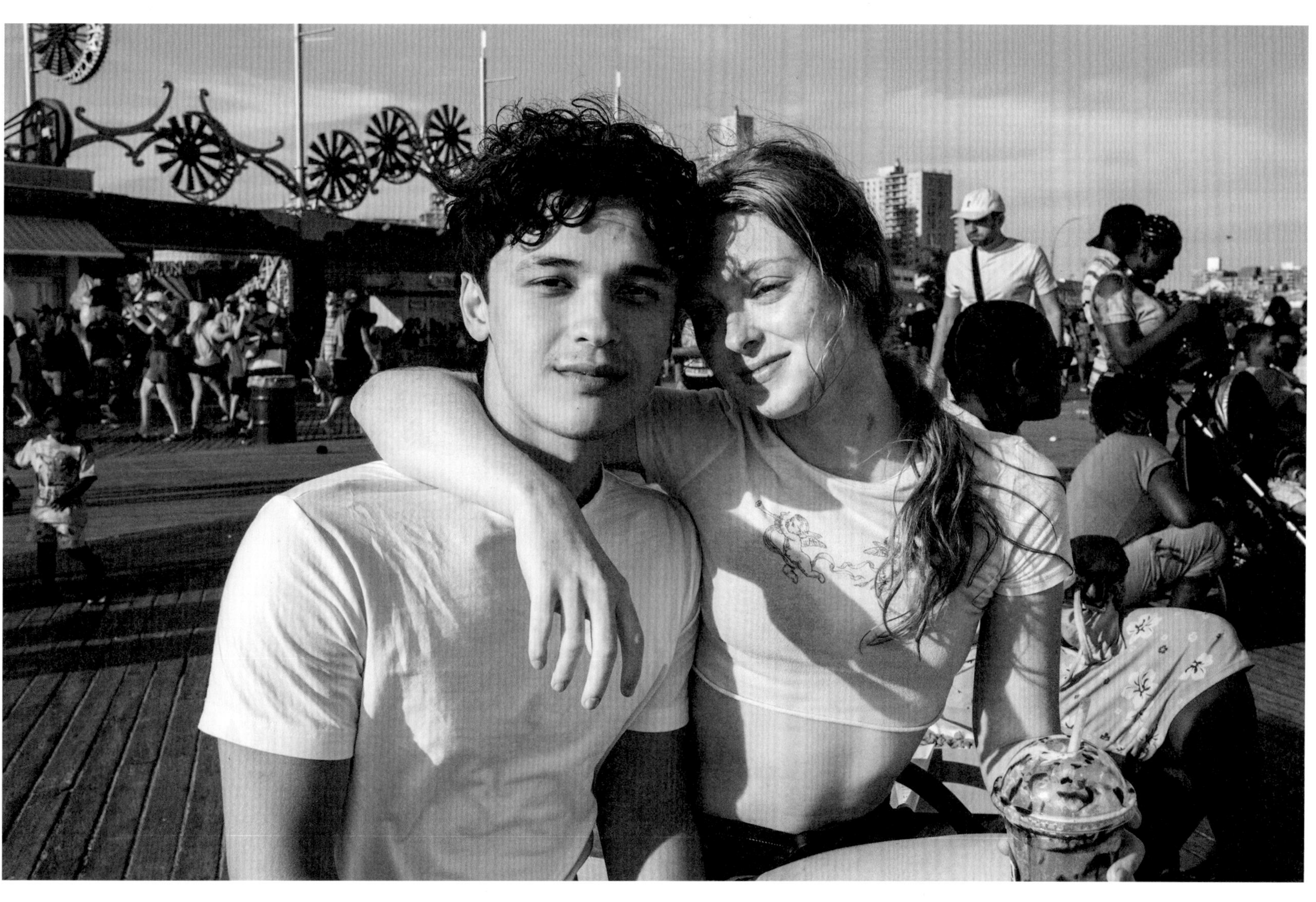

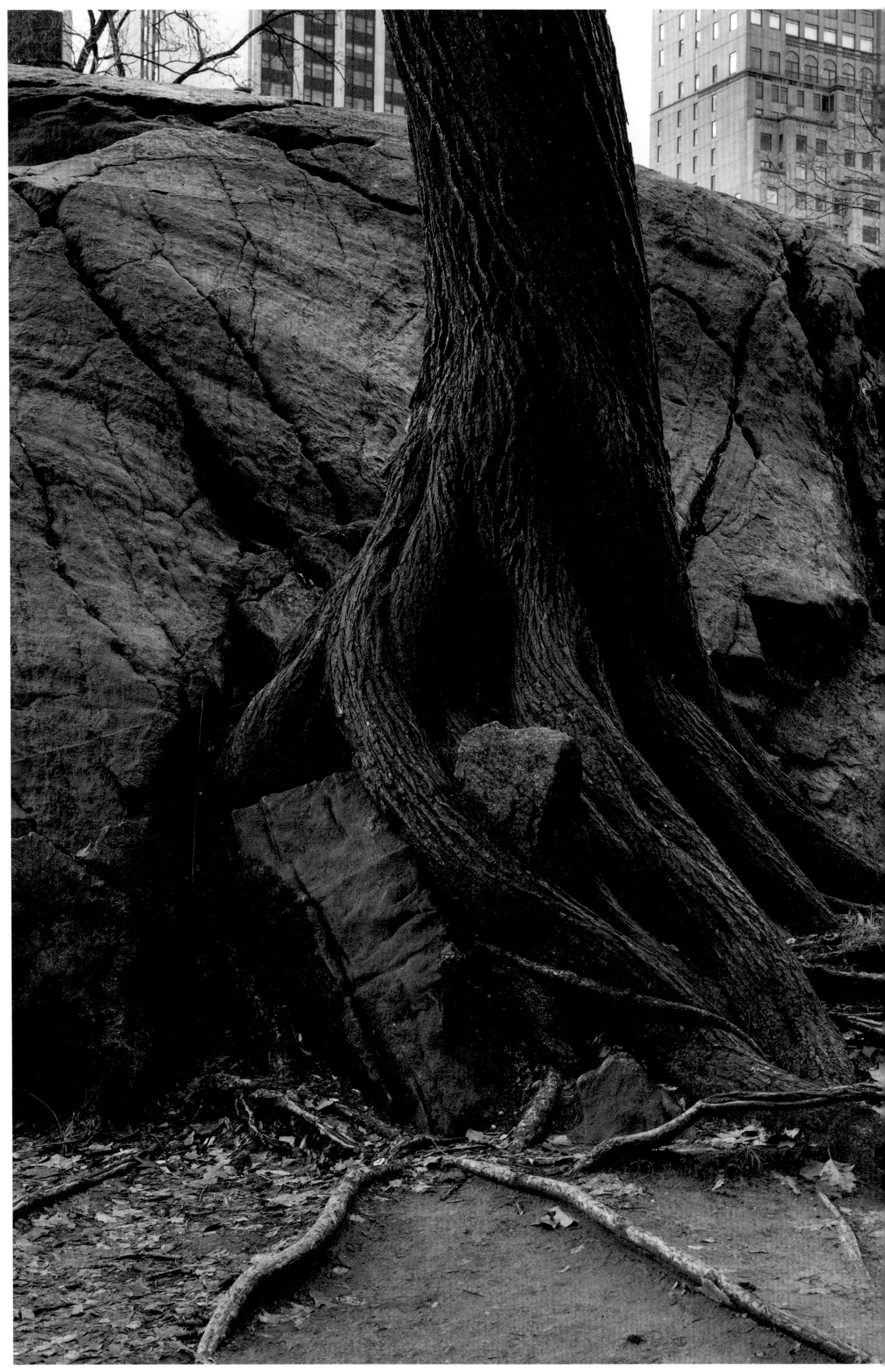

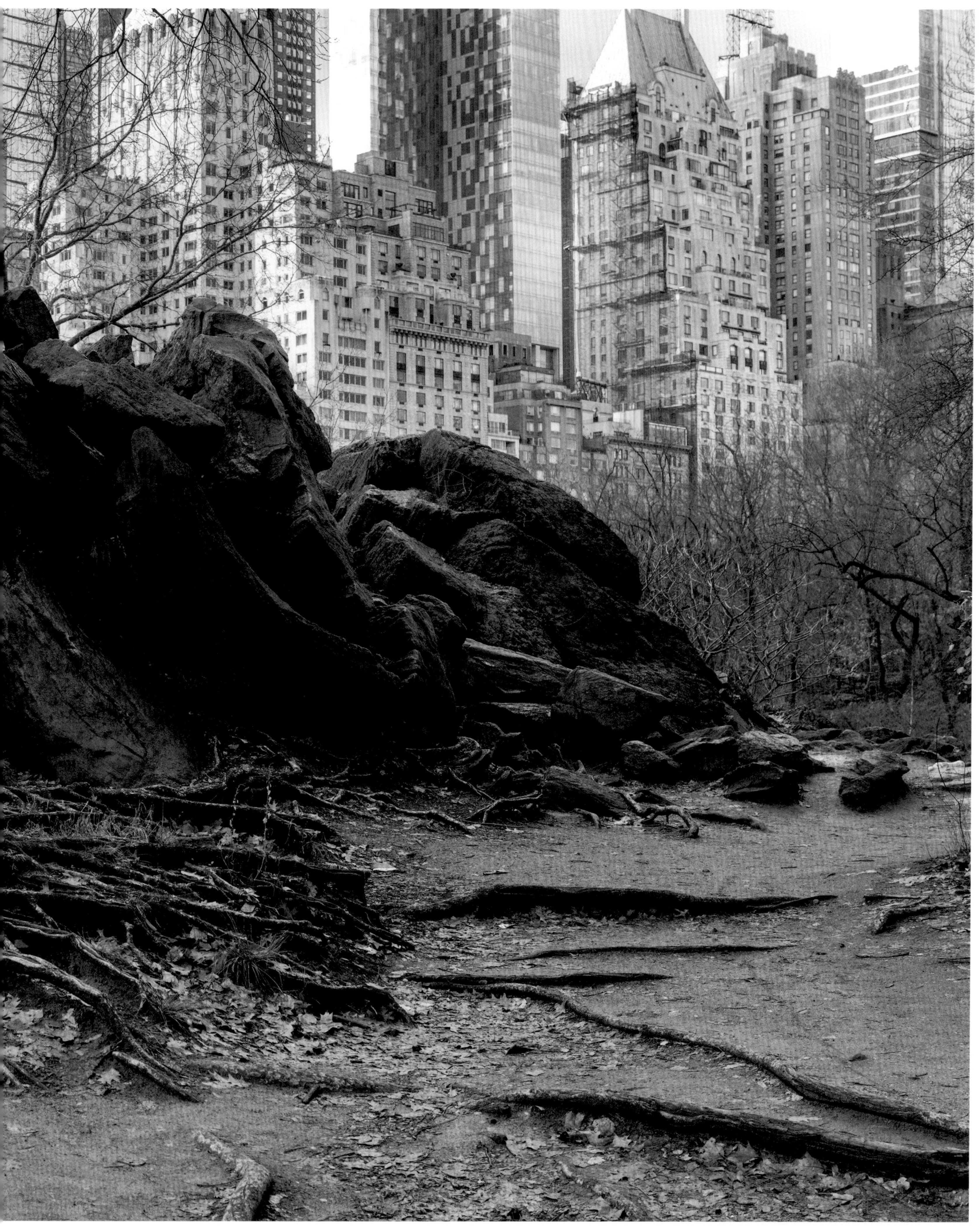

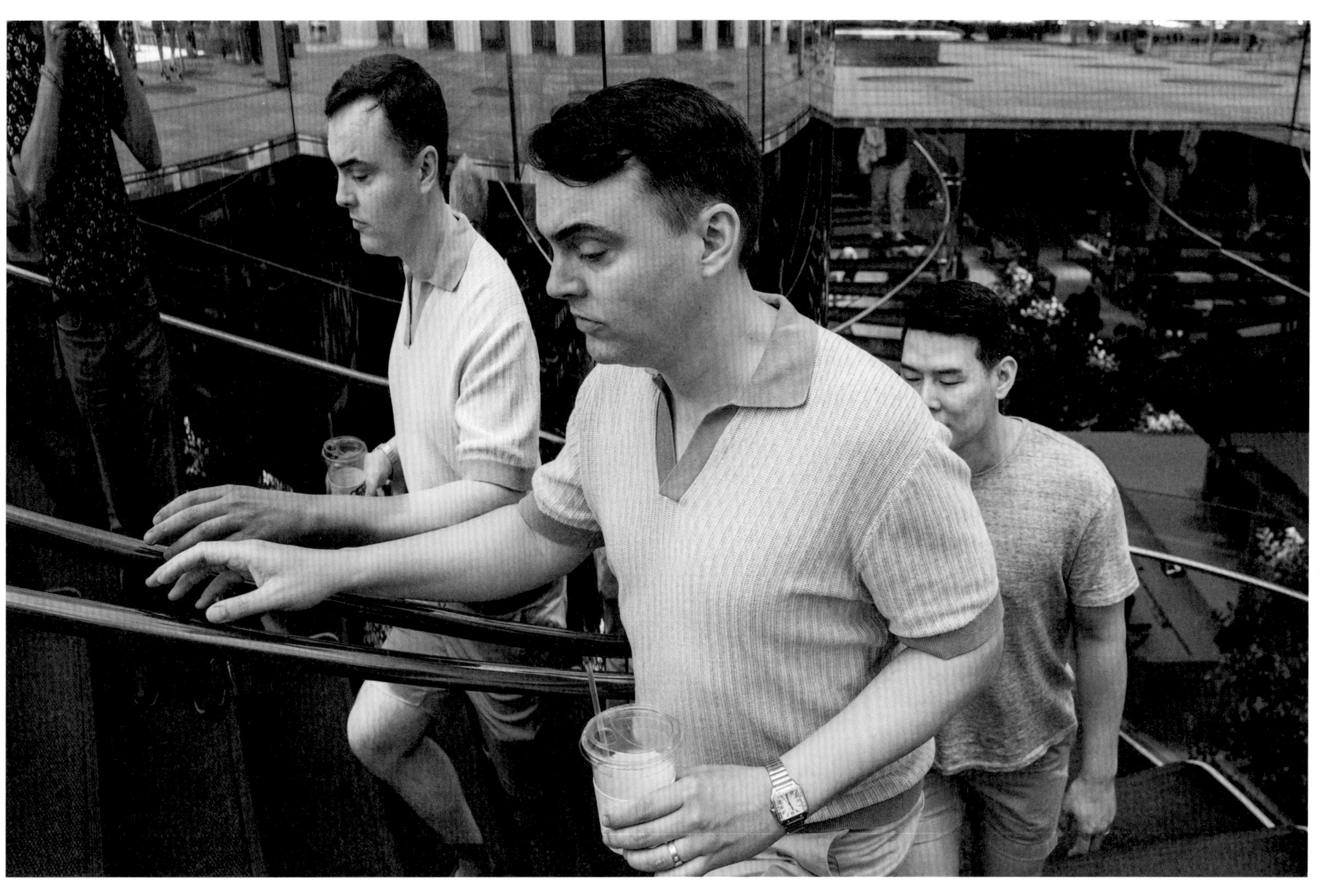

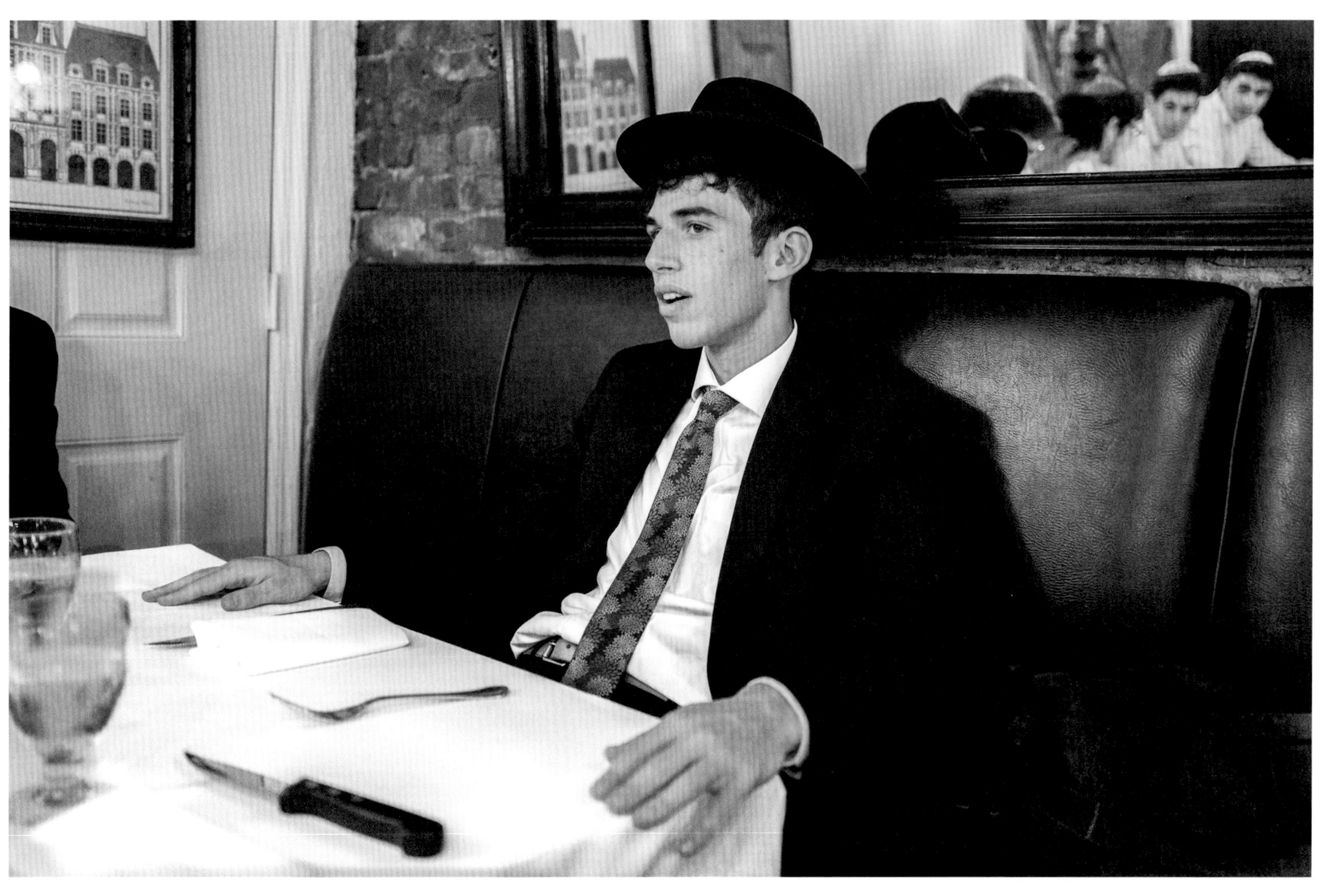

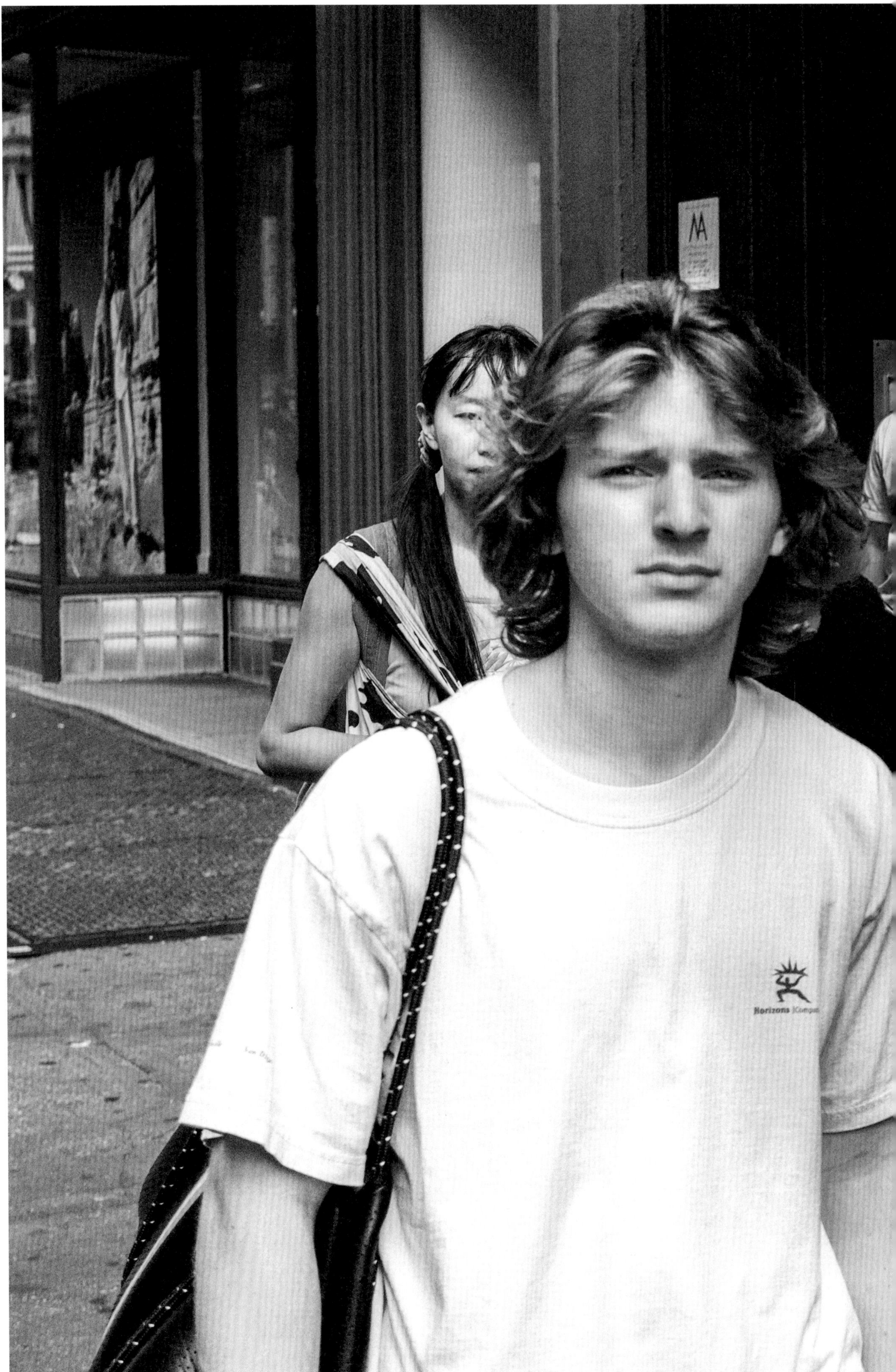
Horizons

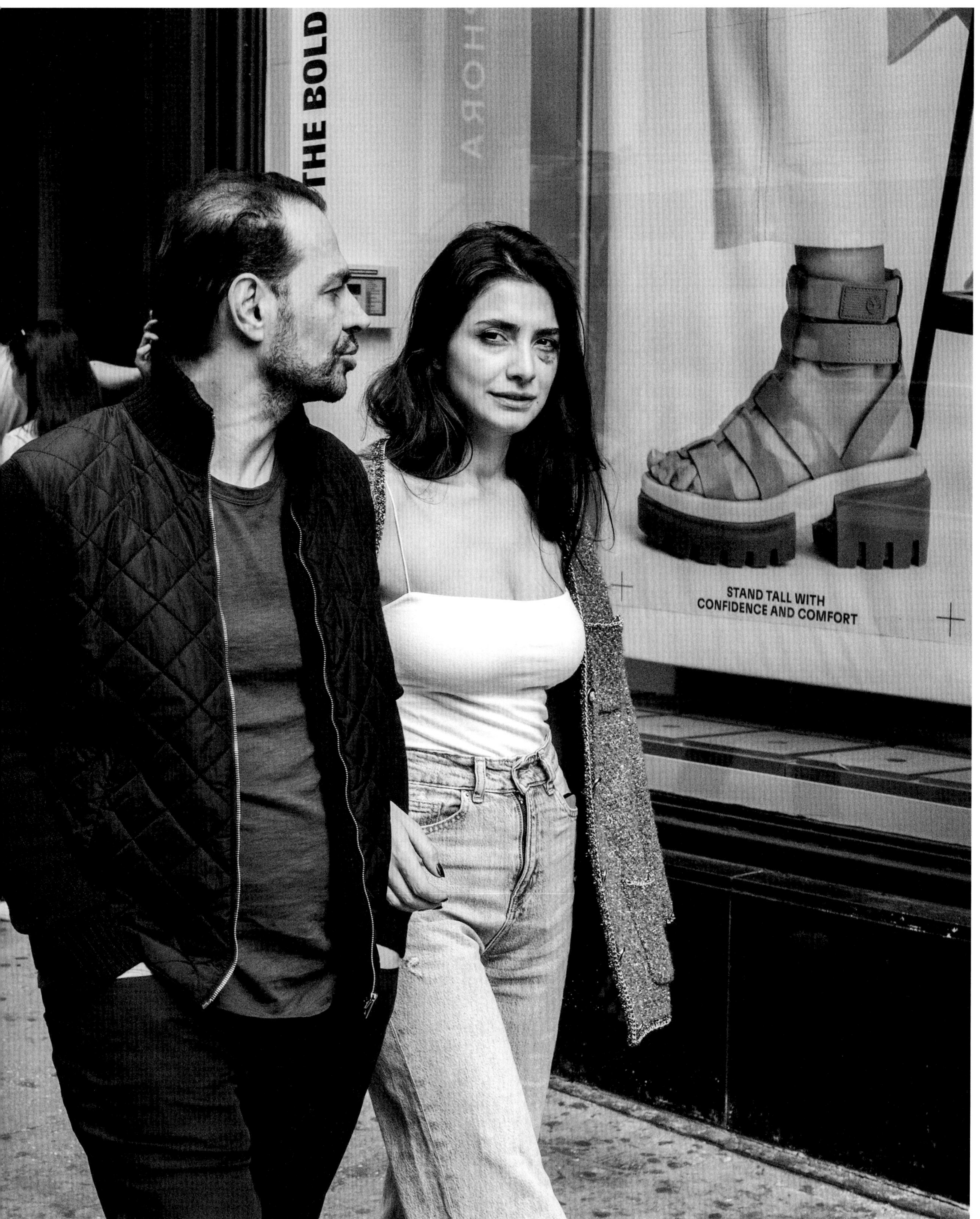
THE BOLD
STAND TALL WITH
CONFIDENCE AND COMFORT

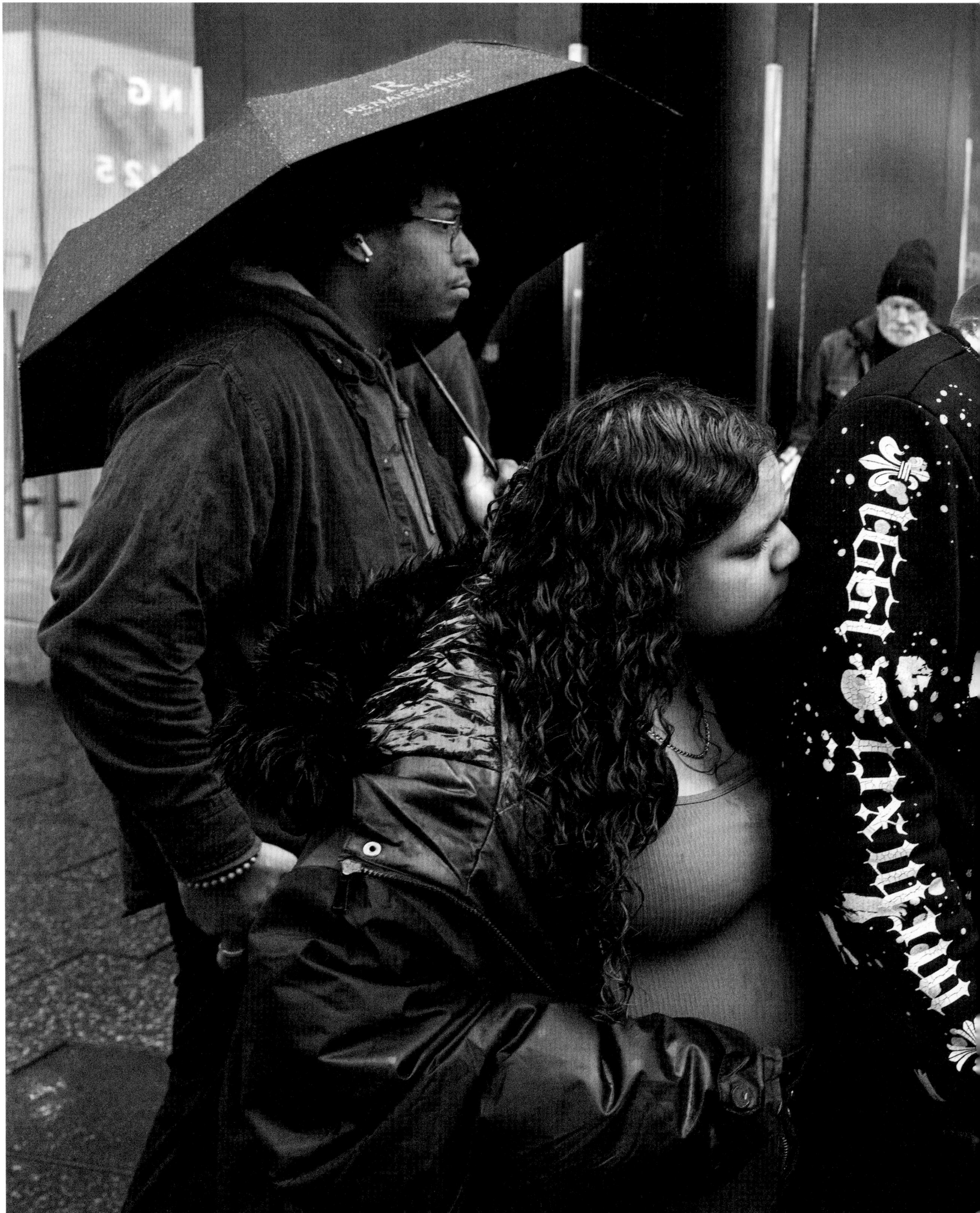
RENAISSANCE

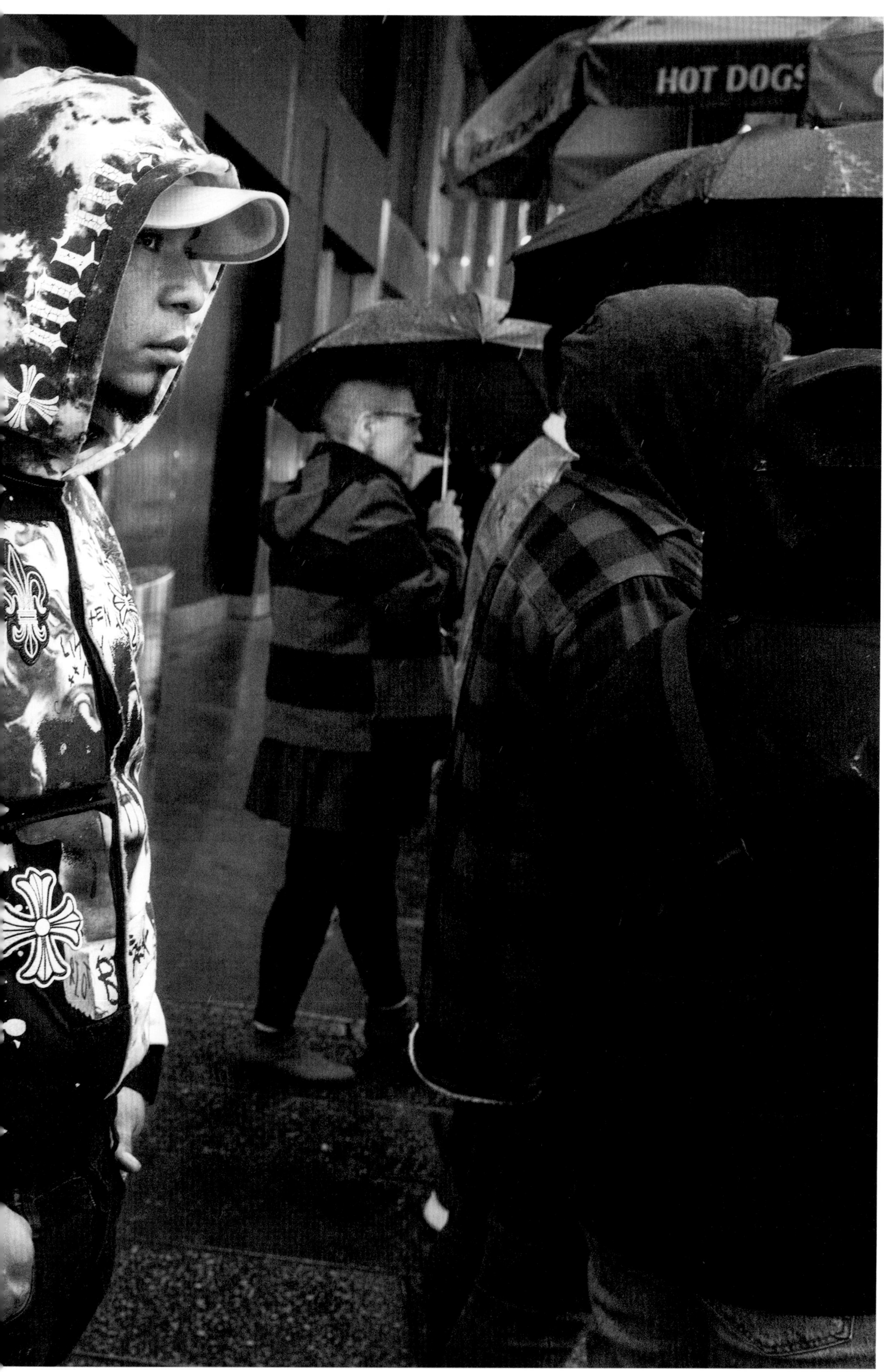
HOT DOGS

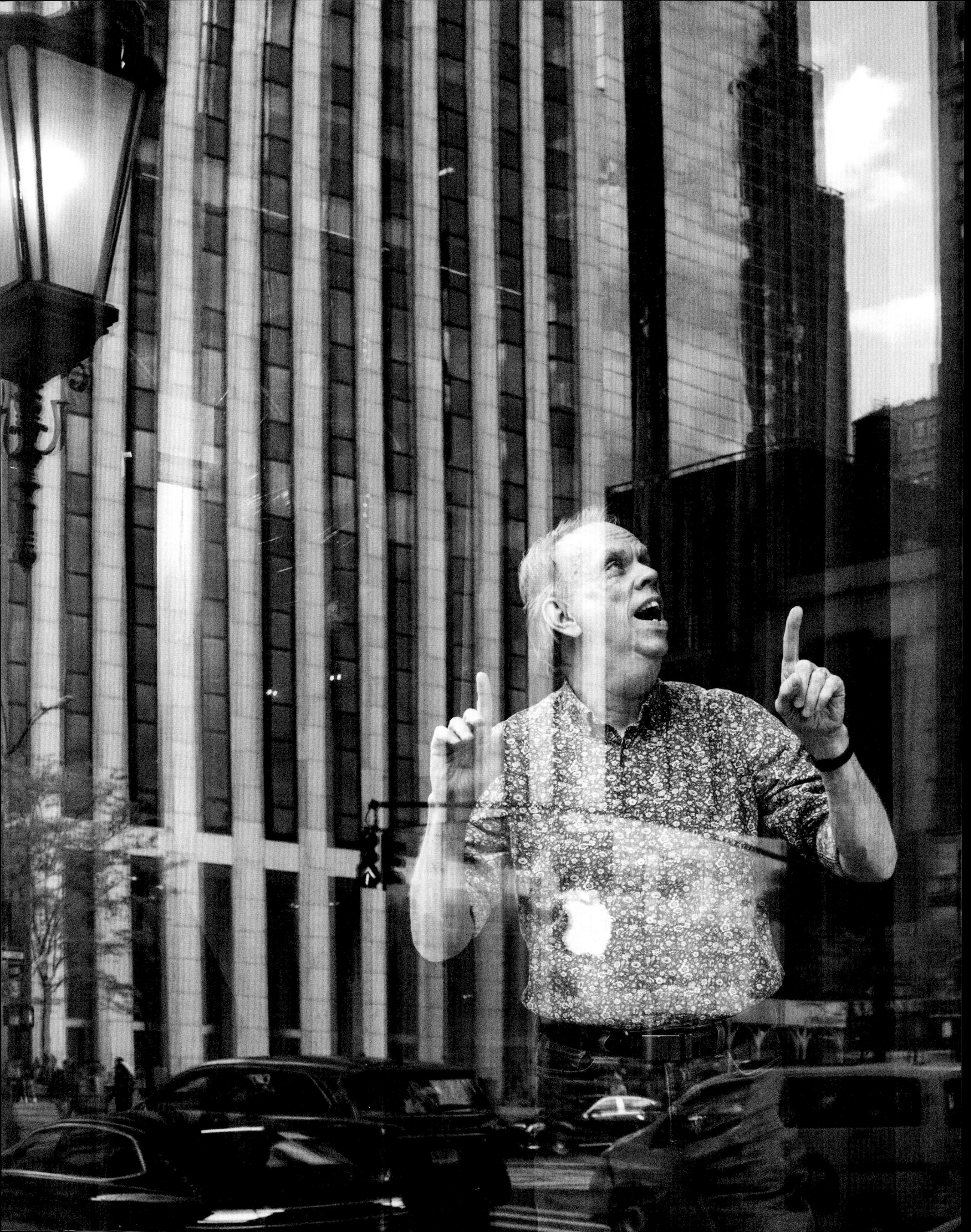

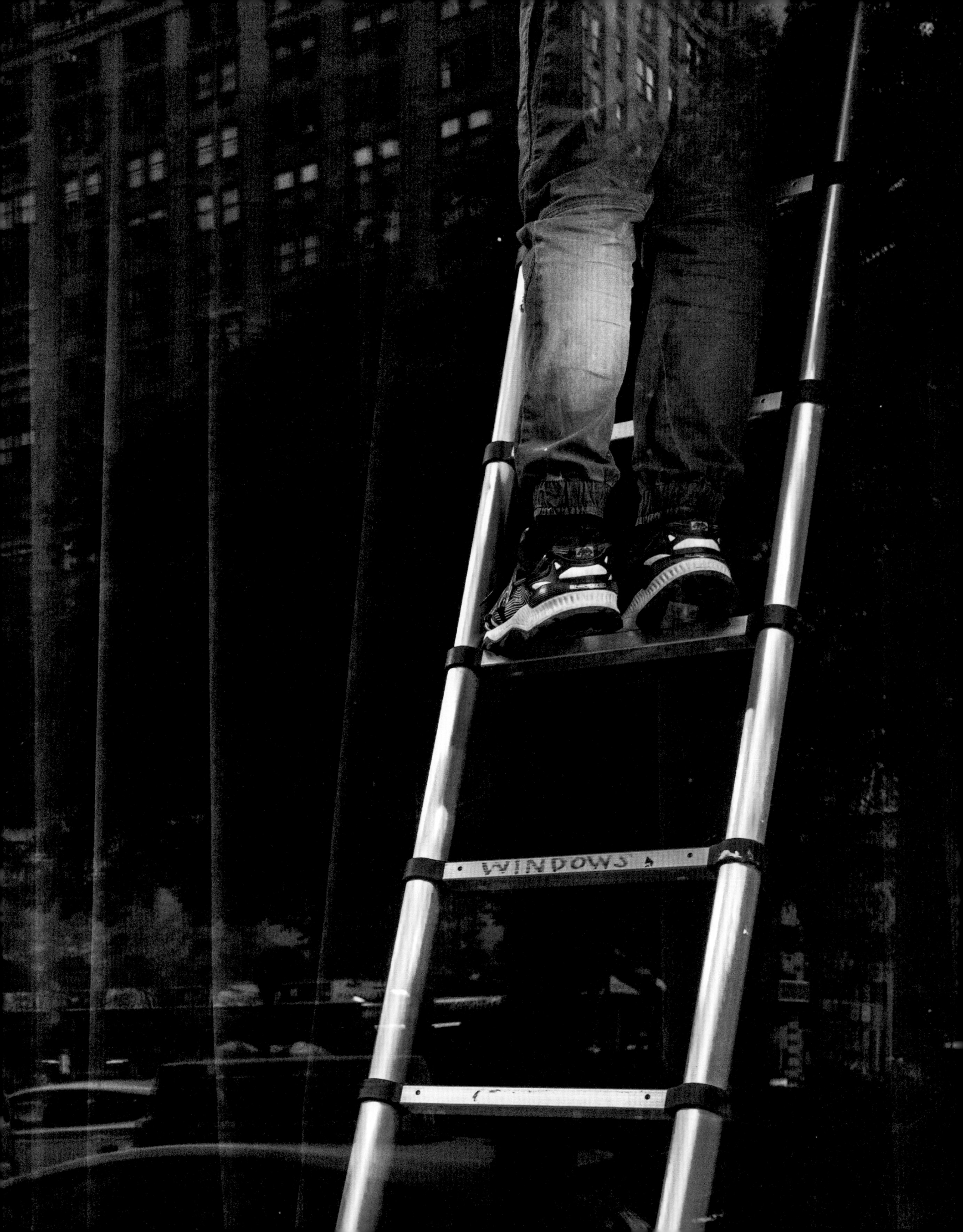
WINDOWS

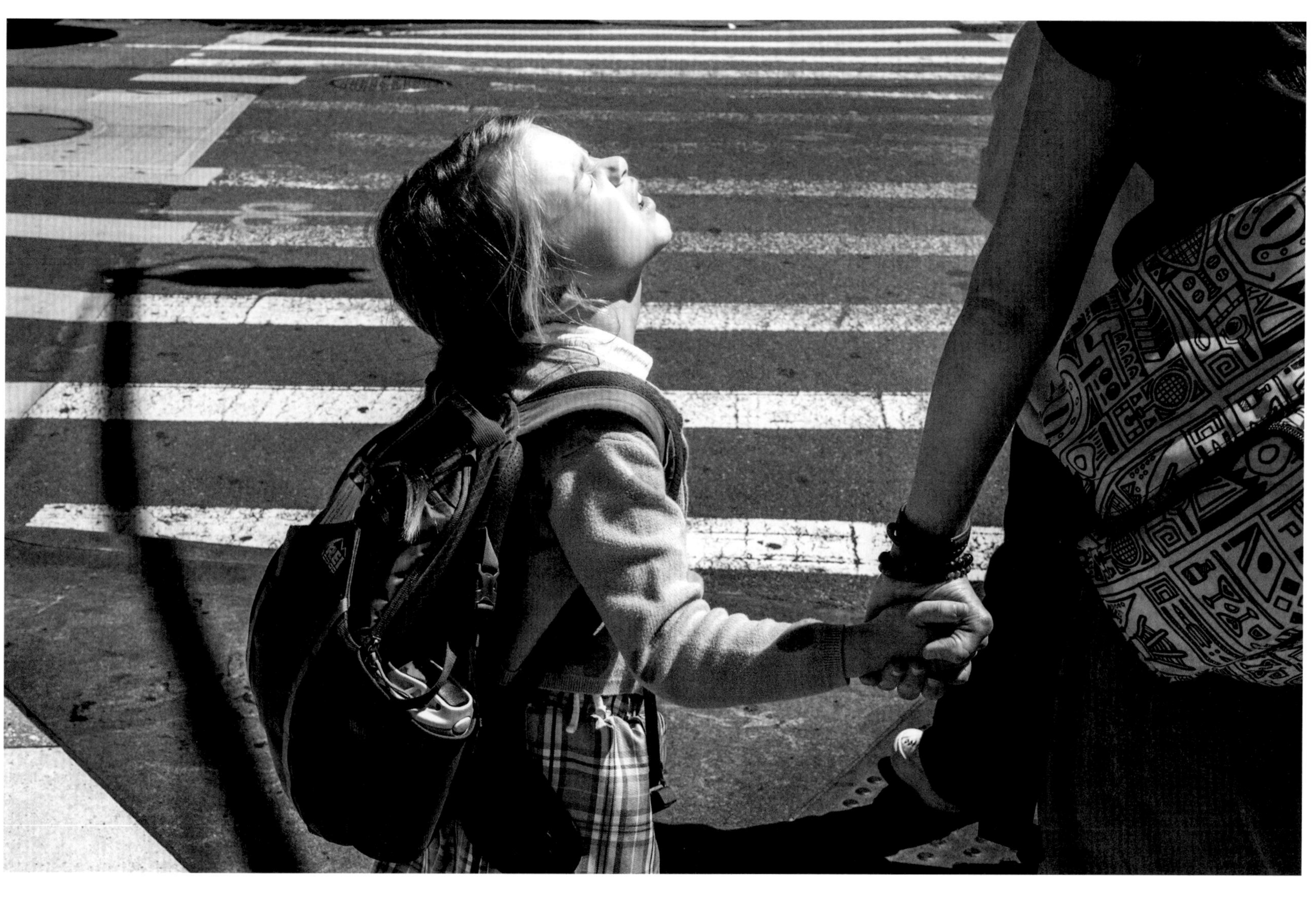

Von Helbra nach New York

Mario Schneider

Die Menschen auf der Straße sind ehrlich zu uns Fotografen, bis sie uns bemerken.

Als Straßenfotograf habe ich oft Situationen festgehalten, deren Protagonisten kurz darauf in einer U-Bahn oder im Gedränge der Stadt verschwunden sind. Kurze Begegnungen, die es mir unmöglich machten, mit ihnen wenigstens einen freundlichen Gruß auszutauschen, geschweige denn und schon gar nicht, mit ihnen ins Gespräch zu kommen. Und doch blieb ein Bild unserer Zusammenkunft zurück.

Die Scham, ungefragt in fremde Leben einzudringen, ohne ihnen etwas dafür zurückzugeben, kennt wohl jeder Straßenfotograf und kann nur durch eine einzige Sache gerechtfertigt werden: durch ein wahrhaftiges Foto. Und da die meisten Protagonisten dieses Buches ehrlich zu mir waren, möchte auch ich nun ehrlich sein und etwas über mich erzählen.

Die Herkunft eines Menschen ist bedeutend für sein ganzes Leben, wie die Schienen für einen Zug. Mit zwei Jahren trat ich eine Reise an, wie sie sonst nur mutige oder enttäuschte Erwachsene machen, alles hinter sich lassend, auf in eine neue Welt. Meine Mutter hatte sich von meinem Vater getrennt und saß nun mit mir im Zug, dessen Gleis aus der flachen Börde in ein Dorf tief im hügeligen Mansfelder Land führte. Dort wartete der Mann auf uns, den meine Mutter liebte.

Schon als Kind ist mir aufgefallen, dass der Name des Dorfes, in dem ich von nun an aufwachsen sollte, etwas Mystisch-Unheimliches an sich hatte. „Helbra“ oder „Hälwer“, wie die Einheimischen es aussprachen, erschien mir wie der Ruf unserer Vorfahren, die wohl gerade erst die Sprache kannten, ein Ruf an eine heidnische Gottheit, voller Selbstbewusstsein, Starrsinn und ohne Furcht. Es soll wohl „Halbe Strecke“ heißen, auch wenn in der Gegend dort jeder etwas anderes behauptet. Aber sollte es wirklich die berühmte „Halbe Strecke“ sein, die einem wie eine Verheißung vorkommen kann, so scheint mir meine kurze Zeit der

From Helbra to New York

Mario Schneider

The people on the street are honest with us photographers, until they notice us.

As a street photographer, I have often captured situations in which the protagonists disappeared into a subway or in a city crowd shortly afterwards; brief encounters that made it impossible for me to at least exchange a friendly greeting with them, let alone enter into a conversation. And yet, an image of our encounter remains.

The shame of intruding into a stranger's life without giving them something back is something familiar to every street photographer, and it can only be justified by one thing: a truthful photo. Because most of the protagonists of this book were honest with me, I also now want to be honest and share something about myself.

The origin of a person is of significance for their entire life, like the rails are for a train. At the age of two, I commenced on a journey that otherwise only courageous or disappointed adults undertake, leaving everything behind me to set off for a new world. My mother had separated from my father and now sat with me in the train, the track of which led from the flat north German plain to a village deep in the hilly Mansfeld Land of southwestern Saxony-Anhalt. There the man my mother loved was waiting for us.

Already as a child I noticed that the name of the village I would grow up in from that point on had something mystically uncanny about it. "Helbra," or "Hälwer" as the locals pronounced it, seemed to me like the call of our ancestors, who had only just learned of language, a call to a heathen divinity, full of self-confidence and stubbornness and without fear. It was said to mean "Halbe Strecke" (halfway), although everyone there in the area claimed something else. However, was it really the famous "halfway"? (Which can seem like a promise.) My brief period of childhood and youth in Helbra today seems like half my life, a

Kindheit und Jugend in Helbra heute wie die Hälfte meines Lebens, eine Hälfte, die niemals kleiner wurde und immer die Tendenz hatte, sich auszudehnen und an Bedeutung zu gewinnen.

Der Teil des Dorfes, in dem ich nun leben sollte, wurde von den Bewohnern „Totendorf" genannt. Niemand konnte mir sagen, warum. Später legte ich mir einige Deutungen zurecht, was nicht schwer war, denn unser Totendorf duckte sich weg vor der Welt, versteckte sich in einer Senke nördlich von Helbra, abseits von Kirche und Gemeindehaus im Schatten eines Berges. Es war still dort, erstaunlich still, denn auf der anderen Seite des Dorfes donnerte und kreischte Tag und Nacht die alte Kupferhütte, in der ich viele Jahre später einmal arbeiten sollte. Es gab bei uns im Totendorf keinen Punkt, von dem aus wir die Hütte hätten sehen können. Nicht einmal ihren über hundert Meter hohen Schornstein, den „langen Heinrich", sahen wir. Nur alle zwei, drei Wochen hörte ich die dumpfen Schläge der Detonationen, mit denen sie dort, wie man mir erzählte, riesige gefrorene Eisenblöcke wegsprengten. Wir lebten in Frieden hier in unserem Totendorf.

Unser gedrungenes Haus aus der Zeit der Bauernkriege war aus Lehm, Stroh und kleinen Schlackebrocken, den geschmolzenen Überresten der Kupferhütte, gebaut. Die meterdicken Wände, außen aufgeplatzt, die graue Farbe abwerfend, machten das Innere des Hauses klein und gemütlich, auch wenn es schwierig war, an ihnen Bilder aufzuhängen oder einen Schrank davor aufzustellen, denn der Lehm warf große Blasen und der Putz wurde stellenweise nur durch die Tapete gehalten.

Wir waren acht in dem winzigen Haus, meine neuen Großeltern, meine Mutter, mein Stiefvater, eine Tante Friede, eine verrückte Alte, die über dem Schweinestall wohnte, ich und bald auch mein Bruder. Es müssen Fremde für mich gewesen sein, denn ich wurde unter sie gemischt, von einem Tag auf den anderen.

Im vergilbten Wohnzimmer rauchte mein neuer Großvater mit seiner verbliebenen halben Lunge sechzig Salem ohne Filter am Tag. Links von ihm die drei

half that never grows smaller and always has the tendency to expand and increase in importance.

The part of the village I was now to live in was called "Totendorf" (the village of the dead) by the inhabitants. No one could tell me why. Later, I worked out a few interpretations, which was not difficult, because our Totendorf cowered away from the world, concealed itself in a depression to the north of Helbra, apart from the church and the parish hall in the shadow of a mountain. It was quiet there, astonishingly quiet, considering that the old copper foundry I would work in many years later thundered and screamed day and night on the other side of the village. There was no place in Totendorf from which we could have seen the foundry. We could not even see its more than hundred-metre-tall smokestack, the "langer Heinrich" (Tall Henry). I only heard the dull blows of the detonations every two or three weeks, with which they, as I was told, blew away gigantic, frozen blocks of iron. We lived in peace here in our Totendorf.

Our squat house from the era of the Peasants' Wars was built of clay, straw, and small chunks of slag, the melted residue of the copper foundry. The metre-thick walls, burst open outside, casting off grey paint, made the inside of the house small and cosy, although it was difficult to hang pictures from the walls or set up a cabinet in front of them, because the clay produced big bubbles, and the plaster was in some places only held in place by the wallpaper.

There were eight of us in this tiny house, my new grandparents, my mother, my stepfather, an Aunt Friede, a crazy old woman who lived above the pigsty, myself, and soon also my brother. They must have been strangers to me because I was mixed in with them from one day to the next.

In the yellowed living room, my new grandfather smoked sixty unfiltered Salems a day with his remaining half a lung. To the left of him, the three packs of cigarettes on the table, like a stack of wood that had to be chopped, to the right the small schnapps glass—in his final years I only still saw him sitting, smoking and drinking, the cigarette stub clamped between his thumb and the remains of his index finger.

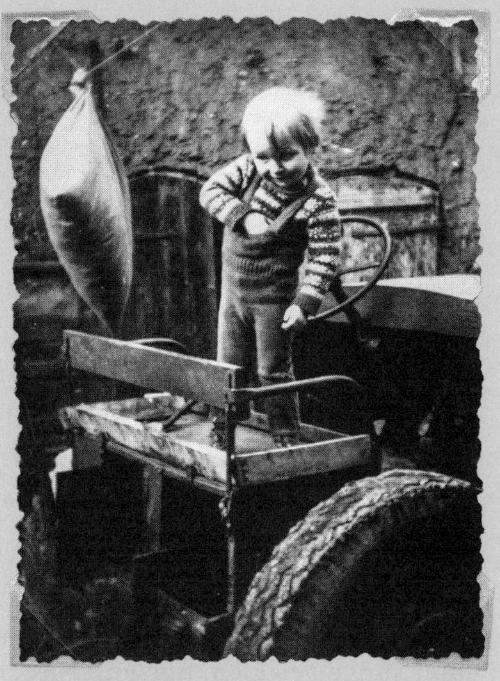

Zigarettenschachteln auf dem Tisch, wie ein Stapel Holz, der gehackt werden musste, rechts das kleine Schnapsglas – in seinen letzten Jahren sah ich ihn nur noch sitzend, rauchend und trinkend, den Zigarettenstummel zwischen Daumen und den Rest seines Zeigefingers geklemmt. Er hatte sich eines Winters beim Holzmachen vier Finger seiner Hand abgesägt und erzählte mir stolz, dass die Hühner kamen und an ihnen herumpickten.

Meine neue Großmutter, in Kittelschürze in der Küche Borschtsch und Pelmeni kochend und an ihren Versuchen verzweifelnd, die Wohnzimmergardinen wieder rein und weiß zu waschen, blieb mir lange fremd, bevor ich sie aus einer scheuen Distanz heraus lieben lernte. Ihr Mittagschlaf auf dem kleinen Kanapee in der Küche war für mich wie eine stete Gewissheit, dass alles um sie herum in Ordnung gebracht war und sich selbst überlassen werden konnte.

Tante Friede hatte keinen Mann. Und einmal, als sie während einer Feier auf die schüchterne Frage eines Herrn in schroffem Ton, ohne ihn anzusehen, blaffte: „Ich tanze nicht!", wusste ich, dass sie immer bei uns bleiben würde – und das beruhigte mich. Sie fuhr mit einem großen Lastwagen die Post auf dem Land aus und ich durfte mit. Dann saß ich auf dem Motorblock im Inneren des „Ello" mit Blick auf die vor uns liegende Straße und sang ihr alle Lieder vor, die ich kannte. Wenn wir im Sommer Pause machten, kletterte ich auf das Dach des Postwagens und pflückte uns Kirschen. Als ich vier oder fünf Jahre alt war und zu groß, um noch bei meinen Eltern im Zimmer zu

He had sawed off four fingers of his hand one winter while cutting firewood and proudly told me that the hens came and picked away at them.

My new grandmother, making borscht and pelmeni in her house dress in the kitchen and despairing in her attempts to get the living room curtains clean and white again, remained strange to me for a long time, before I learned to love her from a shy distance. Her afternoon nap on the small couch in the kitchen was like a constant certainty for me that everything around her had been brought into order and could be left to itself.

Aunt Friede had no husband, and once, at a party, she responded in a sharp bark to the shy invitation of a man, without even looking at him: "I don't dance!" I then knew that she would always stay with us and felt relieved. She delivered the mail in the countryside with a big truck, and I was allowed to accompany her. Then I would sit on the engine block inside the "Ello" with a view of the road ahead of us and sing all the songs I knew to her. When we took a break in the summer, I climbed onto the roof of the mail truck and picked us cherries. When I was four or five years old, and too big to still sleep with my parents in their room, they made me a bed in the narrow and slanted attic room across from them and directly behind that of Aunt Friede. From that point on until I was ten, we were comrades in sleep.

It did not take long for me to start moving about quite naturally in the house. It is said that I was curious and somewhat reckless, as I was often found sitting

schlafen, stellten sie mir ein Bett in die gegenüberliegende, schmale und schräge Dachkammer, direkt hinter das von Tante Friede. Von da an bis zu meinem zehnten Lebensjahr waren wir Schlafgenossen.

Es dauerte nicht lange und ich bewegte mich ganz selbstverständlich im Haus. Man sagt, ich sei neugierig und etwas lebensmüde gewesen, denn man fand mich häufig auf dem Spitzdach sitzend oder über das Geländer der Bahnbrücke balancierend. Ich sei ein guter Junge gewesen, nur unterbrochen von kurzen Momenten, die ich schreiend und um mich tretend auf den Fußböden im Haus oder den Bürgersteigen im Ort verbrachte, ohne Aussicht auf Linderung meiner Wut und Verzweiflung. Niemand in meiner neuen Familie kannte das besänftigende Wasser, mit dem man diesen Brand hätte löschen können. Alle fragten sich, was um Gottes Willen der Junge nur hat.

Wir lebten in sehr einfachen Verhältnissen. Meine Mutter sah nicht, wie wir hausten, wie ein Foto beweist, auf dem sie stolz in ihrem selbst genähten Hochzeitskleid vor der Haustür steht, ihre Hand auf meinem Kopf und die Liebe zu meinem Vater im Herzen. Es gab kein warmes Wasser und keine Heizung im Haus, nur drei kleine Öfen, die meisten Zimmer blieben ungeheizt. So wie auch das Plumpsklo, das hinten im Garten stand, voller Spinnen und einem dampfenden Haufen, dessen unaufhaltsames Wachstum mich immer wieder erstaunte. Wir hatten kein Telefon und versammelten uns um das des Bestatters drei Häuser weiter, wenn wir zwischen den Särgen mit unseren Westverwandten diskutierten. In einem Zimmer auf dem Dachboden über dem Schweinestall lebte eine verrückte Alte, die der Krieg dort vergessen hatte. Wenn es donnerte und blitzte, stand sie mit gepackten Koffern bei uns im Hausflur und hielt sich die Ohren zu. Sie war ein vertrautes Hausgespenst und immer wütend, mit erhobenem Arm meinen Bruder und mich von ihrer Treppe scheuchend.

Wenn zum Geburtstag meiner Großmutter der Mercedes unserer Verwandten aus Westdeutschland im Hof stand und den Schmutz um ihn herum anstrahlte, wurde uns bewusst, wie reich sie waren und

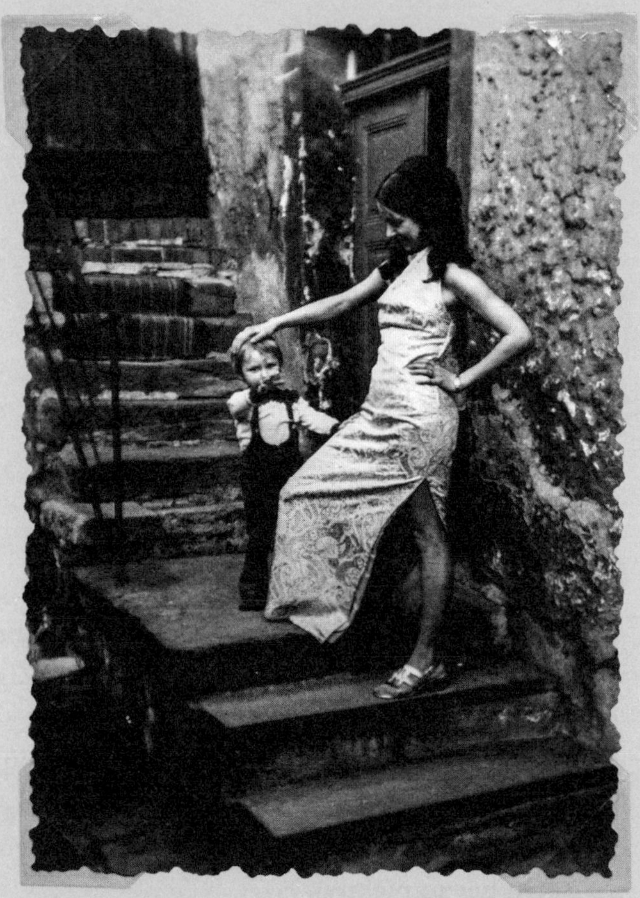

on the pointed roof or balancing on the railings of the railway bridge. I was a good boy, only interrupted by the brief moments I spent yelling and kicking on the floor in the house or on the sidewalks of the village, without any prospect of relieving my rage and desperation. No one in my new family knew about the calming waters with which one could have extinguished this fire. Everyone just asked themselves what in the world was wrong with the boy.

We lived in very simple circumstances. My mother did not see how we lived, as is shown by a photo, in which she proudly stands in front of the house door in the wedding dress she tailored herself, her hand on my head and her love for my father in her heart. There was no hot water and no heating in the house, only three small stoves. Most of the rooms were kept unheated. Just like the outhouse out back in the garden, full of spiders and a steaming pile, the unstoppable growth of which always astonished me. We did not

wie bescheiden wir lebten. Sie wurden auch nicht müde, uns zu erklären, dass eine Existenz unter diesen Umständen würdelos und traurig sei. Aber um nichts in der Welt hätten wir mit ihnen getauscht.

Damals störte es mich nicht, dass wir nur unser eigenes Land sehen würden, die Mauer trennte noch Ost von West. Meine Ferien und Urlaube verbrachte ich auf Rügen oder Usedom, an Flüssen und Seen. Wir badeten nackt, zelteten schwarz und paddelten über das Wasser. Im Winter fuhren wir Ski im Harz. Die westliche Welt existierte nicht für uns, sie war eine Tatsache, aber sie betraf uns nicht.

Wenn ich aus der Schule kam, setzte ich mich neben meinen Großvater in das dunstige Wohnzimmer, wo ich eine Stunde fernsehen durfte. Die Antenne war gen Westen ausgerichtet. Es war das Fernsehen des imperialistischen Feindes – und ich liebte es. Vor allem liebte ich die amerikanischen Filme und Serien, *Columbo*, *Die Straßen von San Francisco*, *Matlock*, *Hart aber herzlich* und *Magnum*. Ich liebte die Wolkenkratzer in den Städten, die goldenen Fahrstühle und Drehtüren, ich liebte die Schauspieler, die mit hinter sich her baumelnden Spiralkabeln der Telefone von der Küche in die Wohnzimmer liefen und mit Jack oder Kate telefonierten. Ich liebte die Cadillacs und Chryslers, die vor den Wolkenkratzern parkten. All das liebte ich wie die Ringe des Saturns, die ich auch nie sehen würde. Eine Rakete wollte ich bauen und ein U-Boot, aber das Ziel war der Mond oder die tiefste Stelle im Bad Anna, wo angeblich ein Panzer aus dem Zweiten Weltkrieg vor sich hin rostete. Unsere Welt war überschaubar für mich, sogar als Kind. Es fühlte sich an wie eine sehr kleine und verlässliche Gesellschaft.

Meine Eingewöhnung in die neue Familie ging so weit, dass ich den Mann, der sich um meine Liebe bemühte, bald Vater nannte. Und irgendwann ist es im Laufe der Jahre geschehen, oder innerhalb einer Minute, ich weiß es nicht, irgendwann vergaß ich, woher ich gekommen war, dass ich einmal Zug gefahren bin und es irgendwo einen Mann gab, den ich nur ein einziges Mal wiedersehen sollte. Alles, was ich, bevor ich drei

have a telephone, and we gathered around that of the undertaker's three doors down, where we stood between the caskets while in conversation with our relatives from the West. In a room in the attic above the pigsty lived a crazy old lady who the war had forgotten there. When there was thunder and lightning, she would stand in our hallway with packed bags and cover her ears. She was a familiar spirit and was always angry, chasing away my brother and I from her stairs with a raised arm.

When the Mercedes of our relatives from West Germany stood in the courtyard on my grandmother's birthday and shone on the dirt around it, we became conscious of how rich they were and how modestly we lived. They also never grew tired of explaining to us that an existence under these conditions was undignified and sad. However, we would not have traded places with them for anything in the world.

At that time, it did not bother me that we would only see our own country, with the Wall still separating East from West. I spent my holidays and vacations on the islands of Rügen or Usedom, next to rivers and lakes. We swam in the nude, went wild camping and paddled on the water. In winter we went skiing in the Harz Mountains. The Western world did not exist for us. It was a fact, but it was not relevant to us.

When I came home from school, I sat down next to my grandfather in the smoky living room and was allowed to watch television for an hour. The antenna was pointed to the west. It was the television of the imperialist enemy—and I loved it. I especially loved the American films and series, *Columbo*, *The Streets of San Francisco*, *Matlock*, *Hart to Hart*, and *Magnum P.I.* I loved the skyscrapers in the cities, the golden elevators, and revolving doors. I loved the actors who walked from the kitchen to the living room with the spiral cords of the telephones hanging behind them, in conversation with Jack or Kate. I loved the Cadillacs and Chryslers parked in front of the skyscrapers. I loved all of that like the Rings of Saturn, which I would also never see. I wanted to build a rocket and a submarine, but the destination was the moon or the deepest point in the

Jahre alt wurde, erlebt hatte, war in einer Grube versunken, die ich erst viel später wieder auszuheben begann. Fremde hatten mich an sich gezogen, jeder auf seine Art, aber alle ganz selbstverständlich, als wäre es schon immer so gewesen. So lernte ich, neben der Angst, alles verlieren zu können, auch das Vertrauen kennen, das Vertrauen in die Menschen.

Als sich zwölf war und mein Vater eine Dunkelkammer einrichtete, begann ich, mit seiner Kamera umherzuziehen und zu fotografieren. Mein erstes Foto war eine Pusteblume. Ich nahm sie aber nicht von oben auf. Ich legte mich auf den Rasen, das Kinn im Gras, hinunter zu ihr, alles um sie herum unscharf. Ich wollte mich in ihre Welt begeben, um Teil von ihr zu sein.

Anna lake, where a tank from the Second World War was allegedly rusting away. Our world was surveyable for me, even as a child. It felt like a very small and reliable society.

My settling in with the new family went so far that I soon called the man who was striving to win my love "father." And at some point, over the years, or within the course of a minute, I don't know, but at some point, I forgot where I had come from, that I had once travelled in a train, and that there was a man somewhere that I would only see one more time. Everything I had experienced before I was three years old was buried in a pit that I would only begin to excavate again much later on. Strangers had drawn me to them, each in their way, but all of them quite naturally, as if it had always been so. Thus, I had also become familiar with, in addition to the fear of losing everything, trust—trust in people.

When I was twelve and my father set up a darkroom, I began to wander around with his camera and take photographs. My first photo was of a dandelion. However, I did not take the picture from above. I laid myself down on the lawn, my chin in the grass, everything around it blurry. I wanted to enter its world, to become part of it.

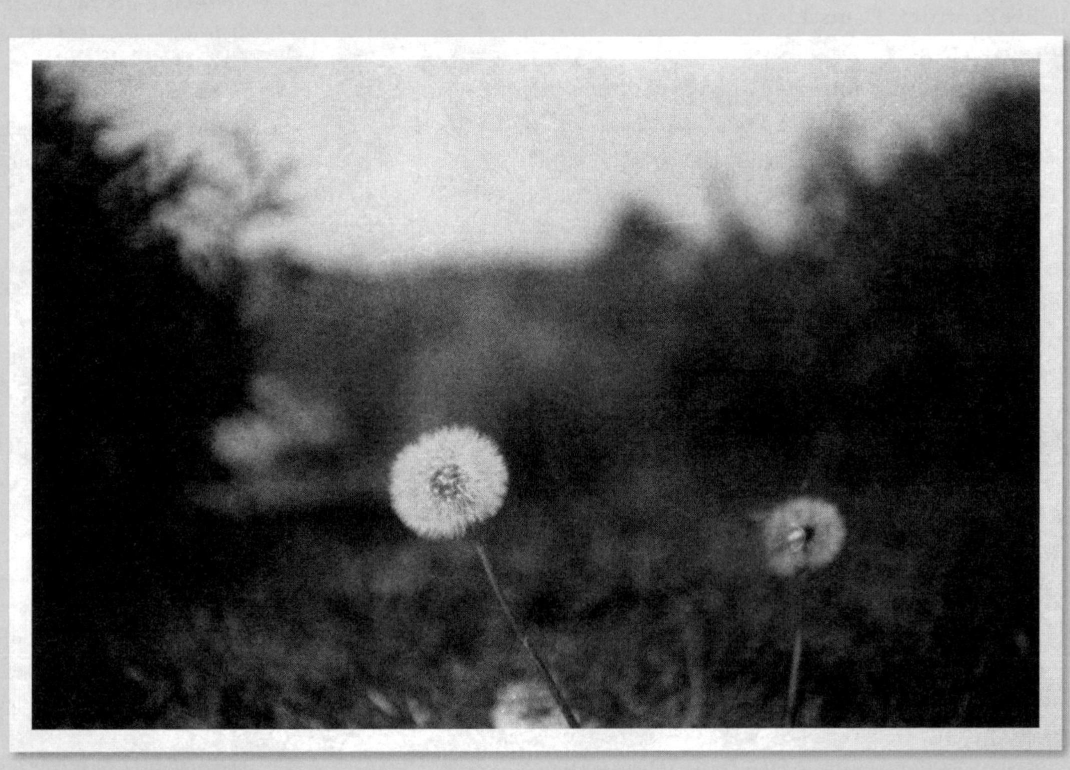

Sergio Purtell, geboren in Santiago de Chile, erhielt 1980 einen BFA in Fotografie an der Rhode Island School of Design und 1982 einen MFA an der Yale University. Nach mehrjähriger Tätigkeit als Dozent für Fotografie zog er nach New York, wo er als Werbefotograf für Designstudios, renommierte Zeitschriften und Verlage arbeitete. Purtell gründete ein eigenes Labor, um sich seiner Leidenschaft für die Entwicklung von Fotografien widmen zu können, unter anderem fertigte er Abzüge für den Walker Evans Estate an. Er lebt und arbeitet in New York.
Sergio Purtell was born in Santiago, Chile, and received a BFA in photography from Rhode Island School of Design in 1980 and an MFA from Yale University in 1982. After teaching photography for several years he moved to New York to work as a commercial photographer, shooting for design studios, prestigious magazines, and publishers. Purtell established a studio to pursue his love for printing, working among others for the Walker Evans Estate. He lives and works in New York.

Andreas Reimann ist einer der bedeutendsten deutschen Dichter der Gegenwart. Zurzeit erscheint eine Gesamtausgabe seiner Werke in der Connewitzer Verlagsbuchhandlung Leipzig. Der auch als Grafiker tätige Lyriker wurde mit zahlreichen Literaturpreisen ausgezeichnet, zuletzt 2023 mit dem renommierten Lessing-Preis. Seit 2015 ist er Mitglied des PEN-Zentrums Deutschland.
Andreas Reimann is one of Germany's most important contemporary poets. A complete edition of his works is currently being published by Connewitzer Verlagsbuchhandlung Leipzig. The poet, who also works as a graphic artist, has been honoured with numerous literary awards, most recently the prestigious Lessing Prize in 2023. He has been a member of the PEN Centre Germany since 2015.

Mario Schneider arbeitet als Fotograf, Regisseur, Autor und Filmkomponist. Er absolvierte zunächst eine Lehre als Metallurge für Hüttentechnik und begann im Anschluss, Philosophie, Kunstgeschichte und Musikwissenschaft zu studieren. Nach einem Studium der Filmkomposition wandte er sich danach der Regiearbeit zu. Schneiders Dokumentarfilme sind international bekannt und wurden mehrfach ausgezeichnet. Sein erster Fotoband, *Tourist*, erschien im Jahr 2020.
Mario Schneider is a photographer, director, writer, and film composer. He first completed an apprenticeship as a metallurgist and then studied philosophy, art history, and musicology. After studying film composition, he turned to film directing. Schneider's documentary films are internationally acclaimed and have won several awards. His first photo book, *Tourist*, was published in 2020.

Elin Spring ist Gründerin und Herausgeberin des Online-Fotomagazins *What Will You Remember?*. Darüber hinaus schreibt sie Rezensionen für verschiedene Zeitschriften sowie Beiträge für Bücher und Ausstellungskataloge. Als unabhängige Kuratorin ist sie Jurymitglied bei Fotowettbewerben und Ausstellungen. Spring führt regelmäßig Portfoliobesprechungen auf nationalen Fotofestivals, an Hochschulen sowie in Museen durch und präsentiert neu entdeckte Arbeiten online.
Elin Spring is founder and editor of the online photography review magazine *What Will You Remember?*. In addition, she contributes reviews to various magazines and provides essays for books and exhibition catalogs. As an independent curator, she has served on the jury for photography competitions and exhibitions. Spring regularly conducts portfolio reviews at national photography festivals, colleges, and museums, highlighting newly discovered work online.

Ich danke / Thanks to:
Richard Kalvar, Elin Spring, Sergio Purtell, Andreas Reimann, Klaus Kehrer, Sylvia Ballhause, Alexa Becker, Wolfgang Zurborn, Sandra Buschow, Gudrun Plenert, Helle Kammer e.V., Anja & Maria

Texte / Texts:
Sergio Purtell, Andreas Reimann, Mario Schneider, Elin Spring
Verlagslektorat / Copy Editing:
Kirsten Limberg, George MacBeth
Übersetzungen / Translations:
Christian Breuer, Kenneth Friend
Projektmanagement / Project Management:
Kehrer Verlag (Sylvia Ballhause)
Gestaltung / Design:
Sisters of Design, Halle (Saale)
Bildbearbeitung / Image Processing:
Kehrer Design (René Henoch)
Herstellung / Production Management:
Kehrer Design (Tom Streicher)

Bibliografische Information der Deutschen Nationalbibliothek
Die Deutsche Nationalbibliothek verzeichnet diese Publikation in der Deutschen Nationalbibliografie; detaillierte bibliografische Daten sind im Internet über https://dnb.dnb.de abrufbar.
Bibliographic information published by the Deutsche Nationalbibliothek
The Deutsche Nationalbibliothek lists this publication in the Deutsche Nationalbibliografie; detailed bibliographic data is available on the Internet at https://dnb.dnb.de.

Printed and bound in Germany
ISBN 978-3-96900-194-3

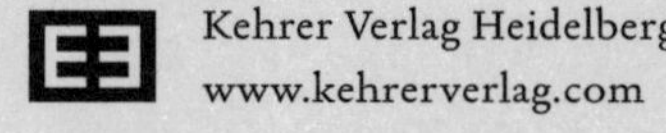
Kehrer Verlag Heidelberg
www.kehrerverlag.com